"The only real stumbling
block is fear of failure.
In cooking you've got
to have a what-the-hell
attitude."
/////////////////////////////////
JULIA CHILD

"I've found from past
experiences that the tighter
your plan, the more likely
you are to run into some-
thing unpredictable."
/////////////////////////////////
MACGYVER

"Give me liberty or...
OOOooo...a jelly donut!"
/////////////////////////////////
HOMER SIMPSON

EATS 2

THE MIDDLE YEARS

ALTON BROWN

STEWART, TABORI & CHANG

NEW YORK

CONTENTS

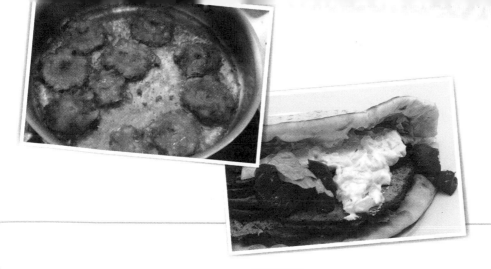

// SEASON 9 ///////////////////////////////

// SEASON 10 ///////////////////////////////

INTERVIEW

Alton Brown Interviews Alton Brown on *Good Eats 2: The Middle Years*

ALTON BROWN: So, the last time we chatted it was for the opening of *Good Eats: The Early Years.* How did that work out for you?

ALTON BROWN: Okay, but I won't be happy until every home in America has one . . . or two. Two would be better.

AB: What can readers, viewers, and fans expect from *Good Eats 2: The Middle Years*?

AB: Well, it's heavier—three pounds, eight and a half ounces.

AB: Volume 1 was no lightweight.

AB: Three pounds eight ounces, to be exact.

AB: So are *Good Eats* books proving to be coffee table books for the kitchen?

AB: No, they're more like kitchen table for the coffee books, which is a critical distinction.

AB: Since Volume 1 dealt with episodes 1 through 80 of *Good Eats*, is it safe to assume that this new tome will take us through episode 160?

AB: Actually, we turned it up to 164. I really wanted to get episode 163, "Fry Turkey Fry," in there, but 163 is a funny number. So we went to 164, which brought us that extra half-ounce.

AB: Have you changed your modus operandi from the first to the second volume?

AB: No, but I did change pencils. The one I used on the first book had gotten quite short. But I do think I condensed information more effectively in this volume. I refined it a bit more, which is good, because it translated to fewer words. Fewer words are almost always better—just ask Hemingway.

AB: As long as they're the right words.

AB: Or big words. Polysyllabic, for instance.

AB: Looking back at the material, were there any highlights, any revelations?

AB: Well, for one thing, the shows in this bunch are just plain better. The food's foodier, the applications are more applicable, and the rigs are way riggier. And the comedy is more commodious.

AB: I see. Now, during this period you moved from a location kitchen to a set and then eventually to your own studio, right?

A B : We did, and in more than a few episodes, we were driven by that shifting reality. Episode 88, for instance—our barbecue show—had to be filmed in and around the Airstream trailer I used as an office because our set wasn't finished yet and we didn't have anywhere to shoot. Once the set was finished, it was still a pain, though, because we had to use a rented sound stage, which meant putting the set up and taking it down three times a year and storing it. . . . Oh, and we had no prep kitchen, so we'd set up ovens and tables in a loading dock. We used a hose for water and had to cover everything in plastic because insulation fell off the ceiling into the food. It was like camping with Mad Max.

A B : Except camping is fun.

A B : Exactly. But when we moved to our own studio, things got much better. A sound stage gives you control, and in our case that translated to putting more money on the screen.

A B : No more insulation in the food?

A B : No, but my culinary staff does occasionally sneak something in there if they know I'm going to taste it on camera . . . just for giggles.

A B : Care to share any details?

A B : No.

A B : Any personal favorites? Shows, that is?

A B : Well, the fried turkey show was and remains a high point. It's a great rig and a really good bird. I also enjoyed our salt special.

A B : That was your first one-hour show since "Down and Out in Paradise," right?

A B : That's right. You're a very well-prepared interviewer. I appreciate that. Oh, I'm also fond of the popcorn show and the piece we did on doughnuts. A lot of fun. Waffles, leeks, dark leafy greens too. And pie.

A B : What about the recipes themselves?

[There's a long pause.]

A B : I thought we'd worked this out before. We call them *applications*.

A B : It was a slip. Sorry.

A B : It's cool. Oh, I'm also a big fan of our chili episode.

A B : You play a cowboy in that one.

A B : That's right—Gus. But I was really just the straight man for my sidekick Rusty, who was played by Daniel Petrow, the same guy who plays my neighbor Chuck. We both had fake mustaches, which really make the man, if you ask me.

A B : So Volume 2 is bigger and better. And Volume 3?

A B : Could we use Roman numerals? Literary works never use Arabic.

A B : Sorry, and Volume III?

A B : Volume III will chronicle episodes 165 to . . . whatever 165 plus 84 is.

A B : 249?

A B : If you say so. One thing I can tell you: I'll probably make the last show in the set about Chinook salmon.

A B : Because?

A B : That way I can title Volume III *The Return of the King*.

A B : Good luck with that.

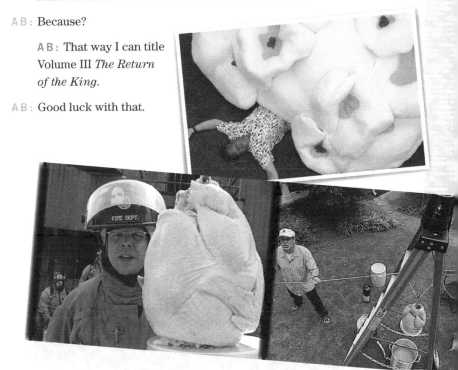

THE EPISODES

GOOD EATS | THE MIDDLE YEARS

USE YOUR NOODLE II: FRESH PASTA

EPISODE 81 | SEASON 6 | GOOD EATS

I've always regretted not making this a two-part show about fresh pasta. Sure, ravioli are fun to make (and even more fun to eat), but this dough is capable of infinite shape shifting: Fettuccini, tagliatelle, and pappardelle are easily within its scope, and I wish I'd made that more apparent in the episode. In fact, one of my favorite applications for this dough is to roll and cut thick, wide noodles, then simmer them in chicken stock for Chicken Noodle Soup (page 61). Regardless of how you roll, cut, shape, or stuff it, this dough is as versatile a multitasker as you're likely to encounter.

TIDBIT The word *macaroni* is derived from the Greek *makar*, meaning "blessed."

Assembled thusly, the average residential ironing board provides up to five feet of rolling space. And since it's portable, you can roll pasta in any room of the house, even outdoors!

PARTS LIST

Atlas model (or equivalent) manual pasta roller

Nuts that fit U-bolt

Steel plate with holes

U-bolt (I prefer a 5-inch model)

Ironing board

KEEP A SEPARATE COTTON BOARD COVER JUST FOR ROLLING PASTA.

Culinary lore holds that the Venetian adventurer Marco Polo first brought pasta to Italy from far-off China in 1295. The fact that fettuccini and ravioli were already popular dishes in Rome at the time should have put the matter to rest. The reason the legend persists is that it isn't very old. In fact, the earliest reference to it I've been able to unearth is a rather whimsical article by S. Gibbs Campbell in the October 1929 edition of *Macaroni Journal* that tells of a sailor on Marco Polo's expedition named Spaghetti, who had seen a Chinese girl preparing long strands of pasta. Marco Polo did bring knowledge of the foods and culture of Asia to Europe, but not of the noodle.

TIDBIT For an even more ridiculous version of the same story, check out Gary Cooper in the 1938 flop *The Adventures of Marco Polo*.

Dry pastas contain nothing but flour and water, and their flavor and body alike stem from the use of high-protein flour ground from durum wheat. Fresh pastas, on the other hand, can be made from a wide array of flours (including all-purpose) because they contain eggs, which increase the protein content of the dough considerably. The yolks also contain fat, which tenderizes the noodles or dumplings and helps to amplify any fat-soluble vitamins present, including A, D, and E.

When pasta dough is first formed, it's brittle and prone to tearing. An hour in the refrigerator will give the flour granules time to hydrate—that is, absorb moisture from the eggs. The result will be plastic and elastic and easy to handle.

Although the rolling pin is still the choice of purists and Italians everywhere, I'm neither purist nor Italian, so I prefer the mechanized version. The classic manual pasta roller, commonly called an "Atlas" after the company that first drew up the design back in 1938, is to my mind still the best machine for the home cook because it's small and stout.

This knob changes the space between the rollers, which in turn changes the thickness of the dough. The roller settings are indexed, meaning that they snap into place when positioned properly. Regardless of what thickness you're shooting for (many recipes reference Atlas roller numbers), you'll want to start on #1 and gradually work your way thinner. Impatience will only buy you torn, rough dough, and that's rarely good eats. Most manual machines come with a cutting attachment that converts sheets into "ribbons" of varying size.

Of course, if a pasta machine's going to do you any good at all, you've got to be able to securely anchor it to a respectable range of real estate, which is a challenge in many modern kitchens. It doesn't help that the wimpy clamps Atlases and their ilk use for anchorage further limit positioning. My answer: Skip the counter altogether and go with an ironing board.

NOTE: In the years since this episode was filmed, I have tested various scenarios seeking to convert my Atlas from manual to automatic. After-market motors made to fit the unit are worthless and weak, and my attempts to put a cordless drill to the task were iffy at best. After reading some reviews, I used that newfangled World Wide Web to order up a roller/cutter made to fit the accessory outlet on the front of my KitchenAid mixer. Although the position is awkward (as in too high), the machine's got the guts for the job. The docking assembly's on the weak side, but if you've got a KitchenAid, this is a decent alternative to hand cranking.

EGG

FLOUR

ABOUT 1 POUND PASTA DOUGH;
ENOUGH FOR 30 RAVIOLI

// SOFTWARE //

10	ounces	all-purpose flour	plus extra for rolling
2	large	eggs	
3	tablespoons	H_2O	
1	teaspoon	olive oil	
½	teaspoon	kosher salt	

// PROCEDURE //

HAND METHOD:

1. Mound the flour on a clean counter or cutting board and form a well in the center (like a really wide volcano, or a really narrow atoll, depending on how you look at it).

2. **Whisk** the eggs, water, oil, and salt together in a **small bowl**.[1]

3. Gently pour the egg mixture into the mouth of the flour volcano.

4. Hold your fingers thusly ⟵ and slowly stir the egg mixture around while pushing flour in with your other hand. As the dough forms, more and more flour will be pulled into the mix. You'll know it's taken in enough when it forms a firm paste. Don't try to work in more flour after this point or you'll end up with a dry, unworkable dough.

5. Push the rest of the flour away and knead for 3 to 4 minutes, or until just barely sticky. Form the dough into a disk, wrap in **plastic wrap**, and stash in the refrigerator for 1 hour.

FOOD PROCESSOR METHOD[2]:

1. Combine the flour and salt in a **food processor** with 2 or 3 quick pulses.

2. Measure the water and oil into a **liquid measuring cup**, then **whisk** in the eggs. Activate the processor and introduce this mixture to the dry team in a slow, continuous stream until the dough begins to pull away from the sides of the bowl. When that happens, stop adding the liquid immediately.

3. Pulse several more times to bring the dough together.

4. Remove the dough as soon as it comes together, wrap with **plastic wrap**, and stash in the refrigerator for at least 1 hour so that the flour granules can hydrate.[3]

NOW THE FUN PART:

1. Divide the dough into two equal pieces and rewrap one with the plastic. Lightly flour the first half and use the heel of your hand to shape it into an oblong, roughly 5 by 2 inches. Slowly turn the crank and feed the dough through, catching it with your other hand as it comes out.

2. Fold into thirds as you would a wallet, turn 90 degrees, and pass through the machine again on the same setting. Fold into thirds, turn 90 degrees, and pass through the machine one last time, still at the widest setting.

3. Set the rollers to the second setting and send the dough through one time. (No more wallet folding at this point.)

4. Continue passing the dough through at narrower and narrower settings until the desired thickness is reached. By the time you get to #6 on the dial you will have a sheet of pasta approximately 3 feet long.

NOTE: Once the dough is rolled you have some choices to make. You can trade out the roller attachment for one of the cutters that no doubt came with your machine and cut noodles. I often cut the sheet into 1-foot lengths before passing them through the cutters. As soon as the cut noodles come out, I toss them in a bit of flour or cornstarch, twist into a—well, a twist, and park on a sheet pan. When the pan is covered I slide it into the freezer. The next day, I move the twists to zip-top bags, four per bag. Back in the freezer, they'll keep for up to a month. To cook, add to salted boiling water (½ gallon of water minimum) and cook until al dente, which won't take very long at all.

TIDBIT | Water is not an ingredient in dry pasta. It is used to shape the dough and then removed during the drying process.

TIDBIT | Pasta's original use was as an extender in soups and some desserts.

[1] Not that it matters, but in case you were wondering this is technically an emulsion in which the oil and water are held together by phospholipids in the egg yolks.

[2] This is indeed a faster yet less satisfying operation. The resulting dough is a bit tougher than hand-mixed dough, but that also translates to resilience, which means it'll be easier to shape and stuff—but just barely.

[3] An hour is the minimum. You can leave the dough in this state for up three days. Let it rest on the counter for an hour or so to take the chill off so it'll be pliable enough to feed through the machine.

IF STUFFING IS YOUR GOAL:

1. Spread the rolled pasta sheet out on a lightly floured counter and gently mark the sheet lengthwise down the middle using a yardstick, but don't press so hard that you split the dough.

2. Use a measuring teaspoon to deliver a dollop of filling (see application on right) every couple of inches along one side of the mark down the middle, spacing them evenly at least 1 inch from each other.

3. Brush the pasta sheet with egg wash (1 egg, lightly beaten together with 1 tablespoon water) on one edge lengthwise down the entire sheet and in between the piles of filling. Fold the un-egg-washed side of the sheet over and seal, removing any air bubbles as you go.

4. Cut into even squares using a sharp paring knife or pizza cutter.

5. Place the finished ravioli on a parchment paper–lined half sheet pan and cover with a damp towel.

6. Repeat the procedure with the remaining dough half.

7. Add the ravioli to the boiling water 6 to 8 at a time and cook until they float, 6 to 8 minutes. Remove with a spider and set on a half sheet pan lined with parchment. Repeat until all the ravioli have been cooked.

NOTE: I never boil more than 8 pieces at a time in 1 gallon of boiling salted water.

TIDBIT | Examples of other stuffed noodles around the world:
POLAND: Pierogi
CHINA: Gao gai or wonton
JAPAN: Gyoza
UKRAINE: Varenyky
JEWS: Kreplach
KOREA: Mandu
SIBERIA: Pelmeny

TIDBIT | From 1700 to 1785, pasta shops quadrupled in Naples, resulting in pasta drying everywhere, including in the streets and on rooftops and balconies.

SHAPING OPTION: TORTELLINI

SPINACH AND RICOTTA FILLING

ENOUGH FILLING FOR ABOUT 30 RAVIOLI

// SOFTWARE ///

½	cup	ricotta cheese	
1	ounce	Parmesan cheese	grated
2	tablespoons	cooked spinach	chopped
1	large	egg	
¼	teaspoon	black pepper	freshly ground
1	pinch	nutmeg	freshly grated

// PROCEDURE ///

Combine all the ingredients in a **medium mixing bowl**. Cover and chill for 30 minutes.

TIDBIT Franco-American, the first company to can pasta and sauce, boasted that they were using a French recipe.

TIP Since fats attract potentially nasty aromas, frozen items containing them, such as ravioli, should be carefully packaged in airtight containment to be stored long-term. Toss in a small amount of cornstarch to prevent sticking. Place 10 to 12 in a zip-top bag and suck the air out.

SUB-APPLICATION — RAVIOLI IN BROWNED BUTTER

Although Chef Boyardee may toss his ravs in tomato sauce, I prefer a quick sauté:

// SOFTWARE ///

6	tablespoons	unsalted butter	
30		cooked fresh ravioli	see page 12
3	tablespoons	fresh sage	chiffonade[4]
	to taste	black pepper	freshly ground

// PROCEDURE ///

1. Place a **12-inch sauté pan** over medium heat and add 2 tablespoons of the butter. The butter will melt, then foam as the water cooks out, then begin to brown as the milk solids cook.

2. When the butter just starts to smell nutty, turn the heat down to low, carefully add 8 to 10 ravioli and fry, tossing often, until they start to turn brown around the edges.

3. Add a little sage and a grind of pepper and toss to coat. Remove from the heat and grab a fork. Repeat with the remaining butter, ravioli, and sage.

[4] Small shreds or ribbons. To cut, roll up the leaves like a cigar and slice across the roll.

1
2
3

1. Cut into circles and place filling in center.

2. Moisten edges, fold over, and seal.

3. Place against a finger or the handle of a wooden spoon. Bring corners of folded sides together.

SALAD DAZE II:
LONG ARM OF THE SLAW

EPISODE 82 | SEASON 6 | GOOD EATS

When I wrote this show

I'd just come off a long book tour during
which I was forced to endure multiple
appearances on bad local TV morning
shows across the country. The scene was always the same:
A third-rate weatherman and a bleached-blond news reader
took turns barraging me with irrelevant questions and tortur-
ous attempts at humor on garish sets awash with bad coffee
and heavy makeup. The sole saving grace: low viewership. Of course, since I'm a cook, they
all wanted a demo but they never had working kitchens beyond the occasional hotplate. So,
in an act of desperation I started making slaw. When the tour was over I started thinking that
slaw would make a fun *Good Eats* episode, especially if it goofed on those bad bouts of morning sickness. The result was *Rise and Shine with Reggie and Suzy* and, boy, did the fans hate
it. Never before (or since, I'm happy to say) have we received so much negative email regarding our work. I'm okay with that as long as you don't take it out on slaw, which is, in fact, one
of my favorite foods, accounting for nearly 100 percent of my personal cabbage intake.

KNOWLEDGE CONCENTRATE

▷ The word *coleslaw* comes from the Dutch *koolsla*, *kool* meaning "cabbage" and *sla*
meaning "salad." Although cabbage is the classic base, the term has come to refer
to any shredded salad served cold in either a creamy dressing or acidic marinade.
That said, there's no reason a coleslaw can't be served hot and still be called coleslaw.

▷ Slaws marinated in acidic pickles or brines harken back to the Roman tradition of
soaking raw vegetables (shredded and otherwise) in salt and vinegar until they wilted.
The word *salad*, in fact, comes from the Vulgar Latin *herba salata* or "salted herbs."
Since mayonnaise didn't come along until the eighteenth century, slaws built upon it
are a relatively recent addition to the menu.

America's slaw heritage got a boost when Dutch settlers in New Netherlands (modern-day New York) planted cabbage all across the Hudson River Valley. Although the people we call the Pennsylvania Dutch weren't actually Dutch (the word is a lazy bastardization of Deutsch, as in German), their deep love of pickled vegetables prompted them to heavily hack the slaw concept to their taste. Many of the slaws that are popular today on the Eastern Seaboard are descendants of these early experiments.

Brining a vegetable like cabbage pulls moisture out of the cell structure. When a slaw is salted the resulting strands become quite floppy, but because of the compression of the cells, they remain dense and crunchy. Slaws that have been presalted or "purged" before dressing keep much longer in the fridge because the dressings don't become diluted by moisture seeping out of the vegetation.

Mayo may be the standard slaw dressing base in the United States, but I never send it into battle alone; it's too fatty and, frankly, not nearly flavorful enough on its own unless it's homemade, but that's another show. For all mayo-centric salads I use two parts low-fat buttermilk to one part mayo (because you can't beat that texture) and one part low-fat plain yogurt (for tang and viscosity).

Although most modern food processors come with grating blades, they tend to mutilate rather than shred, so I only use one if I'm making a pulpy slaw such as the one I like to mound on the slaw dogs I so adore in summer months. (In winter, I reach instead for kraut—which is of course nothing but fermented cabbage.)

Box-style graters come in dozens of different configurations, and as far as I'm concerned they're all flawed. The problem stems from the fact that they're all designed to sit straight up and down on a counter or cutting board. This puts the shredder in a mercilessly difficult position. I get around this to some degree with the use of a simple device I call the Slaw Dog.

Although several members of the cabbage family, including kale and collards, aren't fitting for slaw, almost every other member of the *Cruciferea* family is:

CHINESE CABBAGE (sometimes called Napa or celery cabbage): Makes some of the best summer and fall slaws.

GREEN, RED, OR WHITE CABBAGE: Although available year round, it is best to avoid large heads, which tend to be very bitter, especially in late winter.

SAVOY CABBAGE: Another excellent choice for summer or fall slaw.

BOK CHOY: Sometimes mistakenly referred to as Chinese cabbage, but still makes a tasty slaw.

BROCCOLI, BRUSSELS SPROUTS, AND CAULIFLOWER: Sliced thinly, these are tasty slaw choices indeed, but that's definitely another show (or two).

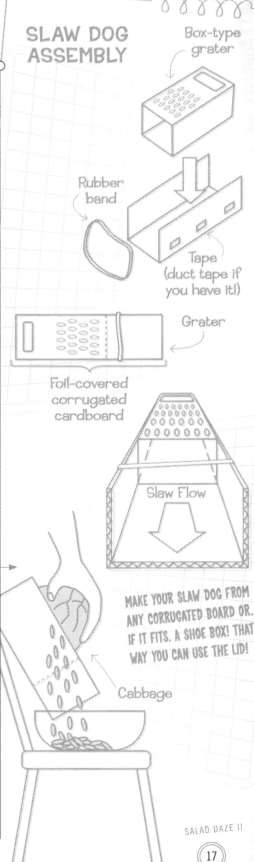

SLAW DOG ASSEMBLY

Box-type grater

Rubber band

Tape (duct tape if you have it!)

Grater

Foil-covered corrugated cardboard

Slaw Flow

MAKE YOUR SLAW DOG FROM ANY CORRUGATED BOARD OR, IF IT FITS, A SHOE BOX! THAT WAY YOU CAN USE THE LID!

Cabbage

COLESLAW, AMERICAN STYLE

8 TO 10 SERVINGS

If you plan on putting this on hot dogs, you may want to consider breaking out the food processor and grating the cabbage, but it's not a must.

TIP | The best tools to mix a cabbage slaw are at the ends of your arms. Just make sure they're clean and that you've got a plenty big bowl.

// SOFTWARE //

1½	pounds	green cabbage	thinly sliced, not grated
1	pound	red cabbage	thinly sliced, not grated
2	tablespoons	kosher salt	
½	cup	buttermilk	low-fat
¼	cup	plain yogurt	low-fat
¼	cup	mayonnaise	
1	tablespoon	sweet pickle juice	as long as it isn't from kosher pickles, you're good to go
1	teaspoon	dry mustard powder	I prefer Coleman's
½	teaspoon	black pepper	freshly ground
1	large	carrot	peeled and grated
1	tablespoon	fresh chives	finely chopped

// PROCEDURE //

1. Combine the green and red cabbage in a **large colander**, toss with the salt, and set in the sink to drain for 3 hours.

2. Thoroughly rinse the cabbage under cool running water for at least 1 minute. Then transfer the cabbage to a **salad spinner** to dry thoroughly.

3. **Whisk** together the buttermilk, yogurt, mayonnaise, pickle juice, mustard powder, and pepper in a **large bowl**. Add the cabbage, carrot, and chives and toss to combine. Serve immediately or store in the refrigerator for up to 3 days.

TRIVIA | This is my favorite W scene ever. She's frozen like a deer in the headlights.

I'M SICK OF THIS SLOP AND I WANT SOME SLAW!

GERMAN HOT SLAW

4 TO 6 SERVINGS

I like this with pierogi (really need to do a show on those) and, of course, bratwurst.

// SOFTWARE //

6	rashers	thick-sliced bacon	
1	small	onion	grated
	to taste	kosher salt	
3	tablespoons	apple cider vinegar	
1	tablespoon	dark brown sugar	
1	pound	green cabbage	shredded
1	teaspoon	caraway seeds	thinly sliced
	to taste	black pepper	freshly ground

// PROCEDURE //

1. Crisp the bacon in a **12-inch straight-sided pan** over medium heat. Remove and reserve the bacon. Remove all but 2 tablespoons of the bacon fat. Add the onion and a pinch of salt and sweat until semi-translucent, 2 to 3 minutes.

2. Pour in the vinegar and add the brown sugar, bring to a boil, reduce the heat slightly, and simmer for 1 to 2 minutes, until reduced and slightly thickened. Pour the dressing into a **small bowl**.

3. Return the pan (and any bits of dressing still left in it) to medium heat. Add the cabbage and caraway and sauté until warm and slightly browned but still crisp, 2 to 3 minutes. Return the bacon and dressing to the pan and toss to coat. Taste, season with salt and black pepper, and serve immediately.

TRIVIA My prop guy Paul drove the limo (he usually plays my hapless apprentice).

A CAKE ON EVERY PLATE

EPISODE 83 | SEASON 6 | GOOD EATS

This episode was *CSI* before CSI. There's mystery, a messy autopsy, showy demonstrations of scientific know-how . . . everything but the little flashlights those guys always whip out instead of just turning on the lights. But this show bedeviled me too because I tried to roll too much theory into one poor little cake. I made all my points, but I think the cake suffered a bit. I think we've fixed that in this current incarnation.

TRIVIA The aluminum suits were made by my costumer Amanda Kibler. To rotate me in the shots I stood on a large lazy Susan spun by a couple of grips just out of frame.

KNOWLEDGE CONCENTRATE

▷○ Although it was long held that the word *cake* derived from the Latin *coquere*, meaning "to cook," it actually stems from a much older Norse word, *kaka*, and probably referred originally to a small, flat bread sweetened with honey. For most of European history, a cake wasn't really a cake if it didn't contain hunks and chunks of either dried fruit or nuts.

▷○ Cakes are a Zen-like balancing act of opposing forces that strive to toughen, tenderize, moisten, and dry the final product. Too much of one and not enough of another could spell dessert doom.

TOUGHENERS, including flour and eggs, contain protein, starch, or both and give a cake its structural integrity.

TENDERIZERS, like shortening, butter, and the cocoa butter in both chocolate and cocoa powder, tenderize cakes by coating flour particles. Sugar tenderizes by holding onto water. Chemical leavenings tenderize by changing the pH of the batter and by increasing the size of the bubbles in the batter.

MOISTENERS include water, milk, syrups, and egg yolks—quite the multitaskers, those eggs.

DRYERS include powdered milk, flours, cocoa powder, and other starches that absorb moisture. Egg whites, which contain considerable protein, are also drying agents.

Although ingredients such as extracts, salt, citrus zests, spices, and liqueurs bring a lot of flavor to the party, they play little or no role in the structural equation of the cake.

Keeping a cake moist is not always about adding more liquid. For instance, egg whites can't hog as much water in a batter if plenty of sugar is included because sugar is hygroscopic and binds to the sucrose, preventing the proteins from getting to it.

On weighing: Ever wonder why European bakers are, by and large, better than American bakers? Because they weigh their ingredients (and, of course, they use the metric system, which is far more precise than the standard U.S. system). But even if you're into pounds and ounces, weighing is the way to go. Flour is highly compactable, so scooping to measure it is highly inaccurate.

Although there are many methods for assembling a batter, most American cakes are put together via the "creaming" method, and the one following is no exception. Such cakes derive their texture from the way the sugar and fat are beaten or "creamed" together. The concept is simple: The mixer cuts the sugar granules into the butter, forming microbubbles, which expand during cooking, partly because of the expansion of water vapor and partly due to CO_2 produced by chemical leavening. Sounds simple, and it is—but a lot can go wrong. If the butter is too cold, the sugar won't work in. If it's too warm, the bubbles collapse. Typically, though, the issue is time. Most cooks just don't cream long enough. Watch for the following to know when to stop:

Fat lightens in color (if you're using shortening, you're out of luck on this one).

Fat changes consistency (looks a little like whipped cream).

Fat increases in volume (by about a tenth; not much, but it matters).

Whatever you do, don't go by a clock alone. A creaming time in a recipe can put you in the right ballpark, but only visual inspection can tell you when the mixture is thoroughly creamed.

On fats: Since it remains solid over a wide range of temperatures, shortening is a favorite of professional bakers because it's very reliable and creams easily. I used to be a huge shortening fan, but over the years I've come to favor flavor over all, and in that regard butter is king and shortening is a ghost. So the application following has been adjusted accordingly.

On cake pans: I prefer heavy aluminum pans with a dull matte finish. Aluminum is an excellent conductor, and the understated finish allows heat to move in at a perfect pace, resulting in a good rise, a nice golden color, and a good set.

A FEW WORDS ABOUT CAKE FLOUR

Cake flour is made from soft winter wheat and it has 8 grams of protein per cup, compared to the 10 to 12 grams in all-purpose flour. Less protein makes for a more tender cake. That also means that more starch is available to swell and stabilize the cake. Also, cake flour is very finely milled, and that helps batters come together quickly, which means less gluten formation, and that translates to tenderness. Finally, cake flour is chlorinated and therefore slightly acidic, a condition that helps to coax the proteins in the flour to set faster—and that too helps to create a finer texture.

GOLD CAKE

2 (9-INCH) ROUND CAKES

4

5

6

1

2

3

Align (folded) point of fan
with center of pan and
cut off whatever sticks
out over pan edge

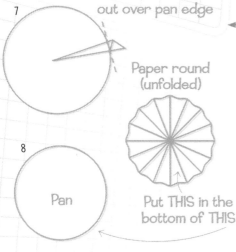

7

Paper round
(unfolded)

8

Pan

Put THIS in the
bottom of THIS

π HELPS WITH PIE: 9 × π = 9 × 3.141592653589793 =
28.27433388230139 = 28.5

¹ For this, I'm partial to a flexible device known as a
dough blade or (aptly enough) bowl scraper.

² I'm very bad at eyeballing this, so I use a scale to
split it right down to the gram.

// SOFTWARE

12	ounces	cake flour	plus extra for the pans
½	ounce	baking powder	aluminum free
1	cup	unsalted butter	at room temperature, plus extra for the pans
12	ounces	sugar	
¼	teaspoon	fine salt	
8	large	egg yolks	at room temperature, lightly beaten
¾	cup	whole milk	
1	teaspoon	vanilla extract	

// PROCEDURE

1. Place an oven rack in the top third of the oven and crank to 350°F.

2. Butter the bottom and sides of **2 (9-inch) round aluminum cake pans**, line with parchment circles (see left), lightly flour the sides, and set aside.

3. Sift the flour and baking powder together onto a **paper plate or flexible cutting board** and set aside.

4. Beat the butter in a **stand mixer fitted with the paddle attachment** for 1 minute at low speed.

5. Add the sugar and salt, boost the speed to medium, and beat for another 4 minutes, or until the mixture is very light and fluffy. You'll have to stop and **scrape** down the sides of the bowl at least twice during the process.[1]

6. Turn the mixer down to medium and add the egg yolks one at a time, mixing until each is completely incorporated before adding the next; this should take about 2 minutes.

7. Kill the mixer, scrape down the sides one last time, then turn it back to low and very slowly add half of the flour mixture.

8. Add half of the milk and all of the vanilla, stopping to scrape the sides of the bowl.

9. Finally add the remaining flour, followed by the remaining milk, again stopping to . . . you know.

10. When everything is fully incorporated, divide the mixture evenly between the two pans.[2] Bake for 25 to 30 minutes, until the cakes reach an internal temperature of 210°F or a toothpick inserted into the center comes out clean.

11. Remove from the oven and cool the cakes on a **cooling rack** for 15 minutes. Invert to de-pan onto the rack and cool completely before frosting.

COCOA WHIPPED CREAM

ENOUGH ICING FOR 1 (9-INCH)
2-LAYER CAKE

Although this frosting isn't anywhere close to being as rich as, say, buttercream, it has a fresh flavor that won't overpower the cake. Just remember to store any cake it sits atop in the chill chest.

// SOFTWARE ///

2	tablespoons	H_2O	
1	teaspoon	unflavored powdered gelatin	
2	cups	heavy cream	
½	cup	Hot Cocoa Mix	(see sidebar, right)
1	teaspoon	vanilla extract	

// PROCEDURE ///

1. Put a **stand mixer work bowl** or, if you're using a hand mixer, a **large stainless-steel bowl** in the freezer to chill.

2. Stir the water and the gelatin together in a **metal measuring cup or a very small saucepan** and set aside for 5 minutes.[3] Then, dissolve the gelatin over low heat, about 2 minutes.

3. Retrieve the mixing bowl from the chill and pour in the cream, cocoa mix, and vanilla. Mix on low speed until thoroughly homogenized.

4. Drizzle in the dissolved gelatin solution, boost the speed to high, and whip until medium peaks develop.

5. To apply: Dump on top of cake and use a **rubber or silicone spatula** to smooth across top and down sides. Or, use a **piping bag** like the one I made a mess with on *Letterman*.

GE HOT COCOA MIX

Combine 2 cups confectioners' sugar, 1 cup unsweetened cocoa powder (preferably Dutch process), 2½ cups nonfat dry milk powder, 2 teaspoons cornstarch, 1 heavy pinch fine salt, and 1 pinch ground cayenne pepper in a large airtight container, lid, and shake vigorously. Enjoy 2 tablespoons in a cup of warm milk or water.

[3] The gelatin must soak before it can be thoroughly dissolved. The process is called "blooming."

Pastry bag o' frosting

Cake layers

DON'T PUT NEEDLE ON CAKE!

Cake Vox!

Old record player

*AS SEEN ON THE LATE SHOW WITH THAT DAVE GUY!

THE FROSTING MAN COMETH

Cake is one of my favorite desserts. Devil's food, butter, pound, genoise . . . doesn't matter. If it's cake, it's welcome at my table, especially if it's adorned with thick waves of frosting. Not icing, not glaze. Frosting. What's the difference? Although several otherwise reliable dictionaries imply or out-and-out state that frosting and icing are synonymous, any true cake lover knows this is nonsense. Frosting is fluffy, whippable, spreadable, rich, and often resembles waves breaking across the top of the cake. Icing is thinner, more sugary, translucent, and gooey—or at least more gooey than frosting. The stuff you see on cinnamon buns is icing. Then there's glaze, which is a lot like icing only it sets into a solid coating that can shatter and break into little shards. Think glazed doughnut. They're all good, I'll grant you. But frosting is special.

CAKE-FROSTING HARDWARE

▸ All the pros build their cakes on these corrugated bases called cake rounds. There is simply no other practical platform for building a cake. You can buy them at any bakers' supply and off the Internet. Do not try to substitute a paper plate. I tried that . . . once.
▸ A large offset spatula is the best tool for spreading frosting, bar none.

▸ In order to frost the sides and top of a cake, you've got to be able to get to it from a lot of different angles. To do that, pros use a heavy-duty cake turntable like this.
   Must one invest in such a device? Not if you have a lazy Susan and a cake pan.

Although there are hundreds of different branches on the frosting/icing family tree, most fall into one of these categories:

Beat enough sugar (usually confectioners') into heavy cream, and you've got a light, refreshing WHIPPED CREAM FROSTING, which, due to its lightness, can be piled on to great effect. The cream can be stabilized with a starch, like cornstarch or even gelatin (in which case it's more of a mousse, really). But even when refrigerated (and all cakes frosted with a whipped cream must be kept on chill), whipped cream does not do well over time. Choose this only if you plan on serving the cake right away and don't see having a lot of leftovers.

GANACHE is a fancy French word for "melted chocolate in cream," and that's all it ever is, equal portions (by weight) of cream and chocolate. Although ganaches can be whipped, they're usually poured directly over a finished cake, thus creating a smooth, shiny layer. Cooled and whipped ganache also forms the base for truffles.

Most simple MERINGUE FROSTINGS, such as the classic 7-minute frosting, are typically composed of egg whites whipped with sugar over a double boiler until cooked. They've fallen out of favor in the last decade or two because they are notoriously unstable, weeping in very humid or cold conditions, and because they're not always cooked to the temperatures needed to kill every possible pathogen in the eggs. Still, coconut cake would not be coconut cake without 7-minute frosting.

BUTTERCREAMS are built on sugar syrups, butter, and eggs. There are many different ways to assemble a buttercream, and various culinary traditions have laid claim to particular procedures.

American buttercreams are extremely simple. Butter and confectioners' sugar are creamed together. A raw egg or milk may be added to create a smoother texture. Flavorings such as extracts and/or chocolate are often added.

French buttercream follows a different course. White or whole eggs are whipped, and then a hot sugar syrup is gradually added. Then the butter is added. Most pastry chefs use this method because it's very stable and keeps extremely well. This is the model we followed in the original show application, but it requires more procedural precision than the updated version.

Swiss buttercreams are meringue based. Egg whites and sugar are heated and whipped together, then the butter is added. The cooked meringue phase helps stabilize the frosting. This is the method we've used in the following application.

Italian buttercream is similar to the French version (which was probably derived from it), although whole eggs are typically used, making it the richest of the buttercreams.

As the water cooks out of the solution, the sucrose molecules draw closer together. Their goal: to make a crystal.

Corn syrup molecules get in the way. Since they have a different molecular shape, the sugar can't bond.

TIDBIT There are 100 calories in 1 tablespoon of butter.

TIDBIT Royal icing, the traditional icing for British wedding cakes, is made of icing sugar (British for "confectioners' sugar"), egg whites, and a drop of lemon juice.

BUTTERCREAM REDUX

ENOUGH ICING FOR 1 (9-INCH)
2-LAYER CAKE; ABOUT 1 QUART

A few of you out there had trouble with this application as it appeared in the show. Okay . . . a lot of you. And I blame myself (most of you blame me too). Most ended up with butter-soup rather than buttercream. We've modified the procedure from a French-style buttercream to a Swiss-style buttercream, which is more reliable.

// SOFTWARE ///

4	large	eggs	at room temperature
8	ounces	sugar	
½	cup	dark corn syrup	
2	cups	unsalted butter	cubed and at room temperature
	pinch	kosher salt	

// PROCEDURE //

1. Put an inch of water in a **pot** that's big enough to hold the **work bowl of a stand mixer** double-boiler style (meaning it can sit in it without touching the water). Bring to a rapid simmer over medium-high heat.

2. Meanwhile, in the mixer work bowl combine the eggs, sugar, and corn syrup and set the bowl over the simmering water. **Whisk** constantly until the sugar dissolves, the mixture becomes thin and foamy, and it reaches 160°F, about 5 minutes.

3. Move the bowl to the **stand mixer fitted with the whisk attachment** and whisk on high speed until the mixture doubles in volume, thickens, lightens in color, and cools, about 15 minutes.

4. Decrease the speed to medium and add the butter one piece at a time, making sure each piece is fully incorporated before adding the next; this should take about 6 minutes. The mixture may appear to "curdle" before it comes together, but that's okay. Add the salt, increase the speed to high, and beat until the buttercream is smooth and creamy, 2 minutes.

5. Use immediately or store in the fridge for up to 3 days. Bring chilled frosting back to room temperature before using.

TIDBIT | Sixty-nine percent of Americans eat the cake before the frosting.

TIP | For more ganache recipes, see "Art of Darkness III: Ganache," page 196.

APPLICATION ____ **GANACHE**

1½ CUPS

// SOFTWARE ///

3	tablespoons	light corn syrup	
1½	cups	heavy cream	
12	ounces	good-quality dark chocolate	finely chopped
½	teaspoon	vanilla extract	

// PROCEDURE //

1. Combine the corn syrup and cream in a **3-quart saucier** set over medium-high heat and bring to a bare simmer.

2. Remove the pan from the heat and cool for 1 minute. Add the chocolate and vanilla extract and stir until smooth. Cool slightly before using. Store in an **airtight container** for up to 3 days.

APPLICATION ____ **WRITING CHOCOLATE**

1 CUP

Okay, this isn't a frosting, but if you're going to frost a cake, you might just want to write on it (cakes being the only food we commonly scribble messages on). In that case, this may come in handy.

// SOFTWARE ///

12	ounces	semisweet chocolate chips	
2	teaspoons	canola or vegetable oil	

// PROCEDURE //

Microwave the chocolate chips and the oil in a **small microwave-safe glass bowl** on high for 1 minute. Remove, stir, and cool for 1 minute. If any chocolate solids remain, return the mixture to the microwave for 10-second intervals, stirring between each. (Microwave ovens vary in power, so cooking time may vary as well.) Transfer the mixture to a **squeeze bottle** with a narrow tip and use to decorate cookies or write on cakes.

SIMPLE CHOCOLATE FROSTING

APPROXIMATELY 1 QUART

Here's one that we really like but just couldn't squeeze into the episode. Technically this is an American buttercream, but in this case much of the butter has been replaced, either with melted chocolate or mayonnaise, which is a great way to get cooked egg stability into a cake without a lot of fuss.

TIDBIT | For our Cocoa Whipped Cream application, see the previous chapter.

// SOFTWARE

1½	cups	unsalted butter	at room temperature
1	ounce	mayonnaise	
6	ounces	semisweet chocolate	melted and cooled
1	pound	confectioners' sugar	
1	teaspoon	vanilla extract	
	pinch	kosher salt	

// PROCEDURE

1. Beat the butter and mayonnaise in a **stand mixer fitted with the paddle attachment** on high until light and fluffy, 3 to 4 minutes.

2. With the mixer on low, slowly pour in the melted chocolate. Continue mixing on low speed until all of the chocolate is incorporated, stopping to **scrape** down the sides of the bowl as needed.

3. Turn off the mixer and add ½ cup of the sugar. Mix on low to combine. Stop to scrape down the sides of the bowl. Repeat until all of the sugar has been incorporated.

4. Add the vanilla and salt and continue to beat until the frosting is smooth and lightens slightly in color, 2 to 3 minutes. Use immediately or store in an **airtight container** at room temperature for up to 4 hours or refrigerate for up to 1 week. Bring to room temperature before using chilled frosting.

WE GO THROUGH A LOT OF STYROFOAM!

DOING THE DEED:

1. Cut a notch to help realign the layers.

2. 1-by-2-inch fence pickets.

3. Use pickets as a guide for "topping" and splitting the cake.

4. Instead of an expensive knife, I use a saw blade.

5. Arrange the layers (see notch).

6. Apply the ganache filling.

7. Apply a thin primer layer or "crumb coat."

8. Apply the frosting.

9. A stipple finish.

10. Using a frosting comb.

11. Applying nuts.

12. Writing chocolate sends a message.

BEET IT

EPISODE 85 | SEASON 6 | GOOD EATS

Although the beet is embraced in many

regions of the world, especially Eastern Europe and Russia, in America . . . not so much. Maybe it's the blood-red juice, the working-class aura, or the fact that far too many of us were exposed to unsettlingly squishy canned beets during childhood. Although they've enjoyed a recent pop-spike as of late (due, I suspect, to frequent pairings with goat cheese, which makes everything taste good), beets have never been part of our daily bread, which is odd when you consider how much we love sweets. And so with this episode we hoped to persuade America to eat to a different beet.

TRIVIA | The couple in the Spanish-language soap opera were played by our camera operator and head chef. You gotta multitask if you're gonna work on *Good Eats*.

KNOWLEDGE CONCENTRATE

▷ Although beet taxonomy is quite complex, most beet-heads recognize four main types of beet, all evolved from one great-grandbeet called *Beta maritima*, or "sea beet," which still grows wild along the Mediterranean coasts of Europe and Africa, and was originally foraged not for its swollen root but for its greens. The big four are . . .

The MANGELWURZEL or MANGOLD BEET: A large, pale root used today strictly as animal fodder, although the Brits are fond of flinging them from time to time.

SWISS CHARD/SPINACH BEET: Harvested for its greens, much like its ancient ancestor.

SUGAR BEET: Used almost exclusively for sugar production. Rarely, if ever, consumed as a vegetable.

GARDEN BEET: The beet that most of us think of when we think of beets, which isn't as often as it oughta be.

▷ Within the garden beet category there are dozens of subvarieties. Besides the standard red beets, there are golden beets, white beets, even candy-cane beets, which are variegated white and red on the inside. Also, miniature or "baby" beets are available early in the season, harvested about forty-five days after planting. Personally, I don't think you can beat plain old-fashioned red beets when it comes to sweetness and texture.

I always buy beets in bunches with the greens intact. The greens are great indicators of health. Healthy greens usually mean fresh beets. Of course, the greens also taste good. More on that later.

Although beets can grow as big as melons, I never buy any larger than tennis balls. Any larger, and you start getting a lot of fiber, and they take forever to cook. If you're forced to choose from a bin of bulk or loose beets, always look for specimens that are nice and smooth with no cracks or wrinkles.

How long fresh beets keep depends a great deal on how old they are to begin with and how you store them. If you buy them early in the season, when they've still got nice, tight greens on them, they'll keep quite a while in a root cellar. Problem is, I don't have a root cellar. Luckily I can make one in my refrigerator—and so can you, if you're really, really kinda freaky about this sort of thing.

Step 1: Get yourself a 1-gallon container (with a lid).

Step 2: Get yourself 2 pounds of play sand (not—I repeat not—cat sand).

Step 3: Stick your beets in the sand.

Step 4: Stick your new root cellar in the bottom of the fridge.

The sand will keep the beets in the dark and help to wick away any damaging moisture. I've had good luck storing turnips and carrots the same way. But then I'm kinda freaky about this sort of thing.

Regardless of their final culinary destination, I never peel beets before cooking them for the simple reason that when properly cooked the skins slide right off like the cover of an old baseball. Also, any chink in the armor will open up a spigot of red liquid, which can stain your clothes (though it usually washes out). For basic cooking, cut the greens back to about an inch long (save the greens) and then give the beets a scrub under running water with a scrubby pad. (I prefer the green ones made by 3M—and, no, they don't pay me to say that.)

Now, unlike our grandmothers, who were taught to cook beets in boiling water, I generally reach for the roasting pan and go with dry heat, which actually intensifies the earthy sweetness. The one exception is if a recipe calls for peeled, raw beets. In that case I drop them in the steamer for a couple of minutes or until the outer coat slides right off.

The red in beets comes from a pigment called betacyanin. It's heat-stable and highly soluble in water, which is why it's been used as a dye for fabrics and as a food coloring. It will generally wash away with soap and water if it hasn't been in contact with your shirt or hands or whatnot for too long. This is why I generally undertake beet cookery with gloves. Not dishwashing gloves, but medical examination gloves. Drugstores and many hardware stores carry such gloves, which are also good for medical experiments if, you know, you're into that.

Plastic storage container (angled entry)

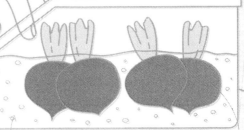

AB'S PATENTED BEET BOX

AS SEEN ON THE ELLEN DEGENERES SHOW!

Beets stay in dark sand, which sucks away moisture

Play sand (from hardware store)

Beets, turnips, rutabagas, etc.

BEET IT

PICKLED BEETS

2 QUARTS

I know what you're thinking, and I insist you stop it this instant. Beets are perfect pickle fodder and again, roasting, along with the use of shallots and tarragon wine vinegar (easily found at most megamarts), makes all the difference.

//SOFTWARE ///

2	pounds	medium beets	with 1-inch stems remaining, scrubbed clean
2	large	shallots	peeled
2	sprigs	fresh rosemary	
2	teaspoons	olive oil	
1	large	red onion	thinly sliced
2	cups	Tarragon Chive Vinegar	see page 101
1½	teaspoons	kosher salt	
3½	ounces	sugar	
2	cups	H_2O	

// PROCEDURE ///

1. Crank your oven to 400°F.

2. Toss the beets with the shallots, rosemary, and olive oil in a **large bowl**. Wrap in a pouch made of **heavy-duty aluminum foil** and roast for 60 minutes, or until a **paring knife** can be pushed into the beet with minimal resistance. Discard shallots and rosemary.

3. Remove the skin from the beets and slice into thin rounds. Divide the sliced beets between **two 1-quart jars,** alternating layers with the onion. Boil the vinegar, salt, sugar, and water in a **2-quart saucepan**. Remove from the heat and pour over the beets. Tightly lid the jars and cool for 2 hours at room temperature. Place in the refrigerator for at least 3 days before serving. Pickled beets can be stored in the fridge for up to a month.

TIDBIT | Beets are known for their ability to purify the blood and liver.

BEET GREEN GRATIN

When they're nice and bright green and fresh, beet greens are every bit as good as Swiss chard (which is also a beet).

// **SOFTWARE** ///

1	tablespoon	unsalted butter	plus extra for the pan
12	ounces	mushrooms	sliced
2	cloves	garlic	minced
1	pound	beet greens	cleaned, stemmed, and roughly chopped
½	teaspoon	kosher salt	plus additional to taste
	to taste	black pepper	freshly ground
4	large	eggs	lightly beaten
1	cup	ricotta cheese	
1	ounce	Parmesan cheese	freshly grated or ground
2	ounces	butter crackers	crumbled

TRIVIA I learned a lot making this show. Like how it's really tough to put a tight medical glove on someone else's hand.

// **PROCEDURE** ///

1. Heat the oven to 375°F.

2. Melt the butter in a **12-inch sauté pan** over medium heat. Add the mushrooms and garlic and sauté for 1 to 2 minutes. Add the beet greens and cook, stirring occasionally, until the greens begin to wilt, 2 to 3 minutes. Remove from the heat and season with salt and pepper. Set aside to cool slightly.

3. **Whisk** together the eggs, ricotta, Parmesan cheese, and ½ teaspoon salt. Fold the cheese mixture into the slightly cooled greens.

4. Pour this into a lightly buttered **9-by-11-inch glass baking dish** and top with the crumbled crackers.

5. Cover with **heavy-duty aluminum foil** and bake for 30 minutes. Uncover and bake for an additional 7 to 8 minutes, or until the crackers are nicely browned. Cool for 5 minutes before serving.

TIDBIT Beet greens contain protein, calcium, fiber, beta-carotene, and vitamins A, B, and C.

TIDBIT Borscht (beet soup) is the national dish of the Ukraine.

FIT TO BE TIED

EPISODE 86 | SEASON 6 | GOOD EATS

Alton Brown

The first time I had a roulade I was about six. It was at a neighborhood Italian place in Los Angeles where my parents were meeting some friends. I was the only kid, but I didn't mind because I really loved eating in restaurants, especially with my dad, who was a serious chowhound. Anyway, the roulade comes, an Italian braciole, to be exact, featuring layers of cheese and spinach rolled up in flank steak. I thought it was a fantastical feat of edible legerdemain wherein a trio of sorcerers—the breeder, the butcher, and the chef—had conjured a cow capable of growing vegetal matter inside its muscles. (Since cheese already comes from cows I didn't figure that was too much of a trick.) When I questioned the adults as to what variety of bovine would come equipped in such a manner, they howled with laughter . . . the kind of laughter that makes all inquisitive kids grow dark and brooding. I sulked the rest of the night, but rest assured, I finished my braciole.

TIDBIT | *Chowhound*, by the way, is not necessarily synonymous with *foodie* or *gourmet*. A chowhound is far less discriminating than either of the latter but tends to enjoy food even more thanks to a complete lack of critical judgment. My father delighted as much in my mom's spag bol with liberal shakings of the stuff in the green can as he did fancy French food. My dad died when I was ten (not food related), and I don't remember him being happier than when he tucked into a good plate of kibble.

TIDBIT | The French term *paupiette* may replace the word *roulade* on menus.

TIDBIT | One of the most popular preparations of flank steak is London broil.

STUFFING IS EVIL

KNOWLEDGE CONCENTRATE

This episode is relatively technique heavy, as roulade construction involves a fair amount of layering and rolling and tying. But once you get the hang of the maneuvers, these dishes (and any you may dream up along the way) will no doubt become favorites for entertaining. And remember, when you serve them to kids, tell them the critter in question grew that way.

Of all the tasty cuts of cow, only one is perfectly suited to rolling: the flank steak.

It lies just behind the skirt steak and contains a majority of the diaphragm. The flank is lean, boneless, and easy to handle, and the grain runs all in one direction, which means that when rolled, cooked, and cut, the meat fibers are going to be nice and short and, therefore, easily chewed. And the flank is flat, a key attribute where roulades are concerned. Of course, flatter would be even nicer, and that requires pounding.

As you can see, manufacturers have kindly provided us an arsenal of meat-mangling mallets, hatchets, and bludgeons, oh my.

I personally prefer the more placid pounding disk (right, fourth from left), which flattens without all the tearing, ripping, and marauding associated with Viking battle axes. Always remember when using such a device to let the weight do the work, and always hold the tool so that when it makes contact with the meat it's parallel to the counter. Otherwise you'll end up with gouges and tears like this:

NO MANGLED MEAT!

Meat-friendly pounder.

Deadly sharp "horns"

Chuck

Rib

Short loin

Sirloin

Round

Brisket

Plate

Flank and Skirt

Glue

LITTLE-KNOWN FACT: COWS HATE BUTTERFLIES AND HAVE BEEN KNOWN TO CHASE THEM SO HARD THEY FOAM AT THE MOUTH.

FIT TO BE TIED

4 TO 6 SERVINGS

Behold: the surgeon's knot.

// SOFTWARE //

2½	ounces	seasoned croutons	
1¼	ounces	Parmesan cheese	grated
2	large	eggs	
1	tablespoon	fresh parsley	chopped
1	tablespoon	fresh oregano	chopped
1	teaspoon	fresh rosemary	chopped
1	teaspoon	fresh thyme	chopped
1	clove	garlic	chopped
1	pound	flank steak	trimmed
2	tablespoons	vegetable oil	divided
½	teaspoon	kosher salt	
¼	teaspoon	black pepper	freshly ground
3	cups	tomato sauce	at room temperature

// PROCEDURE //

1. Heat the oven to 350°F.

2. Pulse the croutons, cheese, eggs, herbs, and garlic until they form a paste in the bowl of a **food processor** and set aside.

3. Sandwich the steak in **two large pieces of plastic wrap** atop a **cutting board**. Gently pound using a **round meat pounder** until the steak is about ¼ inch thick. Use even blows and let the pounder do the work, to avoid gouging the meat.

4. **Brush** the pounded steak with 1 tablespoon of the oil and season with the salt and pepper, then spread the filling evenly over the meat.

5. Roll tightly and tie with **butchers' twine**, finishing with a surgeon's knot (top left). Brush the outside of the roll with the remaining oil.

6. Place a **10-inch cast-iron skillet** over medium-high heat for 3 to 4 minutes. Add the roll and sear on all sides until well browned, about 2 minutes per side.

7. Carefully transfer to a **13-by-9-inch glass baking dish** and pour the tomato sauce over it, turning the meat a couple of times to ensure coverage.

8. Tent the baking dish with **aluminum foil** so that the foil isn't touching the meat. Cook for 45 minutes, or until the meat is done.

9. Rest for 10 minutes, then slice[1] and serve.

[1] Although any long slicer will do, I use an electric knife because it tends to keep the filling intact.

FISH ROLL

This is a real showstopper, not only visually but texturally and flavorally. Okay, *flavorally* isn't a word, but you get the picture. This is definitely a frighten-and-amaze-your-friends-and-family dish. I really feel the electric knife is key.

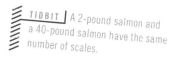

TIDBIT | A 2-pound salmon and a 40-pound salmon have the same number of scales.

// SOFTWARE //

2	thin	salmon fillets	about 11 inches long
3		flounder fillets	about 8 inches long
8		sea scallops	
1	teaspoon	kosher salt	
½	teaspoon	black pepper	freshly ground
1	tablespoon	fresh dill	chopped
1	tablespoon	fresh parsley	chopped
1 to 2	teaspoons	vegetable oil	

// PROCEDURE //

1. Lay out a **sheet of parchment paper** at least 15 inches long and top it with a slightly longer layer of **plastic wrap**.

2. Place the fillets of salmon lengthwise, tails away from you. Overlap the fillets of flounder about 1 inch over the tails of the salmon. Then place the scallops on a **metal skewer** and set at the end of the flounder farthest from you. Season the seafood with the salt and pepper and sprinkle with the herbs.

3. Using the plastic wrap, pull the fish toward you so that the plastic begins to pull the flounder over the scallops. Be sure not to roll the plastic into the fish roll. Use a **half sheet pan** to push the roll tightly as you pull the plastic toward you. The roll should be tight and you should be able to remove the sheet of plastic. Then roll the fish in the parchment away from you so it is completely encased in the parchment, like a sausage, twisting the ends slightly. Refrigerate for 1 hour.

4. Heat the broiler to high and position an oven rack 6 inches from the heat.

5. **Brush** a **broiler pan** with oil.

6. Extract the metal skewer from the fish roll. Then, with the paper still in place, portion the roulade into 1-inch rounds using an **electric knife or long slicer**.

7. Arrange the rounds on the prepped broiler pan and then peel off the paper. Brush each round with more oil.

8. Broil for 6 to 9 minutes, until the rounds reach an internal temperature of 130°F.

9. Serve with Hollandaise Sauce (page 149).

This is one of those shows I dove into for my daughter's sake. I have always been a crab lover, mind you, but it has always been a love I satisfied away from the domestic environment. I'd order it in a restaurant, but cook it? Heck no. Everyone knows crab is just not worth the work. But the kid is crazy for crab and asks for it at least once a week. And so the applications in this show were born. I have to say, as simple as it is, the microwave trick on page 42 is one of the best shortcuts on these pages.

TRIVIA The "crab" wrangler was pathetically played by our assistant editor Brett. Poor guy . . . it was his first time on the show and, man, was he green. He's developed nicely and has gone on to recurring roles as my lawyer Twitchy, an elf, and, surprisingly, a long list of unattractive female characters including the infamous Little Dutch Girl from episode 111 ("Circle of Life").

WHEN DECAPODS ATTACK!!!

Good Eats scraps (under gills)

Good Eats hunks

Good Eats chunks

Good Eats bits

Crabs have been scuttling along floors of the world's silent seas for some 200 million years, and during that time they have diversified into over four hundred distinct species, many of which lurk in the waters surrounding the United States. What kind of crab ends up on your plate is largely a function of where you are on the planet.

If you happen into the Northeast you're likely to happen upon a sand crab or two hiding among the lobsters in the megamart tank. Chefs didn't show this crab much respect until some marketing guru somewhere decided to re-christen it the PEEKYTOE. Now it's all the rage.

The more common East Coast crab also has a fancy moniker, at least in Latin. The *Callinectes sapidus*, or "beautiful swimmer," a.k.a. BLUE CRAB, proliferates prodigiously from the coast of Maryland all the way down to Florida. Of course, down there folks prefer the STONE CRAB, which as far as I can tell is the only crab that is merely maimed during harvest. From mid-October to mid-May, they're hauled, liberated of one large claw, and tossed back to grow another.

On the West Coast we meet up with the blue crab's regional doppelgänger, the DUNGENESS CRAB, which when paired with a little sourdough and a nice white wine is the true San Francisco treat. Head north to the frigid waters of Alaska, and you'll see strange things indeed, like the SNOW CRAB and that deep-diving decapod the KING CRAB, which at six feet across looks as much like a monster as anything you'd ever hope not to see.

For those of you unfamiliar with this critter, allow me to introduce and elaborate on the Dungeness crab. Named for a spit on the Olympic peninsula, Dungeness, or dungies, pretty much rule the Pacific Coast market, which thanks to several overlapping regional seasons is pretty much year round. Most dungies are cooked as soon as they come onto the dock, which helps preserve their fresh flavor. Whole specimens are about 25 percent edible, depending on who's doing the picking, and, actually, that isn't bad for a crab. When purchasing, watch out for shell breaks or punctures, which are bad. And if you've got a choice, go for one that feels heavy for its size. Lightweights have generally molted recently and so contain less meat. And look out for dangling legs, which usually signal a crab that was dead before it was cooked—not a good thing. Many markets will crack and clean your crabs for you, but it's always good to know the basics, especially if you want to reserve some of the shell for either presentation purposes or making crab stock.

TIDBIT The Japanese spider crab can measure up to 26 feet when its legs are fully extended.

TIDBIT Crabs have a 360-degree field of vision and see twice as well as humans.

CRAB DISASSEMBLY

If the idea of dismantling a deep-sea beetle in order to extract the succulent meat that lies within its shell gives you the heebie-jeebies, well, just skip ahead a page. The rest of us are going to play Crustacean Quincy. Your autopsy kit should include:

▶ FLATHEAD SCREWDRIVER (for twisting open . . . stuff).

▶ TWEEZERS (really big ones for getting meat out of cracks and crevices).

▶ WOODEN MALLET (rubber will do too; for crushin' . . . stuff).

▶ CLEAN SIDE TOWEL or DISH TOWEL (because this is going to be messy).

▶ HALF SHEET PAN (to disassemble on).

▶ TWO BOWLS (one for the good eats, one for the non-eats).

1. Flip the crab on its back. You see by the size and shape of this apron that this is a boy crab, which makes sense, because girl Dungenesses are illegal to harvest. We're just gonna crack that off.

2. Now we reach right in that little hole, and we're gonna pry off the back, or carapace, of the crab. Right away I'm gonna rinse off all the stuff on the inside. Right now nothing in here looks like good eats, but your patience will be rewarded. Look around under the hood, and you'll see a lot of these little gray finger things. Those are the gills, also called "dead man's fingers." They pop right off.

3. Twist off all of the legs and set them aside. Then crack the remaining body piece in half.

4. Tasty and delectable pockets of goodness lurk in a honeycomb structure of shell, and you can use the tweezers to pick them out. Since the meat in the body is about three times sweeter than the leg meat, I'd argue that the effort is well warranted.

5. Now spread the legs on the sheet pan, cover with the towel, and lightly bang with the mallet. Once breached, you can simply scoop the meat out with your thumb.

At this point, you could break out some good homemade mayonnaise, chop up some sweet pickles, and make yourself a crab sammich. Or we could go just a hair more sophisticated . . .

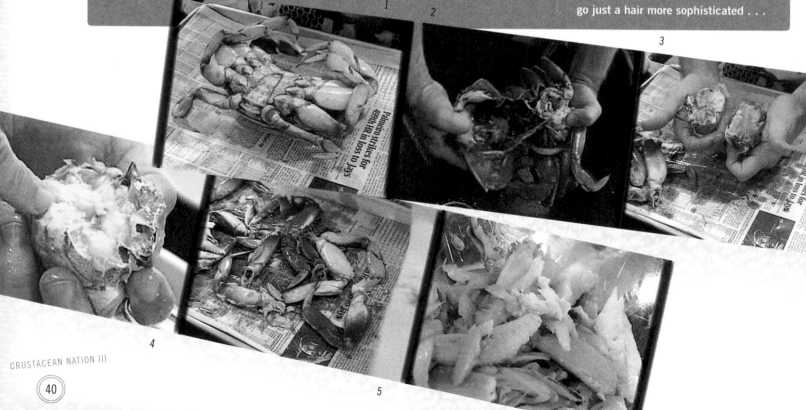

1

2

3

4

5

MARINATED CRAB SALAD

4 TO 6 SERVINGS

// SOFTWARE //

¼	cup	extra-virgin olive oil	
¼	cup	red wine vinegar	
1	clove	garlic	minced
½	teaspoon	kosher salt	
¼	teaspoon	black pepper	freshly ground
½	cup	fresh parsley	chopped
¼	cup	fresh tarragon	chopped
½	pound	cooked lump crab meat	
½	pound	cooked special crab meat	
6	cups	mixed greens	
4 to 6		lemon wedges	

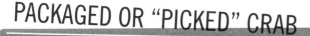

// PROCEDURE //

1. Combine the oil, vinegar, garlic, salt, pepper, parsley, and tarragon in a **large nonreactive bowl or zip-top bag**. Add the crab meats, toss, and refrigerate. Toss every hour for 4 hours.

2. Serve on a bed of mixed greens and top with a squeeze of lemon just before eating.

PACKAGED OR "PICKED" CRAB

Although I enjoy the whole crab-picking scene, the truth is, a cooked blue crab yields only about 15 percent of its weight in edible meat—and that's an awful lot of work for not very much good eats. A professional picker can blaze through one of these guys in about 40 seconds. I can manage it in 4 minutes if I'm in competition form, which isn't very often. That's why, more often than not, I buy cooked and picked blue crab, which comes in several market varieties, all pasteurized to extend shelf life and all requiring refrigeration.

Unfortunately, the name game is unregulated, so one fishmonger's JUMBO is another fishmonger's LUMP, IMPERIAL, or COLOSSAL. In any case, these are all words to represent the biggest pieces of white meat culled from the body.

This is as good and as expensive as it gets. Which is why I often cut it with BACKFIN meat, a.k.a. REGULAR or SPECIAL crabmeat, which comes from the body but is composed of smaller pieces than the lump. Then there is

FLAKE, which is made of the tiniest, teensiest pieces of meat left over from the body after the BACKFIN and LUMP have been removed. Then there is CLAW meat, which I don't really like because it's dark brown and kinda tough . . . like crab jerky. Then there's krab with a "K," which isn't crab at all but SURIMI, a processed fish paste usually made from pollock that's been flavored, colored, and shaped to pass for crab. Kids love it but, hey, they don't know any better.

STEAMED ALASKA KING CRAB LEGS

2 SERVINGS

MICROWAVES

There's nothing wrong with employing a microwave oven in the pursuit of serious culinary goals as long as you don't ask it to do things it can't. Let's take a moment to review what makes the devil box tick. Upon activation, a thingy called a magnetron tube generates waves of electromagnetic energy. Such waves are produced any time electricity moves through a circuit or even a simple wire, but what makes the magnetron special is that it creates oscillating waves, which can be directed at a target. In the case of a microwave oven these waves are shot down a long tube, bounced off a spinning metal fan, and scattered into the cooking chamber. They penetrate the target food to a depth that depends upon a pageful of math and cause polar molecules to dance to the rhythm of the oscillation. This movement generates heat via friction. Now, the most common asymmetrical molecule in crab legs—or any food, for that matter—is water, and there's a lot of it so the heat builds quickly. But since microwaves can't really produce heat in excess of the boiling point of water, they can't brown foods the way dry heat can.

Given their less-than-convenient size and shape, and the location of the fisheries, most snow and king crabs are cooked, dismantled, and flash frozen as soon as they get to the processing plant, which is usually aboard ship. If the shell is orange or red, you also know that they've been cooked, and most have. Now, I don't have a problem with this, given the fact that crab is extremely perishable. What I do have a problem with is stores selling them in a thawed state, which just restarts the countdown timer on decay. It's like throwing someone a culinary hand grenade; odds are, it's going to go off before you can do anything with it.

So, if king and snow crab legs have already been cooked and frozen, "cooking" them is really just a matter of reheating, and in reheating we have two goals:

1. To bring the consumable to a temperature that is both pleasingly palatable and safe from a microbial standpoint, which, to my mind, means reaching 145° to 160°F.
2. To lose as little moisture as possible.

// SOFTWARE //

3		cooked king crab legs	broken into 2 sections each
3	sprigs	fresh dill	

// PROCEDURE //

1. Tear off a 30-inch-long piece of **plastic wrap**.
2. Thoroughly moisten **two paper towels** and stack one upon the other on the wrap.
3. Lay the leg sections on the paper toweling, along with the dill.
4. Wrap the paper towels around the leg sections, then wrap in the plastic, forming a nice, tight parcel. You shouldn't be able to see any of the shell peeking out.
5. Microwave on high for 2 minutes.
6. Be ready with the Ghee (right).

TIDBIT | Once thawed, cooked crab should be consumed within 24 hours.

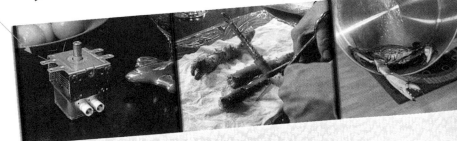

GHEE

SLIGHTLY LESS THAN 1 POUND OF GHEE

When it comes to dressing up pricey shellfish I'm not much for fancy-shmancy sauces. On one hand, plain melted butter is, well, just fat. Ghee, on the other hand, provides an ever-so-slightly nutty counterpoint to crab and lobster, and since the water and milk solids have been removed it's got the shelf life of uranium.

// SOFTWARE ///

2	cups	unsalted butter	

// PROCEDURE //

1. Put the butter in a **2-quart saucepan** over low heat. As soon as it liquefies, turn the heat up to medium.

2. When it finishes foaming, turn up the heat a little bit more and wait for it to foam a second time.

3. Cook until the butter fat turns gold and dark-brown bits of milk solids form on the bottom of the pan, 7 to 8 minutes.

4. Gently pour through a **fine-mesh strainer or folded cheesecloth** into a **heatproof container with a tight-fitting lid**. Ghee will keep for up to a month at room temp, a few months in the refrigerator, and until the universe collapses in the freezer.

TIDBIT According to Greek mythology, Hercules was attacked by a giant crab during his labors.

TIDBIT Referring to certain tumors with spidery arms, the word *cancer* comes from *karkinos*, the Greek word for "crab."

Barbecue. **I can think of no other word** in the American culinary lexicon that inflames such passion. To my mind, barbecue is a process, a life-style, and a dark art. It's midnight moppings to the tinny strains of Junior Kimbrough on a one-speaker boom box, toasting with bourbon from paper cups. It's lawn chairs and lies illuminated by a greasy-handled double–C-cell red Eveready flashlight. It's drooling dogs and ashes in the eyes and, dang it, I'm gettin' all misty just thinking about it. Q is to food what jazz is to music, intricate, primal, and 100 percent American. This episode was not designed as a definitive guide, of course, but rather an inflammatory pamphlet meant to arouse curiosity and whet the appetite.

Fun for the whole family!

PORK-ORATION

OINK!

JOWL

BOSTON BUTT

CHOPS

FAT BACK

CHOPS

PICNIC HAM

RIBS

TENDERLOIN

RIBS

LOIN

SPARERIBS

BACON

ROAST BUTT

LEG HAM

TRIVIA | This episode was set in and around a 1984 Airstream Ambassador trailer (complete with original 8-track . . . sweet!) parked outside a soundstage supposedly in Hollywood, where we're supposedly getting ready to make *Good Eats the Movie.* Nonsense, of course. It was a soundstage in Atlanta where we were trying desperately to finish the *Good Eats* kitchen set we'd been forced to build when a certain individual living within shouting distance of the *Good Eats* house, swollen with jealousy that his home wasn't on TV, decided to complain to a judge he'd apparently donated a considerable sum to and, well . . . so it goes. Anyway, we had to shoot and I had no set, so my trusty Airstream was pressed into service. I loved that trailer, but eventually sold it to a lawyer from New Hampshire.

TIDBIT | The world's largest barbecue cook-off is held every October in Kansas City.

For most of America not housed within the borders of Texas, barbecue means pork, but not all pork is 'cue worthy. What we want from the final dish is fork-tender, succulent, and digit-lickin' good. This means the target meat must contain enough connective tissue to convert into a considerable amount of gelatin. There also needs to be enough fat on the outside to baste the meat through the long cooking process. Now, hams do barbecue very nicely, but unless you're a professional you'll probably end up with something kind of dry, which means you'll need to add a lot of sauce. Several different rib cuts contain the right stuff, but ribs are a discipline all their own. Loins can be smoked, but there's nowhere near enough connective tissue to make anything close to actual barbecue. That leaves the arm area, known as the picnic ham, which is way too gristly, and the shoulder, or Boston butt.

TIDBIT | So named for the barrels or "butts" that Boston butchers used to pack them in.

The nonnegotiable steps to Q-land:

1. Procure meat, preferably a pork shoulder in the 6- to 8-pound range.

2. Brine shoulder to add flavor and to alter the proteins near the surface of the meat so that they partially denature and prevent moisture loss during cooking.

3. Rub on a spice mixture—oddly called a "rub"—to enhance flavor and (some would argue) smoke penetration.

4. Smoke. That is, cook in smoke. The heat is low, and the presence of a suspended colloid (smoke) essentially fumigates the meat, creating the coveted pink smoke ring in the meat.

The word *barbecue* derives from a very old Caribbean word, *barbacoa*, meaning to cook on green sticks directly over a smoldering fire. It's a method that's been popular with the Indians of Española and that surrounding area since, well, long before Columbus got his first boat. The problem with this kind of cooking is that it's very vulnerable to the whims of weather. The peoples of Polynesia cracked this problem by digging a pit and then lining it with hot rocks and coals. They put a whole pig right on top of that, then covered that with banana leaves, then sand. Of course, the problem here is that there's no convection, so smoke cannot do its mysterious mambo around the meat. Most modern pit masters, of course, have traded in their holes in the ground and racks of sticks for steel.

In barbecue, the smoke acts as a kind of airborne marinade, and what flavor ends up in the meat depends a lot on what you're smoking with. If the wood is soft like pine, spruce, or cedar, the smoke will include resins and creosote, which taste very yucky indeed. Stick with hardwoods like hickory and apple. When smoking something hot and fast—say, salmon—I like sawdust, because it's the best way to produce a lot of smoke very quickly without flames. But when the cooking is low and slow I use chunks of wood, because they last longer and give off smoke very slowly. Think of it as time-release.

TIDBIT | According to the Barbecue Industry Association, 75 percent of all U.S. households have a grill.

TIDBIT | Henry Ford invented charcoal in the early 1920s.

TIDBIT | The United States celebrates National Barbecue Month in May.

// SOFTWARE

6 to 8	pounds	pork butt	
8½	ounces	molasses	yes, by weight, and regular, not blackstrap
12	ounces	kosher salt	finely ground in a **food processor**
2	quarts	H$_2$O	
1	teaspoon	cumin seeds	
1	teaspoon	fennel seeds	
1	teaspoon	coriander seeds	
1	tablespoon	Chili Powder	see page 173
1	tablespoon	onion powder	
1	tablespoon	paprika	although sweet or hot will work, I vastly prefer smoked

TIDBIT | Paprika was brought to Hungary by the Turks in the sixteenth century.

TIP | I always reach for whole spices when I can, because the flavor stays safely in the seeds——or fruits, depending on the spice— until you release those flavors via grinding. Once they're ground you'd better use them quickly, because the aromatic oils are volatile. If you don't use them, you lose them.

// PROCEDURE

1. Combine the molasses, salt, and water in a **large (6-quart) covered container**. Add the pork butt, making sure it is completely submerged in the brine, cover, and refrigerate overnight, 8 to 12 hours.[1]

2. Grind the cumin, fennel, and coriander with either a **mortar and pestle or a blade-style coffee grinder** (I keep one just for spices). Add the chili powder, onion powder, and paprika and process to combine.

3. Remove the butt from the brine and pat dry. Sprinkle the rub evenly over the butt and then pat it onto the meat, making sure as much of the rub as possible adheres. More rub will adhere to the meat if you are wearing **latex gloves** during the application.

4. Heat the smoker to 210°F. Place the butt in the smoker and cook for 2 to 3 hours, maintaining a temperature of 210°F. Heat the oven to 300°F.

5. Remove the butt from the smoker and place it in the center of a large piece of **heavy-duty aluminum foil**. Bring the sides of the foil together to create a pouch around the butt, place the pouch on a **half sheet pan**, and cook for 3 to 4 hours in the oven.

6. The meat is done when a **metal skewer** easily penetrates all the way through to the bone. When that happens, remove from the oven and set aside to rest for 1 hour. Then use **two large forks** to shred the meat. Serve on cheap white bread or hamburger buns with Coleslaw (see page 18) on the side.[2]

[1] If you don't have that much refrigerator space, you can manage the brine step in a smallish cooler by replacing a quart of the water with 2 pounds of ice and simply stashing it in a cool place.

[2] If you've done your job properly no sauce will be required. That said, I never sit down to Q without a bottle of my favorite hot sauce standing by. I'm a fan of Louisiana Gold brand, but that's just me— and they don't pay me to say so.

FLOWERPOT SMOKER

I don't have a problem with grills or smokers. But I do have a problem with sending a grill or a smoker to do a barbecue pit's job. It's true that a charcoal grill can attain nice, low levels of heat, but this kind of fire requires a lot of hand-holding, and it's nearly impossible to keep the heat out of direct contact with the meat. There are some rigs that get around this problem with isolated fireboxes. The problem is, they require quite a bit of know-how and a fair stack of money. Electric smokers are pretty good at maintaining low levels of heat

for long periods of time, but they're still metal, and metal doesn't hold on to heat; it conducts it into the outside world. So, if we're really going to imitate a barbecue pit, we need the insulating powers of earth, but that doesn't mean we have to dig a hole. My answer: a flowerpot smoker.

We've got all the necessary components. A hot plate in the bottom will create the heat, and nice, thick terracotta walls will insulate it. And there's even a hole in the bottom to allow air flow; all we have to do is get it off the

ground a bit, and for that I usually use a couple of pieces of two-by-four, though bricks will do just as well. The hole also gives you a place to run the hot-plate cord. A heavy-duty pan will hold the wood, and a grate from a small kettle grill set up top will hold the butt. Oh, and I almost forgot: At the hardware store, pick up a standard replacement grill thermometer. Drop that right in the hole in the top pot. Total hardware bill: $47.32. Making your own smoker from scratch: priceless.

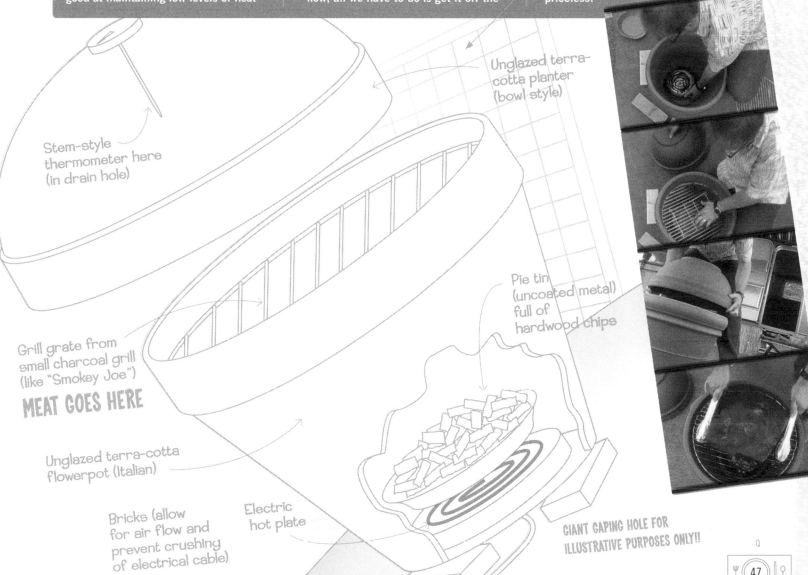

Stem-style thermometer here (in drain hole)

Unglazed terra-cotta planter (bowl style)

Grill grate from small charcoal grill (like "Smokey Joe")

MEAT GOES HERE

Pie tin (uncoated metal) full of hardwood chips

Unglazed terra-cotta flowerpot (Italian)

Bricks (allow for air flow and prevent crushing of electrical cable)

Electric hot plate

GIANT GAPING HOLE FOR ILLUSTRATIVE PURPOSES ONLY!!

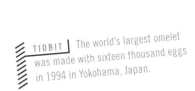

Walk into the average American breakfast joint

and order an omelet and you're likely to receive a rubbery envelope wrinkled as an old man's backside, brown as an L.A. sunset, running with cheese, and packed with hunks of raw vegetables like some kind of salad-bar piñata. Sound yummy? I thought not. My theory is that Americans can't do omelets because omelets are simple, and unfortunately in our language "simple" is synonymous with "easy." And omelets only get easy after you've made a couple hundred and even then they'll sneak up on you now and then. The good news is, an imperfect—heck, even a crummy—omelet made at home is good enough to be called good eats.

TIDBIT | The world's largest omelet was made with sixteen thousand eggs in 1994 in Yokohama, Japan.

KNOWLEDGE CONCENTRATE

Etymologically speaking, *spatula* comes from the Latin *spatha*, meaning a flat, elongated instrument. From that, the Italians get *spada*, or "broadsword," and from that we get *spade*, as well as the term *spay*. Which is not to say you should fix your cat with a sword, but I guess it would do the trick. The diminutive form of *spatha* is *spathula*, and that's where we get *spatula*. Which is best for an omelet? Rubber is okay, but silicone will do an even better job with less bulk.

FRITTATA

6 SERVINGS

TIDBIT | It is said that the Roman epicure Apicius (born in about 2 B.C.) invented the omelet.

Here is an omelet that requires no actual practice. The Italians call it a frittata, and it distinguishes itself from a French omelet because it is flat, rather than folded, and firm rather than creamy. And since you don't have to fold it, you can pile on whatever you want as long as it's either very small or precooked. Think of it as an egg pizza, perfect for any time of day.

// SOFTWARE //

6	large	eggs	well beaten
1	ounce	Parmesan cheese	grated
½	teaspoon	black pepper	freshly ground
1	pinch	kosher salt	
1	tablespoon	unsalted butter	
½	cup	roasted asparagus	chopped
½	cup	country ham	chopped
1	tablespoon	fresh parsley	chopped

// PROCEDURE //

1. Heat the broiler to high. Set a rack in the upper third of the oven.

2. Put the eggs, cheese, pepper, and salt in a **medium mixing bowl** and stir them together using a **fork**. Heat a **10-inch nonstick, oven-safe sauté pan** over medium-high heat for 2 to 3 minutes. When the pan is hot, add the butter to the pan and **brush** it around the surface of the pan. Add the asparagus and ham to the pan and sauté for 2 to 3 minutes, until heated through. Pour the egg mixture into the pan and stir with a **silicone spatula**. Cook for 4 to 5 minutes, until the egg mixture has set on the bottom and begins to set on top. Sprinkle with the parsley.

3. Place the pan under the broiler for 3 to 4 minutes, until lightly browned and puffy. Remove the frittata from the pan and cut into 6 wedges. Serve immediately.

To my taste, a perfect omelet is about the juxtaposition of unrelated forms: a smooth, rich, custardy interior encased in a golden, ever-so-slightly crisp exterior.

// SOFTWARE //

3	large	eggs	
1	pinch	fine salt	kosher is just too chunky for this application
1	teaspoon	unsalted butter	at room temperature, plus more for finishing the omelet

// PROCEDURE //

Although all the actions necessary for the production of an omelet could be squished down into three or four actual steps, I prefer to break it all out into ten small steps, an approach that highlights the importance of small stuff, which is the stuff you want to sweat when you're learning to make omelets.

1. Soak the eggs for 5 minutes in hot—not scalding—tap water. This will ensure that the omelet cooks faster, and the faster an omelet cooks the more tender it's going to be. You don't see this step in French recipes because they don't refrigerate their eggs in the first place.

2. Crack the eggs into a **small bowl (or large, bowl-shaped coffee mug)**. Season with the salt. If you don't have fine salt, just spin some kosher in your food processor for a few seconds. It really makes a difference.

3. Beat the eggs gently with a **fork**. I prefer a fork to a whisk because I don't want to work air into the eggs: Air bubbles are insulators and can slow down cooking if you're not careful.

4. Heat a **10-inch nonstick sauté pan** over medium to high heat. Now, even a nonstick surface is pocked with tiny microscopic crevices and pores that eggs can pour into and grab hold of. Heat expands the metal, squeezing many of these openings shut, so always heat your pan empty for a few minutes before adding anything. How hot? Well, for those of you with an infrared thermometer, I'd say 325° to 350°F. For those of you who don't have infrared thermometers, heat the pan for 2 to 3 minutes, until butter foams briskly upon making contact. Add the butter. Once melted, spread the butter around the pan with a **basting brush** to ensure coverage.

5. Pour the eggs into the center of the pan and stir vigorously with a **silicone spatula** for 5 seconds. (Actually it's not so much a matter of stirring with the spatula as holding the spatula relatively still and moving the pan around to stir the eggs.)

6. As soon as curds begin to form (that's the stuff that looks like scrambled eggs), lift the pan and tilt it around until the excess liquid pours off the top of the curd and into the pan. Then use the spatula to shape the edge and make sure the omelet isn't sticking. Move the spatula around the edge of the egg mixture to help shape it into a round and loosen the edge.

7. Walk away. That's right, let that omelet just sit there unaccosted for 10 long seconds so that it can develop a proper outer crust. Don't worry, your patience will be rewarded.

8. Time for the "jiggle" step. Simply shake the pan gently to make sure the omelet is indeed free of the pan.

9. Lift up the far edge of the pan and snap it back toward you. As soon as you get it there, use the spatula to fold over the one third facing you. Then change your grip on the pan handle from an overhand to an underhand and move to the **plate**, which you might want to lube with just a brief brushing of butter to make sure things don't bind up in transit.

10. Slide the third farthest from you onto the plate and then ease the fold over. Imagine that you're making a trifold wallet out of egg . . . because that's exactly what you're doing. And just ease the pan over.

There, that wasn't so hard. Next time just before the jiggle step you might want to scatter on just a tablespoon of grated cheese and/or fresh herbs, but remember: Fillings do not an omelet make.

N O T E : Many, and I do mean many, omelet recipes call for cooking the eggs in a combination of oil and butter, the logic being that the oil will raise the temperature at which the butter will burn. This is idiotic. Just because I go swimming with Michael Phelps it doesn't make me fast. The solids in butter will burn just as handily in oil as in the pan. So stick with butter, which by the way tastes good.

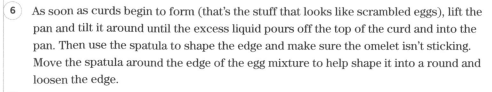

| A nonstick pan is key.

≣ TIDBIT | More people get salmonella from iguanas than eggs. ≣

"SPIKE" (FORMER PET)

// SOFTWARE

10	large	eggs	warmed for 5 minutes in hot H_2O
¼	cup	H_2O	
2	pinches	fine salt	
¼	cup	fresh herbs	chopped, such as chives, parsley, tarragon, or dill
4	teaspoons	unsalted butter	at room temperature, plus 2 teaspoons for finishing the omelets
1	cup	filling	any combination of sautéed peppers and onions, grated cheese, sautéed mushrooms, and cooked and drained spinach

// PROCEDURE

1. Put the eggs, water, salt, and herbs in a **medium mixing bowl** and use a **large fork** to thoroughly combine.

2. Heat a **10-inch nonstick sauté pan** over medium-low heat for 2 to 3 minutes. Add 1 teaspoon butter and **brush** it around the surface of the pan. Using a **4-ounce ladle**, place 1 ladleful of the egg mixture in the center of the pan. Stir vigorously with a **silicone spatula** until curds begin to form. Immediately lift the pan and tilt it around until the excess liquid pours off into empty spots in the pan. You want a thin, even layer of egg. Move the spatula around the edge of the egg mixture to loosen the edge. Cook for 10 seconds without touching it. Place ¼ cup of filling onto the two thirds of the surface of the omelet that are farthest from the handle.

3. Shake the pan to loosen the egg. Using your spatula, fold over the third of the omelet without filling. Slide the omelet onto a **plate** and fold it over so the omelet is a trifold. Coat with ½ teaspoon butter.

4. Repeat the process above for the remaining 3 omelets. You can hold finished omelets on a **half sheet pan lined with parchment paper** in a warm (200°F) oven while you prepare the rest. Serve immediately.

THE MUFFIN METHOD MAN

EPISODE 90 | SEASON 7 | GOOD EATS

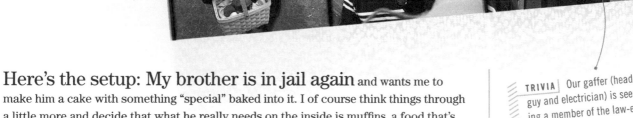

Here's the setup: My brother is in jail again and wants me to make him a cake with something "special" baked into it. I of course think things through a little more and decide that what he really needs on the inside is muffins, a food that's been maliciously mutilated in the past decades by corporate coffee concerns intent on addicting everyone to gooey sweet confections the size of cats' heads. Nope, in this country if you want an honest muffin you'll have to take matters into your own oven.

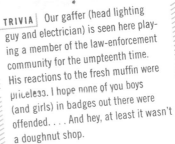

TRIVIA Our gaffer (head lighting guy and electrician) is seen here playing a member of the law-enforcement community for the umpteenth time. His reactions to the fresh muffin were priceless. I hope none of you boys (and girls) in badges out there were offended. . . . And hey, at least it wasn't a doughnut shop.

TRIVIA We never get bored using cheap little rigs on set in place of expensive effects in post-production. One of my personal favorites is the "blanket pull," which we used in this show to illustrate the proper texture of a muffin and what "tunneling" does. Behind the counter a prop person is kneeling on a furniture blanket tied to a rope pulled by our key grip. All they have to do is hold on to the balloons and ride across. It's so simple it's kind of dorky, but I can't get enough of it.

53

I've always held that the baked-goods kingdom should be categorized by mixing method. After all, how a batter or dough is produced is an even more critical determiner of final product than the ingredients that go into it. The most common mixing method in American kitchens is, coincidentally, the muffin method, which goes like this:

Mix all the wet stuff together in bowl A.

Mix all the dry stuff together in bowl B.

Dump bowl A into bowl B.[1]

Mix just until the batter comes together.

Make up.[2]

Bake up.

Cool.

Eat up.

There is but one curious point to remember: In the baking world, sugar is usually treated as a wet ingredient.

Although dried figs, dried apricots, dates, nuts, diced apples, mashed bananas, and even chocolate chips make perfectly good muffin fodder, I am personally a blueberry guy. Since their cell walls have been punctured by ice crystals, frozen berries tend to bleed and weep. When that juice mixes with the muffin batter, the CO_2 (a byproduct of chemical leavening) can make the juice turn green, which doesn't look terribly appetizing. So use fresh berries whenever you have a chance. If you have to use frozen, whatever you do, don't thaw them before they go in the batter. To prevent your berries from diving to the bottom of the muffin, toss them with about a tablespoon of the dry ingredients mixture. Think of this as Velcro, which will bind the batter to the berries, keeping them in suspension.

Beginning bakers often have a tough time knowing when to drop the spoon or whisk and leave a batter alone. A perfect muffin batter still has dry bits and lumps in it, most of which smooth out during baking. Why not mix the heck out of it? Gluten, of course. The more you agitate wheat proteins with water, the more little bungee cords of gluten you form. Whip up enough of them, and the bubbles that form as the chemical leavening goes to work will have to join together into super-bubbles in order to expand. These bubbles will twist and grow, forming tunnels that will completely dominate the texture of the final product . . . and not in a good way.

The word *muffin* evolved from the Old French word *mofle*, meaning "soft." Then again, it may have come from *muffe*, a Low German word meaning "cake." Regardless of where *muffin* comes from, a real *English muffin* is a soft yeast dough cooked on a griddle. The American version is a quick bread, meaning it derives its lift not from biological sources but from chemical reactions. Since baking powder wasn't invented until the mid-nineteenth century, the American version is relatively modern.

TIDBIT Muffin men were such a common sight on the streets of Victorian London that they actually got a nursery rhyme of their very own: "Have you seen the muffin man, the muffin man, the muffin man? Have you seen the muffin man who lives on Drury Lane?"

TRIVIA We made the jail cell in our producer's garage by putting a couple of cots on the wall. My DP, Marion Laney, made the cell seem real by using a cardboard cutout to create bar shadows. And, as usual, my brother was difficult to work with. He's so bad at memorizing lines that we don't even give them to him anymore.

[1] This order prevents dry stuff from flying all over the kitchen.

[2] "Make up" is a bakery phrase that means to get a dough or batter into whatever form is required for baking—i.e., putting it in a pan, piping it into hot oil, dishing it into muffin tins, etc.

BLUEBERRY MUFFINS

12 MUFFINS

// SOFTWARE //

7	ounces	sugar	
½	cup	vegetable oil	
1	large	egg	
1	cup	plain yogurt	
1	teaspoon	vanilla extract	
½	teaspoon	orange zest	grated
12½	ounces	all-purpose flour	
2	teaspoons	baking powder	
1	teaspoon	baking soda	
1	heavy pinch	kosher salt	
8	ounces	fresh blueberries	

// PROCEDURE ///

1. Heat the oven to 350°F. Spray a **standard 12-cup muffin pan** with nonstick spray and set aside.

2. **Whisk** the sugar, oil, egg, yogurt, vanilla, and zest together in **bowl A**. **Sift** together the flour, baking powder, baking soda, and salt into **bowl B** (which by the way should be the larger of the two bowls). Toss the berries with one tablespoon of this dry mixture and set aside.

3. Dump bowl A into bowl B. Stir it a dozen or so times, add 6 ounces of the berries to the batter and stir three more times, then just walk away for 1 minute.

4. Use a **disher** to dose ¼ cup of batter into each hole of the muffin pan.

5. Broadcast the remaining 2 ounces berries on top of the muffins and press down on them ever so slightly.

6. Let the muffins sit for 3 minutes on the counter.[3]

7. Bake on the middle rack of the oven for 25 to 30 minutes, until the internal temperature reaches 210°F or a toothpick inserted into the center of a muffin comes out clean. If your oven has a history of uneven baking, rotate the pan halfway through.

8. Remove from the oven. Cover with a **clean dish towel** and flip the muffins out so that the bottoms are facing up.[4]

9. Serve immediately or store in an **airtight container** for 2 to 3 days.[5]

[3] This is a new step that I've become a fan of in the last few years. I'm convinced that allowing the leavening to have a head start on the counter makes for a better rise in the oven. Keep in mind that the baking powder releases its first shot of gas as soon as moisture is introduced into the equation. Why not let that happen while the batter is still thoroughly pliable?

[4] Since the tops were exposed to dry heat they're relatively set, but the bottoms have not been exposed and are therefore a little on the wet side. Flipping them out will give that vulnerable back side time to dry and set.

[5] At home, they last a week on the counter in a zip-top bag, but I realize some peoples' kitchens simply house more molds than others. The muffins also freeze well.

ENGLISH MUFFINS

12 MUFFINS

Most people will go through life never cooking an English muffin, and that's a shame because all you need is a heavy pan or griddle and a little time. In truth, the English muffin is really just a yeast-risen pancake cooked inside a ring. They are simple, they are wonderful, and that's why this application makes my top-ten all-time *Good Eats* dishes.

// **SOFTWARE** ///

1½	ounces	nonfat powdered milk	
1	tablespoon	sugar	
1	teaspoon	kosher salt	
1	tablespoon	shortening	
1	cup	hot H$_2$O	just off the boil
1	envelope	active dry yeast	
⅛	teaspoon	sugar	
⅓	cup	warm H$_2$O	about 100°F
12	ounces	all-purpose flour	sifted
		nonstick spray	
		cornmeal	for sprinkling

// **SPECIAL HARDWARE** ///

Electric griddle, 4 (3-inch) metal rings

// **PROCEDURE** //

1. Mingle the powdered milk, 1 tablespoon of the sugar, the salt, shortening, and 1 cup hot water in a **medium bowl**. Stir until the sugar and salt are dissolved, and set aside.

2. Join the yeast and ⅛ teaspoon sugar in the ⅓ cup warm water and rest until the yeast has dissolved. Add this to the powdered milk mixture. Add the flour and beat thoroughly with a **wooden spoon**. Cover the bowl and let it rest in a warm spot for 30 minutes.

3. Heat an **electric griddle** to 300°F.

4. Situate metal rings on the griddle and coat lightly with vegetable spray. Lightly sprinkle inside the rings with cornmeal. Place 2 ounces of batter into each ring and cover with a **half sheet pan**. Cook for 5 to 6 minutes, until golden brown on the bottom.

5. Remove the sheet pan and flip the rings using **tongs**. Cover again and cook for 5 to 6 minutes, until golden brown on the second side. Place on a **cooling rack**, remove the rings, and cool. Split with a **fork** and serve.

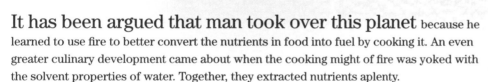

It has been argued that man took over this planet because he learned to use fire to better convert the nutrients in food into fuel by cooking it. An even greater culinary development came about when the cooking might of fire was yoked with the solvent properties of water. Together, they extracted nutrients aplenty.

The Middle Ages saw a steep rise in the popularity of complex brews, and by the eighteenth century meat stocks and broths had become the foundation of all cuisine—meaning, of course, French cuisine. The great sauces, soups, consommés, and bouillons were all born of the simmering pot. The question is, do stocks and stock making have a place in the modern American cooking portfolio?

If you ask me, the answer is you bet. In fact, I'd be willing to say that stocks offer a better return on investment than stocks . . . if you get my drift. Not only are culinary stocks fine examples of edible recycling, they can often replace the texture and mouth-feel of an ingredient that most us would rather feel a little less of: fat.

TIDBIT | The word *stock* comes from an ancient word for "stump" and refers to something that is built on.

TIDBIT | A consommé is simply a stock that has been clarified by simmering with egg whites, ground meat—or sometimes blood.

TIDBIT | The bones of young animals contain more collagen than those of their elders, which is why chefs generally like veal stock best.

TIDBIT | Yes, even bones contain connective tissue. When it's all gone, the bones crumble easily.

57

SPUME

Ever gone to the beach on a really windy day? You probably noticed a considerable amount of foam on the water. That's called spume, and it's essentially bubbles that are reinforced with a lot of protein. The stuff that rises to the surface of a simmering stock is exactly the same. Only it's not called spume, it's called scum, and it's got to go.

Some cooks prefer to do their scumming with a ladle, but I find that a little bit tedious, so I use a fine wire-mesh strainer. Have some cold water nearby to rinse the strainer in between scoops. Just scoop and rinse. That's all there is to it.

[1] If you become friendly with your butcher, and if you ask nicely, you'll be able to get backs, necks, and racks for free.

[2] I have a serious problem with bottled water unless it's in a five-gallon glass bottle inserted in the top of a water cooler. I don't allow plastic water bottles in my home or business.

KNOWLEDGE CONCENTRATE

What exactly is a stock? One thing to get clear on right up front: A STOCK is made from bones and whatever connective tissue and joint material is connected to them at the time they go in the pot. A BROTH is a liquid in which meat has been cooked. A broth may be flavorful, but without bones there will never be substantial body.

In the restaurant environment, stocks are typically built on beef bones (veal, usually) purchased frozen by the case, and believe me when I say there is not a shred or even a molecule of meat left on these bones. Toss them in a pot with some aromatics and simmer long and low for about 3 days, and you've got a stock. In the home kitchen producing a pure veal "stock" is difficult because getting bones that spotless is a tough proposition. And so we usually make chicken or turkey stocks, which, since they usually have a fair amount of meat still clinging to them, are really hybrids with characteristics of broths and stocks, which is fine but not quite as flavor-neutral as what restaurants generally use.

So where does all the lip-smacking goodness come from? Earth's critters may be held down by gravity, but they're held together by connective tissues, like collagen, reticulin, and elastin. These fibrous, extracellular proteins are responsible for making our skin plastic and elastic, holding our muscles to our bones, and keeping our guts from floating all over the place. When some of these, namely reticulin and elastin, are cooked, they can become even tougher than they are when they are raw, which is why we strive to prevent their inclusion in our edibles. Collagen, however, possesses the ability to hydrolyze—that is, dissolve in hot water. When it does, it becomes gelatin, and when gelatin is chilled, it becomes a solid gel. Add some flavorings and color, and you've got America's favorite quivering dessert. When heated, it turns back into a liquid capable of adding unctuous body and lip-smacking goodness to anything from pot roast to chicken soup to Bloody Marys.

Software, in order of importance:

The first ingredient in poultry stock is, oddly enough, POULTRY. Whenever I cook any form of birdage, I save the neck, wings, backs, ribs, and any other part I can salvage and freeze them until I have enough to fill my big stockpot. If, however, you ever find yourself in the unenviable position of needing a stock but having none, a quick stock can be made from a big pack of chicken wings.[1] They're cheap and loaded with collagen.

The second ingredient is WATER. Without it there is no solvent, and no solutes (the proteins mentioned above) will be extracted. If the stuff that comes out of your kitchen faucet is good and tasty and doesn't reek of sulfur or chlorine, if it is neither too soft nor too hard (folks on wells often experience such issues), then by all means use the stuff from the faucet. Otherwise get yourself a filter/pitcher rig of some type and make your water taste better before you cook with it.[2] How much water will you need? Enough to cover everything by about 1 inch. And when it goes in, it needs to be cold.

Next, you need the classic aromatic veggie combo known as MIREPOIX: carrots, celery, onions (and leeks if you've got 'em). Please note that this vegetation should all be of good quality and in good shape. A stock pot is not a trash can, and if you put wilted nastiness into it, nastiness you shall get out.

Finally, HERBS AND SPICES. Although they're strictly optional, I generally throw in peppercorns and a bundle of fresh parsley stems and thyme. I avoid resinous botanicals like rosemary because they get turpentine-y after a few hours in the pot.

Bones, especially bird bones, tend to float because they are hollow, or at least semi-hollow. I put an inverted steamer basket on top of the mass, and then weigh it down with a rock (yes, a clean rock, but really any clean, heavy object will do).

Notes on brewing:

Start the bones in cold water. From a distance, most bones look perfectly smooth, but they're actually packed with a galaxy of pores, which although small are not so small that hydrolyzed collagen cannot pass through them into your stock. If you begin your stock with hot or boiling water, these pores will clog with coagulated protein and no longer will the goodness flow.

BACTERIA LOVE STOCK!

As soon as you see bubbles start to break the surface, drop the heat to medium low. What we're looking for here is a bare simmer with small bubbles just breaking the surface every now and then.

Keep a supply of hot water around too. (An electric kettle is ideal for this.) Even at a bare simmer, you will eventually lose enough water from the pot to beach the bones. Every now and then, add a little bit of hot water, enough to maintain submersion.

How long does it take to actually cook a chicken stock? Well, it depends on a lot of factors. It depends on the age of the birds involved, the size of the batch, and the exact temperature at which it's cooking, but by and large I'd say it takes between 6 and 8 hours.

So what's the first thing you do after creating several quarts of nutrient-rich, low-acidity liquid? Make some soup, enrich some sauces? Heck no. You're going to cool it down as fast as you can to prevent bacteria from moving in like so many microbial pilgrims intent on reaching the promised land. And don't even look at the refrigerator. Water has a very high specific heat, which means it cools down very, very slowly. Putting it in there will only warm up all your other perishables. Then you'll be in a real fix.

What you need is ice, my friend, inside and outside the pot. Once I've strained the stock I dump a few pounds of ice in the sink and set the new vessel right on top. And I keep two big stainless-steel water bottles (not a Thermos, but one of the bottles that everyone should be using instead of plastic for drinking) three quarters full of water frozen at all times. This I simply drop into the pot and stir it around every now and then.

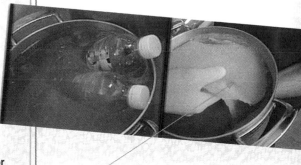

As soon as your stock cools to below 40°F, refrigerate it. The next day you'll have a light yellow Jell-O with a disk of fat on top. Pick up this disk and wrap it in plastic for another day. It's called *schmaltz*, and it is darned good stuff, culinarily speaking.

//SOFTWARE //

4	pounds	raw chicken parts	necks and backs included; wings work well in a pinch
1	large	onion	quartered
4		carrots	peeled and halved
4	ribs	celery	cut in half
1		leek	white part only, cleaned and cut in half lengthwise
10	sprigs	fresh thyme	
10	sprigs	fresh parsley	
2		bay leaves	
8 to 10	whole	black peppercorns	
2	cloves	garlic	peeled
2	gallons	cold H$_2$O	filtered is best

// PROCEDURE //

1. Put all the ingredients except the water in a **12-quart stockpot**. Set an **open steamer basket** directly on the ingredients in the pot and add the water. Cook over high heat until you begin to see bubbles break through the surface of the liquid. *Do not boil.* Turn the heat down to medium-low to maintain a low, gentle simmer. Skim the scum from the stock with a **spoon or fine-mesh strainer** every 10 to 15 minutes for the first hour of cooking and twice each hour for the next 2 hours. Dipping the strainer in cold water will dislodge scum between skims. Add hot water as needed to keep bones and vegetables submerged. Simmer, uncovered, for 6 to 8 hours, until the color deepens and the liquid is flavorful.

2. Strain the stock through **2 fine-mesh sieves** with a few layers of **cheesecloth** in between into another **large stockpot or heatproof container**, discarding the solids. Cool immediately in a **large cooler** of ice or a **sink** full of ice water to below 40°F. Cover and place in the refrigerator overnight. Remove the solidified fat from the surface of the liquid and store in a **container with a lid** in the refrigerator for 2 to 3 days, or in the freezer for up to 3 months.

⎍⎍⎍⎍ CHICKEN NOODLE SOUP

8 SERVINGS

// SOFTWARE ///

1	quart	chicken stock	
¾	cup	onion	diced
¾	cup	celery	diced
1	tablespoon	garlic	minced
2	ounces	egg noodles	cooked
½	teaspoon	fresh tarragon	finely chopped
2	teaspoons	fresh parsley	finely chopped
	to taste	kosher salt	
	to taste	black pepper	freshly ground
		lemon wedges	for serving

// PROCEDURE ///

Bring the stock to boil for 2 minutes in a **large, nonreactive stockpot with the lid on**, over high heat. Add the onion, celery, and garlic. Lower the heat and simmer for 2 minutes. Add the noodles and cook 5 more minutes. Remove from heat and add the herbs and salt and pepper, to taste. Serve with the lemon wedges for squeezing, as desired.

TIP | For a real treat, skip the dry noodles, use the Fresh Pasta on page 12, and just cook it right in the soup.

TIP | Freezing small amounts makes using the stock a whole lot easier. Fill ice cube trays, muffin tins, or small plastic containers of stock to use for various applications—as a base for soups and sauces, for example. Whatever you do, I don't care if you're using fresh stock or frozen stock, bring all stocks to a boil for 2 full minutes before using, just in case any nasty bugs moved into the neighborhood.

HARDWARE

You know, manufacturers tend to call anything over eight quarts a stockpot, but personally, I feel that shape matters just as much as size. A taller, narrower version is better for stock production. A narrower opening means less surface area, and therefore less evaporation. You might want to consider a pot made of the cunning conductor that is aluminum. Anodized aluminum, to be exact. Anodization refers to the process by which a layer of aluminum oxide is deposited onto the surface of an aluminum pot by suspending said pot in sulfuric acid and then passing electricity through it. The resulting surface is (a) super hard, (b) nonreactive so acidic foods are A-okay in it, and (c) being aluminum, lighter than steel. Look for a heavy, tight-fitting lid and nice wide loop handles.

I humbly submit that this country needs a national food to rally behind. We need an edible symbol, to remind us not only of who we are, but of how far we've come. It is my opinion that there is but one food through which we can all celebrate not only our unity, but our individuality: sausage, made at home.

Why advocate homemade sausage when our markets are full of the stuff? "Stuff" is what worries me. Most commercial sausage is packed with additives, flavorings, mystery meats, and far more fat than flavor or texture would warrant. Special tools are indeed helpful in this endeavor, but they are neither expensive nor complex and can be pressed into service when burgers, meatloaf, and the like are on the menu.

TIDBIT | American producers crank out more than 6 billion pounds of sausage a year.

TIDBIT | Of all the sausage-loving nations, Germany wins the prize, with a thousand different varieties of sausages, or *wurst*.

The word *sausage* derives from the Latin *salsus*, meaning "salted." Historically speaking, sausages date back to ancient China, where the pig was domesticated about seven thousand years ago. Some historians believe that the activity of stuffing little bits of meat into casings—that is, the lining of intestines—in order to dangle them over a fire, thus curing them by smoke, preserving them, essentially, might be one of the oldest of culinary activities.

Technically speaking, sausage is any mixture of ground meat, fat, and seasoning. Fillers, preservatives, and colorings are all optional. Culinarily speaking, sausages are divided into two major classes, fresh and cured.

A FRESH SAUSAGE is basically any sausage designed to be cooked and consumed immediately after manufacturing, whether it's in a casing or not. Bratwurst, country sausage, blood sausage, frankfurters, knockwurst, Italian sweet sausage, liverwurst (yum), and breakfast link sausages are all examples of fresh sausages. They must be refrigerated whether they are raw or cooked.

CURED SAUSAGES, like salami, pepperoni, and summer sausages, on the other hand, are dry and at least partially preserved and may therefore be stored in any cool place as long as they remain uncut, which explains the decorations in a lot of delis. Since they're dry, they're a lot firmer than fresh sausages, and the typical cured sausage is highly seasoned and usually smoked. Various chemical additives may be included in the mix to help set the color a nice rosy red. Since cured sausages require a good bit of time and know-how to manufacture safely, we will save them for another day.

Pork has always been the poster-flesh of sausage makers. There are myriad reasons. Pigs are easy and economical to raise, most of their parts are edible, and their flesh has a mild flavor that works and plays well with herbs and spices.

My favorite cut is the shoulder, a.k.a. Boston butt. (If you saw our barbecue show or read episode 88, page 44, you no doubt recognize the cut.) It's economical, it's easy to butcher, and it possesses an average 80/20 lean-to-fat ratio, which is a good starting point for most sausages.

If you need to add fat, and you may, use fatback. This is the fresh, uncured fat from the back of the pig, above the loin. Keep this on hand and you can turn just about anything in your kitchen into sausage. It doesn't take much. If properly wrapped in butcher paper and aluminum foil, it'll freeze for just about ever.

Behold, my grinder.

Medieval-looking, I know, but you have to realize that hand grinder technology hasn't exactly evolved in the last few hundred years. Version 1.0 is still current. The power plant that drives this beauty is the human arm, which is managed by the brain, which can sense a great many factors related to meat grinding—pressure, speed, and so on. Although they're not as rough and tough as hand-cranks, motorized options exist, from attachments made to mate with mixers to stand-alone models that would chew up a Michelin retread if need be. Food processors, by the way, do not count as grinders. They're choppers, and while fine for mousses and forcemeats they should not be trusted with sausage duties.

LINK SAUSAGE

Ever wondered what traditional fresh sausages are stuffed into? Animal intestines, of course, usually from a pig or lamb. Actually it's not the intestine itself—that would be chitlins. Casings are in fact the submucosa, a thin layer of connective tissue harvested from the intestines. Natural casings are superior from a texture standpoint, but have to be stored in a brine in the chill chest, so I typically use man-made casings, which are manufactured from protein—collagen to be precise—like Jell-O. Procurement options: specialty retailers, butcher shops, heck, sometimes even grocery stores. Since they're really, really light, and really, really inexpensive, I usually buy mine dehydrated off of the Internet. For two pounds of meat mixture, you'll need five feet of casing.

BREAKFAST SAUSAGE

2 POUNDS OR 16 (2-INCH) PATTIES

It is a happy coincidence that the sausage most at home on the American palate is also the easiest sausage to put on the American plate. Country breakfast sausage was introduced to these shores by English settlers, and the basic flavor combination of pork, sage, and pepper has remained a favorite for hundreds of years. Which is not to say that there haven't been hundreds of variations. What I really like best about breakfast sausage is that it doesn't need a casing. You just make patties, put them in a pan, and go.

//SOFTWARE

2	pounds	Boston butt pork	(2½ pounds bone-in), diced into ¼-inch cubes
½	pound	fatback	diced into ¼-inch cubes
2	teaspoons	kosher salt	
1½	teaspoons	black pepper	freshly ground
2	teaspoons	fresh sage leaves	finely chopped
½	teaspoon	fresh rosemary	finely chopped
1	tablespoon	light brown sugar	
½	teaspoon	nutmeg	freshly grated
½	teaspoon	cayenne pepper	
½	teaspoon	red pepper flakes	

// PROCEDURE

1. Combine all the ingredients and chill for 1 hour.

2. Using the **fine die of a meat grinder**, grind about 1 cup of the pork mixture at a time, depending on your grinder. Form into 2-inch rounds. Wrap in **butcher paper**, refrigerate, and use within 1 week or wrap in **heavy-duty aluminum foil** and freeze for up to 3 months.

3. For immediate use, sauté a few patties at a time over medium-low heat in a **nonstick pan**. Sauté until brown and cooked through, 10 to 15 minutes, flipping once halfway through cooking.

TIP Grinders have bad reps as congregation points for potential contaminants. Why? Well, they are kind of tough to clean. My secret? Make the machine do most of the work. Feed some stale bread (baguette is especially effective) into the hopper. As the bread moves through the grinder, it will sweep the grease away with it. You'll still have to disassemble and wash the thing in soapy water, but this will make things a lot easier.

TIP Grinders usually come with three different dies, or plates perforated with holes of different sizes that the meat is pushed through. They're notorious for rusting, so most chefs and charcutiers store them in zip-top bags with uncooked rice, which pulls the moisture away from the metal.

ITALIAN SAUSAGE

2 POUNDS OR 10 TO 12 (4-INCH) SAUSAGE LINKS

NOTE: I have to admit that I own a sausage grinder/stuffer attachment for my stand mixer, which I use specifically for filling casings. It's not that my hand grinder doesn't have the attachment because it does. But it's really a two-hand operation and having a motor to actually drive the process is invaluable.

According to Greek mythology, knowledge was delivered to man from Mount Olympus in the form of a fiery coal buried in the middle of a fennel stalk. I don't know about knowledge, but I do know that fennel delivers big-time flavor to a whole host of fresh sausages that hail from the Mediterranean. Now, the bulb (or Florence fennel) can be sliced and diced a million ways, and the feathery tops make a very nice addition to soups and sauces. As for the flavorful "seeds" of fennel, those are actually the fruits of the plant.

// SOFTWARE //

1½	teaspoons	fennel seeds	
2	teaspoons	kosher salt	
1½	teaspoons	black pepper	freshly ground
1	tablespoon	fresh parsley leaves	chopped
2	pounds	Boston butt pork	(2½ pounds bone-in), diced into ¼-inch cubes
5	feet	36-millimeter collagen casing	do not allow this to get wet at any time
		shortening	to lubricate the nozzle of the stuffer

// PROCEDURE //

(1) Toast the fennel seeds in a **10-inch cast-iron skillet** over medium heat, constantly moving the seeds around in the pan until they start to turn light brown, about 5 minutes. Set aside to cool in a **small bowl**. **Grind** the seeds. Combine them with the salt, pepper, and parsley in a **medium mixing bowl**. Add the pork and blend thoroughly. Refrigerate for 1 hour.

(2) Set a **medium mixing bowl** inside a **large mixing bowl** filled with ice and place it under the grinder to catch the meat. Using the **fine die of a meat grinder**, grind about 1 cup of the pork mixture at a time, depending on your grinder.

(3) Set a **half sheet pan** under the **stuffer or stuffing attachment**. Lubricate the stuffer or stuffing attachment with shortening, load the casing onto the attachment, clipping the end with a **clothespin**. Slowly stuff the meat into the casing, trying to avoid air pockets. This should take about 5 minutes.

(4) Lay the sausage out on the counter and tie off one end. Pinch and twist to form 4-inch sausages. Remember to twist the unlinked section, not the other way around. Wrap in **parchment paper** and refrigerate for 2 to 3 hours. Store in the refrigerator for use within 2 to 3 days or freeze for up to 3 months. If freezing, wrap in **aluminum foil**.

(5) To cook: Put the sausages in a **2-quart sauté pan** with ¼ inch of water. Bring the water to boil, cover, and cook for 10 minutes. Remove the lid and continue cooking over medium heat, turning every 2 to 3 minutes, until golden brown. Homemade sausage should reach an internal temperature of 150° to 156°F.

TIP | Fatback can be found at most megamarts and all decent butcher shops, which is also where I'd look for casings. If you strike out, don't worry— artificial casings are easy to find on the web.

TIDBIT | Natural casings can be made from the intestinal linings of lambs, cows, pigs, oxen, even large fish.

I think it's safe to say that John Wayne ate steak.

And if there's a meal more fundamentally American, I don't know what it is. I mean, think about it: Steak is a meal born of wide-open spaces, big skies, and even bigger wallets. Of course John Wayne ate steak! He was a stinkin' millionaire, a movie star! Steak's been the favorite chow of the rich and famous ever since refrigerated boxcars and feedlots made it readily available in the late nineteenth century. Before then, pretty much only cowboys got to eat it. Now I'm not complaining, okay? I mean, a T-bone is sweet, believe me. I just feel that Average Joes like us shouldn't have to fork over a fistful of presidents every time we want to eat one. So, the thing I'm thinking is that we need to give some page time to some often overlooked cuts that when handled deftly deliver delight without delivering you into debt.

Of course, if we want to get top-drawer flavor at bottom-drawer prices, we're going to have to refamiliarize ourselves with offbeat anatomy.

TIDBIT | The United States makes up one fifteenth of the world's population, but consumes one third of the world's meat.

KNOWLEDGE CONCENTRATE

As you may recall from our premiere episode, "Steak Your Claim," the steaks that we buy down at the local megamart are actually cut, or fabricated, from larger cuts, or primals. You may also recall that the real money steaks—tenderloin, ribeye, and whatnot—come from the middle of the cow, on the back. Why? Because it's the farthest from the horn and the hoof. Just make like a cow, and you'll see.

When crawling on all fours you're going to notice that your neck, your shoulders, your arms, and your rump get tired very quickly. It's because they're bearing all the load. Well, it's the same on a steer, which is why the cuts taken from those areas are pretty gosh-darn tough. The only areas that don't get really tired are your back and your abdominals. The back doesn't do a lot of work on a steer, either. And that's why the cuts from those areas are relatively tender—and expensive. As for your abdominals, they may not be bearing any load, but whether you're a cow or a person trying to walk like one, they do work 24/7, doing a job we call breathing. Which is why those cuts will be really, really tough if they're not cooked with care. And it is care worth taking, because the cuts we glean from the area called the plate, namely flank steaks and skirt steaks, are some of the best cuts on the critter.

In the days before World War II, plate-based cuts like the FLANK and SKIRT STEAK were called "butcher's cuts" because butchers had such a hard time selling them that they usually took them home. But following World War II, a flank-based application called London broil became all the rage in America, and the price of flank steak has been going up ever since. But that's okay with me, because I have always preferred skirt steak. Now, if you have ever eaten at a Tex-Mex place, you've probably had fajitas, and therefore skirt steak. But I'm betting that was outside skirt steak, and outside skirt's kind of a scrawny piece of meat, a little tough and greasy, and it's really only good for, well, fajitas.

But inside skirt, that's a whole other animal. What's unique is its grain structure. It's very, very pronounced, and it runs crosswise, rather than up and down, the way it does in, say, a strip steak. This grain provides us with some challenges, and with some real advantages. One steak is usually enough for about six diners. As for all that fat, don't worry about it. It's going to melt right off.

Thin, long, and wide, the skirt steak has more surface area than any other cut of beef and so it lends itself to direct heat. The challenge is that it has a lot of connective tissue, typically the kind of stuff that breaks down only with long, low cooking. So what do you use if you want proper cooking and tenderness? Bi-level cooking, of course. First, cook over very high heat to create char, then remove the heat and wrap with foil to allow low and slow carry-over cooking. I cook the skirt right on top of the coals . . . natural chunk charcoal, of course. Closing the gap between meat and heat means no flare-ups, which is nice, and hey, who likes cleaning a grill grate?

My other favorite "secret" steak is the SIRLOIN, which hails from the transitional neighborhood between the ritzy short-loin, home of the tony T-bone, and the round, home of those big, dry chunks that they carve at cheap weddings. The trick is in hunting out the top sirloin, which is beefy and juicy, while avoiding the bottom sirloin, which is dry and chewy no matter what you do or say.

Think of heat as an army, marching into your meat.

The broiler is the most underutilized hot thing in the American kitchen, and it's a real shame, because a broiler is essentially an upside-down grill in which heat comes from the top rather than the bottom, a fact that has some distinct advantages. When the heat comes from the top, and fat melts on meat, it doesn't drip down onto the coals and catch fire. On top of that, a broiler is a finely adjustable device. You can change the distance between the flame, or the coil, depending on what your oven has, and the food, simply by moving racks around. Most broilers even have high and low temperature settings, further upping the ante. This is all good news to the sirloin, which really, really doesn't want to be cooked beyond medium-rare, lest its pleasantly chewy texture becomes something more shoelike.

Without question this is my favorite *Good Eats* meat application of all time.

// SOFTWARE

½	cup	olive oil	
⅓	cup	soy sauce	
4		scallions	washed, trimmed, and cut in half
2	cloves	garlic	
2		limes	freshly squeezed
½	teaspoon	red pepper flakes	
½	teaspoon	cumin seeds	toasted and ground
3	tablespoons	dark brown sugar	
2	pounds	inside skirt steak	cut into 3 equal pieces
1	large	red bell pepper	julienned
1	large	green bell pepper	julienned
1	large	onion	julienned
2	teaspoons	vegetable oil	
½	teaspoon	kosher salt	
¼	teaspoon	black pepper	freshly ground

// PROCEDURE

1. Put the olive oil, soy sauce, scallions, garlic, lime juice, red pepper flakes, cumin, and brown sugar in a **blender** and puree. Marinade-to-meat contact is key here, so I don't like to do my marinating in a dish or a pan. I like to do it in a **zip-top bag**. Put the steak in the bag and pour in the marinade. Seal the bag, removing as much air as possible, and refrigerate for 1 hour.

BRINES VS. MARINADES

A brine is essentially salty water, as in "briny deep." A piece of meat soaked in a brine absorbs salt and water, and so it tends to cook up moister and more flavorful than a non-brined piece of meat. The word *marinade* comes from the word *marine*, but technically speaking, marinades contain acids, such as wine, vinegar, and citrus juice. Despite the fact that hundreds of horror movies have conditioned us to believe that acids dissolve meats on contact, the truth is, acids coagulate meats. Enzymes dissolve them. Another thing: Acidic marinades, while they bring a great deal of flavor to the party, definitely don't tenderize meat. Even if they had that power they just aren't efficient enough at penetrating meat. No soak can actually tenderize meat, but soaking in a brine can help your meat soak up more moisture, and more moisture means a more tender texture.

(PROP GUYS)

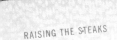

2. Fire up one **chimney starter** of **natural lump charcoal**. When the coals are white and ashy, distribute them evenly in a **charcoal grill**.

3. Put the peppers and onions in a **large mixing bowl** with the vegetable oil and salt and pepper and toss to combine. Set aside.

4. Remove the steak from the bag and pat dry with **paper towels**. Using a **blow dryer**, blow the charcoal clean of ash. Immediately lay the steaks directly onto the hot coals and cook for 1 minute per side. When finished cooking, put the meat in a double thickness of **aluminum foil**, wrap, and rest for 15 minutes.

5. While the meat is resting, put a **12-inch cast-iron skillet** directly on the hot coals and heat for 5 minutes. Add the peppers and onions and cook for 2 to 3 minutes, until the vegetables soften and just start to blacken around the edges. Remove from the heat, cover, and set aside.

6. Remove the meat from the foil, reserving foil and juices. **Slice** thinly across the grain of the meat. Return the meat and the vegetables to the foil pouch and toss with the juice. Serve immediately.

THE RIGHT SLICE

How you slice skirt steak, or even flank steak, matters almost as much as how you cook it. For instance, if you were to take a slice with the grain, it might look very appetizing. But when you put that in your mouth it'll be a lot like chewing on a bunch of pieces of garden hose wrapped up in plastic wrap. Long meat fibers equal a lot of chewing. On the other hand, if you were to take a very sharp knife and cut very thin slices straight across the grain, that would be another story altogether. When you chew a slice containing very, very short pieces of meat fiber it falls apart in your mouth, and that is tenderness. Now, there are some recipes out there that will tell you that this is not the right thing to do, because it doesn't look good on the plate. They'll tell you to cut on a bias, kind of a 45-degree angle. I'll grant you, that

looks very, very pretty laid out on a plate. But because the meat fibers are longer, the piece cut on a bias is going to be a little bit chewier.

Since the grain on a sirloin runs up and down, rather than across the way it does on a skirt steak, it is imperative that you cut on the bias in order to keep all of those meat fibers nice and short. You're always going to be able to control this process better if you cut inward, or toward you. Think of the knife as a baseball bat, rather than a Frisbee, if you get my point.

TIDBIT | *Fajita* comes from the Spanish word *faja*, for "girdle" or "strip."

Long muscle fibers are chewy.

Tender

Pretty

Cutting across the grain makes the fibers shorter and therefore less chewy.

BROILED SIRLOIN STEAK

4 SERVINGS

//SOFTWARE //

1	24-ounce	sirloin steak	1 to 1¼ inches thick
2	teaspoons	olive oil	
	to taste	kosher salt	
	to taste	black pepper	freshly ground

// PROCEDURE //

1. Heat the broiler to high for 15 minutes. **Brush** the steak with the oil and season with salt and pepper. Set a piece of **aluminum foil** on the bottom rack as a drip pan. Put another rack in the position above the foil and put the steak directly on this rack. Cook for 2 minutes. Flip the steak and cook for another 2 minutes.

2. Move the rack with the steak to the top position in the oven, moving the rack with foil and drippings just underneath, and cook for 4 minutes. Flip one last time and cook for another 3 minutes. Transfer the steak to a **resting rig** and rest for 3 to 5 minutes.

   The above times are for medium doneness. Adjust cooking times up or down as desired. Thinly **slice** on the bias and serve.

A resting rig is any arrangement of hardware that keeps the meat relatively warm while allowing char-dissolving juices to run away. Here is one example:

1
2
3
4
5

1. Pot lid
2. Colander
3. Steaks
4. Metal bowl
5. Drippings

TRIVIA Although I've enjoyed considerable discomfort making *Good Eats* episodes in the past, the entire upside-down grill piece was and remains the worst of these experiences. First, we had to get my legs shoved into the pan storage above and provide anchorage for my feet lest I come tumbling out. Then I had to get the lines right, which is surprisingly tough when hanging upside down. I don't remember how many takes it took; I only remember being very glad when it was over. The swing out to the counter left my back sore for three days.

THE POUCH PRINCIPAL

EPISODE 94 | SEASON 7 | GOOD EATS

A wise man named Ferris Bueller once said, "Life moves pretty fast. If you don't stop and look around once in a while, you could miss it." I would add that you can miss a lot of life just by being tied to the stove, oven, or other large kitchen appliance. Although I make a living promoting home cooking, I know full well that sometimes you just need to get some flavor and nutrition on the table with a minimum of muss and fuss. That's what pouch cooking, and this episode, is all about.

TIDBIT | When opening a pouch fresh from the oven, remember to watch out for steam.

Every man needs a smoking jacket with matching fez.

I think of pouch cooking as a hybrid method that combines some of the attributes of a dry heat method, baking, with a moist heat method, steaming. Since you make the cooking vessel yourself, no fancy pots, pans, inserts, or lids are required. Just an oven, and it doesn't have to be a very good one at that. Any food that you would think of steaming, or baking at a relatively low temperature, is a candidate for the pouch, including vegetables, fish, and poultry. Beef and other red meats, which are usually browned or seared somewhere along the line, are generally less suitable to the pouch but even here there are exceptions.

Pouch cooking has been around for thousands of years and may in fact be one of the oldest methods, period. Large leaves (fig and banana) are still used in many parts of the world, including my kitchen, but nine times out of ten, when pouching, I reach for parchment paper: silicone-impregnated paper that can stand high oven temperatures without conducting heat too quickly to the food the way foil does. Also, unlike foil, parchment pouches are microwavable, which can come in very handy.

You can't just drop a Twinkie, a turnip, and a can of kraut in a bag and call it a pouch. The items inside must be compatible from both a flavor and a texture standpoint, and they have to be architecturally sound. Here is my formula for pouch success:

PROTEIN	VEGETABLES	STARCH	AROMATICS	SEASONING	LIQUID
beef	mushrooms	rice	onions	red pepper	soy sauce
pork	artichokes	noodles	garlic	flakes	mirin
lamb	tomatoes	potatoes	scallions	honey	vegetable
fish	peppers	dumplings	shallots	salt	broth
shrimp	snow peas	couscous	celery	black pepper	dashi
chicken	broccoli		fennel	coriander	sesame oil
tofu	bok choy		carrots	cilantro	vermouth
other				lemon	wine
				parsley	chicken
				basil	stock
					fruit juice
					fish sauce

I usually pick one item from the protein column, one or two items (with contrasting textures) from the vegetable column. The starch is optional, but I usually include one on the bottom of the pile to soak up moisture so it won't be wasted. Moving on to the aromatics, I never use more than two, or things get confusing. Seasonings? Anything goes when it comes to seasoning, but since the flavors are relatively subtle I keep the seasoning simple—such as salt and an acid (lime juice, for instance, is a favorite when chicken is in play). Then of course we have a liquid to consider. My favorites are chicken stock, mirin (sweetened rice wine), dashi (a Japanese stock), vegetable stock, and wine (including vermouth).

TIDBIT | Despite the rumors, no one has been able to prove that cooking in aluminum is in any way harmful to your health.

STRIPED BASS EN PAPILLOTE

4 SERVINGS

This application was originally designed for red snapper, a fish that, I'm sorry to say, has become seriously overfished in the last few years . . . to the point that I would not eat it under any circumstances, even if I caught it myself. So consider using a more sustainable whole fish such as farmed striped bass or black rockfish, which is sometimes sold, oddly enough, as Pacific snapper, even though there is no such species. I've also made this with tilefish and whole trout.

// SOFTWARE //

1	cup	couscous	
1	2-pound	whole striped bass or black rockfish	scaled, trimmed, and cleaned
2	teaspoons	kosher salt	plus a pinch for the couscous
½	teaspoon	black pepper	freshly ground
1	small bunch	fresh oregano	
1	small bunch	fresh parsley	
1		lemon	thinly sliced, divided
1	cup	red onion	thinly sliced, divided
2	teaspoons	garlic	minced
1	cup	grape tomatoes	halved
1	cup	artichoke hearts	drained and quartered
½	cup	white wine	
1	tablespoon	unsalted butter	

// PROCEDURE //

1. Heat the oven to 425°F.

2. Rinse the couscous in a **fine-mesh sieve** under cold water, lay it out on a **half sheet pan lined with parchment paper**, and sprinkle it with a pinch of salt. Set aside.

3. Cut another piece of **parchment paper** into a 15-by-48-inch sheet. Fold it in half widthwise and put it on top of **another half sheet pan**. Unfold the paper and put the fish diagonally on top of the parchment. Salt and pepper the fish, inside and out. Put the oregano and parsley inside the cavity of the fish, along with half of the lemon and half of the onion. Pile the couscous around the fish. Put the garlic and the remaining lemon and onion on top of the fish and arrange the tomatoes and artichoke hearts around the outside of the couscous, creating somewhat of a wall. Pour the wine over the fish and dot with the butter.

4. Fold the parchment over the fish, **stapling** the edges if necessary, to create an almost airtight seal. Bake for 30 minutes. Carefully open and serve. (Be aware of bones in the fish.)

Snapper is pretty, but presently overfished, so try striped bass instead.

TIDBIT | *En papillote* is French for "butterfly" and refers to the shape of the paper often used in pouch cooking.

TIDBIT | Other whole fish suitable for pouching: trout, tilapia, arctic char, tilefish.

Although folding is the pouch norm, there's nothing wrong with staples. I wouldn't microwave this, though, because the staples would come too close to the walls of the oven.

THE POUCH PRINCIPAL

SALMON FILLET EN PAPILLOTE WITH JULIENNED VEGETABLES

1 SERVING, EASILY MULTIPLIED

VERMOUTH

Besides being one half of the alchemic tag team that is the martini, vermouth is the perfect wine for this dish because it's aromatic. Like gin, which is an herb-infused spirit, vermouth is an herb-infused and fortified wine. The herbs and flavorings can include cloves, cinnamon, quinine, artemesia (whatever that is), orange peel, chamomile, and a lot more. Vermouth used to be flavored with wormwood, which is where the original word, *Wermut*, came from. Red, or sweet, vermouth is most associated with Italian makers, while clear, dry vermouth is usually a French concoction. The latter is my preference for this dish.

What's that? Oh, you need an easy single-meal option for those Saturday nights home alone, huh? Well, don't feel bad. It happens to everyone sooner or later. That being said, this recipe also multiplies well: Prepare several pouches up to 4 hours ahead, then bake 4 per half sheet pan in a 425°F oven for 12 minutes, or until the fish reaches 131°F. Since you can make them up ahead of time and then just slide them into the oven 15 or 20 minutes before dinner is served, pouches make the perfect party dish.

// SOFTWARE //

⅓	cup	fennel bulb	julienned
⅓	cup	leeks	white part only, julienned
⅓	cup	carrots	julienned
⅓	cup	snow peas	
1	teaspoon	kosher salt	
⅛	teaspoon	black pepper	freshly ground
⅛	teaspoon	coriander	finely ground
1	8-ounce	salmon fillet	pin bones removed
1		orange	separated into suprêmes
1	tablespoon	dry vermouth	

// PROCEDURE //

1. Fold a 15-by-36-inch piece of **parchment paper** in half widthwise. Draw a large heart half on the paper with the fold being the center of the heart. Cut along the line and open up the paper.

2. Layer the fennel, leeks, carrots, and snow peas on the parchment to one side of the fold. Mix together the salt, pepper, and coriander. Sprinkle the vegetables with half of the salt mixture.

3. Put the salmon on top of the vegetables and season with the remaining salt mixture. Top the salmon with the orange sections and sprinkle with the vermouth. Fold the empty side of the parchment over the fish and, starting at the top of the heart shape, fold up both edges of the parchment, overlapping the folds as you move along. When you reach the end, twist the seal closed and tuck the tip underneath to secure tightly. Place on a **microwave-safe plate** and cook in a microwave oven on high for 4 minutes, or until the fish reaches 131°F. Open the pouch carefully and serve for a complete meal.

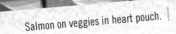

Salmon on veggies in heart pouch.

STONE FRUIT POUCHES

4 SERVINGS

If there's anything I used to dislike about charcoal grilling, it was how terrible I felt squandering all that heat once the grilling was done. After all, some very nice trees gave their all to make this charcoal. The least I can do is not waste it. So while dinner (say, "Over the Coals" Fajitas, page 68) is being devoured, dessert will be a-pouching.

// SOFTWARE ///

10	ounces	gingersnaps	lightly crushed
4		apricots	pitted and cut into eighths
4		plums	pitted and cut into fourths
4	tablespoons	unsalted butter	
3	tablespoons	sugar	
1	pinch	kosher salt	
2		limes	zested and juiced
4	teaspoons	brandy[1]	
4	scoops	vanilla ice cream	optional

Elevation of delicious fruit pouch in process

// PROCEDURE //

1. Heat coals in a charcoal grill or fire pit, or heat the oven to 500°F.

2. Cut 8 (18-by-18-inch) squares of **heavy-duty aluminum foil**. Lay down a double thickness of foil and divide the gingersnaps evenly among the 4 squares. Divide the fruit evenly over the gingersnaps. Dot with the butter.

3. In a **small bowl**, combine the sugar, salt, and 4 teaspoons lime zest. Sprinkle the sugar mixture evenly over the fruit, drizzle with the lime juice and brandy, and seal the packets.

4. When the coals are ash-covered, lay the packets over them and cover with the lid of the grill. If cooking in a fire pit, carefully try to partially bury the packets in hot coals. Cook for 10 minutes on the coals or 12 minutes in the oven. Remove from the heat and open carefully. Serve on plates as is, or spoon the fruit into shallow bowls and top with vanilla ice cream.

[1] If you don't have brandy, use white wine or sherry—but not "cooking sherry"!

We had so much fun with the Frances Andersen character in "Spud II" that I really wanted to give her another shot, so to speak. The problem was there was no way to explain why my character would come within a mile of her. The answer: amnesia, of course. And she just so happens to have inherited a financially troubled health food store. Perfect. Ridiculous, but fun.

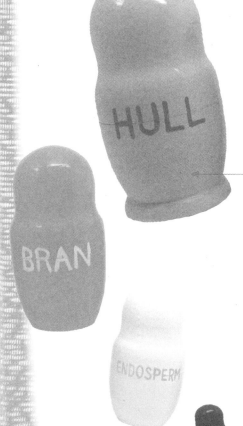

KNOWLEDGE CONCENTRATE

▷ Although the applications in the first half of this episode center around two different forms of wheat—wheat berries and cracked wheat or "bulgur"—many cooking rules apply to all (or at least most) of the whole-grain world.

▷ To qualify as a whole grain, the cereal kernel in question must have these components in place:

ENDOSPERM: This is the big ole solid rocket booster of starch meant to feed the new plant. Refined grains are nothing but endosperm. Ditto the refined flours that are ground from them.

GERM: This is the payload of the seed, containing the genetic information and mechanisms that will actually create the new plant. This small section also contains a majority of the grain's fat and consequently its flavor.

BRAN: This is the kernel's hard protective coating. Bran is very high in dietary fiber. It's also home to omega fatty acids, vitamins, and protein. The bran is arguably the healthiest part of the grain.

Thanks to the presence of the bran and the germ, whole grains deliver high-quality nutrition and a bright, nutty flavor. But thanks to the fat content, whole grains are higher in calories than refined grains and prone to rancidity. Whole grains are also a challenge to cook because it takes time for heat and liquid to penetrate the bran; frustration often ensues.

How much time will be required to cook a particular grain depends to a great extent on the moisture level inside the kernel. Like it or not, whole grains are agricultural products and the moisture levels can vary widely, making it nearly impossible to write reliable applications. If you want to speed the cooking of a particular grain, let it soak for several hours in its cooking liquid before applying the heat. Whole-wheat grains or "wheat berries," spelt berries, and rye berries can soak overnight.

Health and whole grains: A cup of wheat berries contains some 300 calories as well as protein, iron, fiber, manganese, tryptophan, magnesium, and omega fatty acids. I've read through a few hundred pages of research regarding the health benefits of consuming whole grains, including wheat, and it's pretty darned clear that these foods should be on the menu of each and every American each and every day. And yes, I know, it's a carbohydrate. But it's the entire package of germ, endosperm, and bran that conjures the magic. Whether it's the heart, the brain, the blood, the immune system, the gallbladder, or any other little bit of the human body, it seems that whole grains can help it stay healthy.

Wheat berries keep a very long time, years in fact, if stored in an airtight vessel away from heat and light. I've heard that survivalists interested in extremely long-term storage will open a five-gallon bucket of wheat berries and place a softball-sized hunk of dry ice on top. As the ice slowly sublimates, the CO_2 sinks into the bucket, displacing the air. When the dry ice is gone, the vessel is simply resealed, creating its own low-atmosphere storage. Clever. Extreme but clever.

Types: If you really get into wheat berries, as I have, you'll likely come across three varieties. The differences between them are distinct but subtle, and they'll all work in the applications shown here. Keep in mind that any wheat called "soft" will be lower in protein than one labeled "hard."

SOFT WHITE WINTER WHEAT BERRIES: Because of their lower protein content, they tend to swell readily and cook faster. Very good for use in breads.

HARD SPRING WHEAT BERRIES: The protein content can top 15 percent. Can be cooked as a cereal or milled for bread flour (and it makes great pizza dough).

SOFT WHITE SPRING WHEAT BERRIES: Prized by bakers interested in crisp piecrusts and light pastries. Unless you have a grain mill, I wouldn't bother with this stuff . . . it's more a specialty grain.

The second half of the show focuses on another wheat product called couscous, which, in retrospect, I regret. For one thing, couscous should have its own show. For another, couscous isn't a grain. Oh, I know it looks like one and it sorta cooks like one, but it's actually a pasta created by rubbing bits of semolina (a flour ground from "hard" durum wheat) with water. The word *couscous* comes from the Arabic *kashkasa*, which means "to grind or pound." Most of the couscous packaged in the U.S. comes with instructions to soak it in boiling water, which is fine if you just want to render it edible. If, however, you want to make it all light and fluffy and swollen, you're going to have to steam it. In Northern Africa, where couscous is an everyday carb, they use a two-stage pot called a *couscousiere*, but you can get away with a large pot that has a fitted steamer insert. Since the procedure involves a cloth, using a folding steamer basket makes it tough because of the center post.

NOTE: Kids, this is no way to treat a nutritional anthropologist.

BASIC COOKED WHEAT BERRIES

4 CUPS

TIP | As is true with nuts and whole spices, the flavor is going to be a lot deeper if we toast the berries first in a dry pan, which will convert some of the simple sugars into more complex compounds.

// **SOFTWARE** ///

2	cups	wheat berries	
1	quart	H$_2$O	
2	teaspoons	kosher salt	

// **PROCEDURE** //

1. In a **12-inch cast-iron skillet** over medium-high heat, toast the wheat berries for 5 to 6 minutes, until they start to smell nutty.

2. Move the toasted berries to a **pressure cooker**, add the water and salt, and cook over high heat until hissing begins and the pressure rises. Lower the heat to maintain a low hiss and cook for 45 minutes. Release the steam of the pressure cooker according to the manufacturer's instructions (or by running under cool water for 5 minutes). The berries should have a toothy, al dente texture. Drain, if necessary. Cooked wheat berries can be stored in your chill chest for up to 1 week.

APPLICATION

WHEAT BERRY TAPENADE

4 TO 6 SERVINGS

Tapenade. It's a classic Italian olive paste, used as a spread. The problem with most tapenades is that they have a lot of flavor but not a lot of substance. So they don't hang in your mouth very long. The addition of wheat berries solves that problem.

// **SOFTWARE** ///

3	cloves	garlic	minced
1	cup	kalamata olives	pitted and minced
1	teaspoon	kosher salt	
½	teaspoon	Dijon mustard	
1	cup	cooked wheat berries	(see above)

// **PROCEDURE** //

Combine the garlic, olives, salt, and mustard in a **medium mixing bowl**. Fold in the wheat berries. Serve with crusty bread, on a salad, or on its own.

BULGUR GAZPACHO

6 SERVINGS

// SOFTWARE //

1	cup	H₂O	
1	cup	tomato puree	
¾	cup	medium bulgur	
2	tablespoons	balsamic vinegar	
1	clove	garlic	minced
½	teaspoon	cumin seeds	toasted and ground
1½	teaspoons	kosher salt	
1¼	teaspoons	hot sauce	optional, but highly recommended
4		scallions	chopped
1	cup	tomatoes	seeded and chopped
1	cup	cucumber	peeled, seeded, and chopped
¾	cup	green bell pepper	finely chopped
3	tablespoons	fresh cilantro	chopped
1½	cups	tomato juice	

// PROCEDURE //

1. In a **microwave-safe bowl**, combine the water and the tomato puree. Set a **wooden skewer** in the bowl and cook in a microwave oven on high for about 5 minutes, until boiling. (As you'll see later on in the "Myth Smashers" episode, page 217, a wooden skewer placed inside water to be microwaved can prevent sudden boil-overs.)

2. Pour the tomato mixture over the bulgur in a **medium mixing bowl** and cover with **plastic wrap**; set aside for 20 minutes. Fluff the bulgur with a **fork**. Add the vinegar, garlic, cumin, salt, hot sauce, scallions, tomatoes, cucumbers, bell pepper, and cilantro and toss with the bulgur. Add the tomato juice and stir to combine. Chill for 1 hour, then serve.

BULGUR

Bulgur is whole grains of wheat that have been steamed, dried, and then cracked into different sizes or grades. Number one is fine bulgur; number two, a little bigger, is medium bulgur; and number three, a little bigger still, is coarse bulgur. Bulgur's origins can be traced to the Middle East, where evidence of it has been found in Egyptian tombs, Etruscan urns, and Huns' saddlebags. When you think of bulgur, you may automatically think tabouli, because it's a traditional Mediterranean salad. But since bulgur works and plays so well with tomatoes and lends a chewy bite, it's a perfect ingredient for gazpacho.

Bulgar #2 Medium Grind

4 CUPS

// SOFTWARE //

2	cups	couscous	not instant
1	pinch	kosher salt	
½	cup	cold H_2O	

// PROCEDURE //

(1) Rinse the couscous in a **fine-mesh sieve** under cold running water. Dump the couscous onto a **half sheet pan**, sprinkle with salt, and let rest until the grains swell, about 10 minutes. Break up any lumps with your fingers.

(2) Fill a **large steamer pot** or other large pot with 1 inch of water. Bring the water to a simmer. Put a **damp tea towel** in a **steamer basket or metal colander** and add the couscous. Fold the towel over the couscous. Steam, covered, over simmering water for 15 minutes.

(3) Pour the couscous back onto the half sheet pan and sprinkle with the cold water. Toss with a **slotted spatula** until cool and the water is absorbed. Coat your hands with **oil** and spread out the couscous, breaking up any lumps as you go. Set aside for 5 minutes.

(4) Refill the pot with 1 inch of water. Return the couscous to the colander or steamer lined with the damp tea towel and steam, covered, for 10 minutes.

STEAMING COUSCOUS

You can use a *couscousiere* for steaming couscous, but you can't use this fancy French apparatus for anything else. Instead, a good standard two-stage steamer basket will do fine. Put some water in there, and make sure the top of the water is several inches down from the bottom of the steamer basket. If there's not enough space, the couscous is going to be mushy.

This application calls for two steamings. If you were to steam the couscous all the way to doneness at one time, the starch on the outside of the kernels would overgelatinize. And that means they would be very nasty and gummy. By steaming the couscous, giving it a rest, and then steaming it again, we'll have nice fluffy, light, separate kernels. (Grains. Noodles. Well, you know what I'm talking about.) There are even North African recipes that call for three separate steamings.

TIDBIT | Israeli couscous is more than twice the size of regular couscous and resembles tapioca pearls. It cooks more like pasta than traditional couscous.

CHERRY COUSCOUS PUDDING

4 SERVINGS

// SOFTWARE ///

½	cup	whole milk	
3	tablespoons	sugar	
¼	cup	dried cherries	
1		vanilla bean	split and scraped
1½	cups	steamed couscous	(see left)
1	cup	vanilla yogurt	
¼	teaspoon	ground cinnamon	

// PROCEDURE ///

1. In a **small saucepan** over medium heat, bring the milk, sugar, and cherries to a simmer, then remove from the heat. Add the seeds from the vanilla bean and **whisk** to combine; cover and steep for 10 minutes.

2. Pour the milk mixture over the couscous in a **bowl** and add the yogurt. Stir to combine. Divide evenly among **4 custard cups**, sprinkle with the cinnamon, and refrigerate for 1 hour. Serve cold.

Couscous in perforated upper steamer

Just a fancy double boiler/ steamer

Simmering water

FOLLOWING DRAMATIC AMNESIA CONVENTIONS, A SECOND BLOW TO THE HEAD REINSTATES MY MEMORY AND I FLEE FOR MY LIFE!

THE TRICK TO TREATS

EPISODE 96 | SEASON 7 | GOOD EATS

Another episode featuring my "nephew" Elton. His mother is sending him off to a Halloween party dressed like a carrot and armed with healthy stuff like . . . carob (shiver). To save him from a lynching, I whip up a few twists on classic candies, some of which pack as much trick as treat.

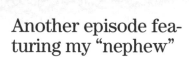

TIDBIT | *Candy comes from the Sanskrit khanda, meaning "chunks of sugar."*

TIDBIT | *Denmark has the highest per-capita candy consumption in the world, at thirty-six pounds per Dane.*

KNOWLEDGE CONCENTRATE

▷ Making candy, be it taffy, toffee, brittle, fudge, caramel, or ice cream, is all about controlling the concentration and crystallization of the sugar in a syrup. Candies can be granular, smooth, and chewy, or hard, clear, and amorphous, all depending on how much sugar is present and whether or not it's allowed to crystallize. Sugar concentration is a function of temperature; the hotter the syrup gets, the higher the ratio of sugar to water. Crystallization, on the other hand, is decided by ingredients and physical agitation.

▷ Once upon a time, before reliable, practical thermometers were developed, confectioners had to calculate the concentrations of their syrups by dropping a bit in cold water and observing how it behaved when it cooled. This is where we get what are called the candy or "ball" stages:

Candy Stage	Temperature	Use
Thread	230°–235°F	syrup, some preserves
Soft ball	235°–240°F	fudge, pralines
Firm ball	245°–250°F	chewy candies
Hard ball	250°–265°F	nougat, marshmallow
Soft crack	270°–290°F	taffy, butterscotch
Hard crack	300°–310°F	brittle, lollipops
Caramel	320°–360°F	caramel sauce

TIDBIT | Amorphous candies, like brittles and taffy, contain no crystals. Crystalline candies, like fudge and pralines, do.

BRITTLES: Brittles are fascinating, because they are essentially the glass of the candy world. I mean, sure, they taste better than glass. But they're brittle like glass. They'll shatter like glass. And sometimes they're even as transparent as glass. Not surprisingly, the manufacturing similarities are uncanny. For instance, when you make glass, you're basically melting down silica crystals—sand—to make an amorphous solid. In brittle making you're melting down a lot of sugar crystals to make an amorphous solid.

Oddly enough, they can both get messed up in the same way. If the vessel they're cooked in is dirty, if the mixture itself is impure, or if it's agitated at the wrong time, little baby crystals can be formed in the mixture. And as they cook, these little crystals can grow into bigger and bigger crystals, and eventually, your nice clear glass starts looking more like a shower door. And your brittle starts looking more like a praline. Which is nice, but it's not a brittle. A couple things will help you avoid this problem:

1. Decent tools.

2. Old-fashioned know-how.

In the case of brittle, you're going to need a nice, heavy-duty pan. I like a saucier because the shape helps to create an environment for evaporation. It's going to need a nice, tight lid. And you're also going to need a good wooden spoon. Why wood? Because wood doesn't conduct heat, and that's good for the candy, as well as the hand that stirs it.

Since syrups get really, really thick, and can't be stirred during most of the cooking process, even heat from below is crucial. Heavy-duty pans, especially clad pans, which contain a layer of aluminum or copper in between the layers of steel, will even out the heat considerably. But if you don't trust your pans, or if your stovetop tends to have hotspots, consider employing an additional pan, preferably cast iron, as a heat diffuser.

ACID JELLIES: Although most of today's confections suffer from an almost overwhelming taste of sweetness, once upon a time the most popular treats actually balanced sweetness with tartness. My favorite of these edible antiques: lemon jellies. Love them—although I do think they could be a little chewier and a whole lot tarter, like gummy bears with a bad attitude. All this requires is upping the gelatin and the lemon. You could even add citric acid to make people really squeal . . . but that would be mean.

TIDBIT | Cast iron diffuses heat well because it's a good conductor and extremely dense.

TAFFIES: As it was for many of my generation, the Tootsie Roll was my favorite childhood candy: It was delicious, cheap, and it lasted all afternoon. Of course, I didn't realize it at the time, but I was really just eating chocolate taffy. Taffy is unique in the culinary world not because of what goes into it, or even how those ingredients are cooked, but because as it cools it's stretched and folded.

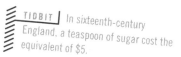

APPLICATION	PUMPKIN SEED BRITTLE

1½ POUNDS

Hulled green pumpkin seeds are often found in the Latin or Mexican ingredient aisle of megamarts as "pepitas." They're delicious and easy to eat, and we used them in our application here. But don't be afraid of roasting your own. After carving a few jack-o'-lanterns I usually have a bucket of seeds. I rinse them to sort out the pulp, spread them on a pan, salt them, and roast them at 300°F until golden brown and just fragrant. Although they're chewy because they're still wearing their outer coat, they're delicious and brittle-worthy.

// SOFTWARE ///

1	teaspoon	vegetable oil	plus additional for hardware
7¼	ounces	hulled pumpkin seeds	those are the green ones
½	teaspoon	cayenne pepper	
½	teaspoon	ground cinnamon	
½	teaspoon	kosher salt	
22	ounces	sugar	
1½	cups	H₂O	

// PROCEDURE ///

1. Heat the oil in a **10-inch sauté pan** over high heat and add the seeds. Toast the seeds, moving the pan constantly, for 4 to 5 minutes, until you smell their aroma and hear some of them begin to crackle. Transfer to a **small mixing bowl** and add the cayenne, cinnamon, and salt.

2. Line a **half sheet pan** with a **silicone baking mat**. Coat the bottom of a **second half sheet pan** with vegetable oil.

3. Set a **3-quart saucier** inside a **large cast-iron skillet**. Add the sugar and water to the saucepan and cook over high heat, stirring occasionally with a **wooden spoon**, until it comes to a boil. Stop stirring, cover, and cook for 3 minutes. Uncover, reduce the heat to medium, and cook until the sugar is a light amber color and reaches 350°F on a **candy thermometer**, about 25 minutes.

4. Remove from the heat and stir in the pumpkin seed mixture. This will greatly reduce the temperature of the sugar, so work quickly. As soon as the seeds are thoroughly incorporated, pour the mixture onto the lined half sheet pan. Using an oiled **spatula**, spread it thinly, working quickly before it hardens. Top with the oiled half sheet pan and press into a single layer. Cool completely, about 30 minutes, then break into pieces. Store in an **airtight container** for up to 2 weeks.

TIDBIT | Recent studies have found no evidence that sugar causes hyperactivity in kids.

TIDBIT | In sixteenth-century England, a teaspoon of sugar cost the equivalent of $5.

ORANGE TAFFY

ABOUT 60 PIECES

// SOFTWARE ///

14½	ounces	sugar	
1½	cups	H$_2$O	
1	cup	light corn syrup	
1	teaspoon	kosher salt	
1	tablespoon	white vinegar	
1½	tablespoons	unsalted butter	plus a tablespoon for hardware
1	teaspoon	orange extract	
6	drops	red food coloring	
6	drops	yellow food coloring	

// PROCEDURE ///

1. Butter a **half sheet pan**, line it with a **silicone baking mat**, and butter the mat as well.

2. Combine the sugar, water, corn syrup, salt, and vinegar and place over medium heat in a **4-quart saucepan**. Stir until the sugar dissolves, raise the heat to high and bring to a boil. Turn the heat down to low, clip a **candy thermometer** to the side of the pan, and cook until the mixture reaches 260°F. Remove the pan from the heat, add the butter, orange extract, and food colorings, and stir to combine. Pour the taffy onto the silicone-lined half sheet pan. Cool until you are able to handle it, approximately 10 to 15 minutes.

3. Don **vinyl gloves**, butter them, and begin to fold the taffy into thirds using the silicone mat to help lift it. Pick up the taffy and fold it back on itself repeatedly, twisting as you go. The taffy is done when it lightens in color, takes on a sheen, and becomes too hard to pull; this will take 5 to 10 minutes of pulling.

4. Roll into a log, cut into 4 pieces, roll each into a 1-inch-diameter log, and cut into 1-inch pieces using **kitchen shears**, making sure to keep the pieces separated or they will stick to each other. Wrap each piece of candy in a square of **waxcd paper**. Store in an **airtight container** for up to 5 days.

NOTE: Although we decided to go with chocolate taffy and peanut brittle in the show, our original working recipes were orange taffy and pumpkin seed brittle, which, to tell you the truth, we like better.

ACID JELLIES

64 (1-INCH) PIECES

// **SOFTWARE** //

1¼	cups	H₂O	divided
2	ounces	powdered gelatin	
½	cup	lemon juice	freshly squeezed
¼	cup	lime juice	freshly squeezed
10	ounces	sugar	divided
2	tablespoons	lemon zest	
2	tablespoons	lime zest	

// **PROCEDURE** //

1. In a **2-quart saucepan**, combine ½ cup of the water, the gelatin, and the lemon and lime juices. Set aside.

2. Combine the remaining ¾ cup water and 8 ounces of the sugar in another **2-quart saucepan** over medium heat. Stir until the sugar dissolves. Bring to a boil, cover, and cook for 3 minutes. Remove the lid, place a **candy thermometer** on the side of the pan, and cook until the sugar mixture reaches 300°F.

3. Remove from the heat and add the sugar mixture to the gelatin mixture. The mixture will clump, but just reduce the heat to low and stir constantly in order to dissolve the gelatin completely. Add the lemon and lime zest and stir to combine. Pour the mixture into an **8-inch square nonstick pan** and cool to room temperature for 1½ to 2 hours. Do not refrigerate.

4. Cut the cooled jellies into cubes using a **pizza cutter** and toss to coat in the remaining sugar. Serve immediately or store in an **airtight container** for up to 4 days. Stored jellies may need to be recoated in sugar before serving.

POTATO, MY SWEET

EPISODE 97 | SEASON 7 | GOOD EATS

This episode introduced a new character, a food agent named Sid who's trying to get work for his new client, the sweet potato. Bogged down for decades in sticky-sweet casseroles, playing second fiddle to marshmallows, the poor kid just needs a break. Sid comes to me because he knows that I've got a history of being afraid of sweet potatoes, which is true. I grew up hating the things. But working on this episode was a real green-eggs-and-ham-style epiphany, and now nary a week goes by that I don't go for one of the recipes herein. The sweet potato waffles are in fact one of my favorite *Good Eats* apps of all time.

TIDBIT | Supposedly, the sweet potato was first cultivated in Peru around 750 B.C.

AB: (reading from a fact sheet) Vitamin C, vitamin E, protein, foliate, six times the RDA of vitamin A. Impressive.

Sid (the agent): And he's a known cancer-fighter!

AB: Well, your client certainly has some handsome nutritional credentials, but—

Sid: And more dietary fiber than a bowl of oatmeal!

AB: Well, fiber's nice, but it's not very sexy, now, is it?

Sid: Um, no.

AB: And let's face it. Your client's just not much to look at, is he?

Sid: Uh-uh, no. But every meal needs a versatile supporting player, someone who can complement a wide range of textures and flavors. My client does it all, Mr. Brown: sweet, savory, you name it! Why, one food critic even dubbed him "the pork of the root world."

AB: "Pork of the root world." Nice accolade. Well, I tell you what. We'll, uh, we'll think about it and get back to you.

TIDBIT | North Carolina ranks number one in sweet potato production in the United States.

87

Despite the name, sweet potatoes are not simply potatoes that happen to be sweet. In fact, botanically speaking, they're not even related to potatoes. They are the root of a vine in the morning glory family. So why do we call them sweet potatoes?

These roots, which Christopher Columbus brought back to Spain in 1493, were called *batatas* by the Indians who lived in the greater Antilles Islands at the time, so in Spain they started calling them *patatas*. The Spanish then introduced them to the English, supposedly by serving a sweet potato pie to Henry VIII.

What about "yams"? Yams are actually a different vegetable, grown in Africa. But back in the 1930s, some Louisiana farmers developed an orange-fleshed sweet potato, and they wanted to differentiate it from the yellow sweet potatoes that dominated the market. *Yam* was already accepted Southern slang for sweet potato, thanks to the slaves, so they decided to stick with it despite the fact that sweet potatoes aren't yams.

Traditionally a cold-weather staple, sweet potatoes are available year round now, but their flavors peak during fall and winter months. Always choose specimens that are a bit heavy for their size, and are free of any soft spots or sprouts. Otherwise, I wouldn't get too carried away with aesthetics because sweet potatoes have never been known for their looks, which is probably why there's never been a Mr. Sweet Potato Head.

Since they're mighty moist when harvested, sweet potatoes are cured, or partially dried, in kilns for a few days to toughen their skins and increase their storage potential. You don't want to undo that cure, so keep them stashed in a dry, cool, well-ventilated area. Try to use them within 10 days, or 2 weeks max. And remember, sweet potatoes bruise more easily than regular potatoes, so be gentle.

A hundred years ago, George Washington Carver set out to plumb the depths of the sweet potato's usefulness, and wound up making everything from flour to vinegar to instant coffee, after-dinner mints, paint, and five kinds of library paste out of the root. Of course, unless you're currently enrolled in kindergarten, that may not qualify as good eats.

Yams

NOW THAT'S A YAM, MAN!

CHIPOTLE SMASHED SWEET POTATOES

4 SERVINGS

Although sweet potatoes can be baked or boiled, steaming is faster, easier, and won't wash away any flavor. In this case, the sweetness is balanced by the smoky heat of the chiles.

// SOFTWARE ///

2	large	sweet potatoes	peeled and cubed
2	tablespoons	unsalted butter	
½	teaspoon	kosher salt	
1		chipotle chile pepper in adobo sauce[1]	chopped
1	teaspoon	adobo sauce	from the pepper can

// PROCEDURE ///

1. Put the sweet potatoes in a **steamer basket** and put the steamer in a **large pot** of simmering water that is 1 inch from the bottom of the basket. Cover and steam over medium-high heat for 20 minutes, or until the sweet potatoes are fork tender.

2. Remove the steamer basket, pour the water out of the pot, and dump the sweet potatoes into the pot. Add the butter and salt and mash with a **potato masher**. Add the chile and sauce and continue mashing to combine. Serve immediately.

[1] A chipotle chile is a smoked jalapeño chile, which is indeed a chile, not a pepper. And yet, as soon as you put them in a can and cook them in a spicy adobo sauce, you get to call them peppers even though they're chiles. This drives me nuts.

TIDBIT | Beacause of their high moisture and sugar contents, sweet potatoes bake beautifully. Simply park a few directly on the oven rack and set to bake at 350°F. You don't have to poke any holes or rub anything on them. Medium-sized specimens will be done in 45 minutes to an hour. For the best results, remove the potatoes and cool them at room temp for 10 minutes before serving. I don't even put salt on mine.

SWEET POTATO PIE

1 (9-INCH) PIE

This pie is everything I ever wanted out of pumpkin pie, only without the pumpkin.

// SOFTWARE ///

20	ounces	sweet potatoes	peeled and cubed
1¼	cups	plain yogurt	
6	ounces	dark brown sugar	
½	teaspoon	ground cinnamon	
¼	teaspoon	nutmeg	freshly grated
5	large	egg yolks	
1	pinch	kosher salt	
1	9-inch	pie shell	frozen or fresh, see page 127
1	cup	pecans	chopped and lightly toasted
1	tablespoon	maple syrup	

// PROCEDURE //

1. Put the sweet potatoes in a **steamer basket** and put the steamer in a **large pot** of simmering water that is 1 inch from the bottom of the basket. Cover and steam over medium-high heat for 20 minutes, or until the sweet potatoes are fork tender.

2. Remove the steamer basket, and dump the sweet potatoes into the bowl of a **stand mixer**. Mash with a **potato masher**.

3. Heat the oven to 350°F.

4. Beat the sweet potatoes in the **stand mixer fitted with the paddle attachment** until smooth. Add the yogurt, brown sugar, cinnamon, nutmeg, egg yolks, and salt and beat until well combined. Set the pie shell (in its pie tin) on a **half sheet pan**, fill with the sweet potato mixture, and smooth the top. Sprinkle the pecans on top and drizzle with the maple syrup.

5. Bake for 50 to 55 minutes, until the pie reaches an internal temperature of 165° to 175°F; the middle should still wiggle slightly. Remove from the oven and cool on a **cooling rack** for 1 hour. Slice and serve. Stash leftovers in the refrigerator.

TIDBIT | In Polynesia, sweet potatoes grow upwards of 100 pounds.

TIDBIT | One cup of sweet potatoes has as much beta-carotene as 23 cups of broccoli.

TIDBIT | Henry the VIII was fond of sweet potatoes, which were believed to be an aphrodisiac.

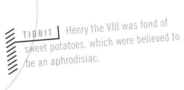

SWEET POTATO WAFFLES

4 (8-INCH) WAFFLES

Sweet potatoes possess a balance of moisture, starch, and sugar that makes them ideal for baked goods, especially those requiring considerable surface browning like waffles.

// **SOFTWARE** //

8	ounces	sweet potatoes	peeled and cubed
1	cup	whole milk	
2	ounces	light brown sugar	
4	tablespoons	unsalted butter	melted
1	tablespoon	orange zest	grated
10½	ounces	all-purpose flour	
1	tablespoon	baking powder	
½	teaspoon	kosher salt	
6	large	egg whites	at room temperature

// **PROCEDURE** //

1. Put the sweet potatoes in a **steamer basket** and put the steamer in a **large pot** of simmering water that is 1 inch from the bottom of the basket. Cover and steam over medium-high heat for 20 minutes, or until the sweet potatoes are fork tender.

2. Remove the steamer basket, pour the water out of the pot, and dump the sweet potatoes into the pot. Mash with a **potato masher**.

3. In a **large mixing bowl**, combine the sweet potatoes, milk, brown sugar, butter, and orange zest.

4. **Sift** together the flour, baking powder, and salt and add to the sweet potato mixture. Stir to incorporate but do not overmix; there should be lumps remaining in the batter.

5. In a separate **bowl**, using an **electric hand mixer**, beat the egg whites until stiff peaks form. Fold the egg whites into the batter one third at a time. The batter will be thick. Using a **disher** (appropriate to your waffle iron's capacity), pour the batter onto a heated, oiled **waffle iron** and cook until lightly browned, 5 to 6 minutes. Serve hot.

   NOTE: I humbly suggest serving these with a drizzle of maple syrup (the real thing, grade B), toasted pecans, and a scoop of vanilla ice cream.

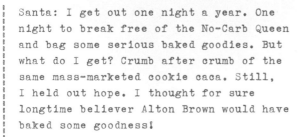

THE COOKIE CLAUSE

It's Christmas Eve. I've fallen asleep on the couch only to be suddenly and unceremoniously roused by a demon in red. Well, not a demon, exactly, but not what you'd classically recognize as Santa, either. What's worse, this dervish from the pole is not happy . . . not at all. Something about the cookies.

Santa: I get out one night a year. One night to break free of the No-Carb Queen and bag some serious baked goodies. But what do I get? Crumb after crumb of the same mass-marketed cookie caca. Still, I held out hope. I thought for sure longtime believer Alton Brown would have baked some goodness!

AB: Well, I...I do believe, but, you know, I ran out of time. I had those---

Santa: Argh! That makes it even worse! That, that's it! I quit!

AB: What? Y...y...you can't! What about all the good little boys and girls?

Santa: I'll just email them and tell them I quit because of you.

AB: You...you...you couldn't! You wouldn't!

Santa: Heh heh. Watch me. Heh heh.

AB: Well, wait, wait, wait. We can-- we can make a deal! Oh, that's it! I'll teach you how to make your own Christmas cookies!

Santa: What?

AB: Yeah! That way you can chow down any time that, you know, the old ball-and-chain's not watching. And all the cookies we make here tonight you can take with you. You can eat dozens by dawn!

Santa: Mm! (grabs AB's ear and pulls him up off the couch) All right. Santa's feeling merciful.

AB: That's nice!

SC: I'll give you exactly thirty minutes to produce some serious...

And so, Santa and I make cookies. Although we considered the obvious gingerbread angle, in the end we went with sugar cookies because they're far more versatile and, despite a certain surface simplicity, are indeed technique driven.

Sugar cookies are brought together via the creaming method, which always follows this order:

1. Beat solid fat at room temperature.

2. Beat sugar into fat.

3. Work in eggs one at a time.

4. Alternately add dry and wet ingredients, starting and finishing with dry.

Sifting is a pain, but it does help to combine and more importantly aerate the dry team. Aerated batters and doughs come together faster, with less gluten production, and that means a more tender baked good.

Until they go into the oven, heat is the enemy of sugar cookies because they are quite short; that is, they contain a high amount of fat, and that fat needs to remain in a solid but malleable state until the leavening starts to do its thing. Firm doughs are also a lot easier to cut and shape, so consider refrigerating the dough every chance you get and keep a cookie sheet or sheet pan in the freezer that you can whip out and park atop the rolled dough before cutting.

TIDBIT The U.S. Postal Service handles about half a million letters to Santa each year, which cost about $185,000 in stamps.

TIDBIT The first cookie cutters were actually wooden molds.

ABOUT 3 DOZEN (2½-INCH) COOKIES

// SOFTWARE //

15½	ounces	all-purpose flour	
¾	teaspoon	baking powder	
¼	teaspoon	fine salt	
1	cup	unsalted butter	at room temperature
8	ounces	granulated sugar	
1	large	egg	lightly beaten
1	tablespoon	whole milk	
2	tablespoons	confectioners' sugar	for rolling out the dough

// PROCEDURE //

1. **Sift** the flour, baking powder, and salt together and set aside.

2. Put the butter and granulated sugar in the bowl of a **stand mixer fitted with the paddle attachment**. Beat on medium speed until light in color, about 2 minutes.

3. Slowly add the egg and milk and beat to combine.

4. Reduce the mixer speed to low and gradually work in the flour mixture, beating until the dough pulls away from the side of the bowl. Divide the dough in half, wrap each piece in **plastic wrap**, and refrigerate for 2 hours.

5. Heat the oven to 375°F and put a **half sheet pan** in the freezer to chill.

6. Use a **small strainer or sifter** to sprinkle a work surface with 1 tablespoon of the confectioners' sugar. Remove 1 piece of dough from the refrigerator. Dust a **rolling pin** with confectioners' sugar and roll the dough out to as close to ¼ inch thick as possible. If the dough tears, quickly stick it back together and keep going. Move the dough around and check underneath frequently to make sure it is not sticking. If the dough has warmed during rolling, place the chilled half sheet pan on top for 10 minutes to chill.

7. Cut into desired shapes,[1] place at least 1 inch apart on a **half sheet pan lined with parchment paper**, and bake for 8 to 12 minutes, until the cookies are just beginning to turn brown around the edges, rotating the pan halfway through.

8. Cool the cookies on the pan for 2 minutes, then transfer to a **cooling rack** to cool completely. Serve as is or ice as desired. Store in an **airtight container** for up to 1 week.

[1] If using metal cookie cutters, chill them before using and always press straight down through the dough, without twisting.

ROYAL ICING

3½ CUPS, ENOUGH FOR ABOUT
3 DOZEN (2½-INCH) COOKIES

// SOFTWARE ///

3	ounces	pasteurized egg whites	
1	teaspoon	vanilla extract	
1	pound	confectioners' sugar	
		food coloring of your choice[2]	as many drops as it takes

TIDBIT | Confectioners' sugar contains a small amount of cornstarch, which prevents clumping by absorbing moisture.

// PROCEDURE ///

1. Combine the egg whites and vanilla in the bowl of a **stand mixer fitted with the whisk attachment** and whip until frothy. Sift in the confectioners' sugar gradually and mix on low speed until the sugar is incorporated and the mixture is shiny. Turn the mixer speed up to high and beat until stiff, glossy peaks form, 5 to 7 minutes.

2. Add food coloring, if desired. Use immediately or store in an airtight container in the refrigerator for up to 3 days. **Whisk** stored icing before using.

[2] Although liquid food colorings are certainly the norm, concentrated gel colorings give you more bang for the buck.

TIDBIT | The first cookies were probably made in seventh-century Persia and flavored with herbs and rosewater.

CHOCOLATE PEPPERMINT PINWHEEL COOKIES

ABOUT 3 DOZEN COOKIES

// SOFTWARE ///

15½	ounces	all-purpose flour	
¾	teaspoon	baking powder	
¼	teaspoon	fine salt	
1	cup	unsalted butter	at room temperature
8	ounces	granulated sugar	
1	large	egg	lightly beaten
1	tablespoon	whole milk	
3	ounces	unsweetened chocolate	melted
1	teaspoon	vanilla extract	
1	large	egg yolk	
1	teaspoon	peppermint extract	
2	ounces	candy canes	or other hard peppermint candies, crushed
2	tablespoons	confectioners' sugar	for rolling out the dough

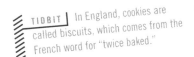
// PROCEDURE ///

1. **Sift** together the flour, baking powder, and salt. Set aside.

2. Put the butter and granulated sugar in the bowl of a **stand mixer fitted with the paddle attachment**. Beat on medium speed until light in color, about 2 minutes. Add the egg and milk and beat to combine.

3. Reduce the mixer speed to low and gradually add the flour mixture. Beat until the mixture pulls away from the side of the bowl.

4. Divide the dough in half. To one half add the chocolate and vanilla and incorporate using your hands in a **large mixing bowl**. To the other half, add the egg yolk, peppermint extract, and candy in another **large bowl** and incorporate. Cover each dough with **plastic wrap** and chill for 10 to 15 minutes. **Roll** out each half to about ¼ inch thick; the chocolate dough should be slightly larger. Lay the peppermint dough on top of the chocolate dough and press them together. Using **parchment paper** underneath, roll the dough into a log. Wrap in **parchment paper** and refrigerate for 2 hours.

5. Heat the oven to 375°F.

6. Remove the log from the refrigerator and using a **thin-bladed knife** cut it into ½-inch slices. Place the cookies 1 inch apart on a **half sheet pan lined with parchment paper** and bake for 12 to 13 minutes, rotating the pan halfway through the cooking time. The cookies will appear dry and darken slightly. Cool the cookies on the pan for 2 minutes, then transfer them to a **cooling rack**. Store in an **airtight container** for up to 1 week.

TIP The dough may crack or break during cutting; use your fingers to press the dough back together and continue slicing.

If the leaf of a plant contains essential oils that can be used to add flavor and/or aroma to a food, we call that leaf an herb. If the essential oils come from other botanical parts—bark, roots, pods, berries, seeds, and the like—that is a spice. Now, I like spices. I like them a lot. In fact, they're a whole other show. But herbs have a few distinct advantages. For one thing, most spices grow overseas . . . way overseas, as in on the other side of the planet. Herbs grow anywhere: kitchen gardens, window boxes, pots—heck, anywhere you're willing to toss a shovelful of dirt. Even boxed-in city dwellers can grow enough herbs to keep themselves in fragrant culinary options all summer long if they make even a meager attempt.

Another thing about herbs is that you can use them in either a fresh or a dry state, something you cannot do with spices, which must typically be processed to some state of dehydration to be of any real use. There are thousands of different culinary herbs grown around the world, but here in America I think you need at least a working knowledge of the Big Ten (there are actually eleven, but that doesn't sound as snappy).

TIDBIT | *Fines herbes* is a seasoning blend consisting traditionally of parsley, chervil, tarragon, and chives.

TIDBIT | Did you know that before science types learned how to synthesize chemical compounds, most drugs were derived from plants? Yup. Most of the herbs we cook with were originally cultivated for their medicinal values.

KNOWLEDGE CONCENTRATE

Although all members of the onion family are technically herbs, only **CHIVES** count in my book. The secret to their use? Snip them with scissors. Never cut them with a knife, which results in too much bruising. They get along especially well with white foods: potatoes, pasta, eggs, and white fish. Nothing says spring like the smell of chives!

Like its cousins basil and thyme, **MINT** comes in a plethora of different flavors: chocolate mint, peppermint, apple mint, and spearmint. It is unique in the herb world in that its flavor plays equally well in savory and sweet applications. For instance, tabouli salad and Mint Chip Ice Cream (page 271).

THYME is my favorite. Common thyme is a very subtle, flexible herb, despite the fact that the tiny leaves can be a beast to harvest. Excellent with meat and seafood, it's a classic bouquet garni participant, and excellent in citrus-based desserts as well.

DILL, a.k.a. dillweed, is actually a member of the carrot family. I think of it as a very sneaky herb, because it's so often confused with fennel, which it tastes nothing like. Although it was first cultivated in India, it has been most embraced by the Scandinavians, probably because it goes so well with beets and potatoes, especially when served cold.

ROSEMARY, which may boast the most identifiable herb flavor in America, comes from an evergreen shrub of Mediterranean origin that can grow up to 15 feet in height if left untrimmed. A lot of landscape architects will use it as a natural deer barrier: Deer just hate this stuff. They won't walk through it and they won't eat it. Probably because it tastes so good with them!

I never make tomato sauce without true, or Greek, **OREGANO**. It also works and plays well with eggplant, chicken, and red meat. Mexican oregano, by the way, is a member of the verbena family.

Although **BASIL** comes in about two dozen varieties, sweet, or Italian, basil is the most common. Which makes sense, because basil is most often thought of as an Italian ingredient and it gets along with cheese and tomatoes so well. Basil should always be added as close to the end of cooking as possible. Ideally, it should just be finely shredded and served raw.

The only member of the daisy family considered to be an herb is **TARRAGON**. Most associated with French cooking, it gets along very, very well with eggs (try it in Omelets, page 50), shellfish, and, as we shall soon see, vinegar.

SAGE'S fuzzy, oval leaves are potent and earthy, and can dominate a dish unless used sparingly. Although sage defines holiday stuffing, the leaves can also be fried in butter and used as a sauce (Ravioli in Browned Butter, page 15).

PARSLEY is perhaps the most misunderstood herb in America. Despite what most folks think, it does have a purpose besides decorating side dishes in diners. Parsley comes in two market varieties: curly and, my favorite, flat-leaf, a.k.a. Italian, which looks a whole lot like . . .

CILANTRO. No, cilantro is not on my Big Ten list, but it is crucial to the cuisines of Southeast Asia, as well as Mexico, so it bears mentioning. Also, it bears mentioning because it's sometimes hard to identify. For instance, young, tender cilantro looks a lot like fennel, but when you go down to the bottom of the plant, and you pick some of the older stuff, it looks a lot like flat-leaf parsley. It's very easy to mistake them for each other, although they do not interchange well in recipes, so take a close look. If in doubt, smell. Cilantro has a strong, almost chemical/soapy aroma that is quite distinct from parsley's rather run-of-the-mill "green" smell.

The goal in herb storage is suspended animation. This requires a bit of added moisture to keep things from drying out, and, since respiration hastens decomposition, a minimum of air.

Take a long piece of paper towel—say, 6 sheets—and spritz with just enough water to barely moisten it.[1] Lay the herbs on top. You can put as many different types together as you like. Very gently, roll up the towel, then wrap with at least two layers of plastic wrap. Stash this bundle in the refrigerator, but not in the crisper drawer, which is usually too cold for herbs. I've always had better luck with the very top shelf because this is typically the warmest place in the fridge. If you're looking for long-term storage solutions for notorious wilters, like tarragon, chervil, and cilantro, take a cue from florists and cut the end off of the bunch, park it in a cup of water, and cover it with plastic. I usually use a plain old plastic drink cup and a shower cap lifted from a hotel. I've managed to keep cilantro for up to a week using this method.

When it comes to getting the flavor of fresh herbs out of the leaves and into the food, you've got two basic options. The first, of course, is to add chopped herbs directly to the dish. The second is INFUSION, and this is a method that can be used for any food that cooks in a water-based liquid. Although many cookbooks suggest a small bundle called a bouquet garni, I prefer the tea bag method, wherein herbs are pouched up in a coffee filter tied off with string or a food-grade rubber band like those you find around broccoli crowns. The other benefit to this method is that you can easily add spices such as peppercorns, cloves, star anise, and so on. I believe that when dealing with infusions, you get the best herbal flavor by adding your pouch to a cool liquid and then bringing said liquid to a simmer.

[1] A spritz bottle is pretty much the only way to do this.

SPRITZ AND ROLL

TIDBIT | To freeze herbs: Put chopped leaves in ice cube trays, cover with water, freeze, then store in zip-top bags.

TIDBIT | Try dried herbs in soups, stews, tomato sauce, and bread doughs.

Whenever I come into a bumper crop of quality herbs, usually at summer's end, I refrigerate some to use fresh and dry the rest. Technically, any herb can be dried, but heartier herbs like oregano, bay, sage, thyme, and rosemary tend to hold on to their essential oils even after they've given up most of their moisture. That said, chives, parsley, even dill are worth drying if you plan to use them within a month or so.

The biggest problem with dried herbs is that they're usually ugly and brown. That's because, as they age, enzymes inside the leaves break down the chlorophyll. But this chemical terminator can be stopped with a quick dip in boiling water.

// SOFTWARE ///

	fresh herbs	
	H_2O	

// PROCEDURE ///

1) Bring a **pot** of water to a boil and blanch the herbs for 15 seconds. Immerse in an **ice bath** for 30 seconds, then drain and spin the herbs dry in a **salad spinner**.

2) Spread the herbs out as evenly as possible on **3 air-conditioning filters**, stacking them on top of one another. Top these with one more empty **air-conditioning filter**. Lay a **box fan** on its side and set the filters on top of it. Strap the filters to the fan with **2 bungee cords**. Stand the fan upright, plug it in, and turn it on high. Dry for 12 hours. Rotate the filters and continue drying for 12 more hours. When dry, remove the herbs from the filters, crumble, remove the stems, and store in an **airtight container** in a cool, dry place. You can either mix them up or keep them in separate containers.

HERB-DRYING RIG

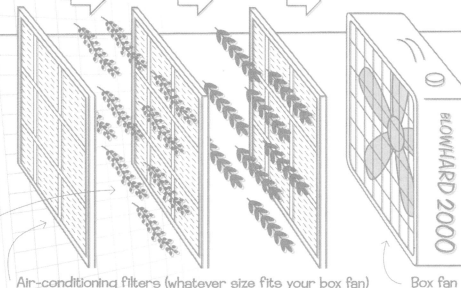

AIRFLOW IS KEY. SO DON'T GO BEYOND FOUR FILTERS. AND MAKE SURE TO LEAVE ROOM FOR AIRFLOW AT EACH STAGE.

BLOWHARD

BLOWHARD 2000

Herbaceous material

Air-conditioning filters (whatever size fits your box fan)

Box fan

TARRAGON CHIVE VINEGAR

6 CUPS

Although herb oils are all the rage these days, making them at home is a tricky proposition because oils have been known to harbor *Clostridium botulinium*, which is never, ever good eats. The acidic environment provided by vinegar is a far safer option.

Use herb vinegar in vinaigrettes, add it to the poaching water for eggs, season tomato sauce, hummus, and other bean purees with it, and use it as a base for marinades.

You will need half of the herbs when you start this recipe and half in 2 weeks. It is best to purchase the second half of the herbs when they are needed. For storage, you will need 3 pint jars or 4 (13-ounce) wine bottles.

// SOFTWARE ///

FOR THE INFUSION

1	teaspoon	household bleach	
12	sprigs	fresh tarragon	
12	shoots	fresh chives	
6	cups	white wine vinegar	

FOR STORAGE

1	teaspoon	household bleach	
12	sprigs	fresh tarragon	
12	shoots	fresh chives	

TIDBIT | The word *vinegar* derives from the French *vin aigre*, meaning "sour wine."

// PROCEDURE ///

1. Make the infusion: Combine **2 quarts of water** and the bleach in a **large container**. Dunk the tarragon and chives in the solution, then rinse in cold water. Pat dry.

2. Put the herbs in a **2-quart container** large enough to hold the vinegar.

3. Heat the vinegar in an **electric kettle**. When the vinegar reaches 190°F, pour the vinegar over the herbs. Cool completely, put the lid on the container, and set in a cool, dark place for 2 weeks.

4. Store the vinegar: After 2 weeks, sterilize the **containers and lids** that you will use to store the vinegar by immersing them in a large pot of boiling water and boiling for 10 minutes. If using corks, purchase pre-sterilized corks, then dip them in and out of boiling water 3 or 4 times.

5. Sanitize the fresh herbs in 2 quarts of water and the bleach, rinse, and pat dry, as described in step 1. Divide the fresh herbs among the containers.

6. Strain the vinegar through a sanitized **funnel** lined with **cheesecloth**. Seal and refrigerate. Discard the old herbs. The vinegar may be stored at room temperature for 5 to 6 weeks or in the refrigerator for up to 6 months.

Garnish, you say? I think not. This is one of those dishes that never fails to surprise and amaze. I sometimes serve it slightly wilted under poached eggs or alongside a particularly stinky cheese.

// SOFTWARE //

4	ounces	flat-leaf parsley	about 2 quarts
2	tablespoons	lemon juice	freshly squeezed
2	tablespoons	lemon zest	
6	tablespoons	walnut oil	
2	teaspoons	dark sesame oil	
1	teaspoon	honey	
	to taste	kosher salt	
	to taste	black pepper	freshly ground
3	tablespoons	sesame seeds	toasted

// PROCEDURE //

1. Wash and dry the parsley. Pick the leaves, and set aside. Discard the stems.

2. **Whisk** together the lemon juice, zest, walnut oil, sesame oil, honey, and salt and pepper in a **large bowl**. Add the parsley and sesame seeds and toss to combine. Allow the flavors to meld for at least 30 minutes before serving.

SPICE CAPADES

EPISODE 100 | SEASON 7 | GOOD EATS

No culinary power on Earth has the ability to transport us through space and time like the mysterious mojo of spice. All of the world's great cuisines are defined by spices. In fact, the world itself was shaped by spice, or rather man's desire for it. After all, Christopher Columbus, Vasco da Gama, and Ferdinand Magellan weren't out there looking for vacation lots. They were searching for spices, which at one time were worth their weight in gold. And all because of their power to convert ordinary everyday food into . . .

TIDBIT | When invading Rome in A.D. 408, the Goths demanded a ransom of three thousand peppercorns.

TIDBIT | Allspice is the dried, unripe berry of a tree native to Jamaica.

THE TRUTH ABOUT SPICES, MEDIEVAL EUROPE, AND SPOILED FOOD

It is said that in medieval Europe cooks in wealthy households poured on the spices to the point of not being able to taste anything else. Some have argued that this was an effort to cover up the fact that most of the meat was in a state of serious decomposition. This would be like saying that you need a helicopter to fly your Yugo around. Households that could afford five pounds of peppercorns could afford to slaughter a small flock of animals before every meal. The reason they used all those spices was because they could. They were showing off, with no regard for tradition or culinary precedent. But that's because there were none. No one in London or Leipzig or Paris knew what to do with cloves or cardamom or nutmeg because they'd never had them before. Today, we have no such excuses. The modern cook has access not only to fine spices but also to accurate records of traditional usage, and before going off willy-nilly I'd strongly suggest that the traditional ways be carefully studied.

▷ A spice is essentially any part of a plant—bark, berry, root, rhizome, or seed—that contains volatile, essential oils that bring desirable flavors and/or aromas to food. The only plant part that's completely ruled out are leaves, which are "herbs." Some plants, like coriander, give us both spice and herb (coriander the herb is more commonly known in the United States as cilantro). Some plants, like celery, give us seeds, herbs, green vegetables, and tubers, but they are rare.

▷ The first step in spice cookery is to find a good source. Since they're perishable, lightweight, and small, I order spices via the Internet from specialty spice vendors who know what they're doing. And, with the exception of some blends, I buy spices whole and grind them myself. Since the oils inside spices are quick to evaporate, whole is the only real way to make them last more than a couple of months. Ground spices tend to go bad before we have a chance to use them.

▷ Since the power of spices lies in volatile compounds, air, heat, moisture, and light are all your enemies when it comes to spice storage. I store mine in small tins that I keep Velcro'd to the back of a cabinet door. That way they're always where I need them to be and there's no confusion. The absolute last thing you want to do is keep them in glass jars stacked in a countertop rack. Bad . . . very bad.

▷ Consider heating whole spices before using them. Coffee is a spice, and think about how you maximize its impact. First you roast the beans to bring out and develop the flavors. Great spicers always heat their spices right before use. This can be done by frying them in oil, toasting them in a pan, broiling them in the oven, or, my favorite, running them through a hot-air popcorn machine. Whatever the method, don't walk away from them, because burning, when it happens, happens quickly. Use your nose. The moment you smell the spice, get it off of or out of the heat.

▷ Grind at the last moment. Once the seed, bark, berry, or what have you has been breached, the clock is ticking. When it comes time to grind, there's plenty of technology to choose from, both electric and man powered. At the bottom of the evolutionary scale is my favorite, the mortar and pestle. The trick is to find the right one. Marble and metal are popular but almost useless because the texture is too smooth and the target ingredients tend to just slide around. I use a pharmaceutical-grade unglazed ceramic set, which has just the right texture. If you have just one, make it a shallow 6-inch model. I have three, and I use them constantly.

Pepper mills and grinders can be used to grind larger seeds and dry berries like, suprisingly, pepper. But my favorite hand-grinding contraption is nothing but a ceramic grinder attached to a glass jar.

In the electrical catagory you can't beat a blade-style coffee grinder. Just look for a model with a deep well and a deep metal cup. In fact, the more metal parts the better, because spices contain oils and oils love plastic and will stick to them like glue. Unless you enjoy really exotic coffee flavors, buy a second grinder for your coffee.

A FEW OF OUR FAVORITE THINGS

1. BLACK PEPPERCORNS, GREEN PEPPERCORNS: White, black, and green peppercorns all come from the same plant, *Piper nigrum*, and are another show.

2. PINK PEPPERCORNS: They're not really peppercorns at all. They're just little pink berries that kind of look like pepper.

3. POPPY SEEDS: There remains a slight misconception that the poppies grown for culinary usage are the same as those grown for narcotics; nonetheless, they are delicious when ground and used as a filling for pastries.

4. ALLSPICE: A native of a Caribbean evergreen, allspice has a clovelike heat that pairs well with poultry, pickles, and pastries.

5. CARAWAY: A member of the parsley family, caraway is most often associated with rye bread and sauerkraut, but works as well with root vegetables.

6. CUMIN: Fennel seeds, cumin seeds, caraway seeds: Why are they interesting? They're not really seeds. They're little bitty fruits, dried.

7. FENNEL: Of course, no sausage is complete without this seed. The bulb and leaves of the plant make excellent additions to salads and slaws.

8. CARDAMOM, GREEN CARDAMOM: Within each pod you'll find approximately twenty-five black seeds whose flavors evoke allspice, pepper, and clove all at once. White pods have been bleached and pack a lightly muted punch when compared to green pods.

9. CINNAMON: The bark of a tree grown almost exclusively for its fragrant flavor. You often find it labeled as Ceylon or bakers' cinnamon in the market, and it's worth the extra pennies, as it's twice as pungent and sweet as cassia, the bark of which is much thinner and more easily ground.

10. CASSIA: Most of the cinnamon that we eat in this country is actually cassia. Still a member of the cinnamon species, cassia is more widely grown and therefore less expensive to process and pack.

11. GINGER: Available fresh and dried, ginger is an easy addition to sweet applications, but be sure you use fresh spice—ground ginger loses its bite quickly. Oh, and it's definitely another show.

12. FENUGREEK: These seeds must be ground for one to appreciate their sweet aromas of nuts and slightly bitter celery taste.

13. BLACK SESAME SEEDS: There is little difference between these and their white counterparts. Sesame has a distinctly nutty and sweet flavor and easily provides texture to baked goods as well as savory noodle dishes.

14. CORIANDER: One of my favorite spices, when planted in the ground it generates an herb we call cilantro.

15. NUTMEG: You'll rarely find me without a nutmeg nut in tow. Whole, these nuts last practically forever (okay, a year) and can be grated as needed. Warm punches, classic béchamel, and eggnog are incomplete without it.

CURRY POWDER BLEND[1]

ABOUT ½ CUP

If you like using spice blends (and I almost always blend) instead of relying on preground powders, try the mix-then-grind technique.

// SOFTWARE //

2	tablespoons	cumin seeds	toasted
2	tablespoons	cardamom pods	toasted
2	tablespoons	coriander seeds	toasted
¼	cup	ground turmeric	
1	tablespoon	dry mustard	
1	teaspoon	ground cayenne	

// PROCEDURE //

Put everything in an **airtight container**. Shake to combine. Store in a cool, dry place for up to 6 months. When ready to use, **grind** and add to dishes according to taste.

TIDBIT | Spices have antiseptic properties, which is why they've been used in preserving since, I dunno, mammoths roamed Montana.

[1] This is a "curry" powder in the English tradition. In India, spice mixes, or masalas, are never assembled ahead of time. And a real curry, by the way, is a soup or gravy, not a flavorant.

GRINDING SPICES BY HAND TAKES FOREVER!

BROILED SALMON WITH AB'S SPICE POMADE

6 TO 8 MAIN-COURSE SERVINGS

Salmon, unlike most fish, can stand up to strong spices without getting lost in the process.

// SOFTWARE //

⅓	cup	vegetable oil	plus 2 teaspoons for the pan
1	3-pound	salmon fillet	pin bones removed
1½	teaspoons	kosher salt	
1	teaspoon	black pepper	freshly ground
1	tablespoon	coriander seeds	toasted
1	tablespoon	fennel seeds	toasted
1	teaspoon	cumin seeds	toasted
1	pod	star anise	
2	teaspoons	onion powder	
1	teaspoon	garlic powder	
½	teaspoon	ground cayenne	

// PROCEDURE //

1. Coat a **half sheet pan** with the 2 teaspoons oil and lay the salmon on the pan. Season with salt and pepper. Set aside.

2. Put the coriander, fennel, cumin, star anise, onion powder, garlic powder, and cayenne in a **blender**. Blend on high speed until the whole spices become powder. With the blender running, pour in the ⅓ cup oil and blend until well combined. Stop the blender to scrape down the sides of the container, if necessary.

3. **Brush** the salmon with the spice mixture. Rest the salmon at room temperature for 30 minutes.

4. Heat the broiler to high. Cook the salmon 6 inches from the heating element and cook until it reaches an internal temperature of 131°F,[2] about 15 minutes depending on the oven.

5. Remove from the oven and let rest for 10 minutes, then serve immediately.

SPICE HARMONY

When consumed all by themselves, most spices taste rather unidimensional, like a single note. Several spices together can work like a chord, supporting each other. If their chemical structures are somewhat similar, then that chord is pleasingly harmonious. Luckily, ages of culinary evolution have worked out some classic combos: Chili powder, five-spice powder, garam masala, and pie spice are all fine examples, but none is better than my personal favorite, curry powder.

[2] The internal temperature of the fish will rise a little as carry-over cooking occurs.

——————————— **DRIED PEAR AND FIG COMPOTE**

ABOUT 2 CUPS

One of my favorite "sweet" spice applications, this works on everything from ice cream to bagels. I've baked pork chops in it (with great success) and stuffed it into duck. It freezes well too.

// SOFTWARE ///

4	ounces	dried figs	roughly chopped
4	ounces	dried pears	roughly chopped
1	cup	apple cider	
½	cup	white wine	
2	tablespoons	honey	preferably orange blossom
6	whole	cloves	
1	stick	cinnamon	
1	1-inch strip	lemon peel	
1	tablespoon	lemon juice	freshly squeezed
½	teaspoon	kosher salt	

TIDBIT | Many culinary spices, such as cinnamon and vanilla, were originally used in making perfumes.

TIDBIT | The original compotes were referred to as "compostes," describing a dish made of stewed fruits.

// PROCEDURE //

1. Combine the dried fruits, cider, wine, honey, spices, lemon peel, juice and salt in a **2-quart saucier**, and bring to a simmer over medium heat. Reduce the heat to low, cover, and simmer for 1 to 1½ hours, until the mixture thickens to the consistency of jam.

2. Remove and discard the cloves, cinnamon stick, and lemon peel. Serve warm or cool. Store in an **airtight container** in the refrigerator for up to 2 weeks.

VEGETABLE CURRY

2 MAIN-COURSE SERVINGS,
OR 4 SIDE-DISH SERVINGS

This is perhaps my favorite way of spicing up frozen vegetables, which I happen to be a big fan of anyway.

// SOFTWARE

1	1 pound	bag mixed frozen vegetables	
⅔	cup	plain yogurt	
1	teaspoon	cornstarch	
2	tablespoons	vegetable oil	
1	teaspoon	cumin seeds	
½	teaspoon	fennel seeds	
½	teaspoon	mustard seeds	
1	teaspoon	ground turmeric	
½	teaspoon	onion powder	
½	teaspoon	coriander	freshly ground
⅛	teaspoon	cinnamon	freshly ground
2	cloves	garlic	crushed
3		dried red chiles	stems and seeds removed
¼	teaspoon	sugar	
½	teaspoon	kosher salt	
	to taste	black pepper	freshly ground

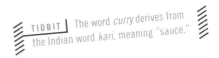

TIDBIT | The word *curry* derives from the Indian word *kari*, meaning "sauce."

// PROCEDURE

1. Poke several holes in the bag of frozen vegetables with a **skewer** and cook in a microwave oven on high for 2 to 3 minutes, or until thawed. Set aside.

2. **Whisk** together the yogurt and cornstarch in a **medium mixing bowl**. Set aside.

3. Heat the oil in a **10-inch sauté pan** over medium-high heat. Add the cumin, fennel, and mustard seeds, cover the pan with a **splatter screen**, and cook, stirring occasionally, until they begin to pop. Once they begin to pop, reduce the heat to medium and add the turmeric, onion powder, coriander, cinnamon, garlic, and chiles. Sauté until the garlic is golden brown, 3 to 5 minutes. Gently add the vegetables, sugar, salt, and pepper and cook for 3 to 5 minutes, until the vegetables are heated through.

4. Pour the vegetables into the bowl with the yogurt mixture and stir to combine. Discard the chiles, if desired, and serve immediately.

This episode wasn't a direct goof on the short-lived series *The Man Show*, but it was an attempt to mine the same ore. I wanted to present new spins on a couple of foods that I know good and well every guy desires in the 2 A.M. of his soul but rarely manufactures himself, namely the corn dog and the mini-burger, or "slider." Of course, the female of the species might equally adore these delicacies but frankly I can't remember the last time I saw one over the age of eight eating a corn dog. Although I'd love to tell you there's a heap of science in this show there really isn't. But there are a few quirky, fully functional techniques that should flip the switch on the male cooking chromosome.

SLIDERS

Great burgers are all about the beef, and flattish mini-burgers like these are best when built of chuck, which possesses deep beefy flavor and enough fat to keep things juicy, generally 20 percent plus or minus a point or two. Chuck also contains a fair amount of connective tissue that will help keep the meat together during patty fabrication. Unless you want to grind your own, I suggest you purchase a big hunk of chuck and ask your butcher to grind it fresh, and be sure to ask for a medium grind on that. If for some reason you must resort to preground, know that things are not always what they seem. Strange though it is, legally speaking, a package of 80 percent–lean ground chuck can contain no more than 20 percent fat, but it doesn't necessarily have to be 100 percent chuck. So buyer beware.

If you are one of the lucky folks who have a built-in griddle on your cooktop, clap your hands and squeal with happiness. If you have such a tool and it's heated by gas, then add hopping to the squealing, for you are capable of the kind of short-order grease flipping that was once the sole right of diner cooks. If you are not one of the happy few, then you should consider purchasing a countertop electric griddle. Plan on spending a hundred bucks and make sure it's the heaviest aluminum model you can find. (Stainless steel is a lousy thermal conductor; ergo, griddles made of it are prone to hot and cold spots.) The thermostat will be built into the power cable, and several long prongs will connect it to the unit. Better models such as the one we used on the show feature removable backsplashes that help minimize splattering of grease. There will also be a grease drain with a catch vessel of some type. Remember, when it comes to electric griddles, heavier is always better . . . and, unfortunately, cost is usually a fair indicator of quality. On a final note, I've tried at least a dozen different griddles designed to be laid across either one or two standard gas burners and I've never really been able to work out the heat management.

THE BIRTH OF THE SLIDER

The mini-burger or "slider" was most likely born on the spatula of a Wichita, Kansas, fry cook name of Walt Anderson, who in 1916 opened a burger stand with a griddle, three stools, and a cash loan of $3.75 for supplies. That stand eventually became the White Castle chain. Although many other chains have attempted to imitate the form, White Castle is, for my money, still the one and only. Although Anderson's partner, E. W. Ingram, became the force behind the brand, Anderson is the one who thought to make the hamburgers square so that he could get more on the griddle at a time. Genius.

CHUCK

TIDBIT One third of Americans have consumed ground beef in the last 24 hours.

This procedure looks to capture the discreet-bourgeoisie charm of the White Castle/Krystal–style burger—i.e., small, greasy, and irresistible. Since the bread/meat ratio is critical, pick your buns, then cut the patties to fit. And remember, they've got to be square. Because, well . . . because.

Note: The onions have been added to the base procedure, and unlike the buns in the show, these are simply heated on the griddle rather than warmed in the oven. Why waste all that heat?

// SOFTWARE ///

½	teaspoon	onion powder	
½	teaspoon	garlic powder	
½	teaspoon	black pepper	freshly ground
½	teaspoon	kosher salt	
1	pound	ground beef chuck	
½	cup	onion	finely chopped
8	3-inch	buns or rolls	split in half
2 to 3	tablespoons	mayonnaise	Duke's is my preferred brand, but then I'm Southern
8		dill pickle chips	preferably ice cold
		yellow mustard	plain, American stuff—not deli mustard or spicy

// PROCEDURE ///

1. Heat your **griddle** to 350°F.

2. Combine the onion powder, garlic powder, pepper, and salt in a **small bowl** and set aside.

3. Line a **half sheet pan** with **parchment paper** and place the ground chuck in the middle of the pan. Cover the meat with a large sheet of **plastic wrap** and roll with a **rolling pin** (a **wine bottle** will do in a pinch) until the meat covers the surface of the pan. Yes . . . it will be very thin. Remove the plastic wrap and sprinkle the meat liberally with the seasoning mixture.

4. Pick up the edge of the parchment and fold the meat in half, widthwise. Roll a couple of times just to seal the two layers, then cut into 8 even squares with a **pizza cutter**.

5. Cook the burgers on the griddle for 2 to 3 minutes per side. Resist the urge to press them with your **spatula**. Squeezing burgers is the culinary equivalent of picking at a scab, and you remember what your mom told you about that. When cooked, stack them on one side of the griddle and cover with **aluminum foil** to keep warm.

6. Spread the onions out on the griddle and fry in the residual beef fat. Turn them every minute or so until they start to brown. Push over to the other side, opposite the patties.

7. Place the buns cut side down on the griddle (don't worry, there will still be some fat there) and lay a **sheet of foil** over them for 2 minutes.

8. Construct burgers thusly: Spread mayonnaise on the bottom bun. The fat will produce a moisture barrier, thus preventing said bun from becoming soggy. The cooked onion is next, followed by the meat. Stack pickles atop and finally the top bun, liberally mustarded. Repeat until there's nothing left to build.

9. Consume mass quantities.

AB'S BURGER ELEVATION

Top bun, toasted

Mustard

Pickles

Meat

Onions

Mayo

Bottom bun, toasted

CORN DOGS

TIDBIT | The word *frankfurter* was dreamed up by a guy from Frankfurt. Hard to believe. He supposedly invented the hot dog bun.

TIDBIT | By the way, the word *wiener* comes from *wienerwurst*, which is German for "Vienna sausage," which is American for "little meat stick you feed kids who don't know any better than to eat them."

Food historians seem to agree that the corn dog rose to popularity during the early 1940s, mostly due to the efforts of Neil and Carl Fletcher (brother vaudevillians turned concessionaires) in Texas, and Jack Karnis in Oregon. Although the Fletchers may have gotten their product into the mouths of thousands during the 1938 Texas State Fair, Karnis (who supposedly came up with the idea while cooking at a logging camp) actually took out a patent for his "Proto Pups" in 1942. Patents are impressive, but I'm inclined to give the props to the Fletcher boys for a couple of reasons. One, cornmeal batters were ubiquitous in Texas by the end of the nineteenth century, and the presence of German immigrant sausage makers in the vicinity of San Antonio would certainly stack the deck in favor of a Lone Star culinary epiphany of just this sort. Also, it's tough to separate the corn dog from the midway. It has always been carnival and fair food. In fact, if you want a freshly made corn dog today, odds are you'll only find it at a fair, unless of course you make it yourself. My version heavily leans toward the Texas pedigree.

Everything I said about griddles goes quadruple for countertop fryers. I am willing to step up and proclaim unilaterally that a decent electric countertop residential fryer does not currently exist. The problem is twofold. First, countertop "small" electrics are governed by regulations designed, as far as I can tell, to protect kindergarteners, who, as far as I'm concerned, shouldn't be messing with fryers to begin with. The second problem is power. Most household outlets deliver between 110 and 120 volts of alternating current at 60 cycles. This isn't in and of itself a problem, but when you start pulling enough of this juice to do any real work, the breakers tend to blow, especially when kitchen outlets are concerned. I really thought when we made this episode that things were looking up in the world of electric fryers, but the demand just isn't there for quality units. When frying my corn dogs at home I stick with a large Dutch oven with a fry thermometer attached.

CORN DOGS

8 CORN DOGS

// SOFTWARE ///

2 to 4	quarts	peanut oil[1]	for frying, depending on the vessel
1	cup	cornmeal	
1	cup	all-purpose flour	
2	teaspoons	kosher salt	
1	teaspoon	baking powder	
½	teaspoon	baking soda	
½	teaspoon	ground cayenne	
2	tablespoons	jalapeño pepper	seeded and minced
1	8½-ounce can	creamed corn	
⅓	cup	onion	finely grated
1	cup	low-fat buttermilk	
8		beef hot dogs[2]	the thicker the better
4	tablespoons	cornstarch	for dredging

// SPECIAL HARDWARE ///

8 sets wooden chopsticks, not separated

// PROCEDURE ///

1. Pour the oil into a **deep fryer or cast-iron Dutch oven fitted with a deep-fry thermometer**. Bring to 375°F over medium-high heat.

2. Combine the cornmeal, flour, salt, baking powder, baking soda, and cayenne in a **medium mixing bowl**. Combine the jalapeño, corn, onion, and buttermilk in **another bowl**. Add the dry ingredients to the wet ingredients all at once, and stir only enough times to bring the batter together; there should be lumps. Set the batter aside to rest for 10 minutes.

3. Carefully push the chopsticks (narrow end up, of course) into the dogs to create a twist-resistant handle.

4. Scatter the cornstarch onto a **paper plate**. Hold the plate bent, like a big taco, and roll each dog in the cornstarch, making sure you cover it completely. Tap well to remove any and all excess starch.[3]

5. Fill a **tall, narrow drinking glass** two thirds full of batter. Quickly dip the dogs in and out of the batter. Immediately (and carefully) place each dog into the oil, and cook until the coating is golden brown, 4 to 5 minutes. Use **tongs** to remove to a **resting rig** for 3 to 5 minutes before serving to a grateful world.

[1] As long as you use standard, refined peanut oil there will be no problems with allergies, as the allergens are in the proteins, which are typically only present in "raw" or "unrefined" oils. I know we've mentioned this before, but it bears repeating.

[2] When I make these at home I use buffalo meat sausages because I figure that's what those early German Texans might have used.

[3] This step is key. The thin layer of starch serves as a primer to hold the batter in place. Skip this step or leave the cornstarch too thick and the batter will slide off.

You know, I can't think of a candy that is more American than fudge. Yet most Americans would rather shell out five bucks for a wedge of someone else's heaven than walk into a kitchen and make their own. And that's a real shame, because if you've got a pot, a thermometer, some basic ingredients, and just a little science in your soul, you too can produce fudge that is really, really . . . (sing *Good Eats* theme here).

KNOWLEDGE CONCENTRATE

Fudge isn't defined so much by its flavor as by its texture, and that texture is defined by crystals—that is, tidy, uniform arrangements of molecular material. The crystals in fudge should be tiny eentsy-beentsy things surrounded by a very concentrated sugar syrup. (Oddly enough, the closest kin that fudge has in the confection world, at least from a structural standpoint, is ice cream, which gets its texture from suspended ice crystals.) So it follows that if we are going to make fudge, we're going to have to make some crystals. The trick is to make them as small as possible, which is a matter of ingredients, temperature, and technique.

To control crystallization we must control the moisture content of the syrup containing the crystal-building material—in this case, sugar. As the moisture content drops, the temperature goes up, so candymaking—and fudge is definitely candy—requires a thermometer that is both accurate and precise.

The diagnostic mercury-bulb thermometer was invented in 1866 by a British physician named Sir Thomas Allbutt. (Ironic, don't you think?) The device is simple enough. The liquid in this reservoir expands when heated, pushing upward into a narrow tube, calibrated to the corresponding temperature. Dr. Allbutt chose mercury because it's one of the only liquids that won't stick to glass, doesn't boil till it hits about 674°F, and conducts heat very quickly.

Make a few adjustments to Allbutt's original, and you've got yourself a darned accurate and economical kitchen thermometer. There are some downsides, however. Bulb thermometers can be difficult to read, especially when doing so means bending your head over a pot of boiling syrup. And if you break one, well, just remember, mercury is extremely toxic. Some bulb thermometers get around this by using alcohol, dyed either blue or red. But such devices are not as accurate as mercury, they're still hard to read, and they're prone to breakage. Despite the fact that they are a snap to read, bimetal, or bonded-coil, thermometers do not cut it in Candy Land, because they are sluggish, notoriously inaccurate, and require frequent mechanical recalibration, which is not nearly as much fun as it sounds. Although digital thermometers are highly accurate, it is very difficult to use them to judge thermal velocity—that is, the speed at which the temperature is changing, which for me is absolutely key to candymaking. And so I'm still using a mercury thermometer, and I hope I never break it because they've gotten very difficult to find.

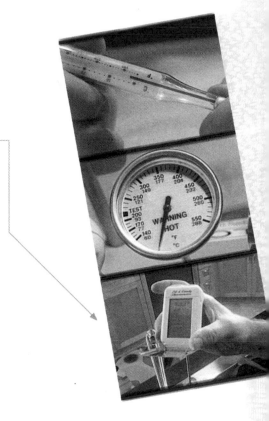

So, you may ask, how did early confectioners judge the concentrations of their syrups without thermometers? Well, it just so happens, when a small dollop of syrup is dropped into cold water, it behaves in a very specific way depending on the sugar concentration (see page 82).

Why include corn syrup? Because it is composed of glucose, which is a type of sugar, but it is not identical to sucrose, or regular granulated sugar. So it can't take part in any of the white sugar's crystallization games. As the syrup becomes more and more saturated, glucose acts as a chemical buffer, preventing crystallization. It's one of the strongest allies in the confectioner's pantry.

The weather does make a difference in candymaking. Sugar is hygroscopic, which means it can and will suck water right out of the air. On humid days, fudge can pull so much moisture out of the air that the sugar crystals will actually start to dissolve, leaving you with a sticky mess. So, if you simply must make fudge in high humidity, compensate for atmospheric moisture by cooking your syrup a few degrees higher than the recipe specifies. Sure, the texture may seem a little on the grainy side at first, but it'll soften up in a day or two.

If you shake, stir, or otherwise agitate the fudge syrup while it's really hot, a few crystals will form, and they'll grow and grow and grow, and your fudge will end up grainy. But if you just let it sit perfectly still, as it cools, the syrup will become thicker and thicker, thus preventing your tiny sucrose molecules from bouncing all over the place. When the time is right, you stir to create the fine crystals that good fudge always features. And the faster you beat the fudge, the finer the crystals are going to be.

Why the wooden spoon? Metal is a relatively efficient conductor of heat, and if a metal tool goes into a hot, saturated syrup, it could potentially pull enough heat out of the syrup to set a chain reaction of crystallization into effect—and that could result in a sandy, gritty texture, not to mention a possibly burned stirring hand. Wood is an insulator, which is why professional fudgeteers always beat their fudges with large wooden spoons.

| Sugar crystals | Fudge crystals |

After this show aired a few times, some viewers wrote to say that although the fudge tasted great the texture was "grainy" and/or "crumbly," adjectives not typically attached to fudge one would consider "good eats." So we went over everything and found that the cooling temperature noted in the online version of the recipe didn't match that in the show. So: bad info management on our part. But then we started thinking that maybe the temperature margin was too tight. So we decided to add a step here where the pot is dipped in 2 inches of room-temperature water to help stop the cooking process faster. Quicker cooling ensures small sugar crystals, which result in a finer, smoother texture. Small changes but with big results. Enjoy your fudge.

GLUCOSE AND FRUCTOSE DANCE TOGETHER IN SYRUP

TIP Roast nuts in a 400°F oven for 5 to 10 minutes.

// SOFTWARE ///

22	ounces	granulated sugar	
4	ounces	unsweetened chocolate	
3	tablespoons	unsalted butter	plus 1 tablespoon for the pan
1	cup	half-and-half	
1	tablespoon	light corn syrup	
1	tablespoon	vanilla extract	
1	cup	nuts	toasted and chopped (optional)

// PROCEDURE ///

(1) Butter an **8-inch square pan**. Trim a piece of **parchment paper** to 8 inches wide and line the pan with this parchment sling, leaving enough overhang on two sides to cover the top of the fudge with later. Fill a **sink or large bowl** with 2 inches of room-temperature water.

(2) Combine the sugar, chocolate, 1½ tablespoons of the butter, the half-and-half, and corn syrup in a **4-quart heavy-bottomed saucepan**. Over medium heat, stir with a **wooden spoon** until the sugar is dissolved and the chocolate is melted. Increase the heat and bring to a boil. Reduce the heat to medium-low, cover, and boil for 3 minutes. Remove the lid and attach a **candy thermometer** to the pan. Cook until the thermometer reads 234°F.

(3) Remove from the heat and set the pan in the room-temperature water. Add the remaining 1½ tablespoons butter but do not stir. Cool the mixture for 10 minutes, or until it drops to 110°F. Add the vanilla and nuts, if desired, and beat with a wooden spoon until well blended and the mixture turns from shiny to matte. Pour into the prepared pan. Fold the excess parchment paper over so it covers the surface of the fudge. Set aside in a cool, dry place until firm.

(4) Cut into 1-inch pieces and store in an **airtight container** at room temperature for up to a week.

4-MINUTE PEANUT BUTTER FUDGE

64 (1-INCH) PIECES

If you've ever made one of the many fudge recipes featured on packages of Baker's chocolate or cans of condensed milk, odds are good you've employed the microwave. How can you possibly make decent fudge in a microwave? You can't. But you can make a darn nice fudgelike candy. And what's even better is that since it steers clear of the cooktop, kids can make it all by themselves . . . if Mom and Dad say it's okay.

// SOFTWARE

1	cup	unsalted butter	plus 1 tablespoon for the pan
1	cup	smooth peanut butter	about 9 ounces
1	teaspoon	vanilla extract	
1	pound	confectioners' sugar	

// PROCEDURE

1. Butter an **8-inch square pan**. Trim a piece of **parchment paper** to 8 inches wide and line the pan with this parchment sling, leaving enough overhang on two sides to cover the top of the fudge with later.

2. Combine the 1 cup butter and the peanut butter in a **4-quart microwave-safe bowl** and cover with **plastic wrap**.[1] Microwave for 2 minutes on high. Stir, re-cover, and microwave on high for 2 more minutes. Use caution when removing this mixture from the microwave, as it will be very hot. Add the vanilla and confectioners' sugar and stir to combine with a **wooden spoon**. The mixture will become hard to stir and will lose its sheen.

3. Spread into the prepared pan. Fold the excess parchment paper over so it covers the surface of the fudge and refrigerate until cool, about 2 hours. Cut into 1-inch pieces and store in an **airtight container** at room temperature for up to a week.

TIDBIT — The average American consumes a little more than 25 pounds of candy per year.

TIDBIT — A Vassar College student supposedly made the first batch of fudge in the early 1900s.

TIDBIT — The largest slab of fudge was made in Ontario, Canada, in 2007 and weighed 5,050 pounds.

[1] Although it may seem like a small step meant merely to prevent a mess in the microwave, if you don't seal the bowl with plastic wrap the heat generated inside the mixture will be insufficient to cook the sugar to the point that the fudge will set, and you will be rewarded with a very tasty soup or ice cream topping.

I don't think any food delivers as much flavor, nutrition, and versatility as nuts . . . at least, not in such a small, easy-to-store, long-lasting, convenient, and almost watertight containment unit. Squirrels know it, which is why they spend all spring and summer hoarding these woody jewels with their spooky little hands. To the average tree rat, a nest full of walnuts, pecans, or cashews could mean the difference between waking up in the spring and ending up a squirrel-sicle. But to the average American, nuts are for bowls on bars and, well . . . that's about it.

PROTEIN! GET YOUR FRESH, HOT PROTEIN! FIBER, ANTIOXIDANTS, OMEGA-3S!

That's right, omega-3s, the very same fatty acids found in fish oil, are also found in nuts. What's more, nuts can lower your risk of heart attack and type-2 diabetes. Sure, tree nuts contain fat, but most of it's that "good" fat you hear so much about, the unsaturated kind that can lower cholesterol and the dreaded LDLs or low-density lipoproteins. And don't forget, nuts are a great source of vitamin E, potassium, magnesium, calcium, folic acid, and zinc.

TIDBIT | Ever wonder why we call crazy people "nuts"? Because in the nineteenth century, *nut* was slang for "head," so a nut-case was off his nut. Eventually, we just boiled that down to *nuts*.

WHO YOU CALLING "NUTS"?

Although most of the "nuts" consumed in the United States are peanuts, peanuts aren't nuts; they're peas. True nuts grow on trees. Brazil nuts, beechnuts, kola nuts, walnuts, pecans, chestnuts, hazelnuts, and almonds all have considerable culinary cred, but my big three are: cashews, pistachios, and macadamia nuts.

CASHEWS are native to South America but are now grown primarily in India, which perhaps makes sense when you consider that they are kin to the mango. Although most of us are familiar with the cashew's crescent shape, the cashew comes from the tree connected to an odd little fruit called a cashew apple, which has various other culinary uses (down in the Caribbean they're soaked in rum).

Each of these fruits has a shell hanging off the end containing a single cashew. The shell itself contains caustic oils often used in furniture varnishes because it repels termites.

Sorry to take that side trip, but when you have an opportunity to put two of your culinary crew in cheap termite suits, you just have to go with it.

The point is that getting even a single cashew to market isn't easy, and that's why they're expensive. Still, because of their unique flavor and high fat content, they're potent players because they can easily be ground into a smooth paste that puts most peanut butters to shame.

The **PISTACHIO** is grown from the Middle East all the way to the far west . . . of Asia, that is, which explains why it's so ubiquitous in Turkish desserts. After spreading slowly across Europe, the pistachio tree was finally introduced to the United States via California in the 1890s.

Pistachio trees seed twice a year, producing clusters of seeds encased in a fleshy yellow-red skin. Traditionally they were harvested by hand, but modern machines can shake ripe clusters from the trees so the seeds can be harvested from the ground. They are then soaked in water (to remove the fleshy coating) and dried in the sun.

The nutmeat of the pistachio is deep green, thanks to the presence of chlorophyll, and in the nut industry, the deeper the green, the more highly valued the nut. (If you've ever seen pistachios with vibrant red shells, that's not nature. That's processors dyeing the meats to make them more attractive, or so, I suppose, they think.)

Most of us buy our pistachios in the shell. With any other nut, this would mean a lot of work. But not so here, because the pistachio splits, or "smiles," when ripe.

The **MACADAMIA NUT** is indigenous to Australia, but centuries of island-hopping through Polynesia brought it to its adopted home of Hawaii, where it's paired with everything from mangoes to marshmallows to mahimahi. What makes the nut so unique is its texture. Bite into a raw or cooked macadamia, and you get a crunchy snap followed by a melt-in-your-mouth succulence that betrays the nut's considerable fat content. As for flavor, it is subtle yet faintly tropical, and when toasted reminds me of coconut. Since it takes a tree seven years to produce a marketable crop, macadamias are expensive. Luckily, a little goes a long way.

```
Termite 1: This wood
tastes nasty.

Termite 2: Like...

Termites 1 & 2: ...cashews!

Termite 1: Let's go get
a box of toothpicks.

Termite 2: Sweet!
```

TRIVIA By the way, these termites are two of my key culinarians. Nice job, ladies.

SOMETIMES YOU FEEL LIKE A . . .

CASHEW BUTTER

1 TO 1½ CUPS

This butter was concocted to give my daughter a tasty way around her peanut allergy.

// SOFTWARE //

2	tablespoons	honey	
⅓	cup	walnut oil	or more if necessary
10	ounces	roasted cashews	
½	teaspoon	kosher salt	

// PROCEDURE //

Place the honey in a **microwave-safe container** and heat in the microwave for 15 seconds. Remove from the microwave and add the oil. Place the nuts and salt in the bowl of a **food processor** and pulse for 5 seconds. Then, with the processor running, very slowly drizzle in the honey and oil. Process until an emulsion is formed and the mixture is smooth; this will take 45 seconds to 1 minute. If the mixture is too thick and doesn't spread easily, add a little more oil. Tightly sealed, this butter will keep in the refrigerator for up to 3 months. And although it's darned tasty in a cashew butter and guava jelly sandwich, it makes a good satay-style sauce as well.

APPLICATION

CASHEW SAUCE

ABOUT 1 CUP

// SOFTWARE //

½	cup	cashew butter	(above)
¾	cup	unsweetened coconut milk	
¼	teaspoon	ground cayenne	
to taste		kosher salt	

// PROCEDURE //

Whisk the cashew butter, coconut milk, and cayenne together in a **medium saucepan** over medium heat. Taste and add salt, if desired. Heat until the sauce is warmed through. Serve over grilled chicken, pork, or rice.

PISTACHIO MIXED-HERB PESTO

ABOUT 1 CUP

Although pistachios are great for out-of-hand eating (and putting into ice cream), believe it or not, they make a really great pesto. Yes, I know, pine nuts make pesto. But pine nuts are darned expensive and burn easily, which is another reason to build this potent paste with pistachios instead.

// SOFTWARE

1	clove	garlic	
3½	ounces	pistachios	roasted
2	cups	fresh flat-leaf parsley	packed
2	tablespoons	fresh lemon thyme leaves	
2	tablespoons	fresh tarragon leaves	
1	tablespoon	fresh oregano leaves	
1	tablespoon	fresh sage leaves	
1	ounce	Parmesan cheese	finely grated
	to taste	kosher salt	
	to taste	black pepper	freshly ground
1	cup	olive oil	

// PROCEDURE

1. Chop the garlic in a **blender** until fine. Add the pistachios and chop coarsely. Add the herbs, cheese, salt, and pepper and blend until chopped fine. With the blender running, drizzle in the oil until the mixture becomes creamy and emulsified.

2. Serve over pasta or use as topping for bruschetta. Store in the refrigerator for up to a week or freeze for up to a month.

TIP | Like stocks and other sauces, this pesto freezes incredibly well. I like to freeze it in ice cube trays for easy thawing and dosing. One standard cube is enough for 1 pound of cooked pasta.

TIDBIT | The queen of Sheba so loved pistachios that she hoarded all that were grown in her country for herself.

SOMETIMES YOU
FEEL LIKE A . . .

───┐ ┌─ **MACADAMIA NUT CRUST**

1 (9- TO 10-INCH) PIE OR
CHEESECAKE CRUST

// SOFTWARE //

5	ounces	macadamia nuts[1]	about 1 cup, roasted and ground
½	cup	Japanese-style bread crumbs	a.k.a. panko
¼	cup	sugar	
2	tablespoons	all-purpose flour	
¼	teaspoon	kosher salt	
3	tablespoons	unsalted butter	melted

// PROCEDURE //

1. Combine the nuts, bread crumbs, sugar, flour, and salt in a **medium mixing bowl**. Add the butter and stir to combine.

2. Press the mixture into the bottom of a **9- to 10-inch cake, pie, or spring-form pan** as a crust for cheesecake or cream pie. Bake according to instructions for cheesecake or pie. If baking for a precooked pie filling, heat the oven to 375°F. Bake on the center rack of the oven for 20 to 25 minutes, until lightly browned.

[1] A 1-ounce serving contains some 22 grams of fat, but over 80 percent of that is monounsaturated, which almost makes up for the fact that 3 grams is saturated.

TRIVIA The squirrel that taunts and tortures me throughout the show was of course inspired by the "varmint" chipmunk from *Caddyshack*.

THE SQUIRREL TAKES
ITS REVENGE!

When this pie was first designed I was quite happy.

The crust was a nice balance of flaky and tender (ouch), the meringue was springy, and the custard filling was in-your-face lemon with a texture that was pliant yet cut-able. Yes, I was happy. I've made this pie quite a few times over the years that have followed and, well . . . I'm not so happy. It's not that the pie doesn't work, because it does. The pie in the show is actually this pie, so that I'm sure of. But it is buggy, which leads me to believe that while the science is sound, the formulae, such as they are, are out of balance. And that is never good eats.

And so, we've taken it apart and put it back together again instituting the changes you'll see outlined in the following applications. And now I really am all the way happy.

GOT SOME EXTRA FOAM RUBBER, POLYESTER BATTING, AND CARDBOARD? WHY NOT BUILD YOURSELF A

LEMON MERINGUE CHAISE LONGUE?

A little slice of history with your pie?

Although our earliest written record of pie—a Roman recipe for a rye crust stuffed with goat cheese and honey—could pass for a dessert, most early pies were decidedly savory. Perhaps you've heard of the medieval mélange known as "humble" pie? "Humble" refers to the bits and pieces left over once all the more edible parts of the animal have been consumed. Therefore, to "eat humble pie" has come to mean eating the very lowest thing— your own words. You may not know that the word *pie* comes from *magpie*. See, early cooks believed that a pie was the culinary version of a magpie, and a magpie is a bird that basically picks up little bits and pieces of everything and shoves them into his nest.

Ever hear of "four and twenty blackbirds baked in a pie"? Well, I bet you didn't know the birds were supposed to be alive, did you? And I don't mean going in . . . I mean coming out. You try finding some blackbirds and getting them into a pie. Just try it sometime!

Here in modern-day America, the most popular pies are fruit pies, and cream or custard pies. Not surprisingly, they were both invented by those masters of desserts, the Pennsylvania Dutch. Here, we're going to concentrate on my favorite cream pie of all time.

Take a close look at a piece of cream pie sometime, and you will no doubt notice that it is composed of three distinct phases. First, we have a light and fluffy meringue: brown on top, white and creamy in the middle. This is firmly anchored to a soft yet cut-able custard, which, in turn, perches atop a flaky, flavorful crust, which must be able to support the entire weight of this device during transfer from pan to plate. Now, the challenge in constructing such a device comes in finding a careful balance between what is best for each individual layer and what is best for the pie as a whole.

Piecrust is a simple thing. Heck, there's nothing in it but some flour, some fat, a little bit of salt, and just enough water to bring it together. Simple! But tricky at the same time, because every little detail matters. Take the flour, for instance. If you were to use pastry flour, well, it doesn't have enough protein in it. It's a very soft flour. So you'd create a crust that just falls apart in the pan. What about bread flour? Well, it's got a lot of protein in it, which means a very, very hard crust. Self-rising flour is no good, because it's got leavening in it. You'll make a biscuit instead of a crust, which isn't the same thing. So, in the end, you're better off with just plain old AP, or all-purpose, flour. It's got a relatively moderate amount of protein in it, so it is perfect for pie.

And now, the fat. Nothing affects the nature of a crust more than the fat that goes into it. Butter has a very low melting point, so it doesn't make a very flaky crust, and it also contains some water, which can definitely throw off your formula. At the same time, nothing browns or tastes better. So I'm definitely going to use some of this. But I'm also going to use lard. Rendered pig's fat has a very high melting point, and a really coarse, crystalline structure, which means that it is ideal for making flaky crusts. And you'll be surprised to know that lard is even lower in cholesterol and saturated fat than butter is. You can find it in most American megamarts, either in the same department as the shortening, or in the Latin food section. And no, it doesn't taste like pork.

1 (9-INCH) PIECRUST

This crust shrunk from time to time and it occasionally tore when I removed the weights. Since starches tend to shrink less when cooked slowly, we dropped the oven temp by 50 degrees. And we reduced the flour-to-fat ratio from 3:2 to 3:1. It's still buttery enough to be tasty but not so greasy that it prevents starches from setting together.

// SOFTWARE //

¼	cup	unsalted butter	cut into cubes
1	ounce	lard	
6	ounces	all-purpose flour	plus extra for rolling
½	teaspoon	table salt	
¼	cup	ice H$_2$O	in a **spritz bottle**
32	**ounces**	**dried beans**	**for blind baking**

// PROCEDURE //

1. Chill the butter and lard in the freezer for 15 minutes.

2. Pulse the flour and salt together 3 or 4 times in a **food processor**. Add the butter and pulse 5 or 6 times, until the texture looks mealy. Add the lard and pulse another 3 or 4 times. Remove the lid of the food processor and spritz the surface of the mixture thoroughly with ice water. Replace the lid and pulse 5 times. Add more water and pulse again until the mixture holds together when squeezed. Place the mixture in a **gallon-sized zip-top bag**, squeeze together until it forms a ball, then press into a rounded disk and refrigerate for 30 minutes.

3. Heat the oven to 375°F.

4. Remove the dough from the refrigerator. **Cut** along two sides of the zip-top bag, open the bag to expose the dough, and sprinkle both sides with flour. Cover with the bag and roll out with a **rolling pin** to a 10- to 11-inch circle. Open the plastic again and sprinkle the top of the dough with flour. Place a **pie pan** upside down on top of the dough and flip the pan and dough over. Use the bag to press the dough into the pie pan. Remove the bag from atop the dough. Trim the excess if necessary, leaving an edge for meringue to adhere to. Poke holes in the bottom of the dough using a **fork** and place in the refrigerator for 15 minutes.

5. Place a large piece of **parchment paper** on top of the dough and fill with dried beans. Press the beans into the corners of the crust and bake for 10 minutes. Remove the parchment and beans and continue baking until golden, 10 to 15 minutes longer. Remove from the oven and place on a **cooling rack**. Cool completely before filling.

BLIND BAKING

Often called "prebaking," blind baking is baking a piecrust before filling it. It's typical of single-crust pies with short baking times or especially moist fillings. While some recipes (such as ours) call for a partial bake, others, like chocolate cream pies, may require a full bake. The raw shell is pricked with a fork to allow steam underneath the dough to escape and prevent humps in the baked crust. Then line the shell with parchment paper (or aluminum foil to prevent over-browning in a full bake) and fill with small weights. Ceramic and metal pie weights are widely available at kitchen supplies stores, but dried beans (I like kidney for their size and weight) are cheaper and even easier to come by—you're just looking for even weight distribution in every crevice. Bake according to the directions and remove the beans using the parchment paper as a sling. Cool the prebaked crust completely on a cooling rack before filling. The beans can be reused as weights (but not cooked to be eaten).

The original application called for nearly constant whisking of the heated base and the addition of the butter and lemon juice after removal of the custard from the heat. I'd based this technique on research regarding starch science and especially the behavior of starches in acidic environments. Like many science types I chased the facts only as far as I needed to prove my point. Bad cook. If I'd pushed on through to the other side I would have found that, indeed, constant agitation does not coax starch granules to drink, any more than acidic ingredients (at these concentrations) interrupt coagulation or gelatinization. In fact, when you think about the swelling of starches, it really doesn't make any sense to add liquids after they've swelled to their fullest. Sure, the final gel might be able to hold the lemon juice in suspension, but then again . . . maybe not.

// SOFTWARE ///

FOR THE MERINGUE TOPPING

4	large	egg whites	save the yolks for lemon filling
1	pinch	cream of tartar	
2	tablespoons	sugar	

FOR THE LEMON FILLING

4	large	egg yolks	2½ ounces
⅓	cup	cornstarch	1¾ ounces
9¼	ounces	sugar	
¼	teaspoon	kosher salt	
1½	cups	H_2O	
3	tablespoons	unsalted butter	
½	cup	lemon juice	freshly squeezed
1	tablespoon	lemon zest	grated

FOR THE CRUST

1	9-inch	prebaked piecrust	see page 127

// PROCEDURE ///

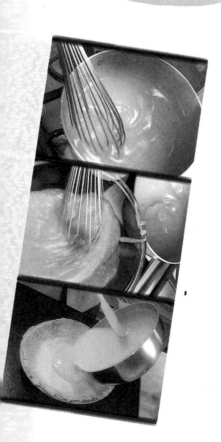

1. Position a rack in the middle of the oven. Heat the oven to 375°F.
2. Place the egg whites and cream of tartar in the bowl of a **stand mixer fitted with the whisk attachment**. Set aside.

3. **Whisk** the egg yolks in a **medium mixing bowl** and set aside.

4. Whisk together the cornstarch, 1⅓ cups sugar, and salt in a **medium saucepan** (this will eliminate any clumps in the cornstarch). Add the water, butter, lemon juice, and lemon zest. Bring the mixture to a simmer, stirring gently, over medium heat.[1] Remove from the heat. One whiskful at a time, add the cornstarch mixture to the egg yolks and stir until you have added at least half of the cornstarch mixture.

5. Return the egg mixture to the saucepan, turn the heat down to low, and cook, stirring gently, for 1 more minute. Pour the mixture into the piecrust.

6. Beat the egg white mixture until soft peaks form, then gradually add the 2 tablespoons sugar and continue beating until stiff peaks form, about 2 minutes. Top the pie with the meringue while the lemon filling is still hot. Be absolutely certain that you take the meringue all the way to the edges of the crust. You should not be able to see even a sliver of the lemon filling underneath.

7. Bake for 10 to 12 minutes, until the meringue is golden. Remove from the oven and cool on a **rack**. Make sure the pie is cooled completely before slicing; this will take 4 to 6 hours. Your best bet is to cool overnight before cutting.[2]

---

[1] Raw eggs contain a starch-eating enzyme called alpha amylase, which can be turned off only by being heated to very close to the boiling point of water for 1 minute. However, watch the pot closely, as there's not much thermal distance between a simmer and a full boil, which could potentially curdle the eggs before the starches have swelled large enough to protect them.

[2] This is definitely a time when not only will patience be rewarded but impatience will be punished. Cutting into the pie in any way before it's completely cooled will result in a breakdown of the fragile starch-protein matrix, and in a few hours you'll have soup rather than pie.

TIDBIT | Since 1950, California has produced more lemons than all of the European countries combined.

TIDBIT | The Meyer lemon is not a true lemon at all, but a hybrid between a lemon and a Mandarin orange.

THE GIANT PIE ATE THE PROP GUY!

TOAST MODERN

There's this great scene in *The Blues Brothers*

where Elwood has brought Jake back to his tiny dive motel room by the El tracks in Chicago. Elwood puts a scratched record on his player and makes white toast by squeezing a slice of white bread onto a bent coat hanger and placing it over a broken-down hot plate. It doesn't get much more elemental than that, but then elemental is the crispy soul of toast and I would argue that toast is the soul of cuisine, or at least of comfort food, which we all know is the best food. In any case, toast is worth making often, and it's worth making right.

TIDBIT | Modern toaster collectors shell out big bucks for rare specimens. There are toaster collector clubs, websites, even a toaster museum.

KNOWLEDGE CONCENTRATE

The perfect slice of toast possesses an evenly brown, crunchy exterior and a warm, slightly moist interior. Creating this requires exposure to temperatures in excess of 310°F. At that point, starches and sugars begin to decompose and turn brown. Science types call this the Maillard reaction. I call it golden brown and delicious. Although Elwood proved that toasting toast requires no real specialized technology, most toast fans prefer that a toaster handle the task.

The first electric appliance to mass-populate American homes was indeed the electric toaster. Released in 1908, it was nothing more than a metal body, a couple of hinges, and some wires. What was special—at the time, at least—was the newfangled chromium nickel resistance wire through which the heat was applied.

Such early machines were of course strictly manual. A little door or a rack held the bread up against the wires. If you wanted both sides toasted you had to flip the bread yourself. If you didn't pay attention, you'd set your toast on fire and burn down the house. "Automatic" models emerged in 1926; these would not only control cooking time but also spit out the toast when it was done. Although the pop-up toaster was a boon to breakfast lovers, the golden age of toasters would have to wait for one more technical development. In 1930, the Continental Baking Company invented sliced bread. The best thing since itself.

There are a lot of toasters on the market and most of them are, simply put, crap. And don't think that a high price tag gets you better performance. Most of the counter candy I've tested in the C-note-plus range generated some of the worst toast. So before you go shopping, look around online for reviews and ratings. Talk to your toast-centric friends, and when the time to purchase draws nigh, keep these thoughts in mind:

Avoid . . .

Expensive machines. There is no reason to pay more than fifty bucks for a toaster.

Metal. Metal gets hot. Metal is hard to clean. Metal is expensive and completely useless in my humble opinion.

Loose crumb trays. Pick up the model in question. Tilt it, shake it, maneuver it around. If the crumb tray falls out, drop it and walk.

Seek out . . .

Compatible design. Think about where this machine will be used. Will it live on the counter or in a cabinet, and will it fit the space available for either scenario? Where are the controls? Do they feel flimsy? Do the body seams meet smoothly? Are the foot pads securely fastened?

Evenly distributed heating coils or bars. Although quartz heating rods are now common in up-market toaster ovens, they're still relatively rare because the close proximity of rod and target food required in a countertop toaster makes evenness difficult. So until toasters featuring moving quartz elements become the norm (I'm working on one right now), you'll probably want to stick to models featuring a nichrome wire element. Look down into the bread slots (which should be wide enough to house half a bagel) and make sure there are the same number of wires on each side of the slot. Some toasters have half as many wires on one side and that means uneven toasting and that's just plain bad.

Controls: light, med, dark is all you need. If you feel you need 10 toast settings, you don't need a toaster, you need medication.

Now that we have the toaster business out of the way, here are two classic, toast-centric applications that don't require any toaster whatsoever.

1. Oven sides
2. Heating element
3. Porcelain hook
4. Gear
5. Timer knob
6. Motor
7. Guide wires
8. Support bar
9. Switch
10. Fan and shaft

RARE MOTORIZED FEED
THROUGH TOASTER

In France, where food itself was invented, they call this *pain perdu*, or "forgotten bread." I suspect this dish really was invented in France because the ubiquitous baguette is composed of a nearly fat-free or "lean" dough, which goes stale very quickly.

// SOFTWARE

8	½-inch-thick slices	country-style bread	such as brioche or challah
1	cup	half-and-half	
3	large	eggs	
2	tablespoons	honey	warmed in the microwave for 20 seconds
¼	teaspoon	kosher salt	
4	tablespoons	unsalted butter	

// PROCEDURE

1. Arrange the bread slices on a **cooling rack** and leave to become stale overnight[1].

2. **Whisk** together the half-and-half, eggs, honey, and salt in a **medium mixing bowl**. This custard can be made up to 12 hours in advance and refrigerated in an **airtight container** until ready to use.

3. Heat the oven to 375°F. Pour the custard mixture into a **shallow dish**. Dip the bread in the custard, soak for 30 seconds on each side, remove to a **cooling rack** set inside a **half sheet pan**, and set it aside to rest for 1 to 2 minutes.

4. Melt 1 tablespoon of the butter in a **10-inch nonstick sauté pan** over medium-low heat. Place 2 slices of bread at a time in the pan and cook until golden brown, 2 to 3 minutes per side. Repeat with the remaining butter and soaked bread. Remove from the pan and place on a **cooling rack** set inside a **half sheet pan** in the oven for 5 minutes. Serve immediately with maple syrup, whipped cream, or fruit.

TIDBIT | In England, French toast is called "Poor Knights of Windsor."

TIDBIT | To make extra-crunchy French toast, dredge the battered bread in crushed corn flakes before cooking.

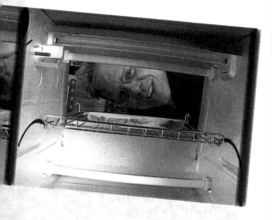

[1] Do not attempt to produce French toast with fresh bread. It will simply turn to mush in the batter.

TIP | I usually make my custard at night, when I put out the bread to get stale. That way, things go quicker come morning.

WELSH RAREBIT

4 SERVINGS AS A SIDE DISH

The English have long enjoyed topping their toast with a wide range of tasty foodstuffs, and no dish captures this tradition better than the eighteenth-century tavern nosh known as Welsh Rabbit, which, oddly enough, contains no rabbit whatsoever. The moniker was designed as a slight by the English, who created the dish, toward the Welsh, whom they considered shifty, shiftless, and usually broke. So broke, in fact, that they might actually call a piece of cheese a rabbit, which doesn't make a lick of sense. As for the "rarebit" variation, we can only assume it was devised in an effort to appease customers angered by the fact that there was no rabbit in their rabbit. Whatever you call it, I certainly would say that any dish that marries beer, cheese, and toast qualifies as good eats. When I make it, I prefer to do so right in front of the fire with my camp stove, which is basically a cast-iron Dutch oven with little feet on it. If you don't have one of these, I'm sure you're going to get one. But until then, just make the sauce in a heavy saucepan over low heat.

RABBIT! GET IT?

// SOFTWARE //

2	tablespoons	unsalted butter	
2	tablespoons	all-purpose flour	
1	teaspoon	Dijon mustard	
1	teaspoon	Worcestershire sauce	
½	teaspoon	kosher salt	
½	teaspoon	black pepper	freshly ground
½	cup	dark beer	such as porter
¾	cup	heavy cream	
6	ounces	cheddar cheese	shredded
2	drops	hot sauce	
4	slices	rye bread	toasted

// PROCEDURE //

1. Melt the butter over medium-low heat in a **small saucepan**. **Whisk** in the flour and cook, being careful not to brown the flour, whisking constantly, for 2 to 3 minutes.

2. Whisk in the mustard, Worcestershire sauce, salt, and pepper until smooth. Add the beer and whisk to combine. Pour in the cream and whisk until well combined and smooth. Gradually add the cheese, stirring constantly, until the cheese melts and the sauce is smooth, 4 to 5 minutes. Add the hot sauce. Pour over toast and serve.

Any chef worth his salt

will tell you that the number-one skill in the kitchen, the skill without which there is no recourse nor repair, is the ability to season food. And by "season" they don't mean spices, or herbs, or anything else that goes "bam." They mean salt. If you can't properly apply salt to food, before, during, and even after the cooking process, then your culinary career is pretty much doomed.

What cooks refer to when they refer to "salt" is sodium chloride (NaCl), a fairly simple ionic arrangement composed of 60 percent chlorine gas, a deadly poison first used as a weapon during World War I, and 40 percent sodium, which, in its pure form at least, explodes if exposed to moisture. Ironically, this marriage of destructive forces forms a nutrient so essential to the human animal that our tongues have actually evolved to bare specific nerves just to taste it.

Salt's influence on humankind is so all-encompassing, so full of science and lore, I didn't even know where to begin. This is how a rock came to be an hourlong special. And truth be told, there's more to salt than will ever fit in these pages, so let's just get to it.

TIDBIT There is enough salt in the ocean to cover the continents 500 feet deep.

TIDBIT All salt is sea salt. True, much of it is mined, but even that salt was laid down as deposits from retreating inland seas.

TIDBIT The world's surface is 71 percent water, with 97 percent of that water being seawater, which is a very good thing because most seawater is about 3.5 percent salt.

KNOWLEDGE CONCENTRATE

▷ Sodium chloride is essential to human life. The list of what salt does, what it enables in our many systems, wouldn't fit in this book, and even if it did, for God's sake, man, I'm a cook, not a doctor! But if for some utterly insane reason you were to doubt salt's considerable bioelectrical influence, then riddle me this: Why did we evolve taste receptors (and strong ones at that) capable of sensing it? Case closed.

▷ Is salt bad for you? I've sorted through dozens of recent medical studies, most of which make frequent use of words I'm hard pressed to understand. But from what I can sort out the answer is a resounding "maybe." Apparently around a fifth of the people walking around the United States (other cultures are quite different) have a genetic predisposition toward hypertension (high blood pressure). And it seems that 1 out of 4 of those (give or take a few) suffer from sodium-related hypertension. As for the rest of us, as long as our kidneys are functioning and we get enough water, it seems that dietary salt isn't that big a deal. But—and this is just me talking here—it seems to me that any sodium issues we may be collectively suffering stem not from salt applied to food in the relative safety of the home but rather packaged and processed goods.

Anyone who's ever flown into San Francisco International Airport from the south has probably looked down and wondered about the many large ponds that range in color from green to bright red. These are salt ponds, and the red comes from a specific form of algae that doesn't mind high salinity.

Whether evaporative or mined, most salt is dissolved into a brine, then refined and recrystallized before packaging. Such salts are very pure.

Type	Origin	Characteristic	Facts
Kosher	Mined or evaporated	Jagged flakes	Is not technically kosher but rather a practical grain shape for applying to raw meat in order to draw out blood and other liquids, a process called "koshering."
Sea	Evaporated	Various grain sizes and shapes depending on processing	Can be refined or left in a "raw" state, or other substances can be included.
Natural	Mined	Usually chunks	Several producers market salt taken directly from the mine with no further refinement. Such salts usually have a pink or orange cast due to trace minerals that have very little effect on the flavor of the salt.
Rock	Mined	Chunks	Although intended for use in crank ice cream machines where it lowers the temperature of ice via endothermic reaction (that's another show) or as a de-icer for sidewalks and such, as far as I know there is no danger in using rock salt as a cooking medium, where its high rate of conduction comes in handy.
Pickling	Usually mined	Very fine crystals	Used in pickles and brines because the fine grain size dissolves readily in cold water.
Smoked	Evaporated	Various shapes and sizes	I only mention this specialty salt because I like it so much. Danish versions are often evaporated in large pans over alder-wood fires, which perfume the crystals in a very pleasant way indeed.
Orange, black, red, etc.	Evaporated or mined	Various shapes and sizes	Whether the crystals contain lava dust or mud from Hawaii, these pretty fads are just that—again, in my humble opinion.

1. Black lava salt
2. Coarse sea salt
3. Fleur de sel
4. Hawaiian sea salt
5. Himalayan pink
6. Kala namak
7. Maldon

EAT THIS ROCK

BRINE-BOILED FINGERLING POTATOES

6 TO 8 SERVINGS

These potatoes are indeed salty, but in a good way . . . like potato chips, or really good French fries. The advantage, of course, is that there is no frying and no oil.

// SOFTWARE //

1¼	pounds	kosher or rock salt	yes, really . . . a pound and a quarter
2	quarts	H_2O	
2	pounds	small fingerling potatoes	cleaned, not peeled
4	tablespoons	unsalted butter	
	to taste	black pepper	freshly ground
1	tablespoon	fresh chives	chopped

// PROCEDURE //

1. Bring the salt, water, and potatoes to a boil in a **large pot**. Cook until the potatoes are fork-tender, 25 to 30 minutes. Remove from the pot to a **cooling rack** and set aside to rest for 5 to 7 minutes.

2. While still hot, toss the potatoes with the butter, pepper, and chives.

TIDBIT | Salts I have in my kitchen right now: kosher, coarse sea salt. The first I can always spin in the food processor or blender to create a finer texture for, say, pickling or popcorn. The latter can be applied to chocolates and pretzels and other surfaces where a big, salty crunch would be appreciated.

SALT TURNS FLAVORS UP TO "11"

Salt has the unique ability to increase the intensity of certain flavors (chocolate, for instance) while downplaying others (salt is better at beating out bitterness than sugar . . . take that, Mary Poppins). Nowhere in literature is this fact made more apparent than in this classic tale, told in many cultures throughout history.

Once upon a time there was a king. And this king had three lovely daughters. One day he called them to him and asked each, "How much do you love me?" Well, the first one said she loved him more than jewels and baby kittens. The second one said she loved him better than a trip to the Caymans. And the last one said, "I love you more than salt." Salt? Something was wrong with that girl. So the king gave cash and prizes to the first two daughters, and to the third daughter he gave banishment from the kingdom forever. And some nice car wax as a parting gift. Having dispensed with his paternal duties, he settled down to a nice meal. But there was something wrong. His food tasted flat. Disgusting. So he screamed for his chef.

KING: Chef!
CHEF: Yes, Sire?
K: What's wrong with my food?
C: Well, Sire, since you placed so little value on salt, I decided to leave it out of your food.

The king realized he'd been a big jerk. So he brought his daughter back amid much celebration and a not-so-surprising marriage to the wiley cook, who did indeed bring salt back to the royal kitchen.

A lesson for us all.

HONEST-TO-GOODNESS SAUERKRAUT

6 TO 8 SERVINGS

This is one of my favorite *Good Eats* applications, not just because I love kraut (mmmmm, kraut) but also because it's such a cool example of cooks learning how to make use of bacteria and yeasts that happen to be all around us all the time. Sauerkraut is technically a pickle, a fermented pickle, in fact, much like kimchi or classic dill pickles. During this type of pickling two different naturally occurring bacteria tag-team the target vegetable, specifically the sugars therein. One ferments to produce CO_2, which paves the way for the second to begin anerobic fermentation that will produce the acid, therefore putting the "sour" in the kraut. Both of these bacteria can tolerate certain saline levels, but the kind of bugs that would throw this process off can't. So in this case the salt is acting as a biological bodyguard, rather than a bouncer.

// SOFTWARE ///

5	pounds	cabbage	shredded
6	tablespoons	pickling salt	divided
1	tablespoon	juniper berries	
2	teaspoons	caraway seeds	
2	quarts	H_2O	

// PROCEDURE ///

1. Mix the cabbage thoroughly with half the pickling salt, the juniper berries, and caraway seeds, using clean hands in a **large mixing bowl**. Set the cabbage aside to wilt for 10 minutes (this will make it easier to pack).

2. Combine the water and remaining pickling salt in a **gallon-sized zip-top bag** and seal tightly. Pack the cabbage mixture down into a **large plastic food container or pickling crock**. Top with a **lid** smaller than the opening of the container and set the zip-top bag of brine on top of this to act as a weight.

3. Place in a cool (65° to 75°F) area overnight. In 24 hours, the cabbage should have given up enough liquid to be completely submerged. If not, add enough brine from the plastic bag to cover the cabbage.

4. Check the cabbage every other day for about 2 weeks and skim the surface of scum if necessary. Pickle for 4 weeks, checking every other day and removing scum. Remove to an **airtight container** and store in the refrigerator for up to a month.

TIDBIT | Number of crystals in a pound of table salt: 5,370,000. Number of crystals in a pound of kosher salt: 1,370,000 . . . give or take a crystal or two.

TIDBIT | To make homemade play-dough, mix ½ cup salt with 1 cup flour, 2 tablespoons vegetable oil, and ½ cup water.

| 10 days later.

TIDBIT | During the Middle Ages salt was used as a symbol of purity not only because it could preserve things but because it was often the whitest thing around.

EAT THIS ROCK

BEEF TENDERLOIN DELIVERED IN AN HERBAL SALT ENVELOPE

10 TO 12 SERVINGS

Although this is hands down my crew's favorite *Good Eats* application of all time, several cooks out in TV land have complained of a mysterious slimy texture on the finished meat. We attempted to replicate the problem and although we weren't terribly successful, several points should be stressed:

1. A thorough sear is crucial. Most electric griddles' heating elements run around the outer edge of the griddle; if you find you are not getting a very dark sear, move the meat out to the edge of the griddle.

2. Rest the meat. The original application called for "at least 5 minutes," but we're upping it here to 10 just to be on the safe side.

3. Don't wrap the meat tightly in the dough. Doing so will only hold moisture right up against the meat, thus stewing the exterior.

// SOFTWARE ///

5	cups	all-purpose flour	plus extra for rolling
3	cups	kosher salt	
3	tablespoons	black pepper	freshly ground
5	large	egg whites	
1½	cups	H_2O	
½	cup	fresh herbs	such as parsley, thyme, or sage, chopped
1	6- to 7-pound	beef tenderloin	trimmed
1	tablespoon	olive oil	

TIDBIT | Some of the first American ad campaigns were for the many salt companies that popped up at the close of the nineteenth century.

TIDBIT | During the Renaissance salt storage boxes or "cellars," crafted for wealthy tables, were often fashioned from gold and jewels.

// PROCEDURE ///

1. Combine the flour, salt, and pepper in a **large mixing bowl**. **Whisk** together the egg whites and water and add to the dry ingredients along with 2 tablespoons of the herbs. Combine with a **potato masher** until the mixture begins to come together, then knead with your hands for 1 to 2 minutes. Transfer the mixture to a **large zip-top bag**, seal, and set aside at room temperature for at least 2 hours and up to 24 hours.

2. Heat the oven to 400°F. In order to achieve uniform cooking, fold over the slender tail end of the tenderloin and tie it with **butcher's twine**. Put a large **electric griddle** at its highest setting; **brush** the tenderloin with the oil and sear on all sides until well browned, about 10 minutes. Rest the meat for at least 10 minutes.

3. Transfer the dough to a floured surface and **roll** out to ¼ inch thick. This should give you about a 24-by-18-inch rectangle. Trim away extra dough and brush away any excess flour, if necessary. Sprinkle the remaining herbs on the center section of the dough and gently press down.

4. Center the tenderloin on the dough. Fold the top part of the dough over, flipping back about 1 inch of dough onto itself. Repeat with the bottom half of the dough. Press together the two flaps of dough and seal. Make sure the dough is not too tight around the tenderloin. At both ends of the tenderloin, press the dough together to create a seal and cut away any excess. Transfer to a **half sheet pan** and roast to an internal temperature of 125°F, 25 to 30 minutes. Remove from the oven; the tenderloin will continue to cook and will gain 10° to 15°F more. Rest for at least 30 minutes and up to 1 hour. Cut away the salt crust at one end and remove the tenderloin from the dough tube using **tongs**. Slice and serve immediately.

TIDBIT | Up until the sixteenth century it wasn't uncommon for convicted criminals to be sentenced to a life spent in the European salt mines.

TIDBIT | English towns that were once salt centers have "wich" in their names (e.g., Norwich, Greenwich). In Germany and Austria, "salz" or "hall" is used.

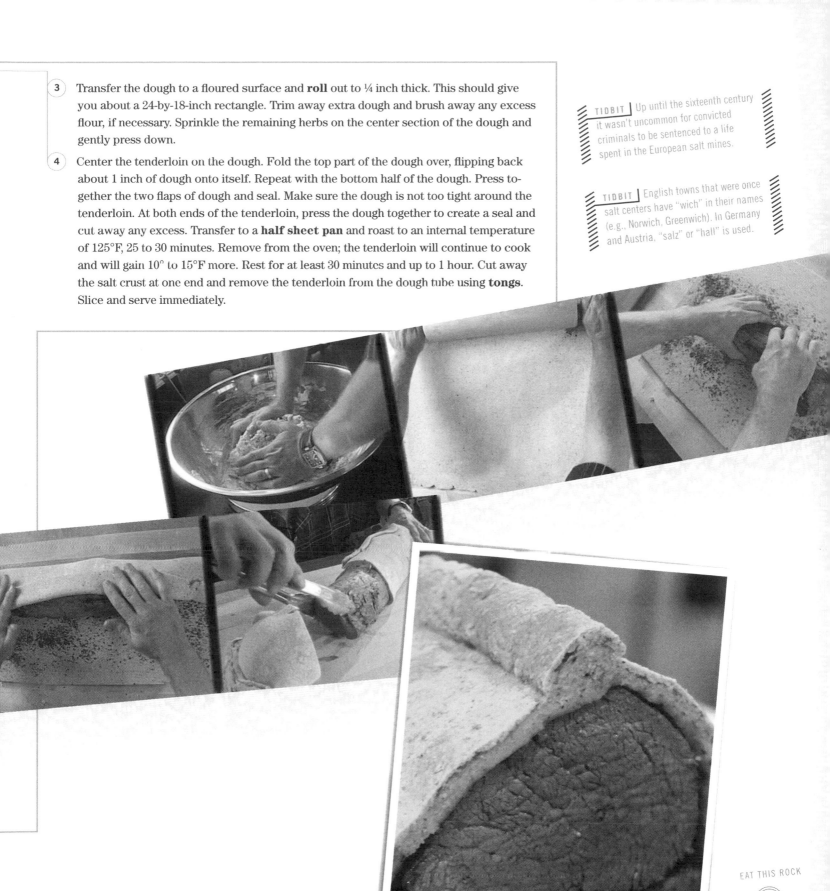

ROCK ROASTED SHRIMP

4 SERVINGS

So simple and so delicious. Not only does the salt season the shrimp, it provides heat transfer in a very unusual manner, which renders the little critters crisp and succulent without washing away any shrimpy flavor.

// **SOFTWARE** ///

4	pounds	rock salt	divided
1	pound	jumbo shrimp	with heads on

// **PROCEDURE** //

1. Divide the salt evenly between two **9-by-13-inch metal pans**.

2. Set the oven temperature to 400°F and put the pans of salt in the oven to heat. When the oven reaches temperature, continue heating the salt for 15 minutes.

3. Put the shrimp on top of the salt in one of the pans. Then cover with all of the salt from the second pan. The shrimp should be evenly and completely covered. Roast for 8 minutes. Remove from the oven and check one shrimp for doneness. The shrimp should be white and pink in color instead of gray. If not done, return to the oven for 1 to 2 minutes. Serve immediately.

TIDBIT | The majority of salt produced in the United States is used to keep winter roads ice-free.

I only include the opening piece of script

because it's one of my favorite scenes in *Good Eats* history. It's not a perfect homage to *Raiders*, but I dare say it's the best one ever to be filmed for a food show.

We open on dense jungle. The camera tracks to a piranha-infested river just as AB and a local guide, Zapato, come into view paddling an old-school rubber raft. They pull up to the bank, check a map, and set off into the jungle.

ZAPATO: (nervous) Tell me, Señor, what do we seek in this horrible place?

AB: The Holy Grail of edible artifacts, my friend. A golden idol so exotic, mysterious, and delicious that many call it "fruit of paradise." That's what we're looking for. And it's close. It's real close.

Zapato notices a nasty-looking spider on AB's back.

Z: Señor! On your back!

AB wipes it off without a second thought. He sees what he's after and picks up his pace.

AB: There they are! Come on!

Z: Señor? I'll wait here. (A creepy screech makes him jump.) On second thought...

AB comes to a banana tree and begins shooting the scene with his camera.

AB: Beautiful, aren't they?

Z: Bananas?

AB: Yeah.

Z: We've been trudging through this forsaken jungle for stinking bananas?

AB: Yes.

Z: Adios, Señor Idiot.

Disgusted, Zapato turns to abandon his employer.

AB: Hey, Zapato, have you ever heard of those really, really big banana spiders?

Z: The ones as big as your head?

AB: Uh huh.

Z: They say they can kill a man with one bite?

AB: Those are the ones.

Z: They are legend. Why do you ask?

AB: No reason.

Z: Adios.

As Zapato turns to go we see a gigantic spider perched on his pack...it's big enough to eat a cat.

AB: Adios, Zapato. I can sympathize with Zapato's disillusionment.

Not too far away, someone screams...horribly.

AB: After all, bananas are cheap, plentiful, and available year round in every megamart between here and the Temple of Doom. When you think about it, no other fruit—or food, for that matter—has gotten under the skin of pop culture like the banana. Maybe it's the color, maybe it's the shape, the flavor, maybe it's the handy wrapper. But there is more to this jungle-born friend than meets the eye. Much more. The banana, which takes many different guises, possesses culinary powers beyond your wildest dreams. In other words, the banana is a treasure well worth pursuing. Not to mention seriously...

Cut to: Good Eats Intro.

FOUR BANANA VARIETIES (BESIDES THE EVERYDAY CAVENDISH) YOU SHOULD SEEK OUT:

BABY/NIÑO bananas are tiny things, 3 to 4 inches long. They're bright yellow when ripe and have a butter-rich texture. The almost floral flavor is the epitome of banana.

MANZANOS are short like the Niños but are significantly chubbier. When ripe, the peel becomes very dark. The flavor is like a fruit salad with berry and apple notes.

BURRO bananas are also short and squat but with blocky, almost sawed-off-looking ends. When ripe, their skins are spotted and the fruit delivers a tangy flavor that's almost like citrus. Great for salads.

RED bananas have nearly black skin and a flesh that's almost like salmon due to a high concentration of beta carotene. I like them in ice cream because everyone expects it to taste like either orange or peach.

The banana's origins have been traced to Southeast Asia, probably India or Malaysia. According to Hindu legend, it was the banana, not the apple, that got Adam and Eve kicked out of paradise. Accordingly, they covered their shame with banana leaves, not fig leaves. It certainly gave them more fashion options. You can also turn banana leaves into a hat, a drinking cup, a cooking pouch, or a pterodactyl. But hey, that's another show. Most historians believe that the Arabs brought the banana to Europe by way of North Africa and then Spain. And we know that a Spaniard, a friar named Tomás de Berlanga, brought them to the New World. He planted one single banana root, or rhizome, in the West Indies around 1516. And that single plant spread so quickly that later European adventurers assumed that the banana was a native tree.

Until refrigerated produce boats came into use in 1903, bananas were a rare sight in North America. But by 1905 banana imports topped 3.5 billion fingers. That's about 40 bananas for every man, woman, and child in the country at the time. They are still our most popular fruit. About a decade after bananas came into this country, they became very popular street foods. Since there were very few trash cans in urban areas, most people just gave them a fling. So many city dwellers were either injured or killed in banana-related accidents that the peel became the poster child for the growing litter problem in America.

Unlike most fruits, bananas actually taste better when allowed to ripen off the tree. This is a good thing when you consider the fact that bananas are harvested and shipped green and firm, with about 50 percent of their carbs still in their young and hard-to-digest starchy form. But as those starches ripen, most of them are going to be transformed into easily digestible sugars like fructose, glucose, and sucrose. Which is why bananas are often the first and sometimes the last solid foods we eat.

If you purchase a green hand, just leave it uncovered at room temperature until ripe. If you're in a hurry, slide it into a paper, not plastic, bag. Plastic traps moisture, moisture begets mold, and mold is not good eats. Not on bananas, at least. If you happen to have a ripe or overripe banana lying around, toss it in. It will provide ethylene gas, which will kick-start the ripening process. Packers use the same trick in their warehouses so that when bananas get to the grocery store, they look good, but they're only partly ripe.

TIDBIT | When truly ripe, a banana's exterior will be striped and spotted with dark brown, which is usually when Americans throw them away as "rotten." Pretty, picture-perfect yellow bananas are nowhere near as flavorful.

PRETTY BUT NOT RIPE...

BANANA ICE CREAM

ABOUT 1 QUART

The texture and flavor of ripe bananas is often compared to that of ice cream, and yet Americans rarely walk their favorite fruit down that frosty path. Shame.

// SOFTWARE ///

2¼	pounds	ripe bananas	about 6
1	tablespoon	lemon juice	freshly squeezed
¾	cup	light corn syrup	
1		vanilla bean	split and scraped
1½	cups	heavy cream	

// PROCEDURE //

1. Freeze the bananas, unpeeled, for at least 2 hours or up to overnight.

2. Remove the bananas from the freezer and thaw for 45 minutes to 1 hour. Peel the bananas and combine with the lemon juice in the bowl of a **food processor**. Process for 10 to 15 seconds. Add the corn syrup and vanilla bean seeds and turn the food processor on. Slowly pour in the cream. Blend until smooth.

3. Chill the mixture in the refrigerator until it reaches 40°F, about 3 hours. Transfer the mixture to an **ice cream maker** and process according to the manufacturer's instructions. Put the ice cream in an **airtight container** and freeze for 3 to 4 hours to firm up before serving.

   VARIATIONS: Clover honey can be substituted for the corn syrup. For Banana Peanut Butter Ice Cream, add ½ cup smooth peanut butter to the food processor along with the corn syrup (or honey) and vanilla.

TOP BANANA

BANANAS FOSTER

2 SERVINGS

Although the banana is most often associated with homey fare, it's got its elegant, sophisticated side too. This is best embodied by a dish that is as simple as it is delicious and as much about theater as cuisine. I speak, of course, of Bananas Foster. Many classic American dishes have histories that are murky at best. Not so Bananas Foster, which was devised in 1951 by Paul Blangé, the executive chef at Brennan's restaurant in New Orleans and subsequently named after a local businessman and Brennan's regular named Stephen Foster.

// SOFTWARE ///

2	tablespoons	unsalted butter	
¼	cup	dark brown sugar	
¼	teaspoon	ground allspice	
½	teaspoon	nutmeg	freshly grated
1	tablespoon	banana liqueur	
2		under-ripe bananas	cut in half lengthwise
¼	cup	dark rum	
½	teaspoon	orange zest	grated

// PROCEDURE ///

1. Melt the butter in a **10-inch heavy skillet** over low heat. Add the brown sugar, allspice, and nutmeg and stir until the sugar dissolves. Add the banana liqueur and bring the sauce to a simmer.

2. Add the bananas and cook for 1 minute on each side, carefully **spooning** sauce over the bananas as they are cooking. Remove the bananas from the pan to a **serving dish**.

3. Return the sauce to a simmer and carefully add the rum. If the sauce is very hot, the alcohol will flame on its own. If not, using a **stick lighter**, carefully ignite the sauce and continue cooking until the flame dies out, 1 to 2 minutes. If the sauce is too thin, cook for 1 to 2 minutes more, until it is syrupy in consistency. Add the orange zest and stir to combine. Immediately spoon the sauce over the bananas and serve with waffles, crêpes, or ice cream.

BASIC FLAMBÉ GROUND RULES

1. No loose clothing.

2. If you've got long hair, tie it back or wear a hat.

3. Since you never know how high the flames may go, do not hold your head over the pan.

4. When working on an open flame, be sure to turn off the flame before adding the alcohol. Otherwise it could evaporate, jump over the side of the pan, and Poof!

5. Always use a long stick-style lighter or a fireplace match.

6. Have a lid standing by just in case things get out of hand, which, if you've observed the first rules, won't happen.

7. Now make sure you have a fire extinguisher around in case things really get out of hand.

8. Oh, and here's my favorite rule: Remember, the dimmer the lights, the flashier the show.

TIDBIT | Bananas are 99 percent fat-free, high in fiber, vitamin C, and vitamin B6, and loaded with potassium, which is essential for regulating blood pressure and keeping your muscles strong and healthy.

FRIED PLANTAINS

4 SERVINGS AS A SIDE DISH

Thanks to the growing popularity of Cuban, Caribbean, and Latin cuisines, most American me-gamarts now carry plantains, which are starchy rather than sweet and can easily stand in for potatoes. The plantain has a tough, rubbery skin, so to peel, cut off one end, cut off the other end, then make a shallow incision down one side, and then repeat on the other side. Take your thumb and squeeze it under the edge of the peel and pull it right off.

// **SOFTWARE** ///

2	cups	H_2O	
3	cloves	garlic	smashed
2	teaspoons	kosher salt	plus extra for seasoning
1½	cups	vegetable oil	
2		green plantains	

// **PROCEDURE** ///

1. Combine the water, garlic, and 2 teaspoons salt in a **medium glass bowl** and set aside.

2. Heat the oil to 325°F in a **12-inch straight-sided pan**. Peel the plantains and cut them crosswise into 1-inch pieces. Fry the slices until golden yellow in color, 1 to 1½ minutes per side.

3. Remove the plantains from the pan to a **half sheet pan lined with parchment paper**, standing them on their ends. With the back of a wide **wooden spatula**, press each piece of plantain down to half its original thickness. Transfer the plantains to the water mixture and soak for 1 minute. Remove to a **tea towel** and pat dry to remove excess water.

4. Bring the oil back up to 325°F, return the plantains to the oil, and cook until golden brown, 2 to 4 minutes per side. Remove to a **plate** lined with **paper towels**, season with salt, and serve immediately.

THE CHARM OF SHOOTING "ON LOCATION"

My producer (the long-suffering Dana Popoff) had researched a banana "plantation" in Clewiston, Florida. The owner had sent some pictures of the various bananas grown and, satisfied, we packed up and flew down. Turns out the "plantation" was essentially a suburban backyard bordered by one of those big drainage ditches that run along the highway. It was . . . not what we expected. But we had to shoot so we bought a raft at the local army surplus and found an angle that made the drainage ditch look like a river.

POOR ZAPATO!

HITTIN' THE SAUCE

EPISODE 108 | SEASON 8 | GOOD EATS

The *Oxford English Dictionary* says that a sauce is "any preparation, usually liquid or soft, and often consisting of several ingredients, intended to be eaten as an appetizing accompaniment to some article of food."

Sauces are extremely popular in America. We have barbecue sauce, steak sauce, salad dressing, salsa (yes, dips count as sauces), ketchup, mayonnaise, and more. They cover a broad spectrum of flavors and viscosities but have one thing almost universally in common: a bottle. In America, sauce isn't something you make, it's something you buy, and that's a cryin' shame because with just a few tools and some basic ingredients . . . well, you know where I'm heading with this.

TIP *Fond* won't form on nonstick surfaces, so if you plan on building a pan sauce, stick to stainless steel or cast iron.

KNOWLEDGE CONCENTRATE

▷ Although any self-respecting Frenchman will tell you that the organization of the sauce world rivals the complexity of tracing the lineage of the French crown, to my mind there are only two divisions:

Sauces prepared independently of the food with which they are to be served (this includes sauces in which foods are meant to be cooked); and

Sauces prepared for a particular food from the leftovers or by-products created by the cooking of said item (including all pan sauces, jus, and the like).

▷ **"Pan" sauces are built upon the brown bits left in a pan after a food (usually meat) is seared, sautéed, or roasted in a pan. The French (who have a name for everything edible) call these browned bits *fond*, or "foundation," and they indeed form the bases for many a dish and sauce. Typically these are the stages of construction:**

1. Remove a majority of the remaining fat from the pan.

2. Deglaze the pan with a liquid such as wine, water, broth, or stock.[1]

3. Reduce.

4. Add a second "flavoring" liquid such as a spirit along with any desired spices.

5. Add a finishing fat, if desired, such as cold butter or heavy cream.

6. Stir in final flavors such as fresh herbs.

TIDBIT | One of the most effective thickeners is Japanese arrowroot, which is actually derived from the kudzu plant.

TRIVIA | I dressed up like a flower with a stem full of packing chips to prove a point about how plants store granules. It occurred to me as I committed botanical seppuku that no one had actually measured the depth of the chips or the length of the sharp blade.

Sometimes the difference between a mere cooking liquid and a sauce is simply a question of viscosity. Let's say you browned some lamb pieces, added some chopped vegetation, and simmered the lot in a combination of red wine, meat broth, and water with some thyme and maybe black pepper. If potatoes are in the mix, odds are good the liquid will thicken up a bit due to the presence of starch. What is starch? Let's review:

Plants manufacture sugar in their leaves via photosynthesis and then they store it in tight little granules we call starch.[2] When exposed to heat and liquid, these granules swell, causing the liquid they're in to thicken, a process called gelatinization. Pour enough heat into these swollen sacks and they burst open, spilling oodles of ultra-long molecular structures (more on those in future episodes) into their surroundings. Oddly enough, this results not in additional thickening but an actual reduction of viscosity until the liquid cools, at which point the molecules knit together into a thick paste—which is what we count on when making a starch-stabilized pie like lemon meringue. The trick in using a starch thickener is understanding that different kinds of starch thicken in different ways.

Here in America, WHEAT FLOUR is the most common thickener. But it has several disadvantages: It clumps worse than any other starch and also it has to be brought to a full boil before it will thoroughly thicken. And it has protein in it, which rises to the surface as scum. Yuck.

Asian cuisines often employ CORNSTARCH, which thickens at lower temperatures than flour, but it isn't very heat stable. If you overcook it even a little bit, you'll end up right back where you started.

TAPIOCA or CASSAVA STARCH is good for pie fillings but very tricky to handle in sauces.

POTATO STARCH works a lot like cornstarch and it's unique among granular starches in that it is kosher for Passover.

My personal favorite thickener has got to be ARROWROOT, which comes (surprise) from arrowroot.[3] One to two tablespoons will thicken a quart of liquid, depending, of course, on the desired viscosity. Introducing such a potent plant matter to a hot liquid is tricky because lumps can form. So always disperse the granules in a cold liquid to form a "slurry" before whisking it into the target liquid. Although water is all that's required, water doesn't exactly intensify flavor, so I often use tomato juice instead. (Arrowroot thickens acidic as well as nonacidic liquids.) And unlike wheat flour, arrowroot thickens at well below a simmer.

[1] Any time a liquid is added to a hot pan for the purpose of dissolving the *fond* stuck to the bottom, it's called deglazing.

[2] Since they're made up of many, many sugars, starches are referred to as "polysaccharides."

[3] Tapioca, cassava, and even potato starch are sometimes sold as "arrowroot starch."

STRIP STEAK WITH PEPPER CREAM SAUCE

4 SERVINGS

// SOFTWARE //

4	6- to 8-ounce	strip steaks	¾ to 1 inch thick
	to taste	kosher salt	
2	teaspoons	black peppercorns	coarsely crushed
2	tablespoons	clarified butter	see page 300
¾	cup	beef stock or broth	
¾	cup	heavy cream	
3	tablespoons	cognac	
1	tablespoon	green peppercorns in brine	drained and slightly crushed

// PROCEDURE //

1. Heat oven to 200°F.

2. Sprinkle the steaks with salt and crushed black pepper. Melt the butter in a **12-inch heavy-bottomed sauté pan** over medium heat. When the butter is hot, add the steaks and cook until brown on both sides, 3 minutes per side for medium. Remove the steaks from the pan, place on a **resting rig** (see page 70), and set in oven.

3. Add the stock to the sauté pan and **whisk** until the crisp bits release from the bottom of the pan. Reduce the liquid for 3 to 4 minutes. Add the cream, cognac, and green peppercorns to the pan. Increase the heat to high and cook, whisking constantly, until the sauce thickens slightly, just enough to coat the back of a **spoon**, 5 to 7 minutes.

4. Season the sauce with salt to taste. Place the steaks on **plates**, top with sauce, and serve immediately.

HISTORY, SAUCED

ITALY, 257 B.C.: Romans, rich and poor alike, are crazy about garam. The sauce, which they put on everything, is a disgusting concoction containing wine, water, salt, and fermented fish entrails. That's right, folks, fish guts. This sauce tends to seek out and destroy the flavor of any food it comes in contact with, which might just be the whole idea.

EUROPE, A.D. 1195: Sophisticated medieval palates favor sweet sauces that showcase the spice rack. The more cinnamon, ginger, nutmeg, mace, cloves, mustard, honey, and, of course, exotic herbs, the better. And for thickening, there's always plenty of stale bread to go around. Perfect for an après-joust dinner party.

INDIA, A.D. 1700: Chefs in the royal kitchens of Mughal courts cook lamb, chicken, and vegetables in korma, a sauce of yogurt and ground nuts richly spiced with toasted coriander and cumin.

FRANCE, A.D. 1813: When it comes to hittin' the sauce, nobody touches the great Antonin Carême, who's developed a system of sauces based on a handful of "mother" sauces: white and brown sauces made from stock, béchamel from milk, tomato sauce, and hollandaise. Carême believes that upon this foundation, hundreds of other sauces can be constructed. As for the father of sauces, well, Carême considers himself to be the Father of All Sauces.

HOLLANDAISE SAUCE

ABOUT 1½ CUPS

Hollandaise, or *sauce hollandaise*, is one of the most elegant and versatile sauces ever concocted. Technically it's a hybrid of a mayonnaise and a classic lemon curd flavored with pepper rather than cup-loads of sugar. Its legendary tendency to break and curdle has been the root of much *sturm und drang* in residential and restaurant kitchens alike. But that's not the sauce's fault. It's the fault of bad recipe writing. All you have to do to successfully mount this classic is to think of it not as a sauce, but as stirred custard, which is what it is.

// **SOFTWARE** //

3	large	egg yolks	
1	teaspoon	H₂O	
¼	teaspoon	sugar	
¾	cup	unsalted butter	cut into small pieces and chilled
½	teaspoon	kosher salt	
2	teaspoons	lemon juice	freshly squeezed
⅛	teaspoon	ground cayenne	

// **PROCEDURE** //

(1) Put 1 inch of **water** in a **large saucepan** over medium heat and bring to a simmer. Once simmering, reduce the heat to low.

(2) Place the egg yolks and 1 teaspoon water in **a medium mixing bowl** and **whisk** until it lightens in color, 1 to 2 minutes. Add the sugar and whisk for another 30 seconds.

(3) Set the bowl over the simmering water and whisk constantly for 3 to 5 minutes, until there is a clear line that is drawn in the mixture when you pull your whisk through or the mixture coats the back of a **spoon**.

(4) Remove the bowl from over the pan, gradually add the butter, one piece at a time, and whisk until all of the butter is incorporated. Place the bowl back over the simmering water occasionally so it will be warm enough to melt the butter. Add the salt, lemon juice, and cayenne. Serve immediately or hold in a **Thermos** to keep warm.[4]

HOLLANDAISE'S KIN

Being one of five classical sauces considered "mother sauces," hollandaise is the basis for many other traditional sauces, including:

▶ **SAUCE AU VIN BLANC**, a traditional sauce for white-fleshed fish, is made by adding a reduction of white wine and fish stock to hollandaise.

▶ **SAUCE BÉARNAISE**, a close kin of hollandaise, starts with a reduction of vinegar, shallots, fresh chervil and tarragon, and crushed peppercorns.

▶ **SAUCE MALTAISE** is hollandaise to which orange zest and blood orange juice is added.

▶ **SAUCE MOUSSELINE**, also called **SAUCE CHANTILLY**, is hollandaise with whipped cream folded into it.

▶ **SAUCE NOISETTE** is a hollandaise made with browned butter.

[4] Continued heating, even on a relatively low flame, will result in disaster. If you don't have a Thermos, cover the pan and set in hot water for up to an hour. Better yet, buy a Thermos.

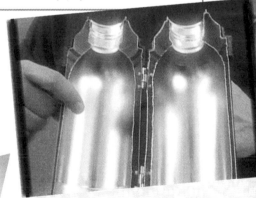

TRIVIA We sawed open this Thermos to help explain how the thin vacuum layer keeps hot hot and cold cold. I think we voided the warranty.

"Was a brave man who first
eat an oyster."
/////////////////////////////////
JONATHAN SWIFT

Oysters are bivalve mollusks, meaning that they basically look like gray blobs encased in tight-fitting two-piece calcareous shells. Besides providing a considerable amount of high-quality nutrition (protein, iron, copper, iodine, etc.), few critters taste more perfectly of the sea (very fresh sea urchin notwithstanding).

KNOWLEDGE CONCENTRATE

▷○ **Oysters were big with the ancient Greeks, who actually used oyster shells as ballots in their elections. Romans gathered them from all over their empire, often sending slaves as far as the English Channel to harvest them. Native Americans munched so many that archaeologists are still finding big piles of shells around ancient coastal community sites. Oysters were once so plentiful on the Atlantic coast of the United States that bars in New York simply gave them away or at most charged a penny for a dozen or two that had been harvested right off of Manhattan. Overfishing and pollution have nearly done these filter feeders in, but careful management has brought the American oyster back from the abyss.**

Although they're considered highbrow by many eaters today due to their relative scarcity and high level of perishability, oysters were once considered fast food for the masses. In Charles Dickens's *The Pickwick Papers*, Sam remarks that "poverty and oysters always seem to go together."

▷○ **Oysters are filter feeders capable of pumping more than twenty gallons of water through their plumbing every day. Oysters derive their distinct flavor, their terroir, from the particular water they're in. So, oysters of the very same species taken from waters even as little as fifty miles apart can taste a world apart.**

Depending on where you live you'll likely encounter four purchasing options:

Live in the shell

Fresh shucked meats in liquor (the liquid from inside the shells)

Frozen shucked meats in either liquor or water

Canned (although the little smoked ones can be useful in hors d'oeuvres, by and large I avoid canned models, which tend to taste like what they're in)

When purchasing oysters, keep the following in mind:

Live oysters should have tightly closed shells or shells that close tightly when tapped. As with humans, permanent "gapers" should be avoided.

Live oysters should always be accompanied by "bed tags" that let you know they were taken from regulated waters.

Fresh shucked oyster meats should be plump and the liquid should be creamy or clear.

Shucked meats will always be stamped with the "date shucked." I wouldn't purchase meats more than seven days after shucking.

Left in breathable containment (a mesh bag or open bucket) in the bottom of the refrigerator, healthy oysters will last five to seven days. Do not ice them, and whatever you do don't put them in water!

Opening (shucking) oysters:

Let me be perfectly clear on this point: If you're not serving them on the shell, there is nothing wrong with buying shucked oysters as long as you're sure of your source and the quality. I tend to buy in the shell because I actually enjoy shucking . . . but I'm weird.

Place the oyster in a protected hand (I like a nonslip glove designed for working in water) with the hinge facing your other hand, which should be holding the oyster knife. Work the tip of said tool into the hinge area. I usually have the best luck with the tip curve facing up, but every oyster is different. Twist the tip gently back and forth until the hinge pops.

Rotate the oyster in your hand, gently working just the tip of the knife around the outside of the shell to separate. Sticking the blade more than half an inch in will damage the meat.

Once the "lid" is removed, sweep the knife under the meat to disconnect it from the shell and serve.

In the days before government regulation, aquaculture, and especially refrigeration, eating oysters in a month without an "r" in its name could be dangerous. Those days are long gone.

4 SERVINGS

A goof on the classic Oysters Rockefeller invented by Jules Alciatore of Antoine's in New Orleans around 1899. It was named for John D. Rockefeller, who was the richest rich guy in America at the time.

// SOFTWARE

6	tablespoons	unsalted butter	
¾	cup	onion	finely chopped
¾	cup	celery	finely chopped
1	teaspoon	kosher salt	divided
1	tablespoon	garlic	minced
1	14-ounce can	artichoke hearts	drained and finely chopped
1	cup	Japanese bread crumbs	a.k.a. panko
2	teaspoons	lemon zest	grated
½	teaspoon	black pepper	freshly ground
1	teaspoon	dried oregano	
4	cups	rock salt	
24		oysters	on the half shell with their liquor

// PROCEDURE

1. Heat the oven to 425°F.

2. Over medium-low heat, melt the butter in a **12-inch sauté pan**. Increase the heat slightly and add the onion, celery, and half of the kosher salt and sweat for 5 to 7 minutes. Add the garlic and cook for an additional 1 to 2 minutes. Reduce the heat to low and add the artichoke hearts, bread crumbs, lemon zest, the remaining kosher salt, the pepper, and oregano. Continue cooking for 2 to 3 more minutes. Remove from the heat and set aside.

3. Spread the rock salt evenly on a **half sheet pan**. Set the oysters atop the salt and, dividing evenly among them, top each oyster with the bread crumb mixture. Bake for 10 to 12 minutes, until the bread crumbs are lightly browned. Serve immediately.

PERSONAL NOTE: I love oysters and used to eat them by the bushel. Then, one day in my late twenties a mere dozen put me in the hospital. Assuming that I'd had a bad batch I tried again a couple months later and again . . . hospital. My doctor concluded that although I am not classically allergic, my body has developed an intolerance to oysters that prevents me from ever enjoying them again. Nature can be so, so cruel. Luckily I still have clams, mussels, abalone, and the like to keep me culinary company.

ANOTHER PERSONAL NOTE: Although I rarely, if ever, prescribe specific beverages for any dish, when it comes to raw oysters there is only one choice: beer, preferably an American pilsner (a lager will do in a pinch). Cooked oysters, however, are best served with wine, and for my money you can't beat a nice flinty Chablis.

OYSTER SOUP

This is as sinfully fatty an application as I've ever developed. A quart of cream! I'd eat this once a year at most and probably at the holidays.

// SOFTWARE ///

1	quart	heavy cream	
1	pint	oysters	with their liquor
1	tablespoon	unsalted butter	
½	cup	celery	finely chopped
	to taste	kosher salt	
½	cup	onion	finely chopped
1	teaspoon	celery seed	
1½	teaspoons	hot sauce	
1	tablespoon	lemon juice	freshly squeezed
2	tablespoons	fresh parsley, chervil, or chives	chopped
	to taste	black pepper	freshly ground

// PROCEDURE ///

1. Bring the cream and liquor from the oysters to a simmer in a **heavy 2-quart saucepan** over medium heat. Remove from the heat.

2. Melt the butter in a **large sauté pan** over medium heat. Add the celery and a pinch of salt and sweat for 3 to 4 minutes. Add the onion and continue cooking until translucent, 4 to 5 minutes. Add the celery seed, hot sauce, and oysters and cook for 1 to 2 minutes, until the edges of the oysters start to curl.

3. Transfer the oyster mixture to the **carafe of a blender** and add enough of the cream just to cover. Puree until the mixture is smooth. Return the remaining cream to medium heat, add the pureed mixture, and cook until heated through.

4. Just before serving, add the lemon juice and herbs and season with salt and pepper to taste.

NOTE: Today, 95 percent of the global oyster supply is farmed and tightly managed, and unlike the situation with, say, farmed salmon or tuna, oysters are considered a sustainability success story here in the States. Although subtle changes in environment may mean that one year the Apalachicolas aren't quite as sweet as the Blue Points, by and large things are good on planet oyster and you can enjoy them with impunity year round. Just make sure you buy from a reliable vendor who has bed tags and harvest information available for review.

1 ¼ CUPS

Lots of folks douse raw oysters with the same tomatoey stuff they dunk shrimp in. I think this sauce is far more oyster-compatible.

// SOFTWARE ///

1	cup	sour cream	
¼	cup	fresh horseradish	grated
1	tablespoon	Dijon mustard	
1	teaspoon	white wine vinegar	
½	teaspoon	kosher salt	
¼	teaspoon	black pepper	freshly ground

// PROCEDURE ///

Combine all the ingredients in a **medium bowl** and **whisk** until the mixture is smooth. Refrigerate for 4 hours or overnight for flavors to meld. Store in an airtight container in the fridge for up to 2 weeks.

Martin Moonstone, III
Oyster Epicure

CONCERNING POPULAR NAMETAGS

There are five types of oysters marketed in the United States:

PACIFIC CRASSOSTREA GIGAS:
A Japanese variety transplanted in waters of Washington State during the 1920s. It's now the most commonly grown oyster in the world. Popular "varieties" include Fanny Bays, Malaspinas, Royal Miyagi, and Steamboats. There are probably as many different regional varieties as there are Eastern oysters, but few make it east of the Rockies—which is kinda nice, if you ask me.
  Characteristics: Small, sweet, delicate.

KUMAMOTO CRASSOSTREA SIKAMEA: Also transplanted from Japan, specifically from Kumamoto

Bay on Kyushu, the southernmost isle of that chain. Until recently the kumamoto was thought to be the same species as the Pacific oyster but is now known to be a separate species, though it's sometimes tough to tell them apart. Grown in parts of California, Oregon, and Washington. Sometimes called "kumos."
  Characteristics: Firm flesh with buttery, sweet flavor. Deep but diminutive shell makes this a favorite for eating on the half shell.

OLYMPIA OSTREA LURIDA/ CONCHAPILA: The Olympia is the only oyster native to the Pacific Coast of North America and ranges from Mexico to Alaska. They're named for Olympia, Washington.
  Characteristics: Small and flat, the

bite-size meats taste "brighter" than any other critter in the sea. If I could eat oysters, these would be the ones.

EUROPEAN FLAT OSTREA EDULIS:
The most famous regional example is the Belon oyster of Brittany.
  Characteristics: Flat shell, sharp mineral flavor, creamy texture.

ATLANTIC/EASTERN OYSTERS CRASSOSTREA VIRGINICAS:
Popular regional types are countless but include Blue Point (Long Island), Apalachicola (Florida), Breton Sound (Louisiana), Chesapeake Bay (Virginia), Malpeque (Prince Edward Island), Wellfleet (Massachusetts).
  Characteristics: The range of size and flavor is simply too wide to render a generalization.

FLAT IS BEAUTIFUL II: FLAT MEAT

EPISODE 110 | SEASON 8 | GOOD EATS

Ever since I came home from school one day to witness my mom pounding out a Swiss steak with the back of a frying pan, I've been fascinated by dishes built on wafer-thin sheets of meat. Aside from the obvious stress-relief potential, wailing on some cuts breaks down connective tissues, thus leading to a more tender dish. Flattening also changes the surface-to-mass ratio, and that means more surface area to be seasoned, browned, and/or sauced. Since they cook very quickly, flat meat dishes are perfectly suited to the modern American's frantically frenetic lifestyle.

The world may not be flat, but there's no reason dinner shouldn't be.

(NOT REALLY RUSSIAN)

155

Although Mom used a pan and a lot of pent-up angst to get the job done, I find that a few well-chosen tools protect my arm, my meal, and my countertops.

Most meat **MALLETS** are "tenderizers." That is, they have heavy heads with jagged teeth, the kind of thing Thor might have carried had he been a chef. Although the flat side of such a cudgel can be used for flattening, when you examine the angle of swing with that of the impact, it's clearly not the best tool for the job. In fact, I'd argue that any meat pounder with a handle parallel to the head like this:

. . . is going to do more damage than good. What you need is a pounder with a wide head and a handle that is not only perpendicular to the pounding surface but one that allows the thrust of the swing to be . . . oh, never mind. Get one that looks like this:

Such a pounder also allows directional control after the head makes contact, allowing the cook to "spread" the meat in whatever direction he or she pleases.

PLASTIC WRAP provides considerable tear protection, which is especially valuable when dealing with more fragile poultry and even fish (although scallops can be flattened to positive effect, most fish disintegrate when pounded). Plastic wrap makes moving and handling flattened meats a lot easier, and also provides a barrier to whatever lubrication is used.

When the mallet strikes it needs to slide across the surface of the meat. This is in fact the part of the action that provides even thinning. Problem is, most meat isn't slippery enough on its own. By spritzing the plastic wrap with **WATER**, you create a slip-'n'-slide situation. I never pick up the mallet with one hand without hefting a water spritzer in the other.

BAD POUNDER
DUE TO ANGLE OF ARM AND WRIST, MALLETS TEND TO DELIVER UNEVEN BLOWS THAT TEAR MEAT

GOOD POUNDER

20-SECOND STEAK

4 SERVINGS

I often serve these thin sheets with a drizzling of extra-virgin olive oil, lemon juice, some shaved Parmesan, black pepper, and arugula, just like a carpaccio. And by the way, since the flattened pieces are seared rather than sautéed, they're technically *paillards*. It's a French thing.

// **SOFTWARE** //

1	pound	beef tenderloin	trimmed
		vegetable oil	
	to taste	kosher salt	
	to taste	black pepper	freshly ground

// **PROCEDURE** //

1. Freeze the tenderloin for 2 hours. (This will firm the meat for easier slicing.)

2. Heat the oven to 200°F.

3. Remove the tenderloin from the freezer and, using an **electric knife**, cut it into ⅜-inch slices. Set the pieces of beef, one at a time, on a **large piece of plastic wrap**, lightly **spritz** the top of the beef with **water**, fold the plastic wrap over the beef, and spritz the top of the plastic wrap with water. **Pound** to no less than ⅛ inch thick. Lightly **brush** each slice of beef on both sides with oil. Season with salt and pepper. Set aside.

4. Heat a **large cast-iron skillet** over high heat for 3 to 4 minutes. Reduce the heat to medium and turn the skillet upside down over the burner. Coat the pan lightly with oil. Place 2 or 3 slices of beef on the pan at a time and sear for 10 seconds on each side. Remove to an **ovenproof platter**. Place in the oven to keep warm. Repeat until all of the beef has been cooked. Serve immediately.

YOU SAY "SCALLOP," I SAY "CUTLET"

When seeking a flat cut of meat at the market you're likely to run into a nomenclature roadblock or two because there are just too many words. Scallop, scallopini, cutlet, and mignon can all mean a thin slice of meat. But please note that these are all thin slices, which are not the same as pieces pounded thin. Truth is, I would never purchase cutlets or scallopini at the market because all that surface area leads to drying. I'd much rather buy a big hunk of beast and do the cutting and flattening myself.

TIP Okay, so this no doubt seems . . . odd. Essentially, the bottom serves as a poor man's griddle, which allows for easier meat access and movement. And I kinda like this better than a griddle because the cooking surface (meaning the underside of the pan) is up off the heat source and therefore heats more evenly.

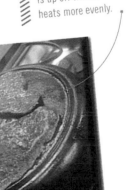

TURKEY PICCATA

Roughly translated, *piccata* means "sharp" in Italian and refers to an entire class of dishes featuring very thin cutlets cooked in a pan and served with an acidic piccata sauce. Classically speaking, veal is the leading cutlet in piccata recipes, but chicken, pork, and even turkey do very nicely as well. In fact, I prefer turkey 'cause it's tasty, cheap, and very easy to cutlet-ize.

// SOFTWARE ///

1	1½- to 2-pound	boneless turkey breast	
	to taste	kosher salt	
	to taste	black pepper	freshly ground
½	cup	all-purpose flour	
2	tablespoons	olive oil	
6	tablespoons	unsalted butter	divided
2	tablespoons	shallots	finely chopped
½	cup	white wine	
⅓	cup	lemon juice	freshly squeezed
2	tablespoons	fresh parsley	chopped

// PROCEDURE ///

1. Heat the oven to 200°F.

2. Cut the turkey breast crosswise into ½-inch pieces. Set the pieces of turkey, one at a time, on a **large piece of plastic wrap**, lightly **spritz** the top of the turkey with **water**, fold the plastic wrap over the turkey, and spritz the top of the plastic wrap with water. **Pound** to no less than ⅛ inch thick.[1]

3. Season both sides of the meat with salt and pepper and then dredge in flour. Shake off the excess flour. Set aside.

4. Heat the oil and 4 tablespoons of the butter in a **12-inch sauté pan** over medium-high heat. When hot, but not yet smoking, brown the turkey, about 1 minute on each side, then remove to an **ovenproof platter**. Place in the oven to keep warm.

5. Reduce the heat to low and add the shallots to the pan. Sauté for 1 to 2 minutes, until they begin to turn translucent. Add the wine and lemon juice to the pan and simmer until slightly reduced, about 2 minutes. Add the remaining 2 tablespoons butter and **whisk** to combine. Season with salt and pepper to taste, if necessary. Pour the sauce over the turkey, sprinkle with the parsley, and serve immediately.

[1] This can be done well in advance of cooking. Simply leave the plastic in place, stack the sheets, and roll for storage.

APPLICATION — CHICKEN KIEV

4 SERVINGS

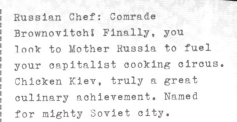

// SOFTWARE //

8	tablespoons	unsalted butter	at room temperature
1	teaspoon	dried parsley	
1	teaspoon	dried tarragon	
1	teaspoon	kosher salt	plus additional for seasoning
¼	teaspoon	black pepper	freshly ground, plus extra for seasoning
4	halves	chicken breast	boneless and skinless
2	cups	Japanese bread crumbs	plus 4 tablespoons
2	large	eggs	beaten with 1 teaspoon water
		vegetable oil	for frying

// PROCEDURE //

1. Combine the butter, parsley, tarragon, 1 teaspoon salt, and ¼ teaspoon black pepper in the **bowl of a stand mixer**. Beat until well combined. Place the compound butter on **plastic wrap or waxed paper**, roll into a small log, and freeze while preparing the chicken.

2. Set the chicken breasts, one at a time, on a **large piece of plastic wrap**, lightly **spritz** the top of the chicken with **water**, fold the plastic wrap over the chicken, and spritz the top of the plastic wrap with water. **Pound** to no less than ⅛ inch thick. Season each piece of chicken with salt and pepper.

3. Lay a breast on a **new piece of plastic wrap** and place one quarter of the compound butter and 1 tablespoon of the bread crumbs in the center of each breast. Using the plastic wrap to assist, fold in the ends of the breast and roll the breast into a tight log, completely enclosing the butter. Repeat with each breast. Refrigerate the breasts for 2 hours or up to overnight.

4. Place the egg and water mixture and the remaining bread crumbs in separate **shallow dishes**. Heat ½ inch of vegetable oil in a **12-inch sauté pan** to 375°F over medium-high heat.

5. Dip each breast in the egg mixture and then roll in the bread crumbs. Gently place each breast in the oil, seam side down, and cook until golden brown, 4 to 5 minutes on each side, or until the internal temperature reaches 165°F. Remove to a **cooling rack** set in a **half sheet pan** to drain and rest for 5 to 10 minutes before serving.

Russian Chef: Comrade Brownovitch! Finally, you look to Mother Russia to fuel your capitalist cooking circus. Chicken Kiev, truly a great culinary achievement. Named for mighty Soviet city.

DEB DUCHON: Not so fast, comrade. Chicken Kiev isn't from Kiev. It's not even Russian. Chicken Kiev is French. French food was very popular in eighteenth-century Russia. Chicken Kiev actually got its name from a bunch of restaurant owners in New York City.

AB, RC: (they look at each other and then the camera) New York City!

DD: They were trying to attract Russian immigrants.

RC: Pretty lady, how could you possibly know these things?

DD: Because I'm a dietalog antropolog.

RC: Then how can you hate Russian cuisine?

DD: I love Russian cuisine. I love the Russians. (moves closer to RC and holds his hand) I spent a year in St. Petersburg in graduate school.

CIRCLE OF LIFE

EPISODE 111 | SEASON 8 | GOOD EATS

Once a culture starts

depending on a commercial entity for a particular food it tends to forget that there was ever another choice. This is especially true of fried foods, which we love to eat but refuse to take personal responsibility for. Doughnuts are a perfect example. Although the corner doughnut (or donut) shop didn't become an icon until the automobile achieved dominance in the mid-twentieth century, I bet there are only a handful of doughnut lovers out there who would even fleetingly consider making their own. And most of them wear plain clothes and take buggies to town. This is indeed a shameful fact because few foods are as "homey" as the lowly doughnut. Oh, I'm not talking about jelly-filled, double-glazed monstrosities showered in sprinkles or even chocolate twist crullers, which are, in fact, darned tricky to make, but straightforward yeast doughnuts, glazed or plain, which are simple and simply . . .

```
"I owe it all to little
chocolate donuts."
/////////////////////////////////
JOHN BELUSHI
```

TRIVIA | We needed a Dutch girl but settled on our assistant editor, Brett . . . and yes, he's a dude. Nice lipstick though.

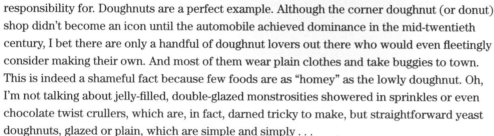

Every doughnut lover out there owes a debt of gratitude to ole Henry VIII. Had it not been for the iconoclast's convenient creation of the Church of England, there would have been no English Separatists. Nor would said Separatists have needed to depart England for the more religiously tolerant climate of the Netherlands. And if they hadn't moved to the Netherlands, these Separatists never would have developed a taste for *olykoeks*, the small pieces of dough, about the size of a walnut, fried in hog fat that were wildly popular with the Dutch. But they did. And when they finally decided to move on to settle a New World rock called Plymouth, the Pilgrims took *olykoeks* with them.

Once stateside, the doughnut underwent rapid transformation. The colonists performed a great deal of physical labor, which required energy, so the mass of the doughnut increased considerably. And then there's the curious matter of the hole.

Although the annals of culinary history offer a plethora of possibilities for the development of the hole, I will recount but two. The first stems from an incident reported in a 1750 edition of the *Cape Cod Gazette* that states that while frying up buns in her family home, a Cape Cod housewife was surprised when an arrow, allegedly fired by a Nauset Indian brave, flew through the open window, passing through one of her buns. (Go ahead and snicker; everybody does.) The shaken woman reported that although the incident was terrifying, the hole in fact improved her pastry. The brave could not be reached for comment.

Do I buy this? Not for a minute. The second story comes from a ship's log entry made by one Hansen Crockett Gregory, who was aboard a schooner anchored off the coast of Maine on Thursday, March 3, 1847. Captain Gregory recalls that on that particular day, the ship had been suddenly seized by terrible storms, requiring that he remain at the wheel well into the night. And at one point he grew so hungry that he called for his ship's cook to send up a fried cake. And just as he started to take a bite of the delight, they were pitched by a horrible rogue wave and he had to grab the wheel with both hands, accidentally impaling the treat upon the wheel. An hour later, when the winds abated, his prize was still there waiting for him. Excellent case of form following function, if it be true. Problem is, a doughnut with a hole already in it won't stay on a ship's wheel nearly as well as if you punched your own. So, why make doughnuts with holes in them? Nope, doesn't wash with me. I happen to subscribe to the theory that the doughnut hole was conceived by those legendary dessert daredevils, the Pennsylvania Dutch. The inventors of everything from cobbler to cream pie. And yes, I've got proof.

GETTING YOUR DOUGHNUTS INTO SHAPE

Doughnut cutters like this . . .

. . . are available in finer cookery stores and on the Internet, along with everything else in the world. These sturdy models do a pretty good job. But, you know, you're kind of locked into the size. And of course this is a unitasker. So I say, skip this and buy yourself a can full of round pastry cutters like this:

For fifteen or sixteen bucks you get twelve rings of differing diameters, which will enable you to cut doughnuts any old size you want, not to mention any other doughs requiring roundness such as cookies and biscuits. They can also be used as molds for salads like tabouli and, say, tuna tartare. That's what I call freedom.

50 DOUGHNUTS (JUST ENOUGH)

True, there are plenty of doughnut recipes out there that call for chemical leaveners, and if faithfully followed they will prepare something that looks like a doughnut—but won't taste or feel like a doughnut. I'd stick with yeast, which creates the texture and flavor that we all crave.

// SOFTWARE //

1½	cups	milk	
3	tablespoons	vegetable shortening	
2	envelopes	active dry yeast	
⅓	cup	warm H₂O	95° to 105°F
2	ounces	sugar	
1½	teaspoons	kosher salt	
1	teaspoon	nutmeg	freshly grated
2	large	eggs	beaten
26	ounces	all-purpose flour	divided
2 to 4	quarts	peanut or vegetable oil	for frying

TIP | The doughnut "hole" dough can be saved and fried after the doughnuts. Fry 10 to 12 holes at a time for 1 to 2 minutes, stirring gently with a spider. Drain and remove to the cooling rack set over a half sheet pan. While still warm, toss in Vanilla Sugar (page 319). Tell the kids you re-rolled the holes into doughnuts and devour these yourself, in private.

// PROCEDURE ///

1. Place the milk and shortening in a **medium saucepan** over medium heat and cook just until the shortening has melted. Move to the refrigerator to cool to 110°F, about 10 minutes.

2. Sprinkle the yeast over the warm water in the **bowl of a stand mixer** and set aside for 5 minutes.

3. Combine the cooled milk mixture with the yeast mixture. Add the sugar, salt, nutmeg, eggs, and half of the flour[1] and combine with the **paddle attachment on low**. Increase the speed to medium and beat until well combined.

4. Replace the paddle attachment with the **dough hook**, add the remaining flour, and beat until the dough pulls away from the bowl and becomes smooth, 3 to 4 minutes. Remove the dough and shape into a smooth round. Transfer to a well-oiled **bowl**, cover, and let rise for 1 hour, or until doubled in size.

[1] I find that flexible plastic cutting boards make the perfect funnels for transporting dry goods to the work bowls even if they are lousy cutting boards.

5. On a well-floured surface, fold the dough over itself twice and roll out to ⅜ inch thick. Cut out using a **2½-inch doughnut cutter**, or use a **2½-inch pastry ring** with a ⅞-inch ring for the center hole. Scrap dough can be re-rolled twice. Set on a lightly floured **half sheet pan** and let rise, uncovered, for 30 minutes.

6. Heat the oil in a **deep fryer (or cast-iron Dutch oven fitted with a deep-fry thermometer)** to 365°F. Drop the doughnuts into the oil 4 at a time and cook for 1 minute per side. Transfer to a **cooling rack set in a half sheet pan**. Glaze (see right) or roll in sugar as desired.

CLASSIC DOUGHNUT GLAZE

ENOUGH GLAZE FOR ABOUT 50 DOUGHNUTS

// SOFTWARE ///

½	cup	whole milk	
2	teaspoons	vanilla extract	
1	pound	confectioners' sugar	

// PROCEDURE ///

1. Combine the milk and vanilla in a **medium metal mixing bowl** and heat over low heat until warm.

2. **Sift** the confectioners' sugar into the milk mixture. **Whisk** slowly, until well combined. Remove the glaze from the heat and set over a **bowl of warm water**. Dip doughnuts into the glaze, 1 at a time, and set aside on a **cooling rack set in a half sheet pan** for 5 minutes before serving.

CHOCOLATE DOUGHNUT GLAZE

ENOUGH GLAZE FOR ABOUT 50 DOUGHNUTS

// SOFTWARE ///

1	cup	unsalted butter	
½	cup	whole milk	
2	tablespoons	light corn syrup	
2	teaspoons	vanilla extract	
8	ounces	bittersweet chocolate	chopped fine
1	pound	confectioners' sugar	sifted

// PROCEDURE ///

1. Combine the butter, milk, corn syrup, and vanilla in a **medium saucepan** over medium heat and heat until butter is melted.

2. Add the chocolate and **whisk** until smooth. Turn off the heat, add the confectioners' sugar, and whisk until smooth. Dip the doughnuts immediately. The glaze will take about 30 minutes to set.

TRIVIA | Ever since my sister Marsha (who of course is not actually my sister since I don't have a sister) made me jump through the cookie hoops in "Three Chips for Sister Marsha," I'd been lookin' to repeat the story structure wherein her complaints generate variations on a theme by me. The Bunny Scout Bake Sale was a cause even I couldn't refuse, what with all those little lasses sporting bunny ears. I also really liked the image of a motorcycle stacked and packed with doughnut boxes. Go figure. By the way, when Marsha parks one of the tykes on my bike in act 4, that is indeed my own flesh and blood making her third *Good Eats* appearance.

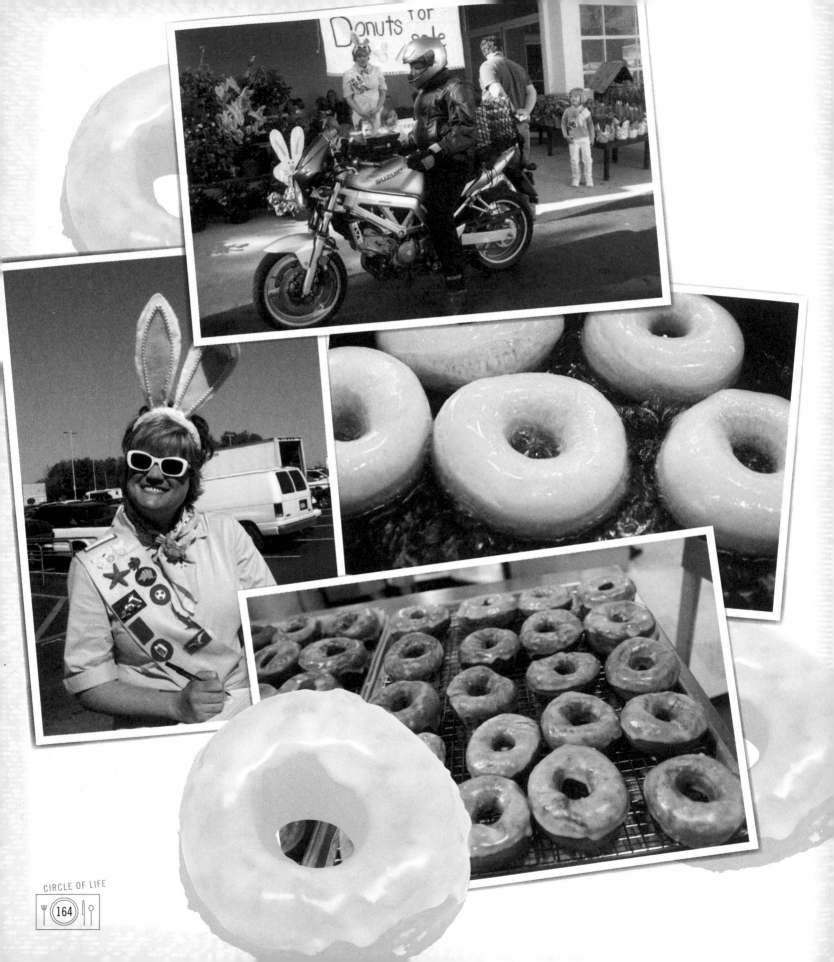

Consider the modern American megamart.

At no time in human history have so many edibles been available to the general population. And yet the average American shopper has a list of fewer than a hundred items from which he or she rarely deviates. We're so busy focusing on our shopping list that we don't allow ourselves to discover new ingredients. And that is a crying culinary shame. Because as you run your usual circuit from cereal to sour cream, you may be walking right past something that could change your culinary life. The cure? Just stop. Step away from the cart. Look around. Look for something that you've never seen before, that you've never tasted or used before. Pick up those wonton wrappers, for instance. Once upon a time I passed them without a second thought and now I can't live without them. Sure, they look innocuous enough, sitting there, but within that envelope lurks a culinary currency capable of converting any standard stuffing into cultured cuisine. You can bake them, broil them, fry them, sauté them, steam them, whatever. Read on, because this hidden refrigerator-case jewel is good eats just waiting to happen.

THE *FAN TS'AI* FANTASY

The Chinese have a desire to achieve balance in all things, culinary and otherwise, hence yin-yang, dark-light, great taste–less filling. In a wonton, this is all wrapped up in the principal of *fan ts'ai*. *Fan*, or starches and grains, need to be balanced by *ts'ai*, meats and vegetables. A good pot sticker has perfect *fan ts'ai* thanks to its balance of filling versus wrapper, thoughtful flavor combinations, and the contrasting *kou gan*, or mouthfeel, that comes from the marriage of crusty golden surface and plump, moist body. Of course, the only way to achieve this is to encourage the food to stick to the pan.

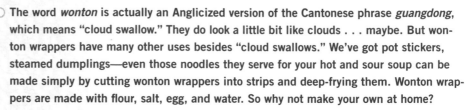

The word *wonton* is actually an Anglicized version of the Cantonese phrase *guangdong*, which means "cloud swallow." They do look a little bit like clouds . . . maybe. But wonton wrappers have many other uses besides "cloud swallows." We've got pot stickers, steamed dumplings—even those noodles they serve for your hot and sour soup can be made simply by cutting wonton wrappers into strips and deep-frying them. Wonton wrappers are made with flour, salt, egg, and water. So why not make your own at home?

I'll give you two reasons. One: It's almost impossible to make the noodle dough thin enough even with a pasta machine. And two, when I'm pressed for time. I'd rather spend my minutes toiling on the payload, not the missile. Since a lot of things that look like wonton skins actually aren't, we should take a moment out for product review.

Actual WONTON SKINS or wrappers usually come in packages of sixty to seventy three-inch squares. I dig the square shape because I think it's versatile and easy to use.

If you'd rather go round, look for GYOZA WRAPPERS or POT STICKER WRAPPERS. They're exactly the same thing as wonton wrappers but round.

Going up in size, we've got SPRING ROLL WRAPPERS and, even larger, EGG ROLL WRAPPERS. They are not made from exactly the same dough as wonton skins and, as they are less flexible and harder to seal, I don't use these for dumpling-type applications.

Next there's RICE PAPER, which is a brittle translucent cousin of the wonton skin. It's ideal for rolling and steaming, but you must remember to soak it before use. You don't keep it in the fridge and it is not interchangeable with wonton skins.

MU-SHU PANCAKES are usually called Chinese tortillas because they look and function much the way Mexican tortillas do, meaning that they're for making tacos.

Shapes vary widely. The easiest shape is a simple right triangle, made by folding the wonton in half diagonally and sealing along the edges. Crimps or pleats can be easily added to secure the seal and add a decorative touch. Its best suited for pot sticker applications, as its flat profile makes it ideal for pan-frying, steaming, or boiling.

For our steamed dumplings we employ a shape reminiscent of a hobo's bundle, sometimes also called a pyramid, by bringing together opposing corners and sealing where the corners meet. Wontons in this arrangement are more frequently used in soup. Small bundles can be made by gathering all sides and sealing just above the filling. This shape is especially well suited for high-heat applications such as frying. Open bundles, often called *shao mai*, are typically made with round wonton papers and steamed.

Round wrappers can also produce *mandu* and *pel'meni* with two simple moves. *Mandu*, typical of Korean cuisine, is a simple half-moon shape created by folding a round wrapper in half over the filling and sealing. From *mandu*, *pel'meni* can easily be secured by moistening the corners of the half-moon shape, overlapping, and pinching.

PORK POT STICKERS

35 TO 40 PIECES (STEAM, FRY, OR PAN SEAR AS YOU PLEASE)

// SOFTWARE ///

8	ounces	ground pork	
¼	cup	scallions	finely chopped
2	tablespoons	bell pepper	finely chopped
1	large	egg	lightly beaten
2	teaspoons	ketchup	
1	teaspoon	yellow mustard	
2	teaspoons	Worcestershire sauce	
1	teaspoon	light brown sugar	
1½	teaspoons	kosher salt	
½	teaspoon	black pepper	freshly ground
¼	teaspoon	ground cayenne	
35 to 40	small	wonton wrappers	
4	tablespoons	vegetable oil	for frying
1¼	cups	hot chicken or vegetable broth or H$_2$O	

// PROCEDURE ///

1. Heat the oven to 200°F.

2. Combine the pork, scallions, bell pepper, egg, ketchup, mustard, Worcestershire sauce, brown sugar, salt, black pepper, and cayenne in a **medium mixing bowl** and stir until well combined. Set aside.

3. To form the dumplings: Remove 1 wonton wrapper from the package, covering the others with a **damp cloth**. **Brush** the edges of the wrapper lightly with water. Place 1 rounded teaspoon of the pork mixture in the center of the wrapper. Shape as desired. Set on a **half sheet pan** and cover with a **damp cloth**. Repeat until all the filling is used.

4. Heat 1 tablespoon of the oil in a **10-inch nonstick sauté pan** over medium heat, just until smoking. Add 10 to 12 pot stickers to the pan and cook, without moving, until golden, 1 to 1½ minutes, then turn and brown the other side. Gently add ¼ cup of the hot broth or water, cover, and cook until the liquid evaporates, about 2 minutes. Remove the wontons to a **heatproof platter** and place in the oven to keep warm. Wipe the pan of any excess liquid or debris and repeat until all the wontons are cooked. Serve immediately.

ABOUT STEAMERS

Steaming is the definitive wonton method, but to do it right you'll need some specialized hardware, namely a steamer capable of housing wontons in single layers. (Try piling them up sometime and you'll have yourself a big, sticky wonton loaf.) Stackable steamers formed of woven bamboo are traditionally sound, but I don't care for them because they're tough, if not impossible, to wash. Stainless-steel versions of the same can be obtained at Asian restaurant-supply shops, but they're usually on the expensive side and very large. Electric countertop steamers are certainly a practical option, but only if you're planning to steam on a daily basis. For my money there's only one practical way to go: the steel lotus.

We actually came up with the steel lotus while working on a show about chicken wings, but it's equally useful for wonton steaming. The lotus is nothing more than three collapsible steamer baskets united by a central shaft composed of threaded stock (basically a rod with screw threads) from the hardware store. A couple of standard nuts keep the whole amalgam stable and secure.

If you're a fan of the show you may remember that the steel lotus didn't actually exist at the time and so I made a multistage steamer basket by prodigiously perforating several disposable pie pans and stacking them with tuna cans from which both ends had been removed. That contraption looked something like this:

This rig works fine, but it's very Sanford and Son compared to the elegance of the lotus. Still, it'll save you if you ever find yourself in a wonton pinch.

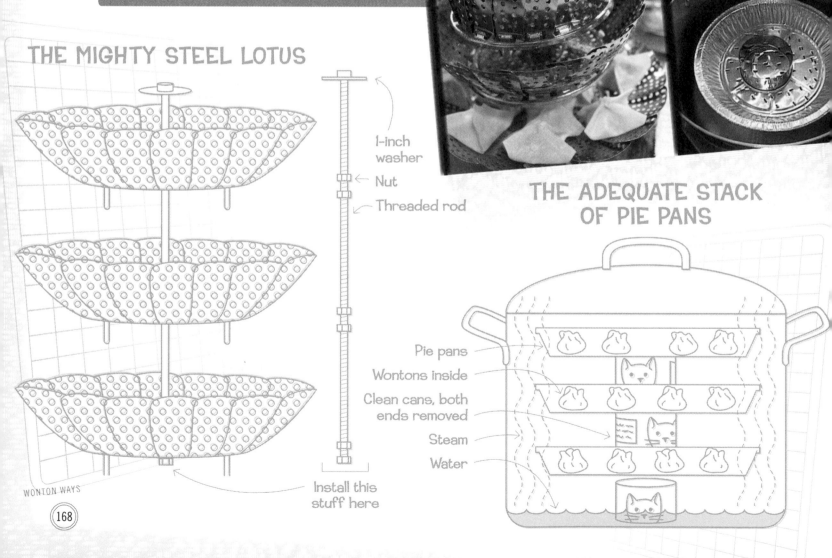

THE MIGHTY STEEL LOTUS

1-inch washer

Nut

Threaded rod

Install this stuff here

THE ADEQUATE STACK OF PIE PANS

Pie pans

Wontons inside

Clean cans, both ends removed

Steam

Water

VEGETARIAN STEAMED DUMPLINGS

35 TO 40 DUMPLINGS

These warm and spicy treats can be served as an app or as a light meal over some Asian-style slaw.

// SOFTWARE

8	ounces	firm tofu	
½	cup	carrots	grated
½	cup	Napa cabbage	grated
2	tablespoons	red bell pepper	diced
2	tablespoons	scallions	finely chopped
2	teaspoons	fresh ginger	minced
1	tablespoon	fresh cilantro	chopped
1	tablespoon	soy sauce	
1	tablespoon	hoisin sauce	
2	teaspoons	sesame oil	
1	large	egg	lightly beaten
1	teaspoon	kosher salt	
¼	teaspoon	black pepper	freshly ground
35 to 40	small	wonton wrappers	

// PROCEDURE

1. Cut the block of tofu in half horizontally and put it between several layers of **paper towels,** set between **two large plates**, and top with a **28-ounce can** from the pantry. Set aside for 20 minutes to extract as much whey as possible.

2. Cut the tofu into ¼-inch cubes and place in a **large mixing bowl** along with the carrots, cabbage, bell pepper, scallions, ginger, cilantro, soy sauce, hoisin sauce, sesame oil, egg, salt, and pepper. Toss by hand to combine.

3. To form the dumplings: Remove 1 wonton wrapper from the package, covering the others with a **damp cloth**. **Brush** the edges of the wrapper lightly with water. Place 1 rounded teaspoon[1] of the tofu mixture in the center of the wrapper. Shape as desired. Set on a **half sheet pan** and cover with a **damp cloth**. Repeat until all the filling is used.

4. Lightly lube a **steamer basket** with **cooking spray**. Position dumplings in the steamer with plenty of space between them and steam for 10 to 12 minutes over medium-high heat. Serve immediately.

[1] It's better to underfill than overstuff a dumpling or wonton.

PEAR WALNUT WONTONS

This ridiculously delicious winter dessert is even better when served hot over vanilla ice cream.

TIP Wontons can also be shaped as ravioli by sealing two wrappers together, or as tortellini; see page 14 for more details.

// SOFTWARE

¼	cup	H$_2$O	
¼	cup	sugar	
1		vanilla bean	split and scraped
1	tablespoon	orange liqueur	
6	ounces	dried pears	roughly chopped
1¼	ounces	walnuts	toasted and finely chopped
25 to 30	small	wonton wrappers	
2	quarts	peanut oil	for frying

// PROCEDURE

1. Bring the water and sugar to a simmer in a **small saucepan** over medium heat, stirring occasionally, until the sugar is dissolved. Remove from the heat and stir in the vanilla bean scrapings and orange liqueur.

2. Process the pears in a **food processor** until finely chopped, stopping to scrape down the bowl if necessary. Add the sugar syrup and pulse just until combined. Transfer the this mixture to a **bowl** and stir in the walnuts. Refrigerate the filling to cool completely, about 1 hour. The filling may be made up to 1 day ahead of time.

3. Heat the oil in a **6-quart Dutch oven fitted with a deep-fry thermometer** to 360°F.

4. To form the dumplings: Remove 1 wonton wrapper from the package, covering the others with a **damp cloth**. **Brush** the edges of the wrapper lightly with water. Place 1 rounded teaspoon of the pear mixture in the center of the wrapper. Shape as desired. Set on a **half sheet pan** and cover with a **damp cloth**. Repeat until all the filling is used.

5. Gently submerge the wontons in the oil, 7 or 8 at a time. Fry until golden, about 2 minutes. Remove to a **cooling rack set in a half sheet pan** lined with **newspaper** and cool for at least 5 minutes before serving, unless of course you go with the ice cream option, in which case hotter is better.

The scene: Two lone cowboys ride the range. Rusty is young, flexible, and energetic. His handlebar mustache is offset by a cheetah-print scarf worn rakishly around the crown of his hat. Gus is a grumpy old trail dog with a perpetual burr up his butt.

GRUMPY GUS: You know, Rusty? Nothing burns me up quite like when folks take a good, honest piece of American kibble and go fussing with it, dressing it up, like it was one of them fuzzy old... (searches for the word)

RUSTY: Poodles!

GG: Poodles is right! Case in point: chili. Do you know, Rusty, there's folks actually compete with chili, like in a culinary rodeo?

R: That don't make no sense!

GG: No, it don't make no sense.

R: How are you supposed to get a saddle on a bowl of red?

GG: What I'm talking about here, Rusty, is the fact that a good, honest bowl of chili don't need no mushrooms. Don't need no 'taters. Don't need no duck fat. Don't need no chocolate, no jujubes, no... Why, it sure don't need none of that tofu.

R: It sure don't need no beans.

GG: No, it don't need no beans. (to camera.) Not that there's anything wrong with beans per se. It's just, well, when a feller's putting his fork into something he expects what he's expecting. And if he don't get what he's expecting a feller's likely to get a little disoriented.

R: Wh... Just like that time I met that saloon girl in Dodge. I could've swore she was...

GG: No. No. No! That ain't what I'm talking about. I'm talking about the fact that chili making is all about taking a few little barely edible bits and pieces and converting it into a sublime gestalt of flavor and texture.

R: I thought it was about cooking.

GG: No sir, it's about...

Next scene: Open range, campfire, night... a mysterious stranger has joined our intrepid duo, who upon close examination remarkably resembles Deb Duchon in a mustache.

GG: Now, the history of chili...

R: ...with an "i"...

GG: Yes, with an "i." (to camera) Used to be foggier than Rusty's head after a night in town. That is, of course, until this mysterious stranger wandered into camp. Go ahead, Mysterious Stranger, tell 'em what you done told us.

MYSTERIOUS STRANGER: Well, nobody really knows how that dish we call chili con carne originated.

GG: Hence, the mystery.

MS: But they do know it didn't come from Mexico.

R: Huh?

MS: However, the predominant flavors—the cumin and the chile peppers and the oregano—they did.

R: (to GG) Look how soft his skin is!

GG: Well, Rusty, he probably uses sunscreen. (to camera) As should we all.

MS: Some nutritional anthropologists say that chili came with a group of sixteen families from the Canary Islands who came and settled near San Antonio in 1731. Other people say that the first recipe for chili con carne...

R: (to GG) That means "chili with meat."

GG: Thank you, Rusty. Now are you going to let the little feller finish?

R: Okey-dokey.

GG: Okay, then.

MS: ...was written by a seventeenth-century nun named Mary of Agrada. She said that recipe came to her when she was in a trance.

R: A nun!

GG: A trance!

GG & R: Mmm hmm!

MS: But I think it was concocted by cooks in the 1850s. They pounded together dried beef and fat and salt and chile peppers into bricks. And those bricks could be reconstituted in hot, boiling water.

R: (to GG) What's "reconstituted"?

GG: Ahh, it's French, I think, for "putting something together." I don't know.

MS: But the real advance in chili making came in 1890, when a spice mix called chili powder hit the market.

GG: Well, I don't know about that. 'Round here we make our own chili powder. But it's a dang good story. Say, stranger, you want some more coffee?

MS: You got decaf?

GG: (looks at Rusty and then slowly looks to camera) You know, stranger, I think maybe it'd be best for all of us if you just rode on tonight.

MS: Well, fine then. You boys smell bad anyway.

R: Smell bad?

(GG and R smell themselves and then watch MS ride off)

R: Side saddle? Strange.

GG: Well, Rusty, I reckon that's why they call 'em "strangers."

R: I better tend to the horses.

GG: Yep. And I better tend to the chili powder. (to camera) And if you're going to make some quality chili powder...

GUS'S POWER GRUMP CHILI POWDER

ABOUT ¾ CUP

// **SOFTWARE** ///

3		dried ancho chiles	stemmed, seeded, and sliced
3		dried cascabel chiles	stemmed, seeded, and sliced
3		dried arbol chiles	stemmed, seeded, and sliced
2	tablespoons	whole cumin seeds	
2	tablespoons	garlic powder	
1	tablespoon	dried oregano	
1	teaspoon	smoked paprika	

// **PROCEDURE** ///

1. Place all of the chiles and cumin in a **cast-iron skillet** over medium-high heat. Cook, moving the pan around constantly, until you begin to smell the cumin toasting, 4 to 5 minutes. Set aside and cool completely.

2. Once cool, place the chiles and cumin in a **blender** along with the garlic powder, oregano, and paprika. Process until a fine powder is formed. Allow the powder to settle for at least 1 minute before removing the lid of the blender. Store in an **airtight container** for up to 6 months.

WHO IS THIS MYSTERIOUS STRANGER?

| Separated at birth.

THE BIG CHILI

4 SERVINGS

// SOFTWARE //

3	pounds	stew meat	beef, pork, or lamb
2	teaspoons	peanut oil	
½	teaspoon	kosher salt	
1	12-ounce bottle	beer	medium ale[1]
1	16-ounce container	salsa	
1	ounce	tortilla chips	about 30 standard chips
2		chipotle chiles	canned in adobo sauce, chopped[2]
1	tablespoon	adobo sauce	from the can of chipotle chiles
1	tablespoon	tomato paste	
1	tablespoon	Chili Powder	see page 173
1	teaspoon	ground cumin	

NOTE FROM GUS ON SERVING OPTIONS: Well, you put the chili in a bowl, you put a spoon in your chili, you put your chili in your mouth. That's the way I see it. But iff'n ya gotta go and fuss with it, then we'll allow a fine brunoise of onion or a squeeze of lime with a chiffonade of cilantro. But that's it!

// PROCEDURE //

1. Toss the meat in a **large mixing bowl** with the oil and salt.

2. Heat a **6-quart heavy-bottomed pressure cooker** over high heat until hot. Add the meat in 3 or 4 batches and brown on all sides, about 2 minutes per batch. As each batch is browned, remove the meat to a **clean large bowl**.

3. When all of the meat is browned, add the beer to the cooker to deglaze the pot. Scrape the browned bits from the bottom of the pot. Return the meat to the pressure cooker along with the salsa, tortilla chips, chipotle chiles, adobo sauce, tomato paste, chili powder, and cumin and stir to combine. Lock the lid in place according to the manufacturer's instructions. When the steam begins to hiss out of the cooker, reduce the heat to low, just enough to maintain a very weak whistle. Cook for 25 minutes. Remove from the heat and carefully release the steam according to the manufacturer's instructions. Season with additional salt, if desired. Serve immediately.

NOTE FROM RUSTY REGARDIN' PRESSURE COOKERS: They's mighty nice, but if you ain't got one, don't despair. Just get yourself a nice, big, heavy Dutch oven. Preferably one that's cast iron. Do your meat browning in there, then add all your ingredients, bring it to a boil, clamp on that lid, and toss it in a 350-degree oven for two to two and a half hours, stirring every half hour. When the meat is fork tender, remove and cool for half an hour before serving.

[1] Note from Gus on beer: Now, light beer ain't hardly beer at all. So that's out. Heavier brews like porter and stout tend to get bitter when you cook with them. So we're just going to stick with a good old middle-of-the-road ale, although a straightforward lager would do just fine in a pinch.

[2] Note from Gus on chiles: Chipotle chiles in adobo sauce ain't nothin' but a piquant mixture of ground chiles, herbs, and vinegar. Chipotles, of course, are nothing but smoked jalapeños, but that's the thing that's challenging about learning your chiles. You see, in Mexican parlance the dried, fresh, and smoked version of the very same pod may all have different names.

TIDBIT In the Old West, cowboys would often throw bulls' eyeballs into their chili.

SANDWICHCRAFT

EPISODE 114 | SEASON 8 | GOOD EATS

This episode was one of two we produced specifically aimed at "cooking with your kids." The mission was to give parents and their offspring some of the tools necessary to get into the kitchen together and really work as a team and to give the younger participants some actual skill goals in regards to tools and techniques. The foods we targeted in these shows (soup and sandwich) are universally adored by kids and adults alike, so they seemed like a good place to start.

I'm convinced that Americans have forgotten how to build an honest-to-goodness sandwich. That's because, as with the hamburger, we've lowered our standards to those of fast-food producers and so-called "delis" that know little, if anything, about the subtle physics of flavor and form required to create the gestalt represented by a truly good sandwich.

TRIVIA This episode marked the third appearance of my nephew Elton, who of course isn't my nephew at all but a fine young man named John Herina, who I believe is currently enrolled at West Point. My sister Marsha is also not my sister but Merrilyn Crouch, an actress of limited scope and skill (just kidding, Merrilyn).

NOTE: I've noticed through the years that parents are very skittish about allowing their kids to handle kitchen tools. My own theory is that if they don't start soon, by the time you think they're ready, they won't want to try. I put a knife (albeit a short one) in my daughter's hand at age five, and she hasn't cut herself yet. I watch over her and try to make sure her technique is sound, but you know what? If the knives are sharp and she's careful, odds are when the blood does flow (and that is inevitable, my friends) a simple bandage rather than a tourniquet will suffice.

Legend states that in the first century B.C., a rabbi named Hillel the Elder took one piece of matzo, placed on top of it a paste composed of fruit, nuts, and spices, with a little bit of wine just to be safe, and stuck another matzo on top, thus inventing the sandwich. In the Middle Ages, we didn't have much in the way of plates, so we often took our suppers on great, greasy slabs of bread we called trenchers. Sometimes when we were really hungry—and that was most of the time—we ate the trencher too. That's not really a sandwich, though, is it? Well, don't feel too bad, my foul-smelling little friend. Truth is, the word *sandwich* didn't even come into existence until 1762. Again relying on legend here, during an all-night marathon card game, the notorious gambler John Montague, the fourth earl of Sandwich, demanded that his manservant bring him a couple of slices of beef in between some bread so that he could take nourishment without having to abandon a winning hand. Well, it seemed to be a pretty good concept, because within days other gamblers were ordering the same as "Sandwich," and the name stuck.

Is any of this actually, verifiably true? No. I doubt that any of it is. The sandwich concept is so simple and so obvious that I feel certain it just happened without any earth-shattering moment in edible evolution.

TIDBIT The modern American sandwich probably would not be possible were it not for events that took place in Chillicothe, Missouri, in 1928, the year the Chillicothe Baking Company started selling bread . . . sliced. The concept caught on, and in 1928 Iowa inventor Otto Rohwedder patented an automatic bread slicer. The rest is . . .

SETTING STRAIGHT SOME NOMENCLATURAL ISSUES

DAGWOOD: A multilayer sandwich constructed on loaf-style sliced bread, often with extra layers of bread added between layers. Named for the comic-strip character Dagwood Bumstead (husband of Blondie), who seems to have derived pleasure in life only from large sandwiches and sofacentric naps. The "club" sandwich is perhaps the most famous of the form.

HOAGIE: A made-to-order that originated in Philadelphia sometime around WWI. It's typically served on an 8-inch-long oblong roll and filled with a combination of meat, cheese, lettuce, and onions liberally lubed with an oregano vinaigrette.

ITALIAN: Layered sandwich on a soft Italian roll or loaf, longer in any case than a hoagie. A real Italian has meat and cheese but no lettuce or any vegetation other than the occasional pickle. The dressing is mustard and oil, salt and pepper. Although Cubans might disagree, the sandwich named after that island is of Italian descent, at least in name.

SUBMARINE: A very long sandwich resembling the craft whose name it bears. The sub is typically cross-cut into smaller sandwiches.

PO-BOY: A sandwich from New Orleans featuring French bread filled with some form of fried seafood. Although many supposed "po-boys" embrace grilled or broiled ingredients, I would argue that if it ain't fried somebody lied. My personal favorite is a calamari po-boy, which, as far as I know, was invented by . . . me.

The name means "wet bread" in French and refers to a sandwich traditionally made in and around Nice. Fans of that area's cuisine will no doubt recognize that this is little more than a *salade niçoise* on bread. Since I've never had a *salade niçoise* that I didn't think would have been mightily improved by the addition of croutons, this is, for me, a perfect storm of a sandwich. When I do encounter a *salade niçoise* at a restaurant I usually ask for it to be served on a day-old baguette, which gets me funny looks, to be sure.

Take a look at the ingredients below, and you'll see that the makings also mimic a traditional tunafish sandwich on a submarine roll.

// SOFTWARE //

1	tablespoon	red wine vinegar	
½	teaspoon	Dijon mustard	
½	teaspoon	kosher salt	
¼	teaspoon	black pepper	freshly ground
3	tablespoons	olive oil	
1	16- to 18-inch	baguette	
12	ounces	canned tuna	packed in oil or water, drained and crumbled
1	small	green bell pepper	cut into thin rings
1	small	red onion	cut into thin rings
2	large	eggs	hard-cooked and sliced[1]
1	cup	kalamata olives[2]	chopped
1		tomato	thinly sliced

// PROCEDURE ///

1. **Whisk** the vinegar, mustard, salt, and black pepper together in a **small mixing bowl**. Continue whisking while gradually adding the oil. Brisk whisking and slow drizzling will be rewarded with a fine emulsion, essentially a vinaigrette. Set aside.

2. **Slice** the baguette horizontally into 2 pieces. Tear out some of the soft bread in the center of each piece, making a shallow well in the bread. Place the tuna, bell pepper, onion, eggs, olives, and tomato on the bottom side of the bread in that order. Drizzle the vinaigrette over the vegetables, top with the second piece of bread, and wrap tightly in **plastic wrap**. Leave at room temperature for 2 hours before serving.[3]

3. Cut into 4 sandwiches and serve.

[1] To achieve the "hard-cooked" condition, I prefer to steam rather than boil my eggs. I find that 12 to 14 minutes does the trick.

[2] Strictly speaking, niçoise olives would be the officially sanctioned choice here, but I rarely keep the little buggers around, whereas kalamatas are always in my kitchen.

[3] This is absolutely critical. Unless the bread has time to soak up some dressing and soften a bit you won't be eating a *pan bagnat*. Besides, if the bread is hard, you'll take a bite and send the filling flying across the room. And you'll probably break a tooth, to boot.

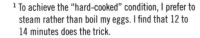

¾ CUPS

As a father I can attest to the fact that by and large the larvae of the species resist the ingestion of vegetation. This condition results from the fact that their taste buds are particularly sensitive to bitter flavors and the fact that the nasty little tots are naturally ornery. This spread is one way to get them to down the goods with a minimum of the fuss that has driven many a parent to nasty cases of the rage shakes.

// SOFTWARE

1		red bell pepper	cut into rings
1	medium	onion	cut into rings
4	cloves	garlic	crushed
1	small	zucchini	sliced
1	tablespoon	olive oil	
8	ounces	cream cheese	
	to taste	kosher salt	
	to taste	black pepper	freshly ground

// PROCEDURE

1. Heat the oven to 400°F.

2. Toss the bell pepper, onion, garlic, and zucchini with the oil in a **large mixing bowl** until well coated.

3. Spread the vegetables evenly on a **half sheet pan lined with aluminum foil** and roast, tossing occasionally, until they are soft and just beginning to brown around the edges, about 45 minutes. Remove from the oven and cool completely.

4. Transfer the vegetables to a **food processor** along with the cream cheese and process until a spreadable amalgam is produced, but stop short of complete smoothness. Kids like chunky, as long as they can't discern the presence of actual vegetables. Do not process until smooth, or they'll probably complain.

5. Taste and season with salt and pepper.[4] To serve, spread on soft bread, such as challah or focaccia, or stuff into a pita. Can be stored in the refrigerator in airtight containment for a week.

[4] Parents tend to undersalt their kids' food because they think that salt is bad for them, which is nonsense. In fact, a touch of salt is actually better at counteracting bitterness than sugar (but that's another show).

CUBAN SANDWICH

4 SERVINGS

Aside from peanut butter and jelly, the Cuban is my favorite sandwich of all time. So take your time and get this right . . . for my sake.

// SOFTWARE

4		hoagie rolls[5]	
2	tablespoons	yellow mustard	
4	ounces	baked ham	thinly sliced
4	ounces	roast pork	thinly sliced
4	ounces	provolone cheese	thinly sliced
10		dill pickles	thinly sliced
1	tablespoon	unsalted butter	at room temperature

// PROCEDURE

1. Split the rolls horizontally in half, leaving one edge intact. Lay the rolls open and spread each side with the mustard. Divide the ingredients evenly among the 4 rolls: Start with the ham, followed by the pork, cheese, and pickles. Close the bread to complete the sandwich.

2. Heat a **panini maker** or **sandwich press**.[6] When it's good and hot, lube the bottom side of the press with butter. Place the sandwiches inside, then butter the top of the buns.

3. Close the lid and press down hard and count to ten. Cook until the cheese is melted and the bread is nicely browned, about 10 minutes. Serve warm to a grateful world.[7]

[5] Aficionados usually agree that the bread is critical to the success of this sandwich. Real "Cuban" bread is very similar to simple Italian white bread, only with fat added, usually in the form of lard. If you live in either Tampa or Miami, Florida, you can scare up the real deal, no problem. The closest thing I can find in my neck of the woods comes out of megamart bakeries as "hoagie" bread.

[6] I don't like naming names when it comes to equipment, but I will say that I would avoid any press that costs less than, say, $75. I also have to say I would avoid any make or model bearing the name of a former boxing great, as they tend to be (ironically) underpowered.

[7] The meat, cheese, and pickle trio won't properly meld without due pressure, and only the biggest commercial presses have lids sufficiently heavy to apply it. So, keep a big hot pad or oven mitt around and use it to apply direct downward pressure on the press whenever you have an opportunity. I actually checked with a bathroom scale once and found that 30 pounds of pressure, applied at least three times during the cooking process, delivered the best results. This squeeze is as critical to success here as the tamp is to a good espresso pull, so don't get lazy on me.

If you don't have a sandwich press, you can wrap 6 fireplace bricks in aluminum foil, heat them in a 500°F oven for 1 hour, and then press the sandwich between them for 10 minutes. This is a bit cumbersome, I'll grant you, but better than having no Cuban at all.

THE *GOOD EATS* UNIFIED THEORY OF SANDWICH PHYSICS

COROLLARY 1: Soft fillings are best served on soft breads, and hard fillings are best served on harder breads.

COROLLARY 2: When wet ingredients, such as tomatoes, are used, a thin coating of mayonnaise, butter, cream cheese, or oil should be applied to the bread as a moisture barrier.

COROLLARY 3: Avoid placing layers of slippery, slide-y substances next to one another, as they undermine stability.

COROLLARY 4: Never, ever use a bread you wouldn't eat on its own.

COROLLARY 5: Most sandwiches are better hot. (This is a recent addition to the theory and I stand by it. Even pb&j is better if the pb is briefly nuked.)

Kids can be tough to feed. As they get older and adopt the modern American mobile mentality, things get even worse. If we're not careful, they'll come untethered from their moorings and drift off into the world without a clue as to how they should feed themselves, which is why they so often fall prey to prepared meal replacement drive-through Styrofoam-encased garbage. Can this fate be avoided? Of course, but only if you're willing to cook and eat with your kids.

I believe that when kids work to produce their own food, they eat better. They learn self-reliance, nutrition, how to work within a team, and even a budget. And unlike anything you can jack into a DS or a Gameboy, cooking'll make better people out of them. You'll get more quality family time, and if you train them right, by the ripe old age of fourteen or fifteen, they'll be cooking dinner for you. And isn't that why we have children to begin with, to take over some of the labor? Well, of course it is. So, where do we start? Soup.

KNOWLEDGE CONCENTRATE

▷○ Soup is delicious and nutritious, and soup making is one of the bedrock skills of the kitchen world. A few decent tools, a humble handful of ingredients, and a smidgen of patience is all that is required to turn your kids into cooks and just about any soup into . . . well, you know.

▷○ Fire may get top billing on the list of man's big, bad culinary breakthroughs, but flames didn't really reach their full potential until they were teamed up with water. That's because water is capable not only of conveying heat but also of extracting both flavor and nutrients.

Nobody knows who actually came up with the idea of cooking in water, but we do know that man was taking soup orders before he actually had a pot to make it in. For instance, in Neolithic Scotland, they used to stretch animal skins over wooden tripods, like big bowls, suspended over campfires. Surprisingly, the skins would not catch on fire because the water inside kept them cool enough to avoid combustion. In other parts of the world, fire-heated stones would be dumped into skin sacks or adobe-lined holes full of water until the temperature rose high enough to cook whatever bits and pieces were tossed in. Luckily, today we have pots and pans. But finding the right one of those can be a challenge too (see sidebar, right).

John Huston, one of my favorite filmmakers of all time, used to say that 90 percent of the job of directing was casting. I believe that 90 percent of cooking is shopping. This is especially true of soup. If you have quality ingredients, all you have to do is not mess them up. With that in mind, I offer a few key tips for seeking out vegetation for the soup below.

Produce should be heavier than it looks like it ought to be.

The tassel at the end of ears of corn should always be moist and kind of sticky.

Stalks (celery), tap roots (carrots), and pods (green beans) should always be bright in color and they should be snappy rather than, well . . . bendy.

To the best of my knowledge, nothing is completely hard when it's ripe—not even a watermelon. The one exception I can think of is garlic. Heads of garlic should be darned hard.

When it comes to fruits and vegetables, bruises are bad. So are moldy spots and just about any other blemish. Spots, however, are not necessarily signs of damage or age. For instance, most bananas aren't truly ripe until their skin turns spotty. But bananas don't go into vegetable soup too often, do they?

If it grows under the ground, it shouldn't have sprouts. This means potatoes, sweet potatoes, and heads of garlic. Some forms of ginger appear to have sprouts but they're rhizomes, so they're different.

You know, if kids and parents are going to coexist in the same kitchen, and work without killing each other—figuratively or literally—we should probably do some kind of preparing for the event. And that really just comes down to three things: space, tools, and time.

If a child can walk up to a countertop and easily rest his elbows, that's the perfect work space. If not, then he can go to the kitchen table. Stools and step units are okay as long as they're safe, secure, and comfortable. The last thing you want is to put a knife in the hand of a kid on a seesaw. Many parents tend to stick their kids at cluttered stretches of counter where obstacles can be distracting and dangerous. Make a clean space and consider getting them their own cutting board to help define that space.

It's very important for kids to have their own set of cooking tools so they can easily handle things. But this doesn't mean you have to buy a bunch of new stuff. Just match the hand to the size of the tool. A paring knife is always a good place to start as far as edgeware's concerned, and you may want to pick up a small wooden spoon and a whisk.

Take time with your kids. Don't get them cooking when the stress of your day and the need to hurry and get a meal on the table is going to overwhelm them. Make the time, take the time, and odds are it will be enjoyable for you and for them. And remember, the trip is more important than the destination. There will be disasters. Nice thing is, most of them will still be edible.

SOUP POTS

I own one soup pot, and here are its specs:

VOLUME: Ten quarts. If I need bigger I break out my turkey-frying pot and cook in the great outdoors. Anything smaller is a waste of space.

MATERIAL: Stainless steel with a reinforced base. Such a vessel is much lighter and less costly than the fully clad version constructed of copper sandwiched by outer layers of steel.

SHAPE: Narrow. Liquids cooking inside a pot that's taller than it is wide will enjoy enhanced convection flow through the pot. Also, since there is less surface exposure, evaporation is minimized, which is especially helpful when making long-cooking stocks. Taller, deeper pots also help to keep the foods within submerged.

Primitive soup pot.

ON KNIFE WORK:

- ▶ Stand comfortably.

- ▶ Cut with whichever hand you write with.

- ▶ Hold the knife firmly but don't stretch your index finger up the spine of the knife. This is a position assumed only by people who actually want to cut themselves.

- ▶ Firm doesn't mean "clutch." Think of it as a putter, not a baseball bat.

- ▶ When in action, the blade should make contact with the board at a 45-degree angle.

- ▶ The knife hand drives the blade, while the "feeder" hand steers the food into it. Remember, unless you're carving a hunk of meat, the blade doesn't chase the food, the food comes to the blade.

- ▶ When cutting veggies for soup, the harder the produce, the smaller the pieces.

- ▶ "Chop" is a bad word because it suggests a force that cuts straight up and down. Never, ever do this. Always slice the blade through the food, because horizontal force plus vertical force is always more efficient.

- ▶ When the knife is not working it should be at rest on its cutting board. Don't walk around with it, wave it, throw it, or anything else with it. And never put it in the dishwasher.

- ▶ Oh, and no open-toed shoes in the kitchen . . . ever.

If you like this finger, don't do this!

BAD

PINCH

REST OF FINGERS WRAP

JUST AS BAD!

Unless you're going into battle with a broadsword, you'll want to skip this grip as well.

A loose but firm grip in which the blade is pinched between thumb and forefinger.

GARDEN VEGETABLE SOUP

6 TO 8 SERVINGS

If your kids never ate any vegetable dishes other than this soup, they'd live to see a hundred.

// SOFTWARE ///

4	tablespoons	olive oil	
2	cups	leeks	white part only, chopped
2	tablespoons	garlic	finely minced
	to taste	kosher salt	
2	cups	carrots	peeled and cut into rounds
2	cups	potatoes	peeled and diced
2	cups	green beans	cut into ¾-inch pieces
2	quarts	vegetable or chicken broth	homemade would be best
4	cups	tomatoes	peeled and chopped
2	ears	corn	kernels cut off, cobs discarded
½	teaspoon	black pepper	freshly ground
¼	cup	fresh parsley	packed and chopped
2	teaspoons	lemon juice	freshly squeezed

// PROCEDURE ///

1. Heat the oil in a **large, heavy-bottomed stockpot** over medium-low heat. Once hot, add the leeks, garlic, and a pinch of salt and sweat until they begin to soften, 7 to 8 minutes. Add the carrots, potatoes, and beans and continue to cook for 4 to 5 more minutes, stirring occasionally.

2. Add the stock, increase the heat to high, and bring to a simmer. Once simmering, add the tomatoes, corn kernels, and pepper. Reduce the heat to low, cover, and cook until the vegetables are fork tender, 25 to 30 minutes. Remove from heat and add the parsley and lemon juice. Season to taste with salt. Serve immediately.

GRAPE GAZPACHO

4 SERVINGS

Technically speaking, a gazpacho is a raw vegetable soup from Andalusia, in Spain, composed of raw vegetables, often with stale bread, olive oil, and garlic. Tomatoes are a rather recent addition, so I don't feel bad about calling this curious creation by that name. I have yet to meet a kid who doesn't love this.

// SOFTWARE //

1	small	cucumber	seeded and chopped, about 1 cup
1		Granny Smith apple	peeled, cored, and chopped, about 1 cup
3	medium	tomatillos	chopped, about 1 cup
1	pound	seedless grapes	about 3 cups
1	cup	walnuts	toasted and chopped
1	cup	plain yogurt	low- or full-fat
1	cup	white grape juice	
1	teaspoon	rice vinegar	
6	large leaves	fresh mint	if you use dry, all bets are off on the whole kids-loving-it thing
	to taste	kosher salt	

// PROCEDURE //

1. Place half of the cucumber, apple, and tomatillos in a **food processor**. Add all of the grapes, walnuts, yogurt, grape juice, vinegar, and mint. Pulse 9 or 10 times.

2. Combine with the remaining half of the cucumber, apple, and tomatillos in a **large bowl**. Season with salt to taste. Chill for 2 hours in the refrigerator before serving. Serve as an appetizer or soup course.

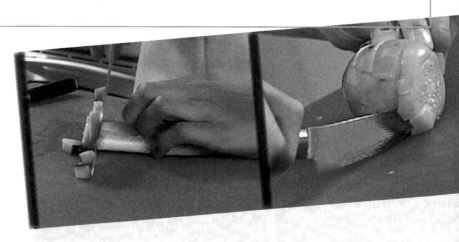

CHRISTMAS SOUP

6 TO 8 SERVINGS

Without fail, this soup is served at the Brown house every Christmas Eve. In other words, it's a tradition. Kids love traditions, so I say, let them make the soup so they can leave a bowl for Santa. Sneaky!

// SOFTWARE //

1	pound	kielbasa	sliced ¼ inch thick, on the bias
	as needed	vegetable oil	
8	cloves	garlic	minced
1	pound	dried red kidney beans	soaked for at least 4 hours or overnight
2	quarts	chicken broth	
1	pound	red potatoes	cut into ½-inch cubes
6	ounces	fresh kale	washed, rinsed, and torn into 1-inch pieces
¼	cup	red wine vinegar	
½	teaspoon	black pepper	freshly ground

TIDBIT The first restaurant opened in Paris in 1765 and served nothing but soups or "restoratives."

// PROCEDURE //

1. Brown the kielbasa in a **7-quart Dutch oven** and set over medium-low heat until it has rendered most of its fat, about 15 minutes. Remove the kielbasa from the pot and set aside. If you do not have at least 2 teaspoons of fat, add enough vegetable oil to make 2 teaspoons.

2. Cook the garlic in the fat for 1 to 2 minutes, stirring constantly to prevent the garlic from burning. Add the beans and chicken broth and cook, **covered**, for 45 minutes. After 45 minutes, stir in the potatoes, cover, and cook for 15 minutes, stirring occasionally.

3. Toss the kale into the pot, cover, and cook for an additional 10 minutes, or just until it is tender, but not mushy.

4. Sprinkle with the vinegar and pepper and stir to combine. Return the kielbasa to the pot and cook just until heated through. Taste and adjust seasoning. Serve hot.

NOTE: I'm ever so disgruntled about the sorry state of the kielbasa available at the average megamart. Specialty shops and Polish butchers are about the only places left to find this garlicky delicacy.

There are as many ways to sort and categorize cheese

as there are for wine. You can sort by type of milk, by country, by style, by age, by size, by shape . . . actually, when you think about it, wine is a heck of a lot easier. This explains cheese lock, the phenomenon of involuntary paralysis that many novice cheese-heads suffer when faced with too many options at the cheese counter. I've contemplated many systems of categorization, but in the end I think the easiest way to sort the *galaxie fromage* is by rinds. Learn your rinds well, and 90 percent of the time you'll know what kind of cheese you're getting yourself into.

KNOWLEDGE CONCENTRATE

▷○ **HARD** cheeses possess thick, dense rinds that are often waxed or even oiled. Cheddar, Parmesan, Gruyère, and, my favorite, Manchego are all examples. They're hard because the curd is cut and pressed before molding, so most of the moisture has been squeezed out. Aging further dries and firms these cheeses, which are usually salty, complex, rich, meaty, and very grate-able.

▷○ The rinds of **SEMI-SOFT** cheeses are almost always brown-orange or brown-gray. But this is a challenging family to identify otherwise because it's really two families in one. Rubbery, meaty cheeses, like Edam, represent some of this country's favorite cheeses because they're so gosh-darned user friendly. Then there are washed-rind semi-softs like Époisses and Langres, which are washed in a special kind of brine that sets the inner texture and encourages specific bacteria to grow. These are some of the strongest cheeses around, and can usually be identified by that sticky, orange rind.

▷○ **SOFT RIPENED** cheeses usually come in disks, loaded with a light, fuzzy mold called *Penicillium candidum*. So much of the milk's original moisture is locked inside these jewels that the cheese literally oozes at room temperature. Brie and Camembert are the most famous of this, my other favorite category. Although the rinds are always white in this country due to the use of pasteurized milk, in Europe the raw milk that's usually used creates a reddish or brown rind.

The easiest cheeses to recognize by sight are **MOLD-VEINED** cheeses like Roquefort, Gorgonzola, and Stilton. The mold that resides inside such delicacies requires air to grow, so the compressed curd is punched with needles, creating micro-tunnels for the fungi. Veined cheeses possess a wide range of flavor and texture. They can be creamy, they can be hard, they can be grainy, they can be just mildly sweet, or they can be tongue-numbingly funky. You know what I mean? Other times they smell like gym socks.

FRESH cheeses like cream cheese, feta, cottage cheese, and chèvre are generally under two weeks old when they're sold so they haven't had time to develop any kind of rind. With the exception of brined feta, which is usually quite crumbly, these cheeses are easy spreaders. And they are sometimes rolled in ash, seeds, or leaves before they're sold. Flavors range from grassy fields to hints of citrus.

Cheese is alive, and as such it has likes and dislikes. It likes to be kept cool but not cold, so the top shelf of your refrigerator is the best place for it. It likes to be moist but not wet, and it likes to breathe, so packaging is very important. When it comes to soft, crumbly, or excessively stinky cheeses, I like to go with a plastic container, and I slide a little piece of damp paper towel or slice of apple in there to provide some moisture. The plastic is also good because it prevents the funkiness from spreading around, if you get my drift. I wrap harder cheeses with waxed paper, secured with a little rubber band.

Whenever you're contemplating the service of cheese, always bring it to room temperature before you dine upon it, because cold hardens the fat—and that will just trap aroma and flavor.

If you decide to have a cheese-tasting party, or to serve a cheese course with your next dinner, and I certainly hope that you will, remember that there are no rules. But I am going to make a couple of suggestions that have helped me in the past. Two of them.

1. Never serve more than three cheeses. As far as I'm concerned, you get past three and everything pretty much just tastes like, well . . . cheese.

2. Try to find a theme, a way of tying the three cheeses together. For instance, choose three made from the same type of milk, or with the same rind style, or of similar ages.

Of course, you can just serve one great cheese—say, a nice block of Parmigiano-Reggiano—with several different contrasting accompaniments so that you can get an idea of the cheese's full range of flavors and aromas. Look to serve about a quarter pound of cheese to each diner. And make sure that every cheese has its own knife.

When one has a cheese tasting, there may be leftovers. Should that be the case, consider the following application.

THE BIRTH OF CHEESE!

No one could possibly really know how cheese came into being, but it probably went down like this somewhere in the Middle East: One day a lone Bedouin set across the desert sands to sell his chicken at the nearest oasis-mart. Knowing that he would get thirsty and hungry along the way, he was careful to pack a freshly tanned calf's stomach chock full of milk. After several hours, he finally did get a little on the parched side, so he reached for his treat. But boy, was he in for a big surprise. A combination of the movement of the camel, the heat of the sun, and the rennet in the stomach lining had coagulated the milk into curds and whey. Luckily, after a moment of tasting, the Bedouin realized it was a lucky mistake, and cheese was born!

FROMAGE FORT

2 CUPS

You may use any leftover cheese you wish, such as Cheddar, Parmesan, provolone, fontina, mozzarella, Camembert, or Saint André. Make sure you use a combination that's not too salty.

// SOFTWARE ///

1	pound	leftover cheeses	at room temperature
¼	cup	dry white wine	
3	tablespoons	unsalted butter	at room temperature
2	tablespoons	fresh parsley	chopped
1	clove	garlic	

// PROCEDURE //

1. Remove any rind and/or mold from the cheese. **Grate** hard cheeses and cut others into ½-inch cubes.

2. Combine the cheeses, wine, butter, parsley, and garlic in a **food processor** and pulse until smooth, 1 to 2 minutes. Serve immediately or refrigerate for at least 1 hour for a firmer consistency. The mixture can be stored in the refrigerator for up to 5 days.

IT'S ALIVE!!!

GOVERNMENT CHEESE

Great though many American cheeses are, when it comes to young, runny cheeses like Brie and Camembert, the Europeans have the edge because they use high-quality raw milk, which can be used in this country only to make cheeses that have been aged at least 60 days before sale. The federal government figures that after 60 days, any potentially dangerous bacteria will have been eliminated. Cheeses aged less than 60 days must be made from pasteurized milk.

Pasteurization is named after the scientist Louis Pasteur. He's the guy who figured out that living critters, albeit small ones, are usually to blame when good food goes bad. Pasteurization utilizes heat to destroy the problematic entities. What's interesting is that different times and temperature combinations can be used. For instance . . .

Holding the milk at 145°F for 30 minutes nukes the nasties while preserving some of the body, the character, the flavor of the milk.

Heating milk to 161°F for 15 seconds kills everything, good, bad, and indifferent. It also shuts down enzymes and knocks off a bunch of nutrients. In other words, it kills the milk. But since that method is a hundred times faster than the method above, it's the one most often employed by the dairy industry. Which is why most American milk tastes . . . white. And it's why young American cheeses never quite reach their potential.

CHEESE SOUP

4 SERVINGS

Cooking with cheese is tricky business. That's because cheeses—all cheeses—are emulsions containing water, fat, and protein in differing amounts. Heat complicates matters considerably. It should be applied slowly and never to a greater degree than absolutely necessary.

// SOFTWARE ///

2	tablespoons	unsalted butter	
1	cup	onion	diced small
1	cup	carrot	diced small
1¼	cups	celery	diced small
½	teaspoon	kosher salt	plus more for seasoning
3	tablespoons	all-purpose flour	
1	quart	chicken stock	
1	tablespoon	garlic	minced
1		bay leaf	
1	cup	heavy cream	warm
10	ounces	fontina cheese	grated
1	teaspoon	Worcestershire sauce	
½	teaspoon	Tabasco sauce	
½	teaspoon	white pepper	
1	teaspoon	Marsala	

// PROCEDURE ///

1. Melt the butter in a **large nonreactive pot** over medium-high heat. Add the onion, carrot, celery, and ½ teaspoon salt and cook for 7 to 10 minutes, until the celery and onion become semi-translucent. Reduce the heat to medium, sprinkle the flour over the vegetables, and cook, stirring constantly, for 2 to 3 minutes.

2. Increase the heat to high, gradually add the stock, and bring to a boil, stirring constantly. Reduce the heat to low and add the garlic and bay leaf. **Lid** the pot and simmer for 30 minutes, or until the vegetables are soft.

3. Fetch out the bay leaf. Remove from the heat, add the warm cream, and puree with a **stick blender** or in a **conventional blender**. Gradually add the cheese one small handful at a time and stir until melted before adding the next handful. Stir in the Worcestershire sauce, Tabasco sauce, white pepper, and Marsala. Taste and season with additional salt, if desired. Return the soup to low heat until warmed through.

AB: Most of the folks walking around on this planet are Lactose intolerant. That means that they lack the enzyme necessary to break down lactose, a sugar that occurs naturally in milk. Now, when these people drink milk, or eat young cheeses, they get a painful punch from...

Lactose Man: I'm Lactose Man!

AB: Yes, from Lactose Man. You know what, Lactose Man? I'm not afraid of you.

LM: Oh, you will be. You will be.

AB: Oh, yeah? Take your best shot!

(LM punches AB in the stomach; the next shot has his fist soaking in ice)

AB: You see, cheeses that have a little age on them have had their lactose, or milk sugar, consumed by the bacteria in the cheese. So there's little, if any, lactose still present.

How's your hand, Lactose Man?

LM: Uh, it hurts.

AB: How's the cheese, Lactose Man?

LM: It's good.

TRUE GRITS

After wheat, more acres of this planet are dedicated to the cultivation of maize (we're just about the only people who call it corn) than to any other grass or crop. But relatively few of those acres are dedicated to sweet, corn-on-the-cob corn, the maize that most of us think of when we think of corn. Truth be told, sweet corn really isn't that important as far as foodstuffs go. Neither is popcorn. The really important stuff is either flint or dent corn, named after the dimples that form in the center of the kernels when it dries. These varieties are low in sugar but high in starch, which means that they're well suited to drying and milling (fresh, they just taste nasty). Although the Internet is probably the easiest place to land top-quality cornmeal, you may be able to dig some up at the local megamart as long as you're willing to do a little bit of label reading.

TRIVIA | The "mom" in the opening sequence is my culinary director, Tamie Cook, and the "dull" young man is my production coordinator, Jim Pace. Both of them turned in some very scary performances.

Although I'm not one to fall for clever packaging gimmicks, I have yet to see a decent cornmeal come out of a box . . . ever. And if the bag doesn't say "stone ground" on the bag, just walk away. Ditto any package that bears the words "quick" or "instant." These are overprocessed goods that cannot be trusted. Most stone-ground meals are whole grain and, as such, contain the fatty germ of the kernel, which will eventually go rancid unless used quickly or wrapped and frozen. So look for an expiration date that is at least six months after the date of purchase.

Stone-ground meals come in fine, medium, and coarse grinds. I typically keep medium on hand for use in cakes, some breads, and for dusting pizza peels and the like. Coarse meal is typically used for cornbread and polenta, which is not a grind size but a dish (see below). Grits are another matter.

TIDBIT Cornmeal was imported to Ireland from the United States to relieve the potato famine in 1846.

Here's a little subject that I allowed to become . . . confused in the episode, when I stated that the real difference between polenta and grits was one of procedure. That's not entirely true. Although the processes do differ, the truth is, coarse yellow cornmeal makes polenta, while grits is composed exclusively of coarsely ground hominy—that is, white corn that has been soaked in a potash (lye) solution prior to drying. The Aztecs and the Maya pioneered the process, called nixtamalization, as a method for easily removing the outer husk from kernels of field maize for grinding. Although they didn't realize it at the time, the potash (or more exactly the alkaline properties thereof) helped to up the niacin content of the meal, making it far more nutritious. (The Europeans who took maize back home missed this trick and ended up unleashing several epidemics of pellagra upon the land.) The resulting kernels, called hominy, are used in soups such as posole as well as in tortillas and grits. These days even coarse white corn that has not undergone nixtamalization is often sold as "hominy" grits, but most old-time Southerners say they can taste the difference. And so my general rule is as follows:

Coarse yellow cornmeal is for polenta.

Coarse white cornmeal is for grits.

And that's that.

TIDBIT Maize was eaten in Italy for the first time in 1650.

TIDBIT China is second only to the United States in corn production.

CHEESE GRITS

4 SERVINGS

// SOFTWARE //

2	cups	whole milk	
2	cups	H_2O	
1½	teaspoons	kosher salt	
1	cup	stone-ground hominy grits	
½	teaspoon	black pepper	freshly ground
¼	cup	unsalted butter	
4	ounces	sharp cheddar cheese	grated

// PROCEDURE //

1. Combine the milk, water, and salt in a **large, heavy-bottomed pot** over medium-high heat and bring to a boil. Once the milk mixture comes to a boil, gradually add the grits, **whisking** constantly. As soon as all of the grits have been incorporated, decrease the heat to low and cover the pot.

2. Remove the lid and whisk every 3 to 4 minutes to prevent the grits from sticking or forming lumps; make sure to get into the corners of the pot when whisking. Cook for 20 to 25 minutes, until the texture is creamy.

3. Remove from the heat, add the pepper and butter, and whisk to combine. Gradually whisk in the cheese a little at a time. Serve immediately.

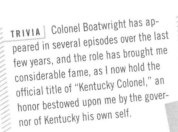

TRIVIA Colonel Boatwright has appeared in several episodes over the last few years, and the role has brought me considerable fame, as I now hold the official title of "Kentucky Colonel," an honor bestowed upon me by the governor of Kentucky his own self.

SAVORY POLENTA

4 TO 6 SERVINGS

// SOFTWARE ///

2	tablespoons	olive oil	plus more if sautéing chilled polenta
¾	cup	red onion	chopped
1½	teaspoons	kosher salt	divided
2	cloves	garlic	minced
1	quart	chicken stock or broth	
1	cup	stone-ground cornmeal	
3	tablespoons	unsalted butter	
¼	teaspoon	black pepper	freshly ground
2	ounces	Parmesan cheese	grated

> **TIDBIT** Every year at the end of Carnivale in Tossignano, Italy, the town consumes over 440 pounds of polenta.

> **TIDBIT** In the first century, Romans made polenta with pearl barley.

// PROCEDURE //

1. Heat the oven to 350°F.

2. Heat the 2 tablespoons oil over medium heat in a **large, oven-safe saucepan**. Add the onion and ½ teaspoon of the salt and sauté until it begins to turn translucent, 4 to 5 minutes. Reduce the heat to low, add the garlic, and sauté for 1 to 2 minutes, making sure not to burn the garlic.

3. Turn the heat up to high, add the broth, and bring to a boil. Gradually add the cornmeal, **whisking** constantly. Once you have added all of the cornmeal, cover the pot and place it in the oven. Cook for 35 to 40 minutes, stirring every 10 minutes to prevent lumps.

4. Once the mixture is creamy, remove it from the oven and add the butter, the remaining 1 teaspoon salt, and pepper. Once they are incorporated, gradually add the Parmesan.

5. Serve as is or pour into a **9-by-13-inch pan lined with parchment paper**. Refrigerate to cool completely.

6. Once the polenta is set, turn it out onto a **cutting board** and cut into squares, rounds, or triangles. **Brush** each side with oil and sauté in a **nonstick skillet** over medium heat until golden brown on both sides.

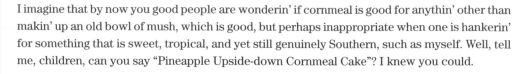

PINEAPPLE UPSIDE-DOWN CORNMEAL CAKE

1 (10-INCH) CAKE

THE COLONEL COOKS!

This next application is one of my favorite desserts of all time . . . sweet, crunchy, caramely, fruity, and undeniably corny. For some unknown reason, I decided to set aside my standard TV persona for this dish and step into the white three-piece suit of Colonel Boatwright, who is an amalgam of Southern gentlemen of a certain age and era. Despite the obvious similarities in haberdashery, hairstyle, and the like, he is in no way meant to be the "Colonel" of fried chicken fame, whom I do admire but never met. I must admit I enjoy the colonel, so I decided to leave the instructions for this fine cake completely and entirely in his words.

I SEE YOU!

I imagine that by now you good people are wonderin' if cornmeal is good for anythin' other than makin' up an old bowl of mush, which is good, but perhaps inappropriate when one is hankerin' for something that is sweet, tropical, and yet still genuinely Southern, such as myself. Well, tell me, children, can you say "Pineapple Upside-down Cornmeal Cake"? I knew you could.

// SOFTWARE ///

1	cup	stone-ground cornmeal	
¾	cup	whole milk	boiling
½	cup	unsalted butter	
1	cup	dark brown sugar	
6	slices	canned pineapple	in heavy syrup
6		maraschino cherries	
⅓	cup	pecans	toasted and chopped
3	tablespoons	syrup	from the can of pineapple
1	cup	all-purpose flour	
2	teaspoons	baking powder	
½	teaspoon	kosher salt	
3	large	eggs	
¾	cup	granulated sugar	
½	cup	canola oil	

// PROCEDURE //

1. Heat the oven to 350°F.

2. We'll start things off by sprinklin' this here stone-ground cornmeal right into this boilin' milk. We're just gonna let that sit and hydrate for 30 minutes.

3. I've got a **10-inch cast-iron skillet** sittin' right on top of medium heat. Yep, there it is. Now, into that we're gonna put that butter. We're gonna let that melt. Not only are we gonna allow that to melt, we're gonna carefully **brush** it all the way up the sides of the pan, so the batter won't stick later on.

4. Our butter's gonna brown just a little bit and we're gonna let that melt all the way. Mmm mmm. Now we're gonna put that dark brown sugar right on top of that butter—gracious me—and just stir that until it melts thoroughly. I reckon that'll take about, oh, I don't know. Looks like 5 minutes is just about perfect.

5. You can see here we've got ourselves a kind of grainy syrup goin', and that's just right, so we're gonna turn that heat all the way off and set our spoon aside safely. Now the fun part. You're gonna very, very carefully place one of these pineapple rings right in the center of the pan. Now we're gonna place more and more circles, right all the way around that first one, just like some kinda gosh-darn planetary orbital thing. One goes there, and it's gonna bubble up a little, that's just from that syrup hittin' the pan.

6. We got ourselves some maraschino cherries, red as a blushin' bride. And we're just gonna put one of them right there in the circle of every one of them pineapples. Now that's gonna be the top of our cake. We're now gonna sprinkle on good Southern pecans. Just sprinkle those right over. Sprinklin', sprinklin', sprinklin' a little bit more, there you go.

7. Last, but by no means least, we're gonna measure ourselves out about 3 tablespoons of this good old pineapple syrup. Just gonna dip right in there and just barely sprinkle that across there. It is gonna hiss at you. Now this just needs to sit here and cool itself down while we go over yonder and deal with that batter.

8. I got my flour in a **big ole bowl**. And I'm gonna **whisk** that up with the baking powder and salt. Alright. We're gonna set that aside.

9. We got ourselves another **bowl**. We're gonna put in it them eggs, and I'm just gonna beat those up just a little bit. And then we're gonna whisk ourselves in the sugar. To that we're gonna add ourselves some good old oil. Just like that, and we'll let them emulsifiers in that egg go to work.

10. We're gonna take our cornmeal milk mush that we done made. We're gonna put that right in this wet mix like that. Oh, well, it's Southern, it's messy. We're gonna mix that up a little, and then we're gonna mosey over to our dry ingredients.

11. And now the secret. This is the secret of the whole operation. The wet stuff goes right on into the dry stuff. Now we're gonna mix 'em together, but we're not gonna overmix 'em. So here we go. One, two, three, four, five, six. Walk away. I said just walk away. That's right. It's gonna be a little lumpy, and I don't care.

12. We're gonna carefully pour our batter directly on the fruit. But do it gently. Do it very, very gently. There we go. This whole contraption is gonna go straight into the middle of the oven for 40 to 45 minutes.

13. When our cakelike device has come out of the oven all beautiful, brown, and crunchy, we're gonna let that cool down now for at least half an hour before you go turnin' its world upside down, or it'll turn yours up, that's for sure. Okay, then, what we're gonna do is we're gonna take a platter or a plate. We're gonna put it right down there over the top, gonna get a good grip, and then as quick as you can, flip that bad boy over. Give it a little thump. "Hello! We're comin' in." Woo! Lookee there. Now I'm gonna take a knife and I'm just gonna cut myself a little wedge.

 TIDBIT Upside-down cakes used to be more commonly known as "skillet cakes."

ART OF DARKNESS III: GANACHE

EPISODE 118 | SEASON 8 | GOOD EATS

Theobroma cacao: **food of the gods.** Few foods fuel the fire of culinary desire quite like chocolate, which is why we decided to dedicate a third episode to its deep brown goodness (see volume 1, *The Early Years*, for the first two). In this case we specifically focus on ganache, which is what the French (in their infinite wisdom) call chocolate and cream that are heated and combined in varying proportions. What I call it is good eats.

Solid "eating" chocolate is amazingly complex stuff composed of cocoa solids, cocoa fat (or cocoa butter), sugar, milk or milk solids, and assorted flavorings. Although chocolate plays by a pretty loose set of rules in Europe, here in the United States, a set of federal regulations called the Standards of Identity govern the composition and nomenclature of chocolate. And here's what they have to say:

UNSWEETENED CHOCOLATE is made from finely ground roasted coca nibs and contains nothing but cocoa solids and cocoa butter, a combination also known as "chocolate liquor" despite the fact that it contains no alcohol whatsoever. Since it also contains no sugar, it's downright disgusting to eat out of hand.

DARK OR BITTERSWEET CHOCOLATE must contain a minimum of 35 percent chocolate liquor, less than 12 percent milk solids, and approximately 30 percent cocoa butter. This classification includes both bittersweet and semisweet chocolates. Although no legal distinction between the two exists, the bittersweet stuff usually contains more chocolate liquor and less sugar than semisweet. All the applications in this show featured bittersweet chocolate, which is a highly predictable and stable form, not to mention darned tasty.

MILK CHOCOLATE must contain a minimum of 10 percent chocolate liquor and 12 percent milk solids. This is America's favorite eating chocolate. But since it's relatively low on cocoa solids and cocoa butter, it's not so great for cooking.[1]

Since it contains no cocoa solids, so-called WHITE CHOCOLATE cannot legally be called "chocolate" in the United States even though it's marketed as "white chocolate" just about everywhere. Go figure. Although I think the flavor is pretty insipid, I do sometimes melt a bar into other chocolate applications to up the cocoa butter content.

French for "coating" or "covering," COUVERTURE chocolate is high-quality chocolate used by professionals for creating confections and, oddly enough, coating and covering them. Couverture chocolate is made with superior beans, ground to a finer particle size, and it also has a higher cocoa butter content than most chocolate for eating (between 32 and 39 percent). Couverture can't be mistaken for a chocolate bar: It is made in 2.2-pound to 10-pound bars or blocks.

I like working with a big bar of chocolate. Most large towns and cities have professional pastry supplies stores where you can pick up couverture chocolate, and there is always, of course, the Internet, which sports a wide range of chocolate resources. Wrapped tightly in foil and kept in a cool place, a big bar will probably last me a year. If you're not up for the megabar, you can always go with the little baby bars you find at the megamart. But just know that you're going to pay a lot more per pound.

Chocolate is hard stuff, and the best way to cut it is with a serrated knife. Instead of forcing the knife through the bar with your hands, use a rolling pin or a mallet on the back of the knife. Chop as evenly as possible, and if you'll be melting the chocolate keep the pieces small. Big chunks will throw off the melting process.

Why reuse the styrofoam mayo model? Because chocolate is essentially the same type of emulsion.

[1] It should be noted that milk chocolate was invented by a Swiss guy name of Daniel Peter in 1875.

BASIC GANACHE FOR COATING AND FROSTING

APPROXIMATELY 3½ CUPS

Here we take advantage of the wide range of fat textures available in both cream and chocolate to create a rich frosting or coating for cakes and cakelike devices.

// SOFTWARE ///

1	pound	bittersweet chocolate	finely chopped
2	cups	heavy cream	

// PROCEDURE //

1. Put the chocolate in the bowl of a **food processor**.

2. Microwave the cream in a **quart-sized microwavable container** (I use a large plastic measuring cup) for 3 to 4 minutes, or until it just simmers. (Keep an eye on it, because with cream a simmer can turn to a frothing boil-over in about 6 seconds.)

3. Slowly pour the cream over the chocolate and leave it alone for 3 minutes.

4. Pulse several times, until the mixture is smooth.

5. Use immediately as a glaze. If a lighter frosting is desired, move the ganache to the work bowl of a **stand mixer** and cool to room temperature, then whip with the **whisk attachment** on high speed for 2 to 3 minutes to integrate air. This can be spread with a spatula.

TRIVIA | Although the girl changes, my key grip Marshall *always* plays the other agent.

CHOCOSICLE

3 CUPS; APPROXIMATELY
8 FROZEN DESSERTS

// SOFTWARE ///

8	ounces	bittersweet chocolate	finely chopped
1½	cups	heavy cream	
1	cup	whole milk	
2	tablespoons	cocoa powder	
2	teaspoons	vanilla extract	

// SPECIAL HARDWARE //

Popsicle Molds: Although plastic molds are the norm, silicone ones are easier to deal with because they're flexible and have better "release" characteristics.

// PROCEDURE //

1. Place the chocolate in a **medium glass mixing bowl**. Set aside.

2. Combine the cream, milk, and cocoa powder in a **medium saucepan** over medium-high heat. **Whisk** constantly until the cocoa is incorporated and the mixture comes to a simmer. Slowly pour the cream over the chocolate and leave it alone for 2 to 3 minutes. Whisk gently until all the chocolate is melted. Whisk in the vanilla.

3. Divide the mixture evenly among ice pop molds and place in the freezer. Freeze for at least 4 hours, until solid. Keep in the freezer in an airtight container for up to a week.

CHOCOLATE TRUFFLES

In culinary parlance the word *truffle* has two distinct meanings.

1. A famed funky fungus found in the ground around the base of hardwood trees—especially oaks—primarily in Italy and France.

2. A small ganache-centered confection that when rolled in a little bit of cocoa powder closely resembles a fungus dug from the base of an oak tree.

// SOFTWARE ///

10	ounces	bittersweet chocolate	finely chopped
3	tablespoons	unsalted butter	
½	cup	heavy cream	
1	tablespoon	light corn syrup	
¼	cup	brandy	
8	ounces	semisweet or bittersweet chocolate	finely chopped
½	cup	Dutch process cocoa powder, finely chopped nuts, and/or toasted coconut	for coating truffles

// PROCEDURE ///

1. Put the 10 ounces bittersweet chocolate and the butter in a **medium glass mixing bowl** and microwave on high for 30 seconds. Remove, stir, and repeat. Set aside.

2. Bring the cream and corn syrup to a simmer in a **small saucepan** over medium heat. Remove from the heat, pour over the microwaved chocolate mixture, and leave unaccosted for 2 minutes.

3. Stir gently with a **rubber spatula**, starting in the middle of the bowl and working in concentric circles until all the chocolate is melted and the mixture is smooth and creamy.

4. Stir in the brandy, then pour the mixture into an **8-inch square glass baking dish** and refrigerate for 1 hour.

5. Scoop the chocolate using a **melon baller or small ice cream disher** onto a **half sheet pan lined with parchment paper** and return to the refrigerator for 30 minutes.

6. Put the cocoa powder, nuts, and/or coconut in separate **pie pans** and set aside.

7. Sandwich a **heating pad** between **two nesting metal mixing bowls** and set the pad to medium. Add the 8 ounces semisweet chocolate to the top mixing bowl. Stir the chocolate occasionally, testing the temperature from time to time, until it reaches 90 to 92°F; do not allow the chocolate to go above 94°F.

8. Remove the truffles from the refrigerator and shape into balls by rolling between the palms of your hands. Use **powder-free vinyl or latex gloves**, if desired.

9. Dip a **large ice cream scoop** into the melted chocolate and turn it upside down to remove the excess. Place one truffle at a time in the scoop and roll it around until it is coated with chocolate. Place the truffle in one of the dishes of either cocoa powder, nuts, or coconut. Move the truffle around to coat; leave the truffle in the coating for 10 to 15 seconds before removing. Transfer the truffle to a **half sheet pan lined with parchment paper**. Repeat until all the truffles are coated. Set in a cool, dry place for at least 1 hour; or store in an airtight container in the refrigerator. Truffles are best when served at room temperature, as cold crushes the aromatic properties and hardens the texture.

TEMPERING CHOCOLATE

Cocoa butter is actually a complex mixture of different fats, each of which crystallizes (solidifies) into one of six different configurations. In order for the chocolate to be solid and snappy at room temperature (like the outside of the chocolate candies Forrest Gump was so fond of), all these fats have to be coerced into the same configuration, which is tricky business because cocoa butter is thermally temperamental. (This explains why the process is called tempering. Or perhaps it's called tempering because so many cooks lose their tempers in the process.)

When you purchase solid chocolate, especially high-quality couverture versions, it is perfectly in temper. The classic approach for using such chocolates as coatings is to melt them to around 122°F, then cool them down to around 89°F to realign the fats, then heat again to 91°F. There are various methods for achieving this, and they're all about as fun as taking a rabid Doberman's temperature. I choose to employ an alternate method in which the chocolate is melted to a suitably liquidous state without crossing above 92°F and thus losing its temper in the first place. I achieve this dream state with the aid of a simple heating pad, as described in the truffle recipe above.

In 1999 we produced the first hourlong *Good Eats* special, "Romancing the Bird," and in that show (which I'm happy to say has become a holiday classic on a par with "A Charlie Brown Thanksgiving"), turkey was, of course, the primary target. One of the axioms I put forth in the preparation of such was that stuffing is evil, pure and simple.

This is because in order to safely avoid running into microbial nasties such as campylobacter and salmonella, which can easily seep into the stuffing via the interior cavity (where the highest percentage of bacteria is typically found), we must cook the bird well beyond the range of what anyone would consider "done": In order to produce tasty and safe stuffing one must essentially kill the messenger. Evil, pure and simple. Oh, and another thing: Due to its bready nature, most stuffing mixtures expand when cooked. Confined to the cavity of a turkey or chicken, expansion is impossible, resulting in a compaction of the mixture that results in something reminiscent of a bad fruitcake, dense and decidedly not good eats . . . again, evil.

Well, little did I know at the time that my proclamation would open a big, fat can of foodie rage. Countless cards, letters, faxes, cables, emails, and texts poured in letting me know in no uncertain terms that I was trampling on seriously sacred ground. And so, after careful consideration I decided to set out to devise a method that would allow stuffing to shed its inherent evilness while actually attaining good eats status.

TIDBIT | The first-century foodie Apicius wrote of Romans stuffing everything from chicken to deer.

TIDBIT | The word *dressing* was introduced in Victorian England, when the term *stuffing* was thought to be improper.

This search ultimately and inevitably took me to *The Tonight Show*—the Johnny Carson version, of course, which represents not only the pinnacle of American late-night television but also the ideal stuffing. That's because although Carson was the foundation flavor on which the show was built, unlike most twenty-first-century chat hosts, Johnny never hogged the spotlight. He held things together without sucking all the air out of the room. In a stuffing, this is exactly what we want from aromatic vegetables.

Typically, aromatic vegetables travel in threes. The combination of onion, celery, and carrot the French call *mirepoix* may well be the most storied of the lot, but when it comes to poultry I prefer the Cajun cousin "trinity," wherein the carrot is replaced by green pepper. Ed McMahon laughed on cue and said things like "Yes!" but mostly he just provided bland bulk just like the bread, rice, potatoes, pasta, or other porous, starchy goods that make up most of a classic stuffing's volume.

Just as the Carson show would have lacked verve without the flamboyant style of bandleader Doc Severinsen, stuffing would just lie there were it not for herbs and spices. Although many modern recipes call for tossing in the entire rack, I prefer to keep stuffing simple. And since it cooks for so long, I actually go with dried herbs.

And what of the band? Well, the band really tied the show together. Bound it, you might say. Stuffing needs a binder too, something to wed the wet and dry. Although I've seen everything from milk powder to mayonnaise used, nothing binds like coagulating proteins suspended in a liquid base. And that means eggs.

On *The Tonight Show*, the first guest was always a big A-list star, onto whom Johnny would lavish most of his attention. In stuffing, this is the lead ingredient, the one the stuffing is usually named for. My favorite is dried mushrooms: small, tasty, and porous as the day is long. Be they porcini, morel, or shiitake, a mere 2 ounces of these fungal mummies will bring plenty of meaty goodness to the party. All you have to do is reanimate them with a little hot water or chicken broth.

Johnny's second guest usually brought some cool animals or technological marvels. And then there a was musical guest who brought, well, noise and big hair. In the stuffing world, both of these would be surprises, ingredients that support the main ingredient and yet retain their own unique flavors and textures.

There you have it:

Aromatics	Binder
Bland starch	Main ingredient
Spices and herbs	Supporting bits and pieces

It worked for *The Tonight Show* and it'll work for your stuffing.

A CASE FOR STUFFING?

Cooks who worked in the big castles and noble houses of sixteenth-century France were expected to not only feed their bosses but also entertain them. One of the devices that they employed for this purpose was the "farce." In a farce, a mouse might very well be stuffed inside a fish, and then that fish might get stuffed into, let's say, a duck, and then the duck into a turkey—or more likely a swan—and then that might go into a pig. And then the pig would go into a cow or a horse, and on, and on, and on. Here's the cool part: The word *farce* comes from *farcir*, which means "to stuff," but the reference is actually a knowing nod to a kind of short play called a farce because it was meant to be stuffed between the acts of a separate long, boring play. The plot of a farce depended on skillfully exploited situations and gags rather than actual character development. So when you think about it, stuffing gave birth to the most adored of all American art forms: the sitcom. Then again, maybe not.

The Tonight Show (in miniature) is a perfect metaphor for stuffing . . . really.

This one goes out to all you poultry lovers who just can't live without your stuffing.

// SOFTWARE

1	10- to 12-pound	turkey	giblets removed
1	quart	chicken broth	
2	ounces	dried mushrooms	
1	cup	onion	chopped
1	cup	celery	chopped
1	cup	green bell pepper	chopped
1	tablespoon	vegetable oil	plus extra for the turkey
1	tablespoon	kosher salt	plus extra for the turkey
3	cups	challah bread	cut into ½-inch cubes
4	ounces	dried cherries	about 1 cup
2	ounces	pecans	chopped
2	large	eggs	beaten
2	teaspoons	dried rubbed sage	
2	teaspoons	dried parsley	
½	teaspoon	black pepper	freshly ground, plus extra for the turkey

TIP To brine this bird, follow the procedure for brining the Deep-Fried Turkey on page 412.

TIDBIT Challah was originally baked by Jewish families in honor of the Sabbath.

// SPECIAL HARDWARE

Getting stuffing in and out of a bird can be tricky and tedious, which is why I use a **reusable organic cotton produce bag**. Stuffing goes into bag, bag goes into turkey, turkey goes into oven, turkey comes out of oven, bag comes out of backside of bird, stuffing comes out of bag. No muss, no fuss.

// PROCEDURE

1. Heat the oven to 400°F.

2. Put the turkey in a **deep bowl** with the stuffing end up. Set aside.

3. Heat the chicken broth in an **electric kettle** (or in the microwave in a **microwave-safe vessel**). Put the mushrooms in a **heatproof bowl** and pour the broth over them. Cover and set aside for 35 minutes.

4. Toss the onion, celery, and bell pepper with the oil and salt in a **large mixing bowl**. Spread the vegetables on a **half sheet pan** and roast for 35 minutes. During the last 10 minutes of cooking, spread the bread cubes over the vegetables, return to the oven, and continue cooking.

5. Drain the mushrooms in a **colander or sieve**, reserving 1 cup of liquid. Chop the mushrooms and put them in a **large microwave-safe bowl** with the vegetables and bread, reserved soaking liquid, cherries, pecans, eggs, sage, parsley, and black pepper. Stir well to break up the pieces of bread. Use your hands to combine, if necessary. Fill the **produce bag**, if using, with the stuffing (a **flexible cutting board** folded into a funnel shape is best for this). Heat the stuffing in the microwave on high for 6 minutes.

6. While the stuffing is heating, rub the bird with oil and season with salt and pepper. Working quickly, place the stuffing in the cavity of the turkey to avoid losing heat (again, a flexible cutting board is best for this). Place the turkey on a **rack** in a **roasting pan** and season with salt and pepper. Roast on the middle rack of the oven for 45 minutes. Reduce the oven temperature to 350°F and cook for another 60 to 75 minutes, until the bird and the stuffing both reach an internal temperature of 170°F. Remove the stuffing if using the bag. Let the bird rest for 15 to 20 minutes before carving. Serve immediately.

TIDBIT | Turducken is a chicken cooked in a duck, cooked in a turkey.

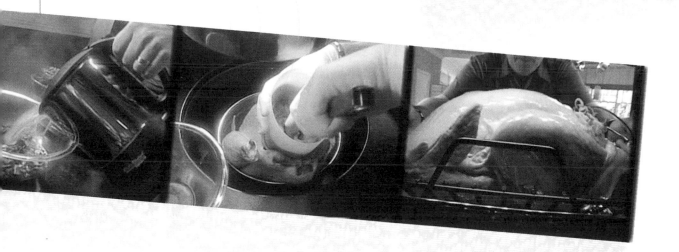

// SOFTWARE

4	small	acorn squash	about 1 pound each
2	tablespoons	unsalted butter	cut into 4 pieces
8	ounces	ground pork	
1	tablespoon	olive oil	
¼	cup	onion	chopped
¼	cup	celery	chopped
¼	cup	carrot	chopped
½	cup	white wine	
1½	cups	cooked rice	
1	10-ounce package	frozen spinach	thawed, drained, and chopped
½	cup	pine nuts	toasted
1½	teaspoons	dried oregano	
	to taste	kosher salt	
	to taste	black pepper	freshly ground

TIDBIT Squash is thought to be one of the first foods cultivated by Native Americans.

// PROCEDURE

1. Heat the oven to 400°F.

2. Cut 1 inch off the top of each squash, reserving the tops, and scoop out the seeds. If necessary, cut off a small portion of the bottom so that they sit upright. Put the squash on a **half sheet pan lined with parchment paper**. Put one piece of butter in the cavity of each squash. Set aside.

3. Cook the pork until no longer pink in a **large sauté pan** over medium heat, 5 to 6 minutes. Remove the meat from the pan and set aside.

4. Return the pan to medium heat and add the oil. Add the onion, celery, and carrot and sauté until they begin to soften, 7 to 10 minutes. Deglaze the pan with the wine.

5. Return the pork to the pan, along with the rice, spinach, pine nuts, oregano, and salt and pepper to taste. Stirring constantly, heat the mixture thoroughly, 2 to 3 minutes. Remove from the heat. Divide the mixture evenly among the squash, top each squash with its lid, and bake for 1 hour, or until the squash is fork tender. Serve immediately.

Pudding. What exactly is it? My dictionary says: "Any of numerous dishes, sweet or savory, served hot or cold, which are prepared in a variety of ways." Thanks!

Unfortunately, etymology's not much help either because the word *pudding* has its root in the Latin *botulus*, which means either "sausage" or "botulism." Luckily we can get some clarification from the British Isles, because four out of five anthropologists who eat pudding do believe that our modern idea of that dessert was born there.

One of the biggest influences from *Monty Python's Flying Circus* is that whenever we need an ugly woman, we put a man in a dress.

Britain's first glimpse of "pudding" probably looked a lot like haggis, which came by way of invading Roman soldiers. It should be noted that the Romans never conquered the Scots (called Picts back then) and went so far as to build a wall to keep them contained up-island. And yet in the end the Scots ended up adopting a Roman food as their national dish. Ironic, don't you think?[1]

Centuries passed, empires fell, and in England the pudding lost its meat and gained more filler, eventually morphing into any bready mass, sweet, savory, edible, or otherwise. Yorkshire pudding (a baked popover) and Christmas pudding (a boiled and booze-drenched fruitcake) are famous examples of such puddings. Somehow, by the dawn of the twentieth century, "pudding" had come to mean just about any dessert you could deliver to an English table. While American kids were shouting, "Hey, Mom, what's for dessert?" English kids were shouting, "Hey, Mum, what's for pud?" Speaking of the other side of the pond, with the possible exception of the colonial cornmeal curiosity hasty pudding, a.k.a. loblolly, American puddings are sweet and spoon-able, akin to mousses and custards. Similarities aside, differences abound. For instance, a mousse gets its light and fluffy texture from the inclusion of whipped egg whites and/or cream. A custard's cut-able curd comes courtesy of the coagulative power of the egg yolk. Puddings, on the other hand—and by that I mean true, American puddings—are always thickened by the gelling action of starch.

Before we get into how that works, we should examine what starch actually is. Plants use photosynthesis to make energy in the form of a simple sugar called glucose.

Let's say for a moment that this battery is a molecule of glucose. Plants store this energy in two different types of structures. Say hello to amylose. Amylose is really nothing but a long—very, very, very long—chain of glucose molecules. The branched version is called amylopectin. When a starch granule swells and bursts in hot liquid, zillions of these molecules are released. They tangle up, trap water, and thicken whatever they're in. However, amylopectin and amylose have different properties, and different types of plants contain varying proportions of each; this is why cornstarch doesn't thicken the same way that potato starch does or the way that flour does. In the end, it's all just sugar. But since these molecules are really, really gigantic, our taste buds can't tangle with them, so they don't taste like anything at all.

My favorite starch sources for puddings are rice, tapioca, and cornstarch.

[1] This style of pudding also continues to thrive in the Cajun tradition of *boudin rouge*, or "blood pudding."

TIDBIT | Trembleque is a creamy pudding made with coconut milk that trembles when turned out of its mold.

TIDBIT | Pease pudding is a thick sauce made from dried legumes.

2 COMMON STARCHES
AMYLOPECTIN   AMYLOSE

STARCHES ARE JUST LONG CHAINS OF GLUCOSE
MOLECULES. STORING ENERGY LIKE D-BATTERIES

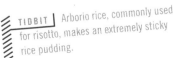

TIDBIT | Arborio rice, commonly used for risotto, makes an extremely sticky rice pudding.

BOMBAY RICE PUDDING[2]

4 SERVINGS

// **SOFTWARE** //

1	cup	long-grain or basmati rice	cooked
1	cup	milk	
½	cup	heavy cream	
¾	cup	coconut milk	
2	ounces	sugar	
¼	teaspoon	ground cardamom	
1½	ounces	golden raisins	
1½	ounces	unsalted pistachios	chopped

// **PROCEDURE** ///

1. Combine the rice and milk in a **large nonstick sauté pan** over medium heat. Heat until the mixture begins to boil. Decrease the heat to low and cook at a simmer, stirring frequently, until the mixture begins to thicken, about 5 minutes.

2. Increase the heat to medium, add the cream, coconut milk, sugar, and cardamom, and continue to cook until the mixture just begins to thicken again, 5 to 10 minutes. Use a **whisk** to help keep the cardamom from clumping.

3. Once the mixture just begins to thicken, remove from the heat and stir in the raisins and pistachios. Transfer the mixture to **individual serving dishes or a glass bowl** and cover with **plastic wrap** directly on the surface of the pudding. Serve chilled or at room temperature.

RICE: IT'S WHAT'S FOR DESSERT

For centuries, rice has been a key dessert ingredient in the cuisines of cultures heavily vested in said cereal. Although many of these cultures have a form of rice pudding, I lean toward those that hail from the Indian subcontinent, where rice is moistened with milk and then subtly flavored with everything from raisins to almonds, pistachios, rosewater, saffron, and cardamom. But first and foremost, we need rice. Rice pudding should never, ever be made with converted rice or boil-in-the-bag rice; those rices have been processed to remove some of the free starch because some people want their rice to not be sticky. Puddings, on the other hand, need stickiness. They need starch.

[2] I've never actually been to India, but ever since I was a kid the idea of Bombay gave me a thrill. Now the city is called Mumbai—not nearly as good a name, if you ask me.

TAPIOCA PUDDING

4 SERVINGS

// SOFTWARE //

½	cup	large pearl tapioca	
2	cups	cold H_2O	
2½	cups	whole milk	
½	cup	heavy cream	
1	pinch	kosher salt	
1	large	egg yolk	
⅓	cup	sugar	
1		lemon	zested

ABOUT THOSE FUNNY LITTLE BALLS

Tapioca is manufactured from the roots of the cassava, a New World plant that today is grown mostly in Africa and Asia. While most of you are probably familiar with the powdered form of tapioca, it's the little pellets or pearls that make tapioca unique. To make these little buggers, cassava roots are smooshed into a kind of pulp and then kneaded and wrung out until the fibers have given up all the starch they possibly can. Then this liquid is kind of dropped onto a hot plate in such a way that it forms pearls as the moisture cooks away. (This is not a procedure that should be undertaken by amateurs.) Quick-cooking tapioca can be found in most major markets. However, landing larger pearls may require taking a trip to the international or Asian foods aisle if you can't find it with the rest of the starches.

// PROCEDURE //

1. Put the tapioca in a **medium mixing bowl** along with the water, cover, and leave overnight.

2. Drain the tapioca in a **sieve or colander**. Put the tapioca in a **slow cooker** along with the milk, cream, and salt. Cook on high for 2 hours, stirring occasionally.

3. **Whisk** together the egg yolk and sugar in a **small bowl**. Whisk small amounts of the tapioca into the egg mixture until you have added at least 1 cup. Then stir the egg mixture into the remaining tapioca in the slow cooker. Add the lemon zest and stir to combine. Cook for an additional 15 minutes, stirring at least once. Transfer the mixture to a bowl and cover with **plastic wrap** directly on the surface of the pudding. Cool at room temperature for 1 hour, then place in the refrigerator until thoroughly chilled.

TIDBIT | Tapioca is an ideal thickener, as it has no flavor of its own and absorbs the essence of the liquid it's cooked in.

TIDBIT | Tapioca tea is also known as bubble tea, boba, pearl tea, and moma.

INSTANT CHOCOLATE PUDDING MIX

3½ CUPS DRY MIX, ENOUGH
FOR 2 BATCHES OF PUDDING

// SOFTWARE ///

3	ounces	Dutch process cocoa powder	about 1 cup
2	ounces	cornstarch	about ½ cup
6	ounces	powdered sugar	about 1½ cups
1½	ounces	nonfat dry milk powder	about ½ cup
1	teaspoon	kosher salt	

// PROCEDURE ///

In a **large bowl or plastic container** with a lid, combine the cocoa powder, cornstarch, sugar, dry milk powder, and salt. Store in an airtight container in the refrigerator for up to 3 months.

APPLICATION

CHOCOLATE PUDDING

4 SERVINGS

// SOFTWARE ///

1¾	cups	Instant Pudding Mix	(above)
2	cups	milk	
2	cups	heavy cream	
1	teaspoon	vanilla extract	

// PROCEDURE ///

1. Put the pudding mix in a **medium saucepan**. Add the milk and cream and **whisk** to combine. Over medium heat, bring the mixture to a boil, constantly whisking gently.

2. Reduce the heat to low and cook for 4 minutes, whisking constantly. Remove from the heat and stir in the vanilla. Pour the mixture through a **fine-mesh sieve** into **individual dishes or a 1½-quart serving dish**. Cover with **plastic wrap** directly on the surface of the pudding. Place in the refrigerator for about 4 hours, to chill completely before serving.

PUDDING GOES "INSTANT"

Instant pudding has an amazing history. It was developed as a restorative by one Alfred Bird, a nineteenth-century English pharmacist whose wife suffered from a wide range of stomach illnesses, including acute allergies to both eggs and yeast. Determined to find a dessert that his wife could enjoy without having any discomfort, Byrd finally struck upon a way to use a flour made from corn to set a flavored mixture much like a custard, only creamier. Mr. and Mrs. Bird started to serve this concoction at dinner parties, and it was such a hit that within a year Alfred Bird and Sons of Birmingham, England, were producing the first instant pudding. We may not have access to the modern industrial instant pudding pantry, but let's see if we can just get by on good old-fashioned know-how.

TIDBIT Instant nonfat dry milk powder contains the same vitamins as whole and low-fat milk.

I think most shoppers face all fruit with a bit of trepidation, but the melon is especially suspicious because it's so guarded, so private, so hidden. Regardless of whether the subject is a watermelon, cantaloupe, Crenshaw, or honeydew, you just know that under that rind Mother Nature is hiding something.

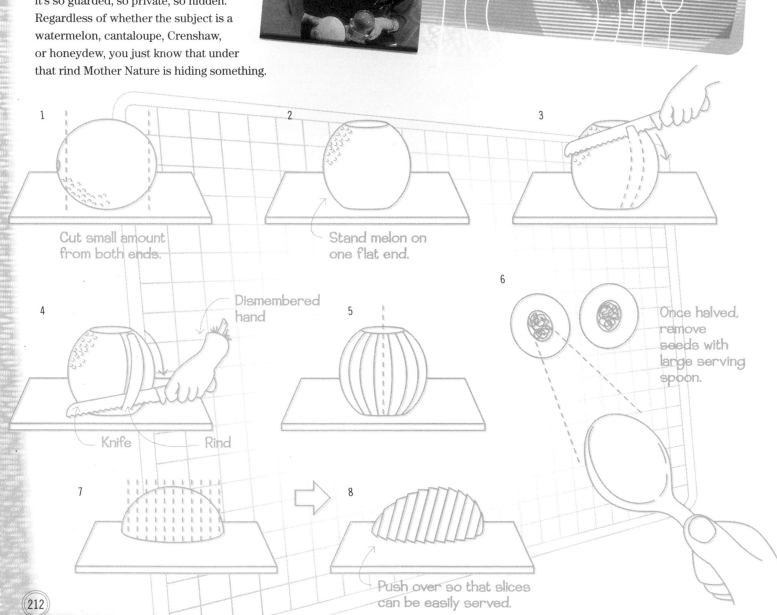

1 Cut small amount from both ends.

2 Stand melon on one flat end.

3

4 Dismembered hand — Knife — Rind

5

6 Once halved, remove seeds with large serving spoon.

7

8 Push over so that slices can be easily served.

Unlike most fruits, melons don't have much in the way of starch reserves, which means that once they "slip" off the vine they aren't going to get any sweeter. So, if you're going to enjoy melons, you're going to have to learn how to pick them right at their peak of flavor.

The best way to detect melon ripeness is with a hand refractometer. If, however, you left yours at home or lent it to an unworthy friend, you'll have to use less absolute means.

Certain varieties such as muskmelons (which most markets in the United States sell as "cantaloupes") will easily break away from or "slip" from the vine when ripe. Oh, wait . . . that's not much help either.

Ripe cantaloupes and honeydew melons will smell sweet, especially at the stem end and especially at room temperature or above.

Slapping or knocking on a ripe melon will create a deep, hollow thumping sound, almost like a drum.

Honeydew melons release their seeds as they mature, so a good firm shake should produce a rattle from within. Unfortunately, muskmelons (cantaloupes) don't cut us the same slack.

My favorite melons I refer to as my three "Cs": Casaba, Charentais, and Crenshaw.

CASABA: Big ole round, yellow thing with a pointy end like an onion. Light, creamy flesh, very juicy, ripe in fall.

CHARENTAIS: Also called French breakfast melons. Some of the finest melon eating anywhere. Striped from pole to pole, like a globe with longitude lines only. Smallish, rarely larger than a big grapefruit. Sweet and floral flavor.

CRENSHAW: Like a casaba but longer. Sweet and fragrant and available as early as midsummer. Best purchased when the blossom end begins to soften. (That's the pointy end.)

Some others worth seeking out:

HONEYDEW: Big, pale-green bowling balls that hit their peak in midsummer. Besides the shake method listed above, you can identify a really ripe specimen if you run your fingers around it; you should feel slight veining on the very surface of the skin.

SANTA CLAUS or Christmas melons ripen in winter, just in time for, you know. Shaped like a blunt-end football, they taste a lot like honeydews.

SPRITE melons hail from North Carolina (or at least that's the only place I've seen them) and are not much bigger than a softball. To me they taste like a crisp combination of a honeydew and an apple—or maybe a pear. Although they're eggshell perfect when unripe, experts on the type will wait for splotchy skin to appear. Perfect to share with a friend with a big spoon, but please serve them warm . . . in fact, all of these melons are best at room temp.

"Fruit is a gamble. I know that going in."
///////////////////////////////////
JERRY SEINFELD

KNOW YOUR MELONS:

inodorous melon with great flavor
Casaba Melon

a winter melon also known as a 'crane'
Crenshaw Melon

santa claus

also known as the Bursa Turkey

HOT MELON SALAD

4 FIRST-COURSE SERVINGS

Use the words *cooking* and *melon* in the same sentence and a lot of melon lovers will look at you like you just got off the ship from, I don't know, Romulus 5. And that is a real shame, because although they are really great when they're raw, melons bloom best when the heat is on. The secret is to use very, very, very high heat. How much heat are we talking? Wok this way.

// SOFTWARE

1½	tablespoons	olive oil	not extra-virgin
1	small	red onion	thinly sliced
1	pound	melon	cubed
1	tablespoon	fresh basil	chiffonade
½	teaspoon	kosher salt	
½	teaspoon	black pepper	freshly ground
2	teaspoons	red wine vinegar	
2	ounces	feta cheese	crumbled
1	tablespoon	pine nuts	toasted

// PROCEDURE

1. Heat a **large sauté pan or wok** over high heat.[1] Once the pan is hot, add the oil, followed by the onion, and sauté for 1 to 2 minutes, moving the pan continuously. Add the melon and sauté for another 1 to 2 minutes, until the melon starts to take on color. Add the basil, salt, and pepper and continue to cook for another minute. Add the vinegar and toss to combine.

2. Pour the mixture onto a **serving platter**, sprinkle with the feta and pine nuts, and serve immediately.

[1] I usually perform this dish in the great out-of-doors in a wok parked over a big propane-powered fryer burner. At night you can see the bottom of the wok glow. I kid you not.

TIDBIT | True cantaloupes are found only in Europe.

TIDBIT | Melons are an excellent source of folate, fiber, and potassium. Some have doses of beta-carotene, vitamin C, iron, phosphorous, and magnesium.

TIDBIT | Melons are members of the cucurbit family, along with gourds, squash, and pumpkins.

MELON SORBET

1 QUART

Heat may be a treat, but the amazing melon can deliver equal pleasure on the opposite side of the thermal wheel. I speak, of course, of the frozen delight known as sorbet. Granted, the juice of just about any fruit can be made into sorbet, but melons are particularly well suited to the dish because their flavor and aroma come through even when they're very, very cold. And since their flesh is very smooth when pureed, you don't have to strain out any pulp. That means more fiber in the juice and that means a smoother texture.

// **SOFTWARE** //

21	ounces	watermelon, muskmelon, or honeydew	diced
3	tablespoons	lemon juice	freshly squeezed
2	tablespoons	vodka	
9	ounces	sugar	

// **PROCEDURE** //

1. Process the melon in the bowl of a **food processor** until smooth. Add the lemon juice, vodka, and sugar and process for another 30 seconds. Refrigerate the mixture until it reaches 40°F, 30 minutes to 1 hour.

2. Pour the chilled mixture into an **ice cream maker** and process according to the manufacturer's directions. Transfer the sorbet to an **airtight container** and freeze for 3 to 4 hours before serving.

CUISINE AS ANTIFREEZE

On the evening of April 14, 1912, the chief baker of the *Titanic*, Charles Joughin, jumped off the back of the ship and started swimming. After frolicking with the ice floes for a couple of hours, he was fished out of the chilly drink by some nice people in a passing lifeboat. When questioned as to how he possibly could have survived in those temperatures, he said that it was probably because he was tanked to the gills on brandy. And he could be right. If he had enough alcohol in his blood, it could have acted as a kind of antifreeze. What does this have to do with making sorbet? By adding some alcohol to the mix we can prevent it from freezing up hard as a rock. Although this could also be achieved with added sugar, the end result would be sickeningly sweet. A little vodka, on the other hand, will hardly be noticed—except by the kiddies, who will sleep better than ever. Come to think of it, Midori would be nice too, seeing how it's made from melon and all.

Synchronized swimmers are a great tool—perhaps the best tool—for teaching how to control ice crystal growth in sorbet.

MELONDRAMA

8 (8-OUNCE) SERVINGS

// SOFTWARE ///

1	pound	watermelon	cut into 1-inch cubes
6	small	fresh mint leaves	
¼	cup	lime juice	freshly squeezed
2	tablespoons	agave nectar	
	pinch	kosher salt	
1	quart	club soda	chilled

// PROCEDURE ///

1. Combine the watermelon and mint in a **blender** and puree until smooth.

2. Strain the watermelon through a **fine-mesh sieve** into a **large pitcher**. Add the lime juice, agave nectar, and salt and stir to combine. Chill for 1 hour or for up to 4 days.

3. To enjoy, combine 4 ounces of the watermelon juice with 4 ounces chilled soda over ice in a tall drinking glass.

TIDBIT Watermelon is one of the only foods that delivers more of the antioxidant lycopene than tomatoes.

TIDBIT According to etiquette books written in the early twentieth century, watermelon-seed spitting is perfectly polite.

TIDBIT The spot where a watermelon rested on the ground will be creamy colored or yellow when ripe. If the spot is white or pale green, it's probably not ripe.

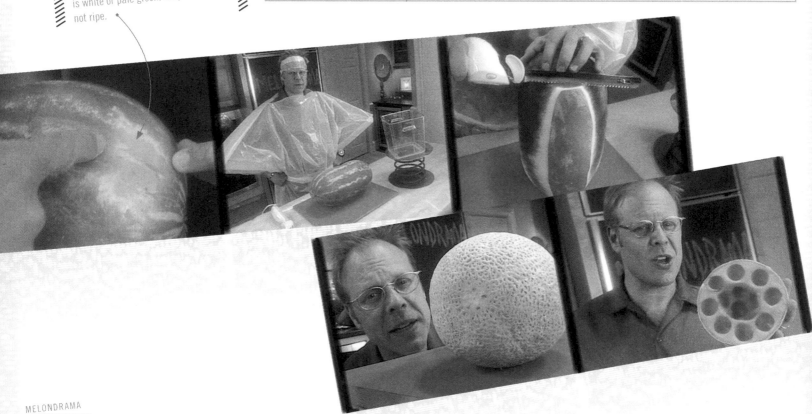

EPISODE 122 | SEASON 8 | GOOD EATS

The culinary world is full of axioms, rules, old wives' tales, and urban legends that are meant to explain why the things that happen in the kitchen happen. This episode was all about proving or disproving as many of them as we could squeeze into a half hour.

```
AB: Hello? (to camera) It's my lawyer. (into phone) Are you
serious? Copyright infringement? Fines? Fine! (to camera) As I
was saying, please stay tuned for what I call "Culinary Myth
Smashers." Because the truth is always...
```

MYTH 1 — SEARING SEALS IN JUICES

It is a generally accepted concept that searing a piece of meat with high heat seals in juices. A chemist by the name of Justus von Liebig concocted this notion back in the nineteenth century, and it's been conventional wisdom ever since. But is it true? This one should be very easy to confront.

Testing this is easy. If a good searing does seal in juices, then it stands to reason that a seared piece of meat should weigh the same before and after cooking, right?

So we took two lovely New York strip steaks. Steak A weighed 307 grams raw, while steak B weighed 296 grams. Each steak was lubed with a wee bit of oil.

Steak A went directly into a 400°F oven. Steak B went into a rocket-hot cast-iron skillet before being transferred to the oven.

Both steaks were cooked to an internal temperature of 140°F. Since it could—possibly—pull moisture out of the meat, salt was omitted altogether.

As we suspected, steak B reached the thermal goal first, and was removed and rested for exactly 5 minutes. Steak A reached temp 4 minutes later and was also rested.

The results? Steak A went from 307 to 266 grams, a net loss of 41 grams or 13 percent of its original weight. Steak B dropped from 296 to 237, for a net loss of 59 grams or 19 percent of its total weight.

The weight loss may seem small, but it's enough to smash the myth. The point being this: Heat damages cells, and when cells are damaged they lose moisture. So, obviously, searing doesn't seal in juices. That said, it does produce an amazing amount of flavor that more than offsets any reduction in internal juiciness.

Roasted Steak 13% loss   Seared Steak 19% loss

NONSTICK COOKWARE PRODUCES KILLER FUMES

For those who monitor kitchen-based urban legends, reports of birds being killed by nonstick pans rank right up there with alligators in the New York City sewer system. But are such reports fact or fiction?

Autopsies performed on several "exotic" birds (gray parrots and cockatoos, to be exact) that died under mysterious circumstances in residential settings were found to have succumbed to fumes produced when polytetrafluoroethylene—or PTFE—is heated in excess of 500°F. As it turns out, birds are extremely vulnerable to toxic gases, which explains why right up to the dawn of the twentieth century miners took canaries with them into the coal mines to act as living gas detectors. If a bird dropped dead, it was time to clear out.

Recent research has shown that the very fumes that can kill a bird may also cause flulike symptoms in people that can last up to a couple of days. So, should we all dig deep holes and bury our nonstick? Hardly. But we should certainly avoid exposing such surfaces to temperatures in excess of 500°F. This means no broiling and no leaving a pan on the cooktop to heat for more than a couple of minutes. Once food goes into the pan, there's somewhere for the heat to go, but when it's empty . . . not so much. As for coated bakeware, I wouldn't worry unless a recipe calls for an oven temperature of 500°F or higher.

One caveat: If you own exotic birds, you should probably skip the nonstick altogether.

TIDBIT | Nonstick cookware accounts for over 80 percent of the cookware purchased in America.

TIDBIT | The cell walls of mushrooms are made of chitin, the same substance that makes up an insect's exoskeleton.

NEVER WASH A MUSHROOM

Most domestic mushrooms come to market dirty . . . only it's not dirt, it's pasteurized horse poop, which should be removed unless you're looking for a little extra crunch. Most cookery manuals instruct us to brush off the offending substrate using a brush such as the one pictured at left. Why not just wash them with water? Supposedly mushrooms, being porous, will drink up any moisture they're placed in contact with. The result: waterlogged fungi. Fact or fiction? As was the case with the seared meat, all you need is a scale to find out.

We set four hand strainers inside four bowls, each containing 113 grams (4 ounces) of common button mushrooms. To the first three bowls we added a liter of water.

After 10 minutes the mushrooms in bowl A were removed, drained thoroughly, and weighed: 119 grams. That means that after a 10-minute soak the mushrooms took on only 6 grams, or 1 teaspoon, of H_2O.

After 10 more minutes, the mushrooms in bowl B were drained in a similar fashion and weighed, to reveal a net gain of 7 grams. Although a teaspoon was absorbed during the first 10 minutes, the second 10 only brought about 10 more drops to the party.

The mushrooms in bowl C were allowed another 10 minutes, for a whopping 30-minute soak. Upon draining and weighing, they tipped the scales at 117.6 grams, for a net gain of 4.6 grams. Now, I am willing to accept that differences in the individual mushrooms may have resulted in this batch soaking up less than the 20-minute batch, but what's important is that after 5 minutes, these mushrooms basically stopped soaking up water.

Finally, the mushrooms in bowl D got a quick spritz from a standard residential sink spray attachment set to half power. Once clean they too were drained and weighed and amazingly showed a net gain of 5.6 grams, a result almost identical to the 10-minute soak.

And so, yes, mushrooms do soak up a little, teensy-weensy bit of water, but nowhere near enough to justify the existence of a mushroom brush.

| Mushroom brush

MYTH 4 — ADDING OIL TO PASTA WATER WILL PREVENT STICKING

Given the lubricative powers of oil, this one makes sense on the surface, but making sense don't make it so.

And so we placed 128 fluid ounces (1 gallon) of water in a stockpot and added 1 tablespoon of olive oil along with two big pinches of salt for flavor's sake. The lid was applied and the vessel put to high heat.

When boilage was achieved, a half pound of spaghetti pasta was added and cooked at medium-high until a state of al dente was reached. During this entire period the oil remained right on the surface of the water despite the convulsive motion produced by the boil. Obviously from that vantage point the oil couldn't lubricate the noodles. But what it did lubricate—quite efficiently, in fact—was the surface of the water, which would have certainly boiled over once enough starch had leached out of the pasta to cause a bubble pileup.

And so, in the end, we decided that adding oil to pasta water is indeed a good idea, just not for the typically accepted reason. Oil helps prevent boil-overs, which have long plagued pasta cookers, but it simply does not lubricate the noodles or prevent stickage.

If you do encounter sticking problems with strand pastas such as spaghetti, try wetting the noodles with cold water before adding them to the pot, and stir frequently as they cook. In recent years I've found that these two maneuvers work to prevent sticking even better than using a large amount of water. I used to strongly advocate bringing at least a gallon of water to a boil before adding pasta, but over time I grew weary of the wait time and wasted energy and dropped that to half a gallon. Prewetting and stirring have rendered the exact same results.

TIP | Do not rinse pasta after cooking. Rinsing washes away the starch that helps sauces to adhere.

MYTH 5 — WATER EXPLODES IN THE MICROWAVE!

It's true, and it's due to a phenonemon called "superheating." Under certain conditions and in certain types of vessels, water can exceed the boiling point without releasing water vapor via bubbles. This can happen because in order for bubbles to form, the vessel or one of the other tools coming in contact with the water needs to possess some scratch or imperfection that can serve as a nucleation site where baby bubbles can be born.

Surface ripples can also affect the birth of bubbles, so vessels with very narrow tops that limit surface area are most prone to surface heating. (In the show I used a

Snapple bottle with the label carefully removed lest someone think I was talking Snapple down.)

When jostled (say, by your hand retrieving the vessel), the water can boil up and out in something resembling a mini geyser, causing nasty scalds.

To prevent such an occurrence, always boil water in a vessel with a wide opening at the top. Give it a stir every minute or so. Placing a wooden skewer or chopstick in the water can help too, but since they tend to float, they're hard to manage.

CUCKOO FOR COQ AU VIN

EPISODE 123 | SEASON 8 | GOOD EATS

Like so much French fare, coq au vin, or "chicken in wine," is *cuisine de bonne femme*—that is, housewife food, mama food, or, in this case, farmer's wife food. Technically speaking, coq au vin is a *fricassee*, a dish in which poultry pieces (the coq) are browned in fat, then stewed in a flavorful liquid such as wine (the vin), along with aromatic vegetables and herbs and spices and whatnot.

DECIPHERING A FRENCH WINE LABEL

A lot of folks won't make coq au vin simply because they don't want to have to deal with a French wine bottle. I know this because we didn't really get into it on the show and more than a few people wrote in to complain about it. So here's everything you need to know in order to locate a bottle of Burgundy for cooking.

1. Look for the phrases "Red Burgundy table wine" or "vin de Bourgogne," either of which indicates that the grape squeezings inside were grown in the region of Burgundy. If said squeezings are red, then you can bet it's the fermented juice of Pinot Noir grapes.

2. Beware a lot of scribbling! Typically the more writing there is on the label, the better the wine inside is. That's because the vineyards of Burgundy are rated, and wines from the top spots (referred to as *grand cru* or even *premier cru*) must include exact info on region, subregion or village, and actual vineyard. Although delicious, most such wines will be costly and their individual peculiarities would likely be lost in cooking.

3. I never cook with a bottle that costs more than twelve bucks. At that point the wine is good enough to drink but not too good to cook with. And I always buy two bottles because I like to drink the same stuff I cook with.

Why would a classic dish call for a tough old rooster? Because the average seventeenth-century French country housewife had a rooster or two, and when one of them was no longer capable of performing its roosterly duties she needed a dish to justify doing away with the old cuss. Now, such a dish would need to take advantage of the rooster's fully developed physiology, specifically a considerable amount of connective tissue, which with long stewing could be rendered into lip-smacking gelatin. Problem is, the great American megamart rarely, if ever, carries rooster. Actually, I'm willing to go out on a limb and just say "never." The next-best thing would be a stewing hen, meaning a year-old female chicken that has suddenly found herself no longer as reliable in the egg-laying department as she used to be. Again, lots of connective tissue, so stewing is really the only option. If your market carries stewers, you're in luck. If not, go with the next-best thing: thighs and legs harvested from broilers or fryers, which are typically between 12 and 15 weeks of age when they head to market. That means they won't have much character but at least there will be some connective tissue and flavor.

While we're on the subject of less-than-common meat stuffs, let's talk about the required seasoning meat for CAV: salt pork. There are a couple of different styles of salt pork, but they're typically cut from the belly, just like bacon. Salt pork is cured in salt, but unlike American-style bacon it's never smoked. Also, it contains a lot less lean meat than bacon. In fact, you may not be able to find any lean in it at all. But that's okay.

Wine is essentially a blending of four elements:

ETHANOL, much of which will be cooked out.

WATER, which converts collagen in the meat to provide body.

FRUIT, which we'd like to concentrate.

TANNINS, which provide astringency, which we want to de-emphasize.

The wine grape that best fits the desired flavor profile for CAV just happens to be Pinot Noir, which just so happens to grow profusely, prodigiously, and profoundly in Burgundy, where goodly wives would have had more wine even than chickens. Once upon a time American cooks would never have actually cooked with a real bottle of Burgundy, but times have changed and good solid French reds often go for far less than squeezings from Napa. So spend a dozen bucks a bottle on two bottles of simple Burgundy.

TIDBIT | Classically, coq au vin is thickened with fresh chicken blood.

Fricassee = Poultry + Wine + Aromatics

Tannin
Fruit
Water
Alcohol
Wine for Cooking

Region: wine of Burgundy (this is the main thing you're looking for)

Producer

Region where grapes were grown (meaning the smaller area within Burgundy)

Alcohol content

If a *Premier Cru*, vineyard listed

Vin de Bourgogne

La Stinky Grand

1962

MÂCON-VILLAGES
→ Le Très Bon
APPELLATION BLA BLA CONTRÔLÉE

Red Burgundy Table Wine

Premier Cru

Alc 12.5% by Volume

750 ml

Vintage

Control statement (the organization that oversees and officiates the production)

If the upper label doesn't make reference to Burgundy, look down here

Volume

CUCKOO FOR COQ AU VIN

(221)

Those who would argue that CAV is complicated and fussy and hard may be forgetting that the process is spread out over two days. The first day is about prep and marinating; the real cooking takes place during day two, and it's neither complicated nor fussy.

TIDBIT | CAV actually tastes better on the day after it's cooked, so you might say it takes three days to prepare.

// SOFTWARE //

24 to 30		pearl onions	
½	cup	all-purpose flour	
4		chicken leg quarters (or one 5- to 7-pound stewing chicken)	cut into serving pieces
	to taste	kosher salt	
	to taste	black pepper	freshly ground
6	ounces	salt pork	cut into lardons or cubed[1]
2	tablespoons	H_2O	
8	ounces	button mushrooms	quartered
1	tablespoon	unsalted butter	(if needed)
2	750-ml bottles	red wine	preferably Pinot Noir, preferably from Burgundy
2	cups	chicken stock or broth	
2	tablespoons	tomato paste	
1	medium	onion	quartered
2	ribs	celery	coarsely chopped
2	medium	carrots	coarsely chopped
3	cloves	garlic	crushed
6 to 8	sprigs	fresh thyme	
1		bay leaf	

// PROCEDURE //

1. Bring **1 quart of water** to a boil. Cut the root end off each pearl onion, then use the very tip of your blade to inscribe a shallow "X" in its place. Blanch the onions in the boiling water for 1 minute. Remove, cool, and pop the skins right off the little buggers by applying pressure to the sides with thumb and forefinger. Set aside.

2. Put the flour in a **large (1- or 2-gallon) zip-top plastic bag**. Season the chicken on all sides with salt and pepper. Dredge a few pieces at a time by putting them in the bag, sealing it, and shaking vigorously. Dancing helps. As the poultry is retrieved, place it on **a cooling rack set over a half sheet pan** or something you don't mind getting messy and leave it there for 5 minutes.[2]

3. Put the salt pork in a **12-inch sauté pan** along with the 2 tablespoons water.[3] Cover and cook over medium heat until the water is cooked out and the pork sticks are golden brown and crisp, 8 to 10 minutes. Remove the pork from the pan and set aside in a **mixing bowl**.

4. Add the pearl onions to the pan (still containing the pork fat), season with salt and pepper, and sauté until lightly brown, 8 to 10 minutes. Transfer the onions to the mixing bowl with the pork. Next, cook the chicken pieces in the pan until golden brown on each side, working in batches if necessary to avoid overcrowding.[4] Transfer the chicken to a **7- to 8-quart enameled cast-iron Dutch oven**.

5. Sauté the mushrooms in the sauté pan, adding the butter only if needed. Cook for about 5 minutes, until they give up most of their moisture. Add the mushrooms to the onions and pork, cover, and refrigerate until ready to use.

6. Pour off any remaining fat and deglaze the pan with about 1 cup of the wine. Pour this into the Dutch oven, along with the stock, tomato paste, quartered onion, celery, carrots, garlic, thyme, and bay leaf. Add all of the remaining wine. Cover and refrigerate overnight.

7. The next day, heat the oven to 325°F.

8. Place the chicken pot in the oven and cook, covered, for 2 to 2½ hours, stirring every half hour. The liquid should barely simmer and when done the chicken should be very tender. Reduce the oven to 200°F when the chicken is done.

9. Remove the chicken to a **heatproof platter or bowl**, cover, and return it to the oven to keep warm. Strain the sauce in a **colander** to remove the carrots, onion, celery, thyme, garlic, and bay leaf, which may be discarded. Return the sauce to the pot, place over medium heat, and cook until it has reduced by one third. Depending on how much liquid you began with, this should take 20 to 45 minutes.

10. Add the pearl onions, mushrooms, and pork and cook for another 15 minutes, until heated through. Taste and adjust the seasoning if necessary, remove from the heat, add the chicken, and serve over egg noodles, if so desired.

NOTE: If the sauce is not thick enough at the end of reducing, you may add a mixture of equal parts butter and flour kneaded together. Start with 1 tablespoon of each. Whisk this into the sauce for 4 to 5 minutes and repeat if necessary.

TIP | Keep in mind that during the deglazing process, an average red wine contains somewhere in the neighborhood of 8 to 10 percent ethyl alcohol, or ethanol, which is being portrayed here by the little red Christmas ornaments (the clear ones are water, sugar, and other stuff). At room temperature, this ethanol is utterly nonflammable. But when the temperature rises and crosses 172.4°F, the ethanol begins converting to vapor, and once it's airborne those fumes are very flammable indeed. So, if you have a gas cooktop and a flame is already present, you might want to turn it off just before the wine goes in; then after the bubbling subsides you can reignite. If you're not willing to do this, at least stand back a little, just in case.

[1] Classic applications of CAV call for the pork to be cut into lardons, which is French for fat, short matchsticks. Trust me when I tell you that these are easier to fabricate when the fat is frigid, so I always store my salt fat in the freezer to keep it firm and cut-able. Remember, though, that fat can absorb flavors directly from the air and freezers can be surprisingly stinky places, so keep it tightly sealed in plastic wrap and a layer of foil.

[2] The resting is important because it gives the flour time to hydrate via juices the salt is pulling out of the meat, resulting in a better sear and crust, which is key to flavor

development. Don't get in a rush and skip this step, or the French will hate us more than they already do.

[3] The water is just there to help render out some of the fat without it burning.

[4] Overcrowding of course leads to trapped moisture and a reduction in temperature. Food cooked this way is more stewed than sautéed.

A TAPROOT ORANGE

EPISODE 124 | SEASON 8 | GOOD EATS

Although carrot roots and greens have been consumed at least since the pyramids were shiny and new, up until the Renaissance this cousin of dill, cumin, parsley, and Queen Anne's lace was thought of more as medicine than cuisine. According to a medicinal manual of the Middle Ages, carrots were especially good for relieving gas and urinary tract infections, as well as the occasional touch of bronchitis.

KNOWLEDGE CONCENTRATE

Today, the carrot is the second-most popular vegetable on earth—the potato is number one. Some experts believe that it's the bright orange color that we actually love so much. But truth is, the original carrots didn't look like this. The original carrots looked like this:

Indeed, the black carrots were cultivated in the Balkans and part of Afghanistan as early as the first century A.D. By the time the seventeenth century rolled around, carrots came in just about every color you could imagine but orange.

And then along came the Dutch, the very same botanical tinkerers responsible for the hundreds of flavors of tulips and green peppers. Dutch growers managed to cross variations of carrots until they isolated a rare mutation from North Africa that displayed a huge amount of beta-carotene, which, of course, is as orange as the day is long.

Why bother doing this? Politics, my friend. You see, at this time, Holland was under the rule of the French House of Orange, and I don't know if they were kissing up for subsidies or just paying homage. Luckily, today colored carrots are back on the scene. In fact, maroon carrots are very, very big in Europe, especially in England.

Carrots are jam packed with fiber and potassium, and there's even some protein, not to mention the fact that your average taproot orange can deliver 20,250 international units of vitamin A . . . well, not exactly vitamin A, but beta-carotene, the naturally occurring orange pigment that, in the lining of your small intestines, is converted into vitamin A, which is especially good news for your vision.

Consider your left eyeball. (Okay, technically this is a kettle grill with a fancy paint job, but we're just a humble cable cooking show on a budget.) Most folks are familiar with the pupil, the iris, the lens, the stuff that brings light into the eyeball. But the real science happens all the way in the back of the eyeball, in the nerve structures that do the actual seeing: the cones, which sense colors and bright images, and the rods, which register black-and-white images in low-light situations. The chemical that rods use to see is called rhodopsin, and if so much as a photon of light hits a molecule of this stuff, it splits into two other chemicals, retinol and opsin. If there's a lot of light available, then all the rhodopsin will split. That's why if you stand in a nice, bright bathroom at night and turn off the light, you're plunged into darkness even though there's still plenty of light around, coming under the door, through the window, and what have you. Wait 20 or 30 seconds and some of the rhodopsin will re-form and your rods will fire up again. But the amount of rhodopsin you can make depends on how much retinol you've got in your system to begin with. And retinol is just another name for vitamin A. And vitamin A is made in the lining of your intestines from beta-carotene, and nothing delivers beta-carotene like carrots.

Whenever possible, I buy bunch carrots with the greens intact because bright green and perky greens are a sure sign of freshness. As soon as you get them home, the greens have got to go, because they'll continue to sap moisture and nutrients out of the carrots. I always leave about an inch of stem intact so that no more moisture than is necessary will be lost from the carrot. As for the greens, well, you could eat them, although I don't think they'd taste very good. Or you could do what women used to do in Victorian England and put them on your hat.

TIDBIT According to Guinness World Records, the largest carrot ever grown weighed a whopping 18 pounds, 13 ounces.

A TAPROOT ORANGE

4 SERVINGS

Down south where I live, carrot salad, or carrot slaw, is a classic side dish. The problem is, most recipes call for grated carrots, which always seem to turn to mush before I get a chance to eat the gosh darn stuff. The way around this is to think "noodles" rather than "slaw." This is darned good stuff—and good for you to boot.

// SOFTWARE //

2	pounds	carrots	12 to 15 medium
½	cup	mayonnaise	
	pinch	kosher salt	
⅓	cup	sugar	
½	cup	canned crushed pineapple	drained
½	cup	raisins	
2	teaspoons	curry powder	
1	teaspoon	minced garlic	
	pinch	celery seed	or caraway (optional)

// PROCEDURE //

1. Wash the carrots and peel them if necessary. Using a **vegetable peeler**, slice the carrots into wide noodle-shaped strips.

2. **Whisk** together the mayonnaise, salt, sugar, pineapple, raisins, curry powder, garlic, and celery seed, if using, in a **large mixing bowl**. Add the carrots and toss to combine. Serve immediately or refrigerate for 1 hour to serve cold.

TIP | If your carrots are less than an inch in diameter, the outer layer will be relatively thin. So just go over it with a dish-scrubbing pad.

4 SERVINGS

When it comes to carrots, what is true for spices is true for herbs as well: They play better with members of their own botanical family. That's because carrots, celery, parsley, caraway, dill, fennel—things like that—all share a unique flavor compound, petroselinic acid. By seasoning carrots with, say, fresh parsley, we not only build a portfolio of contrasting flavors, we actually intensify the carrot flavor itself because we're dosing up on petroselinic acid. Science: It tastes good, don't it?

// SOFTWARE ///

1	pound	carrots	about 7 medium, peeled and cut ¼ inch thick on the bias
2	tablespoons	unsalted butter	
	heavy pinch	kosher salt	
1	cup	ginger ale	go for the good stuff
½	teaspoon	chili powder	
1	tablespoon	fresh parsley leaves	

// PROCEDURE ///

Combine the carrots, butter, salt, and ginger ale in a **12-inch sauté pan** over medium heat. Cover and bring to a simmer. Remove the lid, stir, and reduce the heat to low. Cover again and cook for 5 minutes. Remove the lid, add the chili powder, and increase the heat to high. Cook, tossing occasionally, until the ginger ale is reduced to a glaze, 4 to 5 minutes. Pour into a **serving dish** and sprinkle with the parsley. Serve immediately.

TONIGHT'S IN-FLIGHT MEAL: CARROTS

During World War II, many RAF pilots could be spotted by the orange color of their skin. Management shoveled piles of carrots into the poor chaps to improve their night vision. Problem is, excess beta-carotene is stored in skin and fat cells, so eventually they just started turning into, well . . . carrots. Since this form of vitamin A overload never becomes toxic, the only harm is cosmetic. However, the vitamin A we get from animal tissue can be toxic, especially if it comes from the livers of Arctic critters. Believe it or not, one polar bear liver can kill you quicker than a blowfish fillet. But that's another show . . . or not.

1 (9-INCH) CAKE

England is the one country where carrot consumption beats out potato consumption. When sugar ran short during World War II, the English did not surrender their "pudding." They just did what their ancestors did in the Middle Ages: They turned to the carrot. This is the period that gave birth to the carrot cake, the only dessert I know of based entirely on a taproot.

// SOFTWARE

		unsalted butter	for the pan
12	ounces	all-purpose flour	plus extra for the pan
12	ounces	carrots	grated, about 6 medium carrots
1	teaspoon	baking powder	
1	teaspoon	baking soda	
½	teaspoon	ground allspice	
½	teaspoon	ground cinnamon	
½	teaspoon	nutmeg	freshly grated
½	teaspoon	kosher salt	
10	ounces	granulated sugar	
2	ounces	dark brown sugar	
3	large	eggs	
¾	cup	plain yogurt	
6	ounces	vegetable oil	

// PROCEDURE

1. Heat the oven to 350°F. Butter and flour a **9-inch round, 3-inch-deep cake pan**. Line the bottom with **parchment paper**. Set aside.

2. Put the carrots in a **large mixing bowl** and set aside.

3. Combine the flour, baking powder, baking soda, spices, and salt in the bowl of a **food processor** and process for 5 seconds. Add this mixture to the carrots and toss until they are well coated.

4. In the bowl of the food processor combine the sugars, eggs, and yogurt. With the processor still running, drizzle in the oil. Pour this mixture into the carrot mixture and stir until just combined. Pour into the prepared pan and bake on the middle rack of the oven for 45 minutes. Reduce the oven temperature to 325°F and bake for another 20 minutes, or until the cake reaches 205° to 210°F in the center.

5. Remove the pan from the oven and cool for 15 minutes in the pan. After 15 minutes, turn the cake out onto a **cooling rack** and cool completely before frosting.

CREAM CHEESE FROSTING

ABOUT 2 CUPS

// SOFTWARE ///

8	ounces	cream cheese	at room temperature
¼	cup	unsalted butter	at room temperature
1	teaspoon	vanilla extract	
9	ounces	confectioners' sugar	sifted

// PROCEDURE ///

1. In the bowl of a **stand mixer fitted with the paddle attachment**, combine the cream cheese and butter on medium just until blended. Add the vanilla and beat until combined. With the speed on low, add the confectioners' sugar in 4 batches, beating until smooth between each addition.

2. Refrigerate for 5 to 10 minutes before using.

BAD BUNNY!

SPRUNG A LEEK

EPISODE 125 | SEASON 8 | GOOD EATS

Great Moments
In Leek History

ANCIENT TIMES

"...if you can mock a
leek, you can eat a leek."
////////////////////////////////
W. SHAKESPEARE, HENRY V

I don't know about Henry V, but I do believe that if Fred Astaire had been a vegetable, he definitely would have been a leek. Leeks possess a fine, sophisticated, smooth texture and flavor that isn't afraid to take center stage but is gracious enough to share the glory with other ingredients. The leek is more versatile than either the onion or garlic, and its long, lean shape makes it easier to work with than any of the bulbs. And yet most Americans still pass up this regal stalk.

TIDBIT | After considerable experimentation, I've found that the best way to store a bunch of leeks is to refrigerate them in bubble wrap.

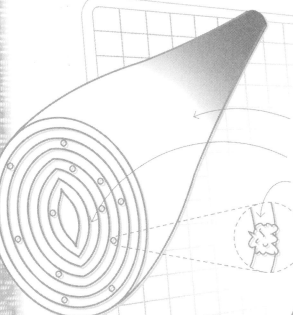

LEEK CROSS SECTION

Looks round
on the outside

Elliptical on the inside

Gnarly grit

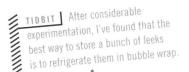

Leeks

Bubble wrap

(230)

The most commonly held misconception about leeks is that they are the mature version of scallions, or green onions, which is patently untrue. Scallions and green onions are just the immature, prebulb version of any of a wide variety of bulb onions. Leeks, on the other hand, are a variety unto themselves. But they do share several common elements with regular old onions.

Leeks are constructed of many concentric layers, which are actually leaves that grow upward in unison, often trapping dirt and sand along the way (which is why an unwashed leek is a crunchy leek). When shopping, always look for a nice, tight skin in the white section and bright, crisp greens up top. Although buying by the bunch is convenient, producemen tend to bundle leeks of various sizes in order to make a preordained weight. I prefer leeks that are right at an inch in diameter so I try to buy them loose by the pound.[1]

When working with leeks the first step is always cleaning, and I don't just mean a cursory exterior spritz. Unlike scallions, leek layers push up out of the ground at slightly different rates, and that means grit gets caught between the layers. An easy way to deal with that would be to simply chop up the leek and toss the bits in some water to flush out the grit. But the idea of running one of my beloved knives through what amounts to tiny rocks . . . well, it gives me the heebees. So, the goal is to make one cut for cleanliness, and to make it count.

First, move the rinsed leek to the cutting board and trim away the root from the bottom of the bulb.

Flip the leek around, and take off the heavy green end.[2]

Observe that the leek is not really round on the inside but rather elliptical. So align your blade so that it runs across the ellipse, corner to corner. Split the leek end to end.

Separate the leaves by running them through your fingers like you're reading a flip book, then swish it around in cold water that's deep enough for the sand to sink away from the leek. (I usually do this in a tall tea glass or beer stein. No reason to fill the sink with water.)

At this point you can dry and continue to fabricate.

TRIVIA One of my major sources of inspiration for making *Good Eats* was *Monty Python's Flying Circus*, and I had long hoped to ape the cut-paper collage style of Terry Gilliam. In this episode I finally got a chance. Although we've done more sophisticated work since, I think these black-and-white bits with their steam punk edge and warbly mechanics are still my favorite.

HISTORICAL NOTE: The leek was revered in ancient Sumeria, Egypt, and Assyria, where it was used as a cure for graying hair. There is no written record indicating whether the leeks were to be applied externally or internally.

[1] If bunches are being sold by the pound I feel free to unwire several bouquets and make my own. This practice would be rather unethical, however, if the leeks in question are priced by the bunch.

[2] Good for inclusion in stock, but not much else.

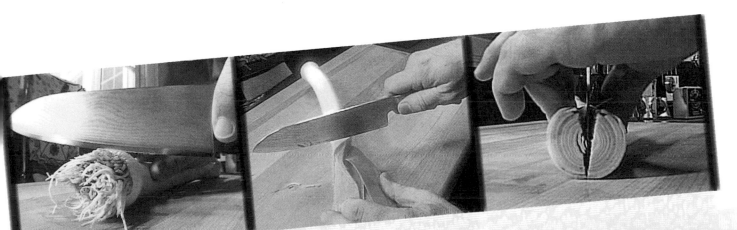

GRILLED BRAISED LEEKS

4 SERVINGS

And now my very favorite leek application of all time, which also happens to be the simplest. If you don't have a grill, a broiler will do. Although grilled and braised leeks are excellent with just a few grinds of pepper, you could add a little bacon and maybe some goat cheese, or some artichokes, or a nice green salad, or maybe some roast chicken. In other words, the sky's the limit. But hey, that's how it is with leeks.

// SOFTWARE

4	large	leeks	dark green tops removed
2	tablespoons	bacon fat	
	heavy pinch	kosher salt	
1	tablespoon	balsamic vinegar	
		crumbled bacon	(optional)
		goat cheese	(optional)

// PROCEDURE

1. Heat the grill to high. Cut each leek in half lengthwise and rinse thoroughly to remove all dirt and sand. Pat dry.

2. **Brush** the cut side of each leek half with the bacon fat and sprinkle with salt. Grill over direct, high heat, cut side down, with the lid closed, until grill marks appear, 6 to 7 minutes. Remove the leeks to a sheet of **aluminum foil**, cut side up. Brush the leeks with the vinegar. Reassemble the leek halves together, wrap tightly in foil, place on the grill away from direct heat, and cook for 10 to 12 minutes.

3. Remove the leeks from the foil and serve immediately, as is or with crumbled bacon and goat cheese.

HISTORICAL NOTE: The year: A.D. 640. The Welsh win a decisive battle over the Saxons, when, at the urging of a monk who would later be known as Saint David, the Welsh army placed leeks in their hats so as to identify each other.

LEEK RINGS

4 SERVINGS

CONSIDERABLY MORE RECENT HISTORICAL NOTE: Once upon a time, supposedly in Texas, a short-order cook accidentally dropped some onion slices into a container of batter, most likely pancake batter. The clumsy oaf retrieved the coated rings, and then headed to the trash. I like to think, however, that upon passing the fry pot, the cook was suddenly tickled by the notion of a possibility and—perhaps coaxed by the inexorable clockwork of evolution—decided to fry the onions rather than discard them.

The problem with frying onions, of course, is moisture. Onions are packed with it. So when they're fried, steam tends to form between the onion and the batter, creating a slimy layer that prevents a true marriage of the two parties involved. So, when you bite into it, the entire onion slithers out like a pale salamander from a hollow stick. Not good eats. This could have been avoided if that man had simply dropped leeks instead.

// SOFTWARE ///

3	quarts	vegetable oil	peanut or canola will do as well
12	ounces	leeks	dark green tops removed, cleaned
1½	cups	milk	
1	large	egg	
2	cups	all-purpose flour	
2	teaspoons	kosher salt	plus extra for seasoning

// PROCEDURE ///

1. Heat the oil in a **heavy 5-quart pot** fitted with a **deep-fry thermometer** over medium-high heat to 375°F.

2. Slice the leeks into ½-inch-wide rings, separating them two layers at a time.

3. **Whisk** the milk and the egg together in a **medium mixing bowl**. Combine the flour and salt in another **medium mixing bowl**. Divide the flour mixture between **2 shallow dishes** and place the milk and egg mixture in a **third dish**.

4. Dip one small handful of the rings first into the first flour mixture, then into the milk and egg, and then into the second flour mixture. Working in batches, fry the rings for 1 to 1½ minutes, until golden brown. Remove the rings to a **cooling rack set in a half sheet pan** and drain for 2 to 3 minutes before serving. Season with additional salt, if desired.

HISTORICAL NOTE: In parts of Northumberland, England, come September, many men's clubs hold leek pageants. The competition is fierce, and in the final days before judging, secret leek plots may be guarded by geezers with shotguns. Before judging, the leek greens are shampooed and the roots are carefully combed.

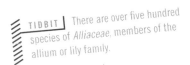
TIDBIT | There are over five hundred species of *Alliaceae*, members of the allium or lily family.

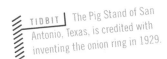
TIDBIT | The Pig Stand of San Antonio, Texas, is credited with inventing the onion ring in 1929.

APPLICATION ───┤ └┤ └┤ ├── **LEEK POTATO SOUP**

6 SERVINGS

// SOFTWARE //

1	pound	leeks	4 to 5 medium, dark green tops removed, cleaned
3	tablespoons	unsalted butter	
	to taste	kosher salt	
14	ounces	Yukon gold potatoes	about 3 small, peeled and finely diced
1	quart	vegetable broth	
1	cup	heavy cream	
1	cup	buttermilk	
½	teaspoon	white pepper	
1	tablespoon	fresh chives	snipped

// PROCEDURE ///

1. Chop the leeks into small pieces.

2. Melt the butter in a **6-quart saucepan** over medium heat. Add the leeks and a heavy pinch of salt and sweat for 5 minutes. Decrease the heat to medium-low and cook until the leeks are tender, about 25 minutes, stirring occasionally.

3. Add the potatoes and broth, increase the heat to medium-high, and bring to a boil. Reduce the heat to low, cover, and gently simmer until the potatoes are soft, about 45 minutes.

4. Turn off the heat and puree the mixture with an **immersion blender** until smooth. Stir in the cream, buttermilk, and white pepper. Taste and adjust the seasoning if desired. Sprinkle with the chives and serve immediately, or chill and serve cold.

HISTORICAL NOTE: Roman emperor and big-time loony tune Nero ate leeks daily because he believed they would protect his fine singing voice. He munched so many that he earned the nickname "Porrophagus," or "leek eater." Crazy though he may have been, his notion about the leeks may have been right, as they were later used in early cough drops.

Ahh, fresh-baked bread.

Crusty on the outside, fragrant, yielding yet chewy on the inside. Tangy. Buttery. Earthy. You know, I don't care what those armies of carbophobes chant; bread is the ultimate comfort food—perhaps the ultimate food, period. Consuming a handcrafted bread is one of life's great primal pleasures. And if you ask me, so is the act of baking it. Now, bread may be pretty simple stuff. But as is usually the case with simple things, every detail counts. If you happen to find yourself armed with a few decent tools, some tried and true techniques, and a handful of carefully chosen groceries, you could soon be filling your home with the intoxicating aroma of freshly baked bread, and your tummy with seriously good eats.

 TIDBIT A bakery in France claims to have been using the same starter since the time of Napoleon.

ONE WAY TO THINK OF A WHEAT KERNEL

Outer skin = bran coat

Endosperm (starch) = fuel

Germ (contains fat and DNA)

Wheat sprout

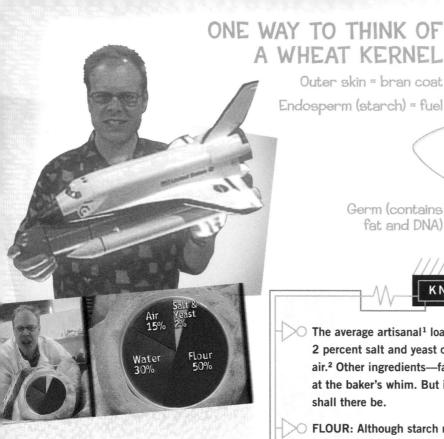

DR. STRANGELOAF

KNOWLEDGE CONCENTRATE

▷ The average artisanal[1] loaf of bread is about 50 percent flour, 30 percent water, maybe 2 percent salt and yeast combined, and somewhere in the neighborhood of 15 percent air.[2] Other ingredients—fat, milk, sugar, nuts, berries, and the like—can come and go at the baker's whim. But if one of the foundation ingredients goes missing, no bread shall there be.

▷ FLOUR: Although starch makes up most of any flour's bulk, the protein content determines what that flour can really do when it comes to baking. That's because when agitated with water, the two distinct forms of protein in wheat—gliadin and glutenin—tangle to form a stretchy, microscopic mesh known as gluten, which yeast can blow up like millions of tiny pieces of bubble gum. The more gluten a flour can bring to the party, the better the quality of the bubbles. Not bigger, mind you, but better. With proper technique a perfectly good loaf can be born of an all-purpose or "AP" flour with a protein content of around 10 to 11 percent. But if you yearn for a strong crust and chewy inner tooth, attributes we will hereafter refer to as the "hearty country loaf profile" or HCLP, you'll need to reach for bread flour milled from a "strong" or "hard" wheat (typically winter harvested and containing upward of 11.5 to 13.5 percent protein).[3]

▷ H_2O: Since it makes up about half of the average dough's weight, water deserves careful consideration here. Municipal hydro is laced with chlorine, which kills microscopic organisms, and that's a good thing—most of the time. But we are going to be baking with microscopic organisms and we'd like to keep them alive until we're good and ready to do them in ourselves. Mineral content, or water hardness, is also a factor in bread baking: Harder waters are better suited to bread than softer. Distilled water or water that's been treated with residential softening equipment, which often employ a lot of sodium, are not your baking buddies. If when passed through a charcoal-based filtration system your water tastes good to you, odds are it'll be fine for bread.[4]

▷ THE BUGS: Real bread is always leavened by the gases created as unicellular fungi called yeast go about their business, a business that converts sugar into carbon dioxide, alcohol, acid, and a few dozen other compounds. In fact, that's all yeast do, other than make little yeast. These collectivities are referred to as fermentation, and without it we would have no decent bread, no beer, no bourbon . . . in other words, life wouldn't be worth living.

Back before baker's yeast became available in the twentieth century, bakers had to either buy yeast from brewers or capture and cultivate wild yeast in sourdough starters, which are indeed named for the fact that the breads created from them are quite tangy.[5] To capture your own, simply mix some water and flour in a big, clean jar or bowl and just leave it lying around, preferably on a porch or by an open window. Unless it's winter or you live near a really smelly mill or factory, odds are that wild yeast will come right on by.

Keep stirring and feeding your starter with a few spoonfuls of flour and water every few days, and if all goes well you'll have yourself a nice, healthy colony of yeast, ready and willing to give your loaf a lift. But what makes sourdough starters really special is that wild yeast usually travel in the company of bacteria such as *Lactobacillus*. Different strains of yeast and bacteria cohabit in different regions, and each team produces a distinct flavor in the final loaf. So San Francisco sourdough isn't famous simply because it's got a good marketing plan but because *Lactobacillus sanfrancisco* thrives around the Bay Area and nowhere else. Other regions, from Italy to Egypt to Tasmania, have their particular microfauna and therefore their own sourdoughs.

For those of us who aren't looking to rustle up our own wild yeast colony, there is a very workable substitute for true sourdough utilizing commercially available over-the-counter unicellular products.

The yeast inside FRESH or CAKE YEAST (named for the cakey form in which the yeast is packaged, not for any intended application) are wide awake, ready to go, and packed away in this nice, big, moist block of yeast chow. This is a favorite form among professionals because as long as it's kept refrigerated and used within a few days, it's highly reliable and it's what most traditional bakeshop recipes are formulated for. For the average consumer, however, it can be wicked hard to find and it doesn't keep, so I rarely use it.

Next up is good old ACTIVE DRY YEAST, which isn't really active at all. In fact, it's mostly dead. Take a look with your USB hand-held microscope (or a really strong magnifying glass if you like lookin' old school) and you'll see tiny extruded rods composed of tightly massed clusters of dead yeast cells, each of which is entombed in an even smaller cluster of dormant but still living cells. Since the dead cells have to be washed away in order for the inner bugs to wake up and get to business, it helps to soak these (a process called "proofing") in warm water before inviting them to the bread party. And since the living population therein is relatively minuscule, it takes a fairly long while to bring up a loaf of bread, because the cells need extra time to replicate. Still, if you're willing to wait, they're able.

INSTANT or "RAPID-RISE" YEAST is dried in a kinder, gentler manner than active dry yeast, so more cells survive. That means this yeast can be added directly to dry dough ingredients without proofing, which is amazingly convenient. The problem with these yeasts is that they ferment so quickly at room temperature they can raise a dough ceiling high before it can actually absorb any of the flavors that yeast produce or the CO_2 itself, which contributes to the overall texture of the bread. My method is to slow the little buggers down by lowering the temperature. Instead of letting the dough rise on the counter or in the legendary "warm place" we've all read about in baking manuals, I send mine to the chill chest, which slows things down considerably.

[1] Meaning made by the hands of a human without addition of chemicals, preservatives, color enhancers, and so on.

[2] Professional bread recipes are written as baker's percentages, where flour equals 100 percent and all other ingredients are calculated as ratios thereof.

[3] Bread flours formulated for bread machines may have an even higher protein content, 13.5 to 14.5 percent. The higher ratio is meant to make up for the fact that machines cannot knead bread as effectively as human hands.

[4] If your refrigerator has a water dispenser and you change the filter frequently, go with that. Otherwise, a pitcher system like those made by Brita and Pur are perfectly fine.

[5] I've heard tell that miners in the Old West often kept a bit of sourdough starter in leather pouches they wore around their necks. Every time they baked up some bread on the campfire, they put some of the leftover dough back in the pouch for the next time. Some of the pouches supposedly became so impregnated with yeast cells that they could actually be used in place of the starter itself. It should be noted that I have not been able to replicate this.

If you take a look at the procedure below you'll see that it starts with a very wet batter with the yeast, honey, water, and a small amount of the flour that is refrigerated overnight. This is called a sponge—or a *biga* in Italy, or a *poolish* in France (in honor of Polish bakers . . . long story)—and it will provide the final loaf with the complex flavors (especially acidity) associated with a full-on sourdough. Yes, this step will take more time and yes, your patience will be rewarded.

// SOFTWARE ///

1	pound	bread flour	plus extra for shaping
1	teaspoon	instant yeast	
2	teaspoons	honey	
1¼	cups	filtered H_2O	
2	teaspoons	kosher salt	
		vegetable oil	for greasing the rising container
2	tablespoons	cornmeal	
⅓	cup	H_2O	
1	tablespoon	cornstarch	

// PROCEDURE ///

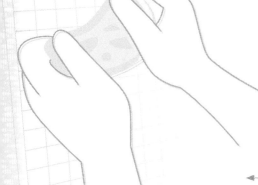

1. Combine 5 ounces of the flour, ¼ teaspoon of the yeast, all of the honey, and all of the filtered water in a **straight-sided container**; cover this sponge loosely and refrigerate for 8 to 12 hours.[6]

2. Put the remaining 11 ounces flour, the remaining ¾ teaspoon yeast, and all of the salt in the bowl of a **stand mixer fitted with the dough hook attachment** and add the sponge from the refrigerator. Knead the mixture on low for 2 to 3 minutes, just until it comes together.

3. Cover the dough in the bowl with a **kitchen towel** and rest the dough for 20 minutes.[7]

4. After 20 minutes, knead the dough on medium speed for 7 to 9 minutes. Most home bakers actually underknead. To make sure this doesn't happen to you, pull off a walnut-sized piece of dough and stretch it between your fingers. The dough is ready when it can be stretched into a thin membrane that light easily passes through. Think of window-paning as using your fingers on the dough in the same way your tongue preps a piece of bubble gum for bubble blowing.

5. While the dough is kneading, pour **1 quart hot water** into a **shallow pan** and place it on the bottom rack of your oven.

6. Lightly lubricate a vessel that's at least twice the volume of the dough with the vegetable oil. Place the dough ball into said container and position it on the rack above the pan of water. Let rise until doubled in size, which, depending on a long list of factors, could take 1 to 2 hours.

7. Once the dough has doubled in size, turn it onto a countertop, lightly dust your hands with flour, and press the dough out with your knuckles. Fold one side in toward the middle of the mass and then the other, as if you were making a tri-fold wallet. Repeat the folding a second time. Cover the dough with a kitchen towel and rest for another 10 minutes.

8. Flatten the dough again with your knuckles and then fold the dough in onto itself, like you are shaping something that looks like the top of a jellyfish. Turn the dough over and squeeze the bottom together so that the top surface of the dough is smooth. Place the dough back on the counter and begin to roll it gently between your hands. Do not grab the dough but allow it to move gently back and forth between your hands, moving in a circular motion. Move the dough ball to a **pizza peel or the bottom of a half sheet pan** that has been sprinkled with cornmeal. Cover with the kitchen towel and let rise for 1 hour, or until when you poke the dough the hole quickly fills back in.

9. Put an 10-inch **unglazed terra-cotta dish** upside down in the oven and heat the oven to 400°F.[8]

10. Combine the ⅓ cup water and the cornstarch in a **small bowl**. Uncover the dough and brush the surface with this mixture. Gently slash the top surface of the dough ball in several places, about ⅓ to ½ inch deep.[9]

11. Add more hot water to the shallow pan in the oven if it has evaporated. Slide the bread onto the hot terra-cotta dish and bake for 50 to 60 minutes, until the bread has reached an internal temperature of 205° to 210°F. Remove to a **cooling rack** and cool for 30 minutes before slicing.

NOTE: As the starch sets and the surface cools, the bread will crack and pop like a bowl of Rice Krispies. The sound used to scare my dog, but don't let it scare you.

[6] I usually make my sponges at night right before going to bed so that I can bake in the morning.

[7] This step, referred to by bakers as autolyse (pronounced "auto-lease"), allows the flour to hydrate and the gluten structures to relax, both of which will make for easier and more efficient kneading.

[8] Baking on a hot, dense mass will ensure a good rise and a crisp crust, but I've never been able to convince myself that shelling out fifty dollars for a pizza stone is the answer. I used to line my oven with unglazed quarry tiles, which is something of a pain. The base of a large (again, unglazed) terra-cotta flower pot is nice and heavy and a lot sturdier than the aforementioned tile. Just make sure you put it in the oven before you turn on the heat to prevent cracking.

[9] Slashing the top of a loaf is not about making it all pretty like, it's about giving the bread someplace to go when it rises in the oven. Skip this, and the outer skin you've created during the rolling and shaping phase is just going to hold everything in and you'll end up with a small, dense loaf. Although pro bakers slash with a device called a lame, a plastic handle with a curved disposable blade, I just can't own a tool called "lame." So I use a serrated knife instead. And I favor the square or "box" cut. Just set the blade on the surface and quickly pull. No downward pressure is required whatsoever unless your knife is dull—and you would never have a dull knife, now, would you? Certainly not.

MY BIG FAT GREEK SANDWICH

EPISODE 127 | SEASON 8 | GOOD EATS

In Greek, the word *gyros* means "turn" or "revolve." From this we get two modern meanings. One is a gyro or gyroscope, a device composed of a weighted flywheel on an axle, which is free to move in any direction. When the wheel spins fast, the gyroscope demonstrates conservation of angular momentum; that is, the axle resists reorientation. Gyroscopes make many modern marvels possible, things like nonmagnetic shipboard compasses, aircraft altitude indicators, and motorcycles, which are stabilized by two gyroscopes, the front and back wheels. Now, since it's been anglicized, *gyroscope* is pronounced with a "j" sound even though the root word, *gyros*, is pronounced with a "y" sound.

The other type of gyro is a highly seasoned composite meat product (like a sausage without a casing) that is cooked on and sliced from a rotisserie (hence the revolving part) and served on pita bread along with tomato, onion, and tzatziki sauce. Despite the fact that this sandwich was most likely invented in New York City, the Greek pronunciation has stuck, by and large, which is why most foodies in the know refer to this excellent edible as a "yee-row."

Most people assume that a gyro sandwich—which, as far as I'm concerned, is the finest sandwich on earth—is impossible to make at home. This, of course, is hooey. All it takes is a little semispecialized equipment, some know-how, and a serious appetite for good eats.

TRIVIA Yes, this episode was completely inspired by *My Big Fat Greek Wedding*—especially the Windex scenes. I'm not much on chick flicks, but my wife dug the movie and I really needed an excuse to do a gyro show.

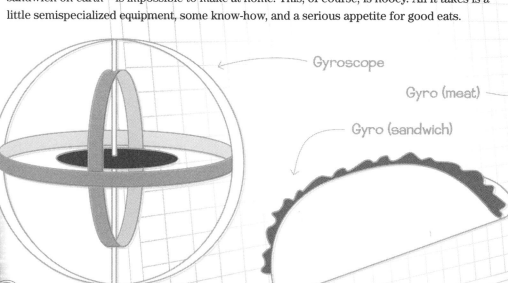

Gyroscope

Gyro (meat)

Gyro (sandwich)

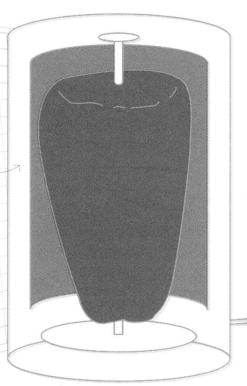

If there is any mystery to gyros—and I'm not saying there is—it has got to be that the meat tastes like lamb but doesn't resemble any familiar cut of that critter. What we've got here is a tightly grained and highly spiced meatloaf.

The gyro loaf is built on a foundation of ground lamb, which just so happens to be my favorite store-ground meat product. It is versatile, it is flavorful, and it's usually a buck or two cheaper than ground beef chuck. If your meat counter doesn't feature said product, simply ask the good man or ma'am behind the counter to grind two pounds of lamb stew meat or, better yet, boneless lamb shoulder steaks.

For most of man's culinary history, the word *roast* has meant "to cook meat near or over an open fire while rotating on a spit." The word *spit* comes from the Old High German *spizzi*, meaning "pointed." Eventually, the spit moved from pit to kitchen, where poor young servant boys called "spit jacks" continuously cranked the huge roasts of "joints" before their masters' fires. (In some households, trained dogs, running on little treadmills, replaced the boy.) Eventually, counterweighted or spring-loaded systems replaced even the best dogs. Leonardo da Vinci actually conceived a spit system that was rotated by a windmill that was mounted inside the chimney, where it was powered by the rising smoke. While the indoor spit, or *rotisserie*, as the French call it, has passed into obsolescence, there's still plenty of rotating magic to be had outdoors.

Although you can create a darned fine gyro-flavored meatloaf without a rotisserie, you can't make a gyro without one. Most American grill manufacturers make rotisseries to go with their models. Some top-of-the-line gas models feature ceramic burners at the back of the grill just to cook whatever's spinning in front of it.

If your grill's manufacturer makes a rotisserie that fits your model, great. If it doesn't, not to worry. There are plenty of aftermarket "universal" models ranging from twenty to a hundred and twenty dollars, and I suggest spending more because you'll get heavier-duty hardware and a bigger motor.

GYROS FROM NEW YORK CITY!

The gyro sandwich isn't very old. In fact, the first time the word appeared in print is about 1970, and although it's got Greece all over it, most nutritional anthropologists agree that gyros were actually invented in one of New York City's Greek communities, possibly at a Greek Orthodox festival. Tzatziki, on the other hand, is very old, and very Greek, and originally made with yogurt from goat's and sheep's milk.

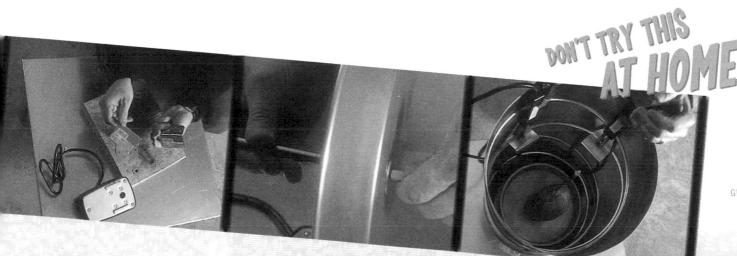

DON'T TRY THIS AT HOME!

GYRO MEAT

6 TO 8 SERVINGS

// SOFTWARE

1	medium	onion	finely chopped
2	pounds	ground lamb	
1	tablespoon	garlic	minced
1	tablespoon	dried marjoram	
1	tablespoon	ground dried rosemary	
2	teaspoons	kosher salt	
½	teaspoon	black pepper	freshly ground
		pitas, Tzatziki Sauce (see page 244), chopped onion, tomatoes, and feta cheese	for serving

// PROCEDURE

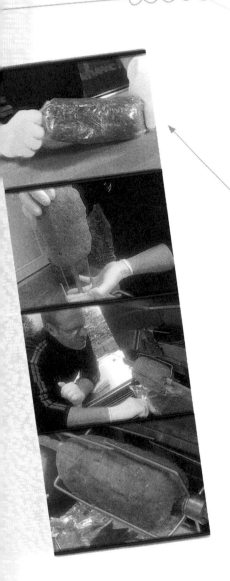

1. Process the onion in a **food processor** for 10 to 15 seconds and turn it out into the center of a **tea towel**. Gather up the ends of the towel and twist into a tight ball. Squeeze over sink to remove as much of the onion juice as possible.

2. Return the onion to the food processor and add the lamb, garlic, marjoram, rosemary, salt, and pepper and process until it is a fine paste, about 1 minute. Stop the processor as needed to scrape down the sides of the bowl.[1]

TO COOK ON A ROTISSERIE, PROCEED AS FOLLOWS:

3. Form the meat mixture into a loaf shape and place it on top of **2 overlapping pieces of plastic wrap that are at least 18 inches long**. Roll the mixture in the plastic tightly, making sure to remove any air pockets. Once the meat is completely entombed, twist the ends of the plastic wrap until the surface is tight. Refrigerate for at least 2 hours or up to overnight, to allow the mixture to firm up.

4. Heat the grill to high.

5. Place the meat on the **rotisserie skewer**. Place a **double-thick piece of aluminum foil** folded into a tray shape directly under the meat to catch any drippings. Cook on high for 15 minutes. Decrease the heat to medium and continue to cook for another 20 to 30 minutes, until the internal temperature of the meat reaches 165°F. Turn off the heat and continue to spin for another 10 to 15 minutes, until the internal temperature reaches 175°F. Slice thinly and serve on pita bread with tzatziki sauce, chopped onion, tomatoes, and feta cheese.

[1] Depending on the horsepower of your processor, you may need to do this in two batches.

NOTE: If serving then and there, I leave the meat on the rotisserie and the grill on. Carefully work with the longest slicer you have and slice thin strips from one end to the other. As new meat is exposed it will brown seductively, and everyone will be happy because they'll get some of that tasty, almost-but-not-quite-burned goodness.

TO COOK IN THE OVEN AS A MEATLOAF, PROCEED AS FOLLOWS:

3. Heat the oven to 325°F.

4. Place the mixture in a **loaf pan**, making sure to press it into the sides of the pan. Place the loaf pan in a hot water bath and bake for 60 to 75 minutes, until the mixture reaches 165° to 170°F. Remove from the oven and drain off any fat.

5. Place the loaf pan on a cooling rack, place a brick wrapped in aluminum foil directly on the surface of the meat, and allow to sit for 15 to 20 minutes, until the internal temperature reaches 175°F. Slice thinly and serve on pita bread with tzatziki sauce, chopped onion, tomatoes, and feta cheese.

TZATZIKI SAUCE

1½ CUPS

Gyros are traditionally dressed with a garlicky cucumber yogurt sauce called tzatziki, which roughly translated means "garlicky yogurt cucumber sauce" . . . I think. Anyway, Greek yogurt is very, very thick and creamy. And if you can find it in your area, you should absolutely use it. If not, you can make a reasonable facsimile by taking 16 ounces of plain, full- or low-fat, American-style yogurt, dumping it right in the middle of a tea towel, and letting it drain.

This is the standard "yee-row" sauce served by every Greek joint on the planet.

// SOFTWARE ///

2	cups	plain yogurt	low-fat is fine, but not fat-free
1	medium	cucumber	peeled, seeded, and finely chopped[2]
	pinch	kosher salt	
4	cloves	garlic	minced
1	tablespoon	olive oil	
2	teaspoons	red wine vinegar	
5 or 6	leaves	fresh mint	finely chopped

// PROCEDURE //

1. Put the yogurt in a **tea towel**, gather up the edges, suspend over a **bowl**, and drain for 2 hours in the refrigerator.

2. Put the cucumber in a **tea towel**, gather up the edges, and squeeze to remove excess moisture; discard the liquid. Combine the drained yogurt, cucumber, salt, garlic, oil, vinegar, and mint in a **medium mixing bowl**. Serve as a sauce for gyros. Store in the refrigerator in an airtight container for up to 1 week.

NOTE: I keep this in a big squeeze bottle with the nozzle cut to ¼ inch in diameter so that all the chunks squeeze out.

[2] If you prefer to use the larger and more costly "English" seedless cucumber (sometimes referred to as a "burpless"), it's okay by me, but use only half of one.

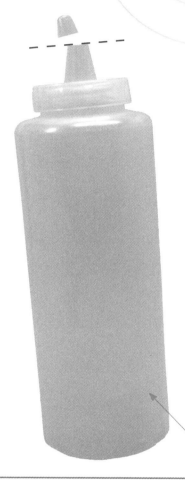

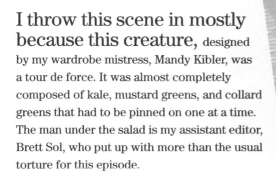

FIELD OF GREENS

I throw this scene in mostly because this creature, designed by my wardrobe mistress, Mandy Kibler, was a tour de force. It was almost completely composed of kale, mustard greens, and collard greens that had to be pinned on one at a time. The man under the salad is my assistant editor, Brett Sol, who put up with more than the usual torture for this episode.

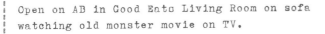

Open on AB in Good Eats Living Room on sofa watching old monster movie on TV.

AB: (chuckle) Hard to believe, but this movie scared the bejeebers out of me when I was a kid. Of course, back then my friends and I had an entire hierarchy of scariness. For instance, Dracula was scarier than Frankenstein because Frankenstein was kind of slow-moving and slow-thinking. Things from space were generally scarier than things that weren't. But nothing—nothing—haunted us like the vegetal apparition that we called "Mean Green."

A horrifying creature lumbers up behind AB. It's like a huge Cousin It but completely composed of (yuck) dark, leafy greens. This...is Mean Green.

AB: Mean Green was a composite monster built out of our collective fear of all foods dark, leafy, and green. Of course, our fears were well founded. These foods were supposed to be healthy. And of course they tasted terrible: bitter, earthy,

composty. Blech. And of course our moms cooked them for days, creating a texture that we were certain could exist only in primordial swamp ooze. Luckily, these unsavory leaves gave off such a stench during their long stewing sessions that you were tipped off to the nature of the evening's meal long before you got home. This gave you time to hatch an avoidance scheme, such as dinner at a friend's, or an appendectomy, or running away to join the French Foreign Legi...

Mean Green attacks AB but instead of recoiling, AB pats him on the head like a friendly dog who plops next to him on the sofa.

AB: But I've learned a thing or two since childhood, about vegetables, cooking, and monsters. And I'm pleased to say that the creature formerly known as Mean Green is—in my house, at least—referred to now as Deep Green. And he's a good friend of mine, not to mention seriously...

TENDER

HEARTY

TIDBIT According to Hippocrates, greens were part of the Greek diet.

TIDBIT John Milton wrote that "turnip greens awaken slumbering desire in even the most quiescent spouse."

KNOWLEDGE CONCENTRATE

▷ **I divide the green and leafy world into two distinct groups:**

— 1. tender

— 2. hearty

Tender greens like beet greens or baby mustard greens wilt quickly when exposed to heat, as does spinach and Swiss chard. Hearty greens like kale, collards, turnip greens, and mature mustard greens all require longer exposure to heat in order to soften. It is these hearty greens with their strong flavors and concentrated nutrition that we will focus on here.

▷ **Kale, mustard, turnips, and collards are brassicas; that is, they are members of the same botanical family as cabbage, cauliflower, and broccoli. But here's the difference: All of these greens bear the scientific moniker *acephala*, which means "headless." These are some of the very oldest of the brassicas and were conceivably consumed by our furrier, more-broad-of-forehead forefathers.**

▷ **While it is certainly true that dark, leafy things keep better and longer when left in a whole state, it's also true that you will be a whole lot more likely to use them if they are prepped and ready to go when you walk up to the old chill chest. And, clean and prepped, they will take up a lot less room in there. The first thing we have to deal with is the stem, which I'm certainly not going to eat. My rule is if a piece of stem or leaf vein is less than ¼ inch wide, I'll leave it be. Anything bigger than that, and it's got to go. Here's how:**

Just lay out the leaf, then fold it over like a big green taco and run a knife right down the stem. You can just pull the stem off with your fingers if it's a thin one. And of course scissors work well too.

▷ **Curly leaves can be kind of torn up and dumped in a sink full of water; just make sure that the water is deep enough for any gunk, dirt, sand, and so on to sink down away from the stuff you're going to eat.**

If, however, you're dealing with a really big, flat leaf, like a collard green, pull off the stems, then stack about eight or ten leaves, fold them, and roll them up. Hold them carefully, cut down the middle, and then cut them perpendicular to the first cut. Move them to the water and slosh them around to rinse.

Letting water cling to these leaves is a fine idea if you're going to cook them right away. But for long-term storage, bone-dry is better. You could use a hand-cranked salad spinner, but it would take all day for the amount you'll need for a pot of cooked greens, so I prefer to use the big electric salad spinner that I've got here in the laundry room. That's right, the clothes washer. Just fill a zip-up pillow bag or pillow cover with your greens and drop it in the washing machine. Turn on the spin cycle, and come back in about a minute.

Small batches of raw greens can be wrapped in a couple of paper towels and stashed in 2-gallon zip-top bags for a couple of weeks as long as you use a straw and suck out every bit of air that you possibly can before sealing the bag.

Somewhere along the line, certain Southerners got the notion that greens such as collards, turnip greens, mustard greens, and such aren't worth eating unless they've been cooked to the point where you could eat them with a spoon, or in extreme cases suck 'em up a straw. This is unfortunate for a whole big bunch of reasons.

Let's say for a moment that we could take a collard leaf and blow it up to thousands of times its normal size. And let's say that we had some technology that would allow us to cut a wee little patch in the side of the leaf so we could peel back the chloroplast and look down into the cell structure inside. What we would see would not be unlike this:

Behold: a lot of little boxes—these are the cells that are made up of pectin substances that are reinforced with lignin and cellulose—and inside, all kinds of structures including nutrients, like vitamins and minerals. Things that we want to get at. The problem is, they're in those cells. Now, cows get around this when they eat grass because they stand and they chew, and chew, and chew all day long, which is why they don't build buildings or powerboats or supercomputers. People, on the other hand, know how to cook. And through cooking, through a combination of water, heat, and time, we can soften these walls and get at the nutrients inside. If we cook longer than it takes just to soften, we can, actually, almost dissolve these walls to the point that the nutrients will run out into the water. And there's nothing wrong with that, as long as you like drinking the "pot liquor," as we call it in the South—and I certainly do. However, if you continue to cook the leaves, these nutrients can begin to break down. Bad things can happen. See, when isothiocyanates cook enough, they form very strong flavors and even stronger smells in the air. And that stinky, rotten-egg smell that comes out of greens all too often can be toxic in large amounts. In fact, it was synthesized and turned into a biological warfare agent used in World War I called mustard gas.

By the way: Isothiocyanates are powerful plant nutrients called phytochemicals. And we love them because they're like hit men against evil free radicals, some of which are proven carcinogens. Not only can they help prevent their damaging effects, such as tumors, they can actually help remove them from our bodies. But you know, you don't have to overcook them to consume the benefits.

POT O' GREENS

4 SERVINGS

// SOFTWARE ///

1	quart	H_2O	
1½	pounds	smoked turkey legs	
2	pounds	stemmed collard or turnip greens	weigh the greens after stemming, but before washing
1	teaspoon	kosher salt	plus extra for seasoning
1	teaspoon	sugar	
1	teaspoon	red pepper flakes	

// PROCEDURE ///

1. Combine the water and turkey legs in an **8-quart pot** over medium-high heat. Cover, bring to a boil, and simmer for 10 minutes.

2. Meanwhile, wash the greens thoroughly; it's best to do this in a sink with at least 5 inches of water. Move the leaves around in the water and let them sit for a few minutes so any sand or dirt will fall to the bottom of the sink. Dry thoroughly in a **salad spinner** and chop the pieces in half.

3. Add the greens, salt, sugar, and red pepper flakes to the pot, reduce the heat to low, cover, and simmer gently for 45 minutes, or until the greens are tender. Move the greens around every 10 to 15 minutes. Taste and season with additional salt, if desired. Serve immediately.

TIDBIT | The word *collard* comes from the Anglo-Saxon term *colewart*, which just means "cabbage plant."

FLAVOR PARTNERS FOR GREENS

Most greens deliver strong flavors and profit from strong partnerships. Consider the following:

▶ PUNGENT as in garlic.

▶ ACIDIC as in vinegar and citrus.

▶ CREAMY as in blue cheese.

▶ SMOKY as in smoked meats. My favorite smoke-injection system is smoked turkey legs, which are available at most megamarts. They impart just the right amount of smoky goodness without overwhelming the natural flavor of the greens, and they contribute a fair amount of collagen, which of course breaks down into gelatin to provide considerable lip-smacking body.

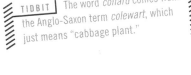

Although here in America hearty greens are most often associated with long, slow cooking methods, in Asia greens such as turnip greens, mustard greens, and kale are often cooked hot and very fast. The key to getting away with this is in using the right technique, bright acidic flavors, and the proper pan.

The big issue in pan selection is surface area. If you've got a big old mess of greens and try to cook them in too small a pan, you'll end up stewing them—and that's not what you want to do. You're looking for more of a sauté. So you'll need a lotta wide-open real estate such as that found in a heavy roasting pan.

// SOFTWARE ///

1 to 1¼	pounds	stemmed hearty greens such as mustard greens or kale	weigh the greens after stemming, but before washing
1	tablespoon	olive oil	
2	cloves	garlic	minced
1		lemon	zested
2	teaspoons	lemon juice	freshly squeezed
1	tablespoon	honey	
1½	teaspoons	kosher salt	
¼	teaspoon	black pepper	freshly ground
½	teaspoon	red pepper flakes	
1	tablespoon	sesame seeds	

// PROCEDURE ///

1. Wash the greens thoroughly; it's best to do this in a sink with at least 5 inches of water. Move the leaves around in the water and let them sit for a few minutes so any sand or dirt will fall to the bottom of the sink. Dry them thoroughly in a **salad spinner** and coarsely chop the pieces.

2. Heat a **13-by-11-inch roasting pan** over 2 burners on medium heat. Once hot, add the oil. Add the garlic, lemon zest, lemon juice, honey, salt, and pepper and stir to combine. Add the greens and sauté for 4 to 5 minutes, tossing continuously. Add the red pepper flakes and the sesame seeds. Toss to combine. Adjust seasoning, if needed. Serve immediately.

TIDBIT | In the South, greens are eaten on New Year's Day in the hopes that they'll bring money in the coming year.

When most Americans think of *Oryza sativa* they think of long-grain, aromatic rices like basmati and jasmine, rices that cook up fluffy and separate, which is fine. But the short- and medium-grain varieties that feed Europe and most of Asia are considerably more versatile. This is due to the fact that their starch content is quite different and therefore they respond to cooking in some very interesting ways. Case in point: risotto. I remember my very first bowl of the stuff, served at a restaurant, which only offered it at the top of the hour because they insisted it took that long to make a decent batch. When it came I practically called the waiter a liar because he insisted the rice wasn't cooked in cream when I knew darn well that it had been. Little did I know that what I was divinely devouring was made possible by the nature of a medium-grain rice.

PARTS LIST: ORYZA SATIVA

- Bran coat
- Husk
- Germ

PARTS LIST: BROWN RICE

- Bran
- Endosperm
- Where germ used to be

By the time white rice is processed and packaged, the outer husk and bran as well as the fat-bearing germ have been ground off, leaving nothing but shiny white endosperm, which is literally a fuel tank.[1] This tank contains energy in the form of starch—that is, glucose molecules held in two different arrangements: amylose and amylopectin.

How a rice behaves during cooking depends to a great extent on the ratio of these two structures. Quite conveniently, the proportions are relative to the length of the grain.

LONG-GRAIN rices contain a high percentage of amylose but not a lot of amylopectin. When cooked, this equation yields grains that are light, fluffy, and remain separate from each other. Long-grain rices have what people in the rice industry call "kernel integrity."

MEDIUM-GRAIN rices contain a higher percentage of amylopectin, which cooks up softer than long-grain. Also, amylopectin tends to leach out of the kernel into the surrounding liquid, a condition that makes dishes like risotto and rice pudding possible.

SHORT-GRAIN rices contain a much higher percentage of amylopectin, which results in a very sticky final product, hence sushi rice. When it cooks, it gives up huge amounts of starch to the surrounding environment.

Some of the finest medium-grain rices come from Italy, where, of course, risotto reigns. If you plan on stirring up your own at home, you'll want to lay in the proper software. ARBORIO rice may be considered indispensable to the dish here in the United States, but other varieties such as CARNAROLI and VIALONE NANO are held in even higher regard in the land of the boot.

Oh, something about the packaging of Italian rices you should know: You'll often see words like "semifino," "fino," or "superfino" on boxes of Italian rice. These are not quality-related terms but rather references to grain length, *superfino* being a fair amount longer than a *semifino*.

And now for something completely different: brown rice. When it's first harvested, rice has an outer coat on it, a seed husk that is utterly, completely inedible. It is removed at the mill via mechanical means.[2] The germ is also removed, leaving us with an endosperm laminated in a thin layer of material called bran. At this point the rice itself is referred to as "cargo rice," or brown rice, and it's far more healthful than white rice because the bran contains riboflavin, vitamin B_6, magnesium, manganese, phosphorus, selenium, even some vitamin E. And then, of course, there's fiber (nature's broom). And it turns out that the oil in rice bran actually helps remove undesirable low-density lipoproteins from the bloodstream.

The problem with the bran—and the reason it's most often milled away to yield white rice, shiny white endosperm that is then "enriched" by having nutrients pushed into the starch matrix—is that it acts like a raincoat, preventing the cooking liquid from working its way into the endosperm. As a result brown rice takes quite a while to cook. In a pan on the stove this protracted exposure to bottom-up heat often results in scorching, mushiness, gumminess, and generally disgusting results. The way around this is to avoid the cooktop entirely.

THE TWO MAIN STARCH FORMS IN RICE

Amylose

Amylopectin

TIDBIT | Rice is now cultivated in over 110 countries, in many different climates and environments.

TIDBIT | In a number of Asian languages, the same word denotes both "rice" and "food."

[1] Remember the discussion of wheat structure a few episodes back? Same thing, only less protein to contend with here.

[2] Some American mills have taken to incinerating the husk material in order to generate electricity to run the rest of the mill.

WILD MUSHROOM AND ASPARAGUS RISOTTO

6 CUPS

This is a fairly simple risotto, as I believe every risotto should be. When it comes to ingredients in addition to the rice, I have two rules: I never add more than two chunky ingredients and I never use vegetation that hasn't already been cooked unless it's of herbal origins.

// SOFTWARE //

3	tablespoons	unsalted butter	divided
2	cups	wild mushrooms	such as oyster, morel, wood ear, porcini, shiitake, or chanterelle; coarsely chopped
1½	cups	asparagus	cut into 1-inch pieces
	to taste	kosher salt	
5 to 6	cups	chicken stock	
1	cup	onion	finely chopped
2	cups	Arborio rice	
1	cup	dry white wine	
1	teaspoon	lemon zest	grated
½	teaspoon	nutmeg	freshly grated
½	cup	Parmesan cheese	grated

// SPECIAL HARDWARE ///

You're going to need a **wide, heavy pot in the 3- to 4-quart range**. Wide is good because it makes it easier to stir the risotto, and heavy is good because it helps to prevent burning; and I don't just mean a heavy bottom, I mean heavy sides, too. Other hardware includes a stirring device of some type. Risotto purists insist that wooden spoons are the only way to go because their insulative power prevents heat from seeping up out of the risotto too quickly. I personally prefer a large rubber or silicone spatula.

1. Heat 1 tablespoon of the butter in a **medium sauté pan** over medium heat. Add the mushrooms, asparagus, and salt and sauté until the asparagus is tender but still crisp and the liquid from the mushrooms has evaporated, 7 to 10 minutes. Set aside.

2. Heat the stock in a **medium saucepan** to a bare simmer and hold it there over low heat.

3. Heat the remaining 2 tablespoons butter in **large, heavy-bottom saucepan** over medium-low heat. Add the onion and sweat until translucent, about 5 minutes. Add the rice and stir with a **wooden spoon** until the grains become opaque, 2 to 3 minutes. Add the wine and stir until the wine is absorbed by the rice.

4. Add enough of the hot stock to just cover the rice. Stir constantly until the liquid is completely absorbed. Add just enough stock to cover the rice and continue stirring as before. There should be just enough stock left to repeat one more time. It should take 30 to 35 minutes for all of the stock to be absorbed.

5. After the last of the stock is added and most of it is absorbed, fold in the mushrooms and asparagus and stir until the risotto is creamy and the asparagus is heated through. Remove from the heat and stir in the lemon zest, nutmeg, cheese, and salt and pepper to taste. Serve immediately.

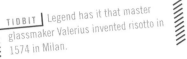

TIDBIT | Legend has it that master glassmaker Valerius invented risotto in 1574 in Milan.

HAPPY RICE!

RISOTTO

In the United States, any medium-grain rice can be labeled or packaged as "risotto rice," so just because you see an Italian word on the box it doesn't mean you're getting Italian rice inside the box. This begs the question: Does a medium-grain rice from Arkansas make as good a risotto as a rice from the Po River Valley? Well, maybe yes and maybe no. What I do know, though, is that when it comes to risotto nothing matters more than technique.

The goal is to cook the rice until it's just tender while coaxing enough starch out into the cooking liquid to thicken it to a loose gravy consistency. To achieve this the rice kernels must remain surrounded with hot liquid but not so much that they cannot rub up next to each other. No rubbing, no releasing of starch. So the risottoist must:

1. make frequent, small additions of hot liquid to the pot, and

2. provide frequent (but not necessarily constant) agitation.

Agitation, by the way, does not necessarily have to come from stirring. Giving the pan a gentle shake every now and then can achieve the same ends, but since the pot is chock full of hotness, care must be taken.

BAKED BROWN RICE

4 SERVINGS

// SOFTWARE ///

1½	cups	brown rice	medium- or short-grain
2½	cups	H_2O	
1	tablespoon	unsalted butter	
1	teaspoon	kosher salt	

// PROCEDURE ///

1. Heat the oven to 375°F. Spread the rice in an **8-inch square glass baking dish**.

2. Bring the water, butter, and salt just to a boil in an **electric kettle or a covered saucepan**. Pour it over the rice, stir to combine, cover the dish tightly with **heavy-duty aluminum foil**, and bake on the middle rack of the oven for 1 hour.

3. After 1 hour, remove the foil and fluff the rice with a fork. Serve immediately.

TIP | Since the bran contains unsaturated oils that can oxidize and go rancid at room temperature, you should tightly wrap brown rice and put it in the freezer rather than on the pantry shelf for long-term storage.

TRIVIA | Kudos to Jim and Brett for putting up with the rice suits and especially Jim for actually being seen in that rain getup: That's a man who's very secure with his masculinity.

BROWN RICE SALAD

4 SERVINGS

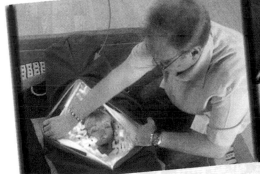

// SOFTWARE ///

6	slices	bacon	
½	cup	red onion	diced
½	cup	white wine vinegar	
½	cup	chicken broth	
2	teaspoons	Dijon mustard	
1	teaspoon	sugar	
1	teaspoon	kosher salt	
½	teaspoon	black pepper	freshly ground
1	recipe	Baked Brown Rice	(left page)
1	tablespoon	fresh dill	chopped

// PROCEDURE ///

1. Fry the bacon until crisp in a **10-inch sauté pan** over medium heat. Drain the bacon, crumble it, and set aside. Pour all but 1 tablespoon of the bacon fat out of the pan.

2. Add the onion to the fat in the pan and cook over medium heat until translucent, 5 to 6 minutes. Add the vinegar, broth, mustard, sugar, salt, and pepper and stir to combine. Add the bacon back to the pan along with the rice, and cook, stirring occasionally, until the liquid is absorbed, 7 to 10 minutes. Stir in the dill. Refrigerate until ready to serve.

   NOTE: When you do break your salad out of the chill chest you'll find it pleasantly chewy but not hard the way refrigerated long-grain (think Chinese take-out) rice would be. That's because as the starch in rice cools, amylose and water come together, creating a structure resembling a crystal, which is why it's hard as a rock. The process of starch retrogradation is reversed when the rice is reheated. When more amylopectin is around, its highly branched, tumbleweed character prevents the molecular alignment necessary for retrogradation to take place, which is why I turn to medium-grain rices for any and all rice applications that are served cold.

TRIVIA | When you see dietician Carolyn O'Neil's face pop out of that grain of rice (actually a duffle bag), it's a bit of a shock. And it wasn't easy to pull off. The rug under the duffle is actually on a platform about a foot off the floor. Carolyn was on the floor and had to shove her head up through aligned holes in the rug and the bag. This required a near Cirque du Soleil—like flexibility on Ms. O'Neil's part—and kudos to her for complaining not one bit.

CAROLYN'S TRICK

Head in a bag

Carolyn

Plywood

Rug

Foam wedge

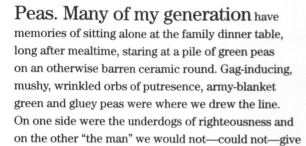

Peas. Many of my generation have memories of sitting alone at the family dinner table, long after mealtime, staring at a pile of green peas on an otherwise barren ceramic round. Gag-inducing, mushy, wrinkled orbs of putresence, army-blanket green and gluey peas were where we drew the line. On one side were the underdogs of righteousness and on the other "the man" we would not—could not—give in to. Those with family dogs had it easier because during the actual meal peas could stealthily be transerred from plate to canine the way the *Great Escape* tunnelers dumped their dirt in the stalag yard. The rest of us dug in and waited for morning. Sometimes we won . . . sometimes the peas won.

Needless to say, very few of us have happy memories of peas. Many of us refuse them to this day.

And that's a shame, because the English garden pea, or sweet pea, and its ancient but versatile ancestor, the field pea, are as good eats as good eats get.

PEAS IN A POD

You don't often see garden peas in their original and intended container, for two reasons. One, peas are at their best during a very slender slice of springtime, usually from late March through May. Two, once picked, peas lose their flavor fast. As much as 40 percent of their sugar can convert to starch in the first day after picking. Long-distance shipping is pretty much out of the question. That means that if you do find these fresh, you want to be sure they're very, very fresh. You want the pods to be nice and firm, a little glossy, and when you rub them together they should squeak. If they rattle, it means that the peas have pulled away from the inner pod and they are therefore past their prime.

One of the reasons that kids, or at least country-born kids, don't care for peas is that unlike snow peas and sugar-snap peas, they have to be shelled—and shelling is a job that can be done by little fingers. (To tell you the truth, I've always kind of liked shelling peas. Is that wrong?) But there is an easy way to do it: Grab the pea and with one end pointing down, press until the seam starts to open and then just unzip it with your thumb.

Then run your thumb down the length of the pea and voilà, no more peas in the pod.

Oh, and another thing: Garden peas take to the deep freeze better than almost any other veggie. They were, in fact, some of the very first foods to ever successfully undergo the freezing procedure. I keep frozen peas on hand at all times. (I might add that they're very good for icing down boo-boos.) Canned green peas, on the other hand, are . . . what's the word . . . ah, yes: evil—evil in every way conceivable. If I ruled the world, they'd be outlawed.

FIELD PEAS, which usually come in yellow and green, sometimes orange, are heartier and starchier than sweet garden peas. And they're historically significant, because they were one of the first foods to be gathered and then dried. A cave-dwelling family who had peas like these would be able to get all the complex carbs, proteins, minerals, and good old-fashioned calories that they would need to survive a winter when the hunting was iffy at best. And because they split naturally when dry, the peas could be cooked without long soaking, an attribute that gives modern cooks a leg up as well. And their starchiness means that once they're cooked, they blend down into very smooth soups.

Early European agriculturists learned that if they were going to live off of staples like wheat and barley, they would have to practice field rotation. That's because cereal crops tend to deplete soil nutrients quickly. So you have a parcel of land, you split it in half, you grow your grains on one side, and you leave the other side fallow so that it can recover through a growing season; and then you rotate the crops. Peas, however, do not deplete nutrients from the land. In fact, they feed it. So if you take the same parcel of land and split it into thirds, growing peas in one, wheat in another, and leaving the last fallow, you could actually double your nutritive output every other year. Peoples who adapted the three-field method, such as the Franks under Charlemagne, eventually came to dominate the economic landscape of Europe. So you could say that peas changed the world.

GARDEN PEAS, OR SWEET PEAS as we know them today, were born when seventeenth-century Dutch agriculturists spotted the occasional mutant mini-pea plants in their fields. And, no doubt building upon the work of Gregor Mendel, they did what they've done with everything from carrots to tulips: They coaxed entirely new varieties of plants out of the gene pool. Unleashed upon Europe, the dwarf pea, or *petit pois*, started a craze in the court of Louis XIV, where lady courtiers took to consuming large plates of the tender goodies right in their beds just before lights out. The Dutch would go on to develop the snow pea, which would become very popular, via the Portuguese, in China and Japan . . . but that's another show.

TIDBIT Today over 90 percent of all peas are sold frozen.

TIDBIT Between 1700 and 1900 the English developed over a thousand varieties of peas.

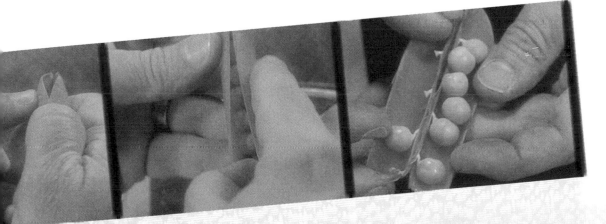

CURRIED SPLIT PEA SOUP

4 SERVINGS

// SOFTWARE //

2	tablespoons	unsalted butter	
1	cup	onion	chopped
	to taste	kosher salt	
1	tablespoon	garlic	minced
12	ounces	dried green or yellow split peas	sorted and rinsed
5	cups	chicken broth	
1	tablespoon	curry powder	
	to taste	black pepper	freshly ground

TIDBIT | In 1670 colonists survived on a ration of one pint of peas a day.

// PROCEDURE //

1. Melt the butter in a **4- to 6-quart saucepan** over medium-low heat. Add the onion and a generous pinch of salt and sweat for 2 to 3 minutes. Toss in the garlic and continue to sweat for an additional 1 to 2 minutes; do not brown the onions or garlic.

2. Add the split peas, broth, and curry powder. Increase the heat to high and bring to a boil. Reduce the heat to low, cover, and simmer until the peas are tender and no longer hold their shape, 45 to 50 minutes. Taste and adjust the seasoning as needed. Using an **immersion blender**, puree the soup to the desired consistency. Serve immediately or keep warm in a **Thermos**.

TRIVIA | Obviously the show (if not its title) is a nod to the scariest horror movie ever made, *The Exorcist*, for which canned split pea soup was used as, well . . . what split pea soup looks like. Although the goof here is a little clumsy, I couldn't pass up any structure that would allow me to fling peas around and give my soundtrack composer Patrick Belden the opportunity to riff on "Tubular Bells," a piece I know he greatly admires and often points out is the first album ever put out by Virgin records. The house where "little Stevie" lives was my own residence at the time, and this was one of the few times we shot there.

SPLIT PEA BURGERS

8 (5-OUNCE) BURGERS

// SOFTWARE //

2	tablespoons	olive oil	plus additional for sautéing
½	cup	onion	chopped
½	cup	bell pepper	chopped
	to taste	kosher salt	
2	teaspoons	garlic	minced
4	ounces	mushrooms	sliced
3	cups	vegetable broth	
1	cup	dried split peas	sorted and rinsed
½	cup	raw brown rice	
1	teaspoon	ground coriander	
1	teaspoon	ground cumin	
1	cup	plain dry bread crumbs	
	to taste	black pepper	freshly ground

// PROCEDURE //

1. Heat 1 tablespoon of the oil in a **large saucepan** over medium heat. Add the onion and bell pepper along with a generous pinch of salt. Sweat for 5 minutes, or until the onion is soft. Add the garlic and mushrooms and continue to cook for another 4 minutes.

2. Add the broth, split peas, rice, coriander, and cumin. Increase the heat to high and bring to a boil. Reduce the heat to low, cover, and simmer for 1 hour, or until the rice and peas are tender.

3. Remove from the heat and gently pour the mixture into the bowl of a **food processor** and process until just combined. Do not puree. Pour this mixture into a **bowl** and stir in ¾ cup of the bread crumbs. Season to taste with salt and black pepper. Refrigerate for 30 minutes.

4. Shape the mixture into patties and dredge on each side in the remaining ¼ cup bread crumbs. Heat the remaining 1 tablespoon oil in a **medium sauté pan** over medium heat. Add 2 burgers at a time and sauté until brown on each side, 3 to 4 minutes per side. To grill, cook on high for 3 to 4 minutes per side. Serve immediately.

PEASE PUDDING

Ever heard the old nursery rhyme "Pease pudding hot, pease pudding cold, pease pudding in the pot, nine days old"? Of course you have. But have you ever taken the time to wonder why it's "pease pudding" instead of "pea pudding"? Well, it turns out that the original singular of the noun was pease. It was twisted by the Saxons, most likely, from the original Latin *pisum* ("PIE-sum"). What happened was that as the English language developed the standard "s" plural, pease became used as a plural and a new word, *pea*, had to be invented as a singular.

Anyway, the original pease pudding was, like most English puddings, just a bunch of mushed-up peas put in a cloth and boiled for hours and hours. I actually believe that this is the device that began the whole kids-hating-peas scenario. Luckily, the natural evolution of this method brings us to a far more kid-friendly form, namely a burger—a pea burger, in fact.

Dateline: Turkey, A.D. 900.

As the moon rises over the barren, desolate plains of Eurasia, bands of marauding Ottomans, tired and hungry from a long day of empire building, settle down to their supper. These guys travel light and rarely eat at a table, much less with a fork, which by the way hadn't been invented yet. And they don't even have anything to sit on. But they are a civilized and inventive lot, so when one of them manages to kill a critter, their swords, spears, and daggers become culinary tools. And thus the shish-kabob, or skewered roasted meat product, was born. Of course, you have to wonder, if the Ottomans were so inventive, why didn't they invent the ottoman, which would have at least given them a place to sit?

TIP | Do not eat the food directly off the skewer, as doing so can result in the contacting of insurance personnel.

TIDBIT | A kabob by any other name: *anticuchos* = Peru, *brochette* = France, *yakitori* = Japan.

TIDBIT | In chemistry, the term *shish kebab* is used metaphorically for a type of crystalline body that grows from a central rod.

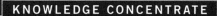

KNOWLEDGE CONCENTRATE

▷ **Although wooden skewers are useful for many small grilled applications such as Japanese yakitori, those will have to wait for a show of their own because here we need big, long metal skewers that resemble the speartips and bayonets on which the original kabobs were cooked.**

Ideally speaking, kabob skewers for use over gas or charcoal will be at least 12 inches long, with 17 inches being vastly preferable. They will be composed of flat 12-grade nickel-plated steel or stainless steel. (Round skewers are useless for kabobs because the food simply spins around on them.) One end will be shaped into a sharp point, while the other will curve into a ring for easy handling. Some especially large skewers designed for use in tandoor ovens may have wooden handles, which are cool to the touch and easy to handle, but also harder to clean—and flammable.

▷ **Although kabobbery be a simple sport, I do find that by following a few basic guidelines you can bolster your chances of success.**

I like to work with latex gloves. That's just because this can get a little bit messy and some marinades will stain if you're not careful. I also have to do less hand-washing this way.

Even though all of the ingredients are going to be cooked through, I keep the meat and vegetables segregated to prevent any possible cross-contamination.

Always sort out the meat and veggies by size before skewering so that like-size pieces end up meeting the heat together.

When it comes to the actual skewering, aim for center mass.

Although meat that's tightly packed onto a skewer will resist spinning during turns over the fire, even a half inch of space will add 50 percent more surface area, and surface area is good.

Veggies with squishy centers such as zucchini should always be cut in at least 1-inch rounds and then be skewered through the side.

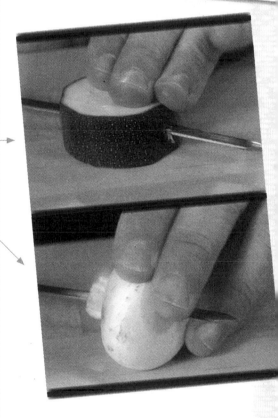

Mushrooms are notorious skewer spinners, so always leave the stem on, and always run through the stem from the bottom.

Onions are very popular on kabobs, but if you cut them into wedges and then try to put them on, they always fall apart. So I suggest going with either big hunks of leeks or large pearl onions.

Peppers are popular kabob fodder because they're tasty and colorful. I like cutting them into rounds; when you run those guys through, they stay nice and even, and you get some charring around the side.

Soak cut pieces of hard vegetables such as sweet potatoes and rutabagas in water for half an hour before skewering to help prevent splitting.

Whenever possible, hold the target food on a flat surface before pushing the skewer through the food. Resist the urge to shove the food onto the skewer like one might impale a marshmallow on a stick.

Although kabobs can be cooked under a broiler, they were invented for the outdoors, and that's where they belong. For most folks this means a grill, hibachi, or fire bowl and either gas, charcoal, or wood can be used. Regardless of fuel source, kabobs should cook via radiation and convection, not conduction, which means ditching the grill grate altogether. Of course, the food will have to rest on something, so either:

Make sure your skewers are long enough to rest on the chasis of the grill; or

Consider "bookending" the skewers with clan bricks (I keep fireplace bricks around for just this sort of maneuver).

DIS-KABOB-ULATED

SPICY BEEF KABOBS

WHY KABOBS?

But seriously, folks, the kabob concept is great because:

▶ Small hunks of meat have far more surface area than large hunks and thus cook faster with (potentially) better flavor development.

▶ When properly handled, kabobbery results in even cooking of multiple pieces of food.

▶ Kabobs can be daring service pieces.

▶ Kabobs can be cooked almost anywhere—in the oven or over charcoal or gas—and they can even be fried.

▶ Kabobbing is flat-out fun.

▶ Kabobs can be used to trick children into eating things they wouldn't ordinarily allow in their mouths.

TIP | Although a very thin coating of oil will help any last-minute seasonings to stick and encourage crust development, do remember that oil burns. If you apply so much that it drips onto the coals, there will be flames—and flames mean soot, and soot is never good eats.

Although many cuts, from the round to the chuck, have kabob potential, I believe the sirloin primal best delivers that perfect balance of beefy flavor and meaty texture that you expect from something as elemental as a kabob. I also like sirloin because it's very easy to fabricate in the home kitchen environment. Oh, and if you've ever heard that story about King Henry VIII having knighted this cut of meat, thus making it Sir Loin, that's crazy talk. The *sir* comes from the French for "under." *Sirloin* actually means "under the loin."

// SOFTWARE //

1½ to 2	pounds	boneless beef sirloin	
3	cloves	garlic	minced
2	teaspoons	hot smoked paprika	
½	teaspoon	ground turmeric	
1	teaspoon	ground cumin	
1	teaspoon	kosher salt	
½	teaspoon	black pepper	freshly ground
⅓	cup	red wine vinegar	
½	cup	olive oil	(not extra virgin)

// SPECIAL HARDWARE //

4 (12- to 17-inch) metal skewers

// PROCEDURE //

1. Cut the beef into 1½- to 1¾-inch cubes and set aside in a **large mixing bowl**.

2. Combine the garlic, paprika, turmeric, cumin, salt, pepper, and vinegar in the bowl of a **food processor**. With the processor running, drizzle in the oil. Pour the marinade over the meat and toss to coat. Refrigerate in an **airtight container or a zip-top bag** and marinate for 2 to 4 hours.

3. Heat a **grill** to medium-high. Thread the meat onto **skewers**, leaving about ½ inch between the pieces of meat. Place on the grill and cook, with the lid lowered, for 2 to 3 minutes per side, 8 to 12 minutes total—8 minutes for rare and 12 for medium. Remove from the heat to **aluminum foil**, wrap, and let rest for 2 to 3 minutes before serving.

4 SERVINGS

Just as meat appreciates a little bit of a soak in a marinade before facing the fire, so does fruit appreciate a little syrup.

// SOFTWARE ///

1		vanilla bean	
8	ounces	dark brown sugar	
½	cup	lime juice	freshly squeezed
	pinch	kosher salt	
1		pineapple	

// SPECIAL HARDWARE //

8 (12- to 17-inch) metal skewers

// PROCEDURE //

1. Split the vanilla bean and scrape out the pulp. Put the bean and the pulp in a **small saucepan**, along with the brown sugar, lime juice, and salt. **Whisk** together, place over medium-high heat, and bring to a boil, stirring just until the sugar has dissolved. Remove from the heat and cool for 2 hours before using. Remove the vanilla bean. Once cool, **funnel** the syrup into a **squeeze bottle or other sealable container**. Store in the refrigerator.

2. Heat a **grill** to high.

3. **Peel** and core the pineapple. Cut the pineapple into eighths, lengthwise, and remove any prickly brown eyes.

4. Thread the pieces of pineapple onto **skewers** lengthwise. Coat the skewered pineapple on all sides with the syrup. Grill on all sides until golden brown, about 4 minutes per side, 12 minutes total, until the pineapple is tender. Serve with any remaining syrup as a sauce.

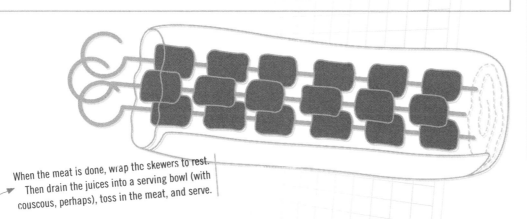

When the meat is done, wrap the skewers to rest.
Then drain the juices into a serving bowl (with
couscous, perhaps), toss in the meat, and serve.

THROW AN OLD-SCHOOL KABOB BASH!

If you want to create a more historically accurate kabob experience, try this:

Find yourself a nice level plot of ground and remove any extraneous, unnecessary plant life or errant combustibles like, say, a house, lawnmower, can of gas, or sleeping livestock.

Carve yourself a shallow trench maybe 4 inches deep, 12 inches wide, and 5 feet long.

Line this trench with sand, encircle it with stones or bricks, and fill it up with hot charcoal.

Remember that kabobs are party food, and it doesn't matter what the party is. You could be celebrating your new job or, I don't know, maybe you laid siege to a fortified town. It doesn't matter; any reason is fine.

Remember that in kabobbery frequent fiddling is absolutely necessary. You've got to keep turning the food all the time and keep testing for doneness. Since a thermometer isn't really practical in this form of cookery, you'll need to use your hands.

But when it comes to trench kabbobing, everyone must supervise his or her own cooking, which takes the responsibility and pressure off you, the host.

URBAN PRESERVATION II: JERKY

EPISODE 132 | SEASON 9 | GOOD EATS

This is one of my favorite *Good Eats* episodes because beef jerky is one of my favorite snacks, and in an age of sugary, starchy snacks it's a nutritional hero. Sure, there's some sodium and some sugar (or honey), but by and large jerky is a low-carb food that's packed with lots of lovely protein. It keeps forever with little care or maintenance and can easily be produced in the home. And no, you don't need a food dehydrator, which is little more than a plastic box with a fan and a heating element. You may even already possess the hardware necessary to produce several pounds of top-quality jerky at this very moment, as I discovered I did a few years ago. The reason I came up with this particular hack is simple and stemmed from a conversation with my wife:

```
Me: Honey, I want to make beef jerky.

Her: That's nice, honey.

Me: So, I'm going out to buy one of those dehydrators.

Her: Oh, no, you're not.

Me: I'm not?

Her: You're not bringing one more piece of junk into this kitchen.

Me: I'm not?

Her: Everybody says you're the MacGyver of the kitchen.
So go MacGyver something.

Me: Fine, I will.

Her: Fine.
```

I stormed off to sulk in the basement, and that's where I found an old box fan that had served as our sole source of air-conditioning during culinary school. Then I saw a stack of furnace filters and a plan started to form. The resulting rig, christened the Blowhard 3000, was originally utilized in "Herbal Preservation" (episode 99) as an herb-drying device. Although it excels at that (and other) chores, jerky was in fact the original application.

264

"Jerky" can be defined as any meat cut into strips, cured, sometimes smoked, then dried to a state of preservation. Such products are pleasantly tough and chewy and, typically, highly flavored. Although jerky is most often enjoyed as a snack or meal replacement, it is also a powerful flavorant in cooking.

Although enzymatic action is somewhat responsible for the decomposition of meat, most of the damage is done by microorganisms that find the moist, warm, nutritious, low-acid landscape of meat to be the perfect place to live, eat, and breathe. To preserve meat we must render it inhospitable to those microscopic nasties. Refrigeration will certainly slow them, and freezing will stop most in their tracks, but if you're serious about preserving meat you've got to think mummification. Consider the steps:

PREP: In the case of mummies this typically meant rippin' the brains out the nose and stuff like that. In the case of jerky it means cutting the meat into long, thin strips in order to maximize surface area.

The best cuts for jerky are those with long, well-delineated muscle fibers such as some sections of the round and especially the diaphragm or flank steak, which is flat, relatively clean of fat and connective tissue, and easy to handle. When preparing meat for jerky, always cut with the muscle grain rather than across it.

MARINATE (embalm): This step introduces compounds that impregnate the target food with salt and sugar and other chemicals that have the ability to suck the life out of microbes via osmotic pressure. Luckily these substances taste good.

Marinating the meat before drying enhances the flavor and also helps to eliminate any nasty micro-critters by drawing out water and increasing salinity.[1]

DRY: Once the moisture level of the meat (referred to by food geeks as "water activity") drops to less than 5 percent, microorganisms cannot thrive in it. Although the marinade process ups the level of solutes, it doesn't remove much water. For that we have to physically dry the meat. If we locate the marinated meat in a sufficiently arid climate (either natural or manmade), no other drying mechanism is required. However, this is rarely possible in the United States, which is, by and large, temperate.

Commercial food dehydrators don't make very good jerky because they utilize heating elements that actually cook the meat rather than simply drying it.

The best meats for jerky:

Beef

Venison

Salmon

Duck

Ostrich/emu

Although wild game can make for tasty jerky, beware . . . many critters such as bear and cougar and such can harbor particularly nasty and hard-to-kill parasites, so do your due diligence and consult an expert on the subject. And remember, the jerky in the application from this episode is still, technically, raw.

[1] Use marinade rather than brine here. A brine— nothing more than salt water—has got a good bit of preservative power. But we can make it an even more potent potion if we add an acidic ingredient. To me, a marinade is basically a salty, acidic liquid.

Smoke

Smoke condensate
(liquid smoke)

Ice in zip-top bag

Upside-down metal mixing bowl
(see-through here)

Bundt pan (or tube pan)

Mexican furnace
"chimney"

Cutaway view (not a hole)

CRITICAL SMOKE
DISTILLATION POINTS:

1. Use hardwood only (like hickory)

2. Keep wood smoldering
(flames = soot)

Your nonflammable porch

Smoldering hardwood

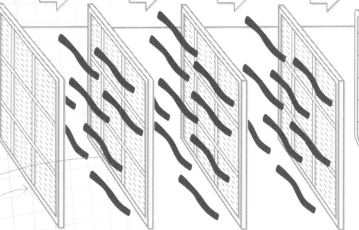

TO MAKE BEEF JERKY, WE USE
THE SAME BLOWHARD RIG FROM
THE DRIED HERBS APPLICATION
ON PAGE 100.

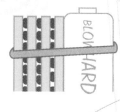

BLOWHARD

BLOWHARD 3000

Marinated
meat

Air-conditioning filters (whatever size fits your box fan)

Box fan

BEEF JERKY

10 TO 12 OUNCES JERKY

// SOFTWARE ///

1½ to 2	pounds	flank steak	
⅔	cup	Worcestershire sauce	
⅔	cup	soy sauce	
1	tablespoon	honey	
2	teaspoons	black pepper	freshly ground
2	teaspoons	onion powder	
1	teaspoon	Liquid Smoke	
1	teaspoon	red pepper flakes	

TIDBIT In the early twentieth century, Liquid Smoke was sold as a preservative. If smoking could preserve foods, the thinking went, why not just brush on some of the liquid version and achieve the same ends? I'll tell you why: Though it may taste great in small amounts, it preserves not a darned thing.

// SPECIAL HARDWARE //

1 box fan, 4 paper air-conditioning filters, and 2 bungee cords

// PROCEDURE ///

1. Trim the steak of any excess fat, put it in a **1-gallon plastic zip-top bag**, and place it in the freezer for 1 to 2 hours to firm up. This makes the meat much easier to slice.

2. Remove the steak from the freezer and thinly slice the meat, with the grain, into long strips.

3. Put the strips of meat, along with all of the remaining ingredients, in the zip-top bag and move them around to evenly distribute all of the ingredients. Put the bag in the refrigerator for 3 to 6 hours.

4. Remove the meat from the marinade and pat it dry. Evenly distribute the strips of meat on **3 of the air filters**, laying them in the grooves and then stacking the filters on top of one another. Top these with one empty filter. Next, lay the **box fan** on its side and lay the filters on top of it. Strap the filters to the fan with **2 bungee cords**. Stand the fan upright, plug it in, and set it to medium. Dry the meat for 8 to 12 hours. (If using a commercial dehydrator, follow the manufacturer's directions.)

5. Once dry, store in an airtight container in a cool, dry place for up to 3 months.

Fan Speed
Filter Density
Meat Thickness
Humidity & Temperature

Back in season one we did our first ice cream show, "Churn, Baby, Churn," which featured what is traditionally known as Philadelphia ice cream—that is, eggless ice cream. Those applications were enhanced by pectin and gelatin from preserves, and they were mighty tasty. But we received no small amount of email stating that what you really wanted to make at home was premium Häagen-Dazs and Ben & Jerry's, which also happen to be personal favorites of mine (Chubby Hubby was, in fact, named after me).

Anyway, what these super-premium ice creams have in common is fat—lots of fat—and eggs. And although raw-egg ice creams used to be quite common, to really get that silky-smooth texture you must make a stirred custard. With the right custard base in hand, flavors can come and go at will.

For centuries now, man has been building devices to deliver ice cream into his bowl. My favorite has an ergonomic handle, a nice heft, and a big, wide, open scoop. The scoop's edges, as you can see, will really cut into the ice cream from the sides.

KNOWLEDGE CONCENTRATE

Let's consider the basic parts list of a premium ice cream:

ICE: Supplies the cold.

SUGAR: Provides sweetness and helps keep ice crystals from becoming too large.

AIR: Prevents overhardening and keeps the ice cream from being too cold in the mouth.

PROTEIN (in this case, eggs): Supports bubble formation.

FAT: Provides smooth mouthfeel while enhancing and carrying flavors.

Having formulated and tested hundreds of different combinations, I have come up with what I consider to be the very best formula for a vanilla custard base for ice cream using precise quantities of certain dairy products, eggs, sugar, and vanilla.

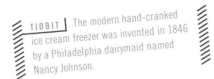 TIDBIT | The modern hand-cranked ice cream freezer was invented in 1846 by a Philadelphia dairymaid named Nancy Johnson.

 TIDBIT | Powdered milk is often added to ice cream mixtures to increase protein content and thereby improve texture.

Now, ingredients are very important and I think the ratio in the following application is perfect, but what really matters is how the ingredients are assembled. Here, then, are the standard steps for creating a stirred custard and transforming it into ice cream.

SCALD THE DAIRY: Bringing the moo-juice to a simmer will kill microbial pests, but since all commercially available dairy in this country is pasteurized, that's not really much of a factor. Heating does alter certain chemicals inside the milk (enzymes, to be exact), making a smoother texture possible, but the real reason we scald is that we want to load the dairy with the exact amount of heat necessary to cook the eggs, or at least mostly cook the eggs.

RIBBON THE EGGS AND SUGAR: The ribbon stage is the point at which a mixture of beaten eggs and sugar falls from a beater in a kind of semiliquid pile reminiscent of fabric ribbon. While the dairy is heating, beat the egg yolks and sugar together. This step dissolves the sugar into the liquid phase of the eggs and also partially denatures the egg proteins so that they won't become grainy when cooked. This step is often skimped on, to the detriment of the final product.

TEMPER THE EGGS: Slow introduction of the hot dairy to the egg-sugar mixture helps to condition the egg proteins so that, in the end, they can be cooked to a higher temperature without curdling (overcoagulating).

COOK THE CUSTARD: Once the eggs and hot dairy are combined, the young custard must be further heated, typically to 170° to 175°F, at which point the custard will be thick enough to thoroughly coat the back of a spoon (what the French call *nappé*). And since salmonella can't survive past 165°F, cooking the custard to 170°F ensures microbial safety.

MATURE THE CUSTARD: Cooling and then chilling the custard for several hours achieves two things. By getting the temperature below 40°F we shorten the amount of time that the custard will need to be in the ice cream churn. That's good, because the faster the custard freezes, the finer its texture will be (see sidebar). The other reason is that allowing the custard to age for a while allows certain enzymatic changes to take place that enhance the overall texture of the finished product. If that sounds a bit vague, it's because dairy scientists haven't exactly figured out the hows and whys of this process.

CHURN THE CUSTARD: The churning process freezes part of the water phase of the custard and works air (overrun) into the mass.

HARDEN THE ICE CREAM: When it exits the churn, the ice cream (or "frozen custard," if you prefer) is only at a soft-serve consistency . . . not that there's anything wrong with that. But if a firmer, scoopable product is desired, the young ice cream must harden by spending several hours in the freezer.

ICE CREAM, LEGALLY SPEAKING

A few of the Food and Drug Administration's rules concerning frozen dairy dessert products:

▶ Ice creams must contain a minimum of 10 percent butterfat.

▶ "French-style" or "frozen custard" ice cream must also contain 1.4 percent egg yolk solids.

▶ "Reduced-fat" ice cream must contain 25 percent less total fat than the original product.

▶ "Light" ice cream must contain 50 percent less total fat or 33 percent fewer calories than the original product. Low-fat ice creams can contain no more than 3 grams total fat per ½-cup serving.

▶ "Nonfat" ice cream must contain fewer than 0.5 grams of total fat per serving.

▶ A gallon of commercial ice cream must weigh a minimum of 4.5 pounds.

▶ Air content, or "overrun," in any of these products may be equal to the total volume of the ingredients. (That's right: Half of the volume of an ice cream you buy can be made up of air.)

1 ½ QUARTS

// SOFTWARE

3	cups	half-and-half	
1	cup	heavy cream	
8	large	egg yolks	
9	ounces	sugar	
2	teaspoons	vanilla extract	

// PROCEDURE

1. Combine the half-and-half and cream in a **medium saucepan** and bring to a simmer over medium heat, stirring occasionally. Remove from the heat and set aside.

2. **Whisk** the egg yolks in a **large mixing bowl** until they lighten in color. Gradually whisk the sugar into the yolks until smooth.

3. Slowly **ladle** one third of the hot dairy into the yolk mixture, whisking constantly. (This is the tempering part.) Return this mixture to the pot containing the rest of the dairy. Cook over low heat, stirring frequently, until the custard thickens slightly, enough to coat the back of a **spoon** (170° to 175°F).

4. Wash the original mixing bowl. When the custard is ready, transfer it to the bowl, stir in the vanilla, and cool at room temp for 30 minutes. Cover and refrigerate until the temperature drops below 40°F. (I usually chill it overnight.)

5. Pour into a prepped **ice cream maker** and process according to the manufacturer's directions. Within 25 to 30 minutes the ice cream will attain a classic soft-serve consistency. Enjoy it as is or move it to the freezer to harden for another 3 to 4 hours.

CHOCOLATE ICE CREAM

One might think that retrofitting this concoction to create chocolate ice cream would simply involve melting chocolate into the original mixture. And, indeed, that can be done. But let's consider for a moment the anatomy of solid chocolate. Most chocolate contains a fair amount of sugar, and we've already got enough of that. It also might contain milk, salt, or extracts. And we don't need any of

that, either. So what it really comes down to are the two primary chocolate components: cocoa solids and cocoa butter. Cocoa butter is composed of a very complex bunch of fats that melt at different temperatures. Although luscious when going from room temperature to inside your mouth, this stuff is rendered waxy and hard by the cold ice cream. So all we really want here is cocoa solids, which we can get easily from good old-fashioned cocoa

powder. Dutch-process or alkalized is best because it disperses in liquid easily. And its color is, well, more chocolatey.

Before adding the cream and proceeding as above, simply whisk 1½ ounces Dutch-process cocoa powder into 1 cup of the half-and-half in the saucepan. (It's actually easier to integrate cocoa powder into a smaller amount of liquid than the full amount.)

MINT CHIP ICE CREAM

1½ QUARTS

My personal favorite ice cream of all time is mint chip, and man, do I love me some mint. So instead of infusing fresh mint leaves I go for the hard stuff: peppermint oil. Oils are typically much stronger, more potent in flavor than extracts. They also have the added benefit of containing no alcohol, although they can go rancid on you if you store them improperly. (Life's full of trade-offs.) Extracts and essential oils contain volatile substances that will simply disappear into thin air if they get too hot, so it's always a good idea to add them after the mixture has had time to cool down a bit.

If you prefer something a little more . . . subtle, go with mint extract instead. (Wimp.)

// SOFTWARE

3	cups	half-and-half	
1	cup	heavy cream	
8	large	egg yolks	
9	ounces	sugar	
1	teaspoon	peppermint oil	
3	ounces	chocolate-mint candies	coarsely chopped

// PROCEDURE

1. Combine the half-and-half and cream in a **medium saucepan** and bring to a simmer over medium heat, stirring occasionally. Remove from the heat and set aside.

2. **Whisk** the egg yolks in a **large mixing bowl** until they lighten in color. Gradually whisk the sugar into the yolks until smooth.

3. Slowly **ladle** one third of the hot dairy into the yolk mixture, whisking constantly. (This is the tempering part.) Return this mixture to the pot containing the rest of the dairy. Cook over low heat, stirring frequently, until the custard thickens slightly, enough to coat the back of a **spoon** (170° to 175°F).

4. Wash the original mixing bowl. When the custard is ready, transfer it to the bowl and cool at room temp for 30 minutes. Add the peppermint oil and stir to combine. Cover and refrigerate until the temperature drops below 40°F. (I usually chill it overnight.)

5. Pour the mixture into a prepped **ice cream maker**; add the candies and process according to the manufacturer's directions. Within 25 to 30 minutes the ice cream will attain a classic soft-serve consistency. Enjoy it as is or move it to the freezer to harden for another 3 to 4 hours.

GOOD VS. CRAPPY ICE CREAM!

○ – Air bubble
+ – Ice
● – Sugar
⸰ – Fat

CRAPPY DISCOUNT OR "LITE" ICE CREAM

THE GOOD STUFF

*NOTICE THE SIZE OF THE AIR BUBBLES, AND THE AMOUNT OF SUGAR AND FAT.

TIDBIT Ice cream was served at England's Windsor Castle as early as 1667.

TIDBIT In 1982 the world's largest sundae was created with 15,000 pounds of ice cream, 120 pounds of chocolate syrup, and 50 pounds of whipped topping.

CHURN, BABY, CHURN II

If you take a look around these days, it seems as though every briefcase, gym bag, purse, and backpack has become home to some form of costly "power bar" or "protein bar" or "energy bar," which, despite delivering as many calories as, and often more fat than, a like-size candy bar (which when you think about it is also an "energy" bar), promise to supercharge consumers on the go with high-level nutrition and plenty of energy. A noble cause, to be sure, but I say real "power" starts in the kitchen: the home kitchen, where, with a little nutritional know-how and the right ingredients, we can create bars that are good for you while still being seriously good eats.

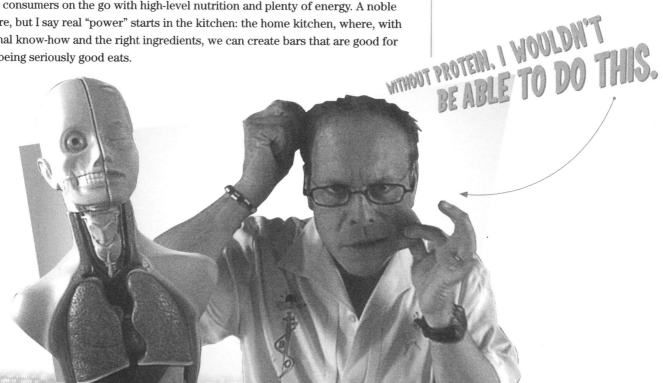

WITHOUT PROTEIN, I WOULDN'T BE ABLE TO DO THIS.

The universe of energy bars is often classified according to the percentages of carbohydrates, fats, and proteins that they contain. Ever wonder what these things do?

CARBOHYDRATES include sugars as well as starches from the plant world. Simple sugars are made up of either one or two molecules; once ingested, they move quickly into the bloodstream, where they are literally burned up in the power plant of your metabolism. Now this is very, very good news if you are running a marathon, chopping wood, or lifting weights. If, however, you are simply lifting the remote control, this isn't so good. That's because when excess glucose doesn't get used up by your body, your pancreas sends out insulin to neutralize it. That means that in a couple of hours you're going to have a glucose deficiency, which your body is going to counter with the hormone adrenaline, which is going to make you feel nasty, cranky, and muddy-headed. What's more, excess carbs easily convert to fat.

Speaking of FATS, they are extremely efficient when it comes to storing energy, a whopping 9 calories per gram. Without fats, your body cannot utilize fat-soluble vitamins like vitamins A, D, E, or K. Nor can it maintain healthy organs or cell membranes. Fats also supply fuel for your muscles when no carbs are available. Oh, and here's another crucial fat fact: Fats are composed of fatty acids, some of which are required for human life, which is why they're called "essential fatty acids."

With the exception of fat, water, and the minerals that make up your skeleton, most of the body is made up of PROTEIN. Three quarters of your dry weight, in fact, is muscle, nails, hair, skin—stuff that has to be renewed and renovated every now and then lest you simply fall apart. Proteins are made out of tiny building blocks called amino acids, twenty of which are required by the human body for life. A healthy body can manufacture eleven of these, but the remaining nine have to be imported from the outside world or the whole system collapses. Now, the challenge is in finding protein sources that provide all nine of these essential amino acids.

ESSENTIAL AMINO ACIDS:

▶ Histidine

▶ Isoleucine

▶ Leucine

▶ Lysine

▶ Methionine

▶ Phenylalanine

▶ Threonin

▶ Tryptophan

▶ Valine

NONESSENTIAL AMINO ACIDS:

▶ Alanine

▶ Arginine

▶ Asparagine

▶ Aspartic acid

▶ Cysteine

▶ Glutamic acid

▶ Glutamine

▶ Glycine

▶ Proline

▶ Serine

▶ Tyrosine

Sucrose and other carbohydrates literally burn up via your metabolism.

CH₂OH

Sucrose

24 (2-INCH) SQUARES

One of the most popular bar categories is the protein bar, favored by body builders looking to add some muscle tissue and followers of the low-carb cult, whose bodies have been tricked into burning fats and proteins, rather than carbohydrates, as major energy sources. I grabbed a random "hi-protein" bar off my local megamart's shelf and this is what I found:

28.65 grams of protein (almost half the RDA for an average-weight man)

365 calories (a regular-size Snickers bar contains 271)

27 grams of fat, 10 of which are saturated

Energy-producing? Yes. Healthy? Not so much. There is, however, a way to get the complete protein we need into a convenient and tasty package without all the calories or all the fat. We use soybeans—or, more exactly, soy protein powder, which is indeed a complete protein.

// SOFTWARE //

		vegetable oil for the pan	
4	ounces	soy protein powder	
2¼	ounces	oat bran	
2¾	ounces	whole-wheat flour	
¾	ounces	wheat germ	
½	teaspoon	kosher salt	
3	ounces	raisins	
3	ounces	dried blueberries	
2½	ounces	dried cherries	
2½	ounces	dried apricots	
1	12.3-ounce package	soft silken tofu	
½	cup	unfiltered apple juice	
4	ounces	dark brown sugar	
2	large	eggs	beaten
⅔	cup	natural peanut butter	

// PROCEDURE //

1. Heat the oven to 350°F. Line the bottom of a **9-by-13-inch glass baking dish** with **parchment paper** and lightly coat with vegetable oil.

2. Combine the soy protein powder, oat bran, flour, wheat germ, and salt in a **large mixing bowl**. Set aside.

3. Coarsely chop the raisins, dried blueberries, dried cherries, and dried apricots and set aside in a **small bowl**.

4 **Whisk** the tofu until smooth in a **third mixing bowl**. Add the apple juice, brown sugar, eggs, and peanut butter one at a time and whisk to combine after each addition. Add this to the flour mixture and stir well to combine. Fold in the dried fruit. Spread evenly in the prepared baking dish and bake 35 minutes, or until the internal temperature reaches 205°F. Remove from the oven and cool completely. Cut into 24 squares and store in an **airtight container** in the refrigerator for up to 1 week. These bars can also be frozen—tightly wrapped—for up to 3 months.

N O T E : These bars are dense, cakey, and delicious—and, I'm pleased to say, darn good for you. Take a look at these numbers: Each bar contains 154.01 kilocalories or calories, 21.08 grams of carbohydrates, 8.41 grams of protein, 4.79 grams of fat, 2.14 grams of fiber, a measly 91.92 milligrams of sodium, and 17.7 milligrams of cholesterol.

ENERGY BARS OF YORE

Although energy bars might appear to be modern marvels, mankind has been seeking out compact nutrition sources for centuries.

For instance, back in the Middle Ages, no well-equipped Crusader would leave the castle without a dense fruitcake, called pan forte, packed with honey, grains, nuts, and dried fruit. Pan forte was the most calorie-laden food of its day, and it delivered vitamins and minerals, energy, and enough fiber to keep even the most noble knight a regular guy.

And then there was pemmican. The Cree Indians taught early American frontiersmen like Alexander Mackenzie how to pound dried deer and buffalo meat with fat, bone marrow, and dried berries, and then to sew up the whole thing in a rawhide sack sealed with tallow. Sounds pretty gross, but the resulting bar—called *pemmican* after the Cree word for "fat"— gave Mackenzie the strength to become the first European to cross the North American continent coast to coast back in 1793.

A couple centuries later, hundreds of bars designed to deliver quick energy were unleashed on the public. These "handy bars" were indeed loaded with calories. But no one really thought to add, you know, good nutrition until 1975, when Nestlé hired an inventor to concoct a healthy, easy-to-carry, tasty bar for the "Me Generation." The result? The granola bar.

BROWN RICE CRISPY BAR

24 (2-INCH) SQUARES

White puffed rice is a popular ingredient for health bar manufacturers, not because it's that healthy but because it takes up a lot of space, thus bulking the bar while cutting calories. Of course, when I bite into anything chewy containing puffed rice I want it to look, feel, and taste like a Rice Krispies treat. I am, after all, only American and human. But with a little tinkering we can make it better—better *for* you, that is.

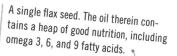

A single flax seed. The oil therein contains a heap of good nutrition, including omega 3, 6, and 9 fatty acids.

// SOFTWARE //

3	tablespoons	flaxseed oil	plus extra for the pan and spatula
3	ounces	puffed brown rice	
1	tablespoon	orange blossom honey	
7	ounces	mini marshmallows	
3	ounces	slivered almonds	toasted
1½	ounces	dried cranberries	coarsely chopped
1½	ounces	dried cherries	coarsely chopped
1	ounce	dried blueberries	

// PROCEDURE //

1. Heat the oven to 425°F.

2. Lightly coat the inside of a **9-by-13-by-2-inch metal baking pan** with oil and set aside.

3. Spread the puffed rice evenly on a **half sheet pan**. Toast in the oven for 4 minutes, stirring occasionally.

4. Place the 3 tablespoons oil, the honey, and marshmallows in a **large mixing bowl** set over a **pot** of gently simmering water. Stir until the marshmallows are melted, 4 to 5 minutes. Once the marshmallows are melted, quickly add the toasted brown rice, almonds, and fruit and stir to combine. Coat your hands or a **spatula** with oil and spread the mixture evenly into the **prepared baking pan**. Once the mixture has cooled completely, cut into squares and store in an **airtight container** for up to 2 days.

   NOTE: Each delicious rice delight has just over 93 kilocalories or calories, just over 15 grams of carbohydrates, 1.16 grams of protein, 3.72 grams of fat, 1.01 grams of fiber, and only 4.31 milligrams of sodium, and it tastes good too! It's like an entire grocery store in a bar.

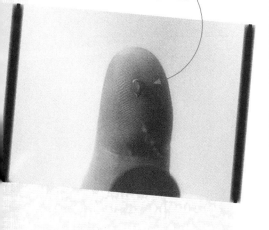

This is what happens if you don't oil your hands.

SILENCE OF THE POWER BAR

During the show I'm trying to decipher the ingredients in a Captain Power Protein Puck, a fictitious product, of course. Requiring some assistance from an expert, I head off to visit Koko Karl, a.k.a. Cocoa Carl, a.k.a. Auntie Pudding, in the Beard Home for the Culinarily Insane. The scene is a complete rip-off of a scene between the infamous cannibal Hannibal Lecter and former FBI agent Will Graham from the novel and film *Red Dragon*. Bart Hansard, who has played many a role on *Good Eats*, was charged with the tough job of channeling Anthony Hopkins's portrayal of Lecter. The scene ended up taking quite a while to film for the simple reason that I could not keep a straight face to save my life. It remains one of my very favorite scenes from the series.

KOKO KARL: Well, well, well. Look what the cat drug in.

AB: Hello, Koko.

KK: To what do I owe the honor? Do tell.

(AB holds up a Captain Power energy bar to the window)

KK: Hmmm. How nice. You brought Karl a goodie. Hmmm, a Captain Power Protein Puck, no less.

AB: You know, Karl, I never would have figured you for health food.

KK: Healthy? Maybe for the captain's bank account.

AB: What do you mean?

KK: No, no. That won't do. Quid pro quo, my dear AB.

AB: All right. Quid pro quo the wrapper.

KK: (takes the wrapper and smells it) Mmmm, yes. A few of my favorite things. (smells again) High-fructose corn syrup. Oh, lots and lots of sodium, and (smells again) oh, oh, lovely (smells again), luscious, palm kernel oil.

AB: What's the big deal with palm oil?

KK: It's the only fully saturated fat that stays liquid at room temperature!

AB: That means that products that contain it can remain moist and unctuous, and still have the shelf life of uranium.

KK: How nice. It can learn.

AB: You know, saturated fats are bad for you. (holds up a piece of the bar)

KK: (eyes the bar) Only if you eat them.

AB: Well, at least this one's packed full of protein. (hands the bar to Koko Karl through the air hole)

KK: (sucking on one end) That's because it's been hydrolyzed.

AB: What do you mean?

KK: Extracted from cow hooves and skins. (disgusting suckling sounds)

AB: Guess that's your way of saying it's low quality, then?

KK: Like eating glue, only tastier. Ohh, Captain, you're a bad boy, yes, you are. You're a ba... (begins to gobble the puck ravenously) Now, if you'll excuse me, I'd like to enjoy my sugar rush in private. (lunatic laughter)

Shocked by the outburst, AB flees down corridors of shadow.

WAKE UP, LITTLE SUSHI

Legend has it that sushi was invented

about a thousand years ago when an old woman who lived in the woods of Japan had just sat down to eat a big pot of rice. She heard some bandits coming, and, fearing they would take her rice, she climbed a tree and hid it in the nest of a large sea bird. By the time the bandits departed and she finally got back up the tree, the rice had partially fermented and it was completely littered with bits and pieces of fish left by the sea bird. She tasted it, it was great, and thus sushi was born.

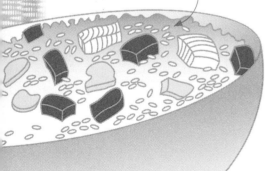

This of course would have been the old *chirashizushi*, or "scattered bowl" sushi form, which happens to be my favorite.

KNOWLEDGE CONCENTRATE

▷ Sushi is one of the rare cases where I suggest spending a fair amount of time in a sushi bar before going home and giving it a try. Since the sushi chef, or *itamae*, practices his or her craft right at the counter, sitting at the bar is kind of like going to culinary school. Watch, learn, eat, ask questions. Show the guys behind the counter that you care, and they'll teach you just about anything. And they'll make sure you get the best stuff in the shop.

▷ When ordering at a sushi bar you really need to know only one word to look like you know what you're doing and be served the best the chef has to offer. Just say you'd like to order *omakase*, which basically means you're entrusting the chef. If you want to really wow the man (and in 99.995 percent of cases it will be a man), then say, "Omakase onegaishimasu," which means "Do me the favor of protecting me." That's it. If you're allergic to something, tell him. Otherwise break out your *hashi* (chopsticks) and get ready for whatever comes across the counter.

▷ The basic sushi kit:

— SHOYU OR DARK SOY SAUCE: The ketchup of Japan. Although I use it in other parts of the kitchen, I always keep a bottle on hand here.

— RICE VINEGAR: A slightly sweetened vinegar that is used on the sushi rice, or *meshi*.

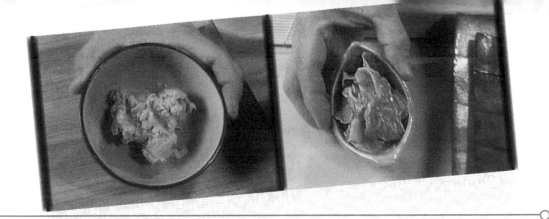

MESHI, OR JAPANESE SHORT-GRAIN RICE: Unfortunately, the Japanese do not export any of their rice, but California grows some excellent hybrids, so you should be able to find it easily at a megamart, an ethnic market, or an online store.

NORI: These bright green sheets are not seaweed. They're algae, harvested from the northern shores of Japan (and Korea as well), dried on racks, and pressed into sheets. Nori is very, very susceptible to moisture, so I generally buy several packages containing just a few sheets rather than one big package. That way, you don't have to open them and let all the moisture in. They come with those little packs of desiccant stuff. You don't want to eat those. Bad eats.

WASABI POWDER: That hot green stuff that's often lurking inside your little pieces of sushi is, in most cases, not wasabi at all but rather horseradish dyed green. Real wasabi is a rhizome that comes from an evergreen member of the mustard family. It's very picky stuff: It grows only in certain kinds of soil and on well-drained—but moist—shaded hillsides. Some wasabi is grown in Oregon and in New Zealand, and it's pretty good. But real sushi aficionados will tell you that the Japanese version is superior in every way. Wasabi is highly perishable, very rare, and hideously expensive. And grating it properly requires a rather specialized sharkskin grater.

PICKLED GINGER, OR *GARI*: Although it's not an absolute necessity when making or serving sushi, it is a common palate cleanser, something you would eat in between pieces of sushi. The manufactured type is usually made with vinegar that's dyed orange or pink. Homemade stuff is usually white, but that's another show.

When buying fish for sushi, only buy from a trusted purveyor or fishmonger you've purchased from in the past. Tell said purveyor that you're planning on sushi and ask for suggestions. Buy the fish the day you plan to make the sushi; otherwise, hang up your apron and go to a sushi bar. Bring a cooler to the market and make sure ice is available.

Remember, too, that most of the fish that becomes sushi in Japan has been frozen, so don't reject fish just because it's been frozen. Although it might be tempting to have your fishmonger cut the fish into strips for you, don't. It will age and oxidize very quickly. Have the fishmonger leave it in large pieces; cut what you need as you need it.

When cutting fish for sushi, always work with your longest, thinnest knife so you only have to cut in one direction. Sawing fish is evil, and you don't want to be evil. Since you'll be using your longest knife, you'll also want to cut on your largest board.

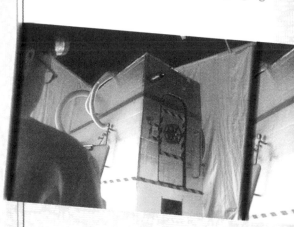

TRIVIA | The "sushi simulator" used to house the sushi bar set was an obvious nod not only to aircraft simulators but also to the holodeck from *Star Trek: The Next Generation*. The exterior was basically an acrofoil box built on a scissor lift. Ultra-low-tech.

TIDBIT | It's not uncommon for a Japanese sushi knife to cost over $5,000.

4 CUPS

// SOFTWARE ///

2	cups	sushi rice	or other short-grain rice
2	cups	H_2O	
2	tablespoons	rice vinegar	
2	tablespoons	sugar	
1	tablespoon	kosher salt	

// PROCEDURE ///

1. Cover the rice with **cool water** in a **large mixing bowl**. Swirl the rice in the water, pour the water off, and repeat 2 or 3 times, until the water is clear.

2. Combine the rice and 2 cups water in a **medium saucepan** and bring to a boil over high heat. Reduce the heat to the lowest setting and cover. Cook for 15 minutes. Remove from the heat and let stand, covered, for 10 minutes.

3. Combine the vinegar, sugar, and salt in a **small bowl** and heat in a microwave oven on high for 30 to 45 seconds. Transfer the rice to the large mixing bowl and add the vinegar mixture. Fold thoroughly to combine and coat each grain of rice. Cool to room temperature before using to make sushi.

MESHI TIPS:

▶ Wash the grains in cold water before cooking. This will remove the nasty, powdery starch residue, which will become a gummy annoyance if left in place. Keep rinsing and draining until the water is clear. Three changes of water usually does the trick.

▶ Sushi rice is usually cooked with an equal portion of water by volume.

▶ Sushi rice is not cooked with salt.

▶ Sushi rice is always seasoned as it's cooling.

▶ Sushi rice should be tossed rather than stirred.

▶ Traditionally sushi rice is fanned as it cools. If you don't have a folding fan, use a Ping-Pong paddle. (I use one of those old cardboard fans that used to be handed out by funeral homes.)

▶ When the rice is finished, cover with a moist kitchen towel, not a lid.

▶ Once sushi rice is cooked and cooled, it should be used. Refrigeration ruins the flavor and texture.

Hold sushi so that FISH, not RICE, is dipped in shoyu.

Dipping rice in shoyu is the #1 way to show everyone you're a big gomer!

NEVER pick up sushi with hashi!

CALIFORNIA ROLL

8 APPETIZER SERVINGS

Once upon a time, a sushi chef in California got a crazy idea. He thought he would take the rice out of the inside of the roll and put it on the outside of the roll, and thus was born America's favorite sushi, the California roll (which has no raw fish in it at all). Serve these with pickled ginger, wasabi, and soy sauce.

// SOFTWARE //

1	medium	avocado	peeled, pitted, and cut into ¼-inch-thick pieces
½		lemon	juiced
4	sheets	nori	
⅓	cup	sesame seeds	toasted
1	small	cucumber	peeled, seeded, and cut into matchsticks
4		crab sticks	torn into pieces
2	cups	Sushi Rice	(left)

// PROCEDURE //

1. Toss the avocado with the lemon juice to prevent browning.

2. Cover a **bamboo rolling mat** with **plastic wrap**. Cut nori sheets in half crosswise. Lay one sheet of nori, shiny side down, on the plastic-covered mat. Wet your fingers with **water** and spread about ½ cup of the rice evenly onto the nori. Sprinkle the rice with sesame seeds. Turn the sheet of nori over so that the rice side is down. Place one eighth of the avocado, cucumber, and crab sticks in the center of the sheet. Grab the edge of the mat closest to you, keeping the fillings in place with your fingers, and roll it into a tight cylinder, using the mat to shape the cylinder. Pull the mat away and set the roll aside. Cover with a **damp cloth**. Repeat until all of the rice has been used. Cut each roll into 6 pieces. Serve immediately.

Nori

Sushi rice

Fish (raw)

MAKI SUSHI

(makizushi)

Rice and fish (or other ingredients) rolled in nori

NIGIRI

In 1809 a sushi maker named Yohei came up with an idea that changed the world: fast food. Now this was Edo—Tokyo, but before it was Tokyo—and it was about the size of London back then, and its population was known to have a lot of taste but not a lot of patience. Yohei wanted to satisfy both of these qualities. So he took a little slice of fish, grated on some fresh wasabi, then flipped it over and pressed it onto a hand-pressed oval of rice. He named the form *nigiri*, sold them by the piece, and they have been popular ever since.

FORMING *NIGIRI*

Although you do want to shape the rice, you do not want to squeeze it too tightly. There needs to be plenty of air between the granules so that when the sushi hits your mouth it just kind of falls apart. I go through the same little ritual, or the same series of movements, each time I do this so that the fish is just adhered on top.

1. Moisten your hands with *tezu* (a weak solution of water, rice vinegar, and salt).
2. Pick up just under 1 ounce of sushi rice and quickly but lightly knead it into a small football shape. The oval should just stay together.
3. Palm the rice ball and pinch some wasabi paste (if using).
4. Pick up a fish slice (1 ounce again is about right) and rub the underside with the wasabi.
5. Use your fingers to mold the fish to the rice.
6. *Nigiri*.

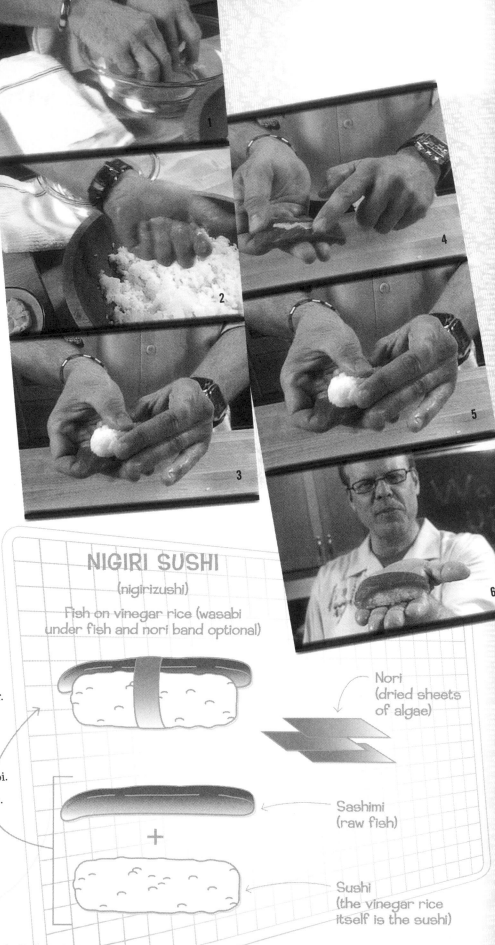

NIGIRI SUSHI

(nigirizushi)

Fish on vinegar rice (wasabi under fish and nori band optional)

Nori
(dried sheets of algae)

Sashimi
(raw fish)

+

Sushi
(the vinegar rice itself is the sushi)

Cobblers are hands down my favorite dessert, a perfect marriage of fruit, spice, and dough—not crust, but dough: brown and crisp on one side, moist and oozy on the other. Cobbler does not aspire to the structural fussiness of pie. It's down and dirty, primordial, and ever-so-slightly naughty. I have found myself in the wee hours of the morning, in the kitchen, in the dark, in my underwear, spoon in hand, eating cobbler. Cobbler knows no shame and cobbler keeps all secrets.

TIDBIT My favorite cobbler fodder:
Peaches (often with ginger)
Rhubarb
Blackberries
Blueberries
Strawberries (especially with rhubarb)
Pears

[1] Those dessert innovators the Pennsylvania Dutch were responsible for many cobbler permutations.

Cobbler was born of English plum pudding, and some say the name comes from the fact that the dough pieces originally topping the fruit resembled cobblestones. Others claim the moniker stems from the verb *cobble*, as the desserts are usually "cobbled" together. Nomenclatural issues notwithstanding, we do know that once the cobbler concept reached American shores, it mutated and spread like a virus.[1] Some lesser-known but delicious branches on the family tree include:

BROWN BETTY: Baked fruit with layers of buttered bread crumbs.

BUCKLE: Fruit cooked with yellow cake batter.

CRISP, KNOWN AS "CRUMBLE" IN ENGLAND: Fruit topped with a mixture of butter, sugar, flour, and nuts or oats and baked.

GRUNT: Fruit topped with biscuit dough; named for the sound it makes as it cooks.

PANDOWDY: Cobbler in which the dough is pressed into the fruit, creating an uneven crust.

SONKER: A mixed-fruit cobbler containing a high fruit-to-dough ratio. As far as I know, sonkers are indigenous only to a small area surrounding Mt. Airy, North Carolina.

All you need to make any number of cobblers is a suitable vessel (anything that can go into an oven or onto a cooktop), fruit, and a sweetened dough assembled via the biscuit method. Depending on the specific application the dough may be relatively dry, as in a pie dough, or wet, as in a biscuit dough.

If you want to know what fruits make for good cobblers, you have only to check out the preserves section of your local megamart. The berries and stone fruits that are so popular with preservists contain reasonably high amounts of pectin, a water-soluble polysaccharide capable of creating gels when cooked in a slightly acidic aqueous solution. This is why pectin-rich citrus, such as lemon, is often added to the fruit mix. There's another reason for adding acidic ingredients (even vinegar) to cobblers: They help to reinforce fruit cell walls so that the cooked fruit doesn't turn to mush. (That said, careful cooking and a reliable timer provide even better mush insurance.)

REGARDING RHUBARB

Rhubarb is in the same botanical family as buckwheat and sorrel and is, therefore, in fact a vegetable.

Rhubarb, which in Latin roughly translates to "root of the barbarians," was originally used as a medicinal product—a hepatic stimulant, to be precise—until about the eighteenth century, when it finally became a culinary ingredient.

Why the long wait? Oh, I don't know . . . could it be because rhubarb is poison?! In this case, the poison comes in the form of oxalic acid, which, besides being a flavorant, is also a darn good bleach and rust remover. All the poison is in the leaves, which taste really lousy raw.

When buying rhubarb, look for the best ruby-red variety in your megamart

in late winter through spring. You always want the stalks to be celery-crisp—they'll have better flavor that way—and as bright red as you can get them. The rest of the year, when ruby-red rhubarb isn't in season, you can buy "hothouse" rhubarb, easily recognizable by the fact that it is not bright red, but rather pink. It's the stuff that's in the frozen-fruits section of the store.

RHUBARB AND PEACH COBBLER

6 TO 8 SERVINGS

The crust of this classic version of cobbler is more like a piecrust than a biscuit. But, since it isn't being shaped and isn't expected to provide structural support (as in a pie), it's much easier to deal with than pie dough.

// SOFTWARE

FOR THE CRUST

2	cups	all-purpose flour	
2	tablespoons	sugar	
1	tablespoon	lemon zest	grated
1	teaspoon	kosher salt	
9	tablespoons	unsalted butter	cut into small pieces and chilled
9	tablespoons	lard	cut into small pieces and chilled
9	tablespoons	ice H$_2$O	

FOR THE FILLING

1	cup	sugar	
2	tablespoons	cornstarch	
¼	teaspoon	kosher salt	
1	pound	rhubarb	chopped into ½-inch pieces
1	pound	peaches[2]	sliced into ½-inch pieces
1	tablespoon	lime juice	freshly squeezed

// PROCEDURE

(1) Make the crust: Put the flour, sugar, lemon zest, and salt in the bowl of a **food processor** and pulse 3 or 4 times. Add the butter and lard and pulse until the mixture just becomes crumbly. Sprinkle or spritz the mixture with the ice water a little at a time and process just until the dough holds together when squeezed in your fist.

(2) Put the dough in a **1-gallon zip-top bag** and form it into a disk. Refrigerate the dough for at least 30 minutes, while you prepare the filling.

(3) Make the filling: Heat the oven to 375°F. Place a piece of **aluminum foil** on the bottom rack to catch any overflow. Butter a **9-inch square glass baking dish**.

(4) **Whisk** together the sugar, cornstarch, and salt in a **medium mixing bowl**. Stir in the rhubarb, peaches, and lime juice.

(5) Remove one third of the crust dough from the bag, pinch into pieces, and distribute it evenly in the bottom of the prepared baking dish. With the remaining dough still in the bag, **roll** it out to a sheet large enough to cover the top of the dish. Pour the fruit mixture into the dish and top with the dough that has been removed from the bag, pressing the dough into the corners of the dish. Bake, uncovered, for 1 hour, or until the dough is cooked through and starting to turn golden. Change the oven setting to broil and continue to cook until golden brown, about 3 minutes. Remove from the oven and cool for 30 minutes before serving.

[2] If using frozen fruit, increase the cooking time to 1½ hours.

COBBLED TOGETHER

Craving cobbler, but find yourself without an oven? Don't despair. Just make like an old-school New Englander and punt, with a grunt. This dish is analogous to a Northern chicken and dumplings, where drop-style biscuits replace the more noodlelike dumplings of the South. Although purists prefer their doughy dumplings poached, I finish my grunt in the oven for a bit of browning.

// SOFTWARE

2	cups	all-purpose flour	
2	teaspoons	baking powder	
1	teaspoon	kosher salt	
¼	teaspoon	baking soda	
4	tablespoons	unsalted butter	cut into small pieces and chilled
1	cup	buttermilk	
19	ounces	blackberries	fresh or frozen
1	cup	sugar	
1	cup	H_2O	
½	teaspoon	ground ginger	

// PROCEDURE

1. Heat the oven to 400°F. Place a piece of **aluminum foil** on the bottom rack to catch any overflow.

2. Put the flour, baking powder, salt, and baking soda in the bowl of a **food processor** and pulse 3 or 4 times. Pour the mixture into a **large mixing bowl** and, using your hands, work the butter into the flour mixture until about half of the fat disappears and the rest is left in pea-size pieces. Make a well in the center of the mixture, add the buttermilk, and stir with a **rubber spatula or wooden spoon** just until it comes together. Turn the mixture out onto a piece of **parchment paper** that has been lightly dusted with flour, shape the dough into a ball, wrap, and refrigerate while you prepare the filling.

3. Combine the blackberries, sugar, water, and ginger in a **10-inch cast-iron skillet** and place over medium heat. Bring to a simmer, decrease the heat to medium-low, and cook, stirring occasionally, for 15 minutes, or until the liquid is thick enough to coat the back of a **spoon**. Retrieve the dough from the refrigerator and gently drop it onto the fruit mixture using a **1-ounce disher or large spoon**, evenly distributing it over the top. Bake for 15 to 20 minutes, until the top is just starting to brown. Remove from the oven and cool the grunt for 15 to 30 minutes before serving.

INDIVIDUAL BERRY CRISPS

4 INDIVIDUAL CRISPS

Perhaps the easiest cooked fruit desserts to produce are crisps, which are little (nothing) more than flour-tossed pieces of fruit cooked under a crumbly crown of cookie or cracker crumbs rubbed into nearly equal portions of butter, flour, and sugar. The most famous version of a crisp topping is streusel, which uses oats instead of cracker crumbs. This version can be made out of anything from animal crackers (fun to serve to vegetarians) to ginger snaps to vanilla wafers. In summer, when fruits are plentiful, I usually keep a tub of the topping around just in case.

// SOFTWARE //

FOR THE TOPPING

½	cup	all-purpose flour	
⅓	cup	sugar	
¾	cup	nuts	walnuts, pecans, or almonds, chopped
¾	cup	crushed crackers	ginger snaps or breakfast cereal can be substituted
4	tablespoons	unsalted butter	cut into small pieces and chilled

FOR THE FILLING

12	ounces	frozen berries	blueberries or raspberries
¼	cup	sugar	
2	teaspoons	cornstarch	

// PROCEDURE //

1. Heat the oven to 350°F.

2. Combine the flour, ⅓ cup sugar, nuts, and crackers in a **large mixing bowl**. Work the butter into the dry ingredients with your hands until the mixture is crumbly. This mixture can be refrigerated for up to 1 week in an **airtight container**.

3. Combine the berries, ¼ cup sugar, cornstarch, and ¼ cup of the crisp topping in a **medium mixing bowl**. Divide the mixture evenly among **4 (7- to 8-ounce) ramekins**. Top each ramekin with ½ cup of the remaining crisp topping.

4. Place the ramekins on a **half sheet pan** and bake on the middle rack of the oven for 30 to 35 minutes, until the fruit is bubbling and the topping is browned. Cool the crisps for 15 minutes before serving.

   NOTE: If you don't have custard cups or ramekins, heavy coffee mugs will do just fine.

GOOD WINE GONE BAD: VINEGAR

EPISODE 137 | SEASON 9 | GOOD EATS

We Americans have gotten pretty hip to herbs and spices these last couple of decades. Our seasoning has improved, as has our overall application of heat and general cooking technique. But with the exception of the occasional homemade salad dressing our relationship with vinegar remains strained. I blame Easter, or more specifically Easter eggs, the dyeing of which exposed all our young, sensitive airborne chemical sensory apparatus to the acrid and acrimonious fumes of distilled white vinegar. After that shock, how could champagne vinegars, sherry vinegars, or even the grossly overpoured balsamic vinegars (which I could live without) ever stand a chance? With this episode, we attempted to undo some of the ancient damage and bring this powerful pantry pal onto friendlier ground.

KNOWLEDGE CONCENTRATE

▷○ **Literally translated, the French word for "vinegar" means "sour wine." The sour in question is provided by acetic acid, and that acid is formed when a very specific family of bacteria called acetobacters metabolizes alcohol in the presence of air. With the possible exception of college-aged males, acetobacters are just about the only critters on earth who can actually thrive in alcohol.**

Besides producing water and acetic acid, certain acetobacters create a strange, slimy disk referred to as a "mother." This unsettling-looking thing is actually almost 100 percent cellulose, the same stuff that makes up plant stems. It's called a "mother" because it is so packed with acetobacters that simply transferring one little piece of it into another alcohol-bearing liquid, like wine, will turn it into vinegar.

▷○ **Although kits are available for home vinegar makers, most of us rely on commercially made vinegar, the best of which is created via a very old method called the Orléans ("or-lee-AHN"), or Orleans method, named after Orléans, France, where it was pioneered. Here it is in a nutshell:**

1. Vinegar culture (the mother, or some young vinegar that still contains live bacteria) goes into an oak barrel.

2. Wine goes in, leaving plenty of room for air.

3. The barrel is sealed but for a small airhole, usually stuffed with cotton or wool to keep "stuff" out.

4. The bacteria is given 12 to 15 months to convert the alcohol. Although different makers have differing standards, 6 percent acidity is an average target.

5. When the product is ready, most of the vinegar is pumped out, but enough is left behind to inoculate the new wine and the process starts all over again.

Just in case a batch goes bad, most vinegar makers keep some of their original mother in storage (dormant) as an insurance policy.

A few vinegars to ponder:

BALSAMIC vinegars hail from the Emilia-Romagna region of Italy, where white Trebbiano grapes are squeezed then cooked down until the sugars concentrate to around 40 percent. The juice is then barreled and placed in very warm aging rooms where the water slowly evaporates. As the liquid reduces and concentrates, it's moved to progressively smaller barrels, a process requiring a minimum of twelve years to produce a "Tradizionale vecchio" vinegar and twenty-five for a "Tradizionale extra vecchio," which would traditionally be enjoyed by drizzling on, say, chunks of Parmigiano-Reggiano or a bowl of berries. These "true" balsamics always come in the official bottles of the Modena-based consortium that oversees production. A great majority of what is sold as balsamic is just regular vinegar with color and sugar added—which isn't to say that they're all bad for making vinaigrettes and the like.

SHERRY vinegars are produced from Spanish sherry aged in a succession of American oak barrels in a process referred to as the solera system, which is quite complex and involves fractional blending of different aged sherries; this, when you think about it, mimics the way sherries are made in the first place. Although comparisons are often made between sherry and balsamic vinegars, I find most sherry vinegars to be much more useful in the kitchen because they're so much lighter than (not to mention cheaper than) true balsamics.

CIDER vinegar is produced from apple juice (no peels or cores allowed) that is fermented first into cider, then vinegar. Cider vinegar is a workhorse in my kitchen because its fruity, rounder flavor gets along well with so many foods, especially pork. Down south you can't make a decent barbeque sauce without the stuff, which is available in filtered and nonfiltered versions.

RICE vinegars are from a simple form of rice "wine" or sake and are typically light, white, and lower in acidity than other vinegars. They are ideal for use in Asian-style pickles and dipping sauces for fried foods such as tempura. I often add rice vinegar to soups that need just a little brightening. When shopping, keep in mind that Chinese rice vinegars can be considerably stronger than the Japanese versions that dominate the American market.

WHEN VINEGAR ISN'T GOOD EATS

Although it could be argued that the Orléans method produces the world's best vinegars, it takes time—and time is money. And that's why a clever industrialist came up with another way, a way that is faster and, of course, cheaper. What you do is you take yourself a big vat of wine and you inoculate it with a free-floating form of acetobacter, one that doesn't create a mother. Then you just percolate oxygen into that tank continuously until it turns into vinegar, which is usually one, maybe two days. The problem is, this liquid will never, ever possess the kind of flavor and body delivered by the Orléans method.

SAUERBRATEN

4 TO 6 SERVINGS

Legend has it that sauerbraten, the greatest meat and vinegar dish of all time, was invented in Germany, around A.D. 800, by none other than Charlemagne. I believe this just like I believe that Catherine de Medici invented the fork, and Claude Monet invented chocolate mousse . . . or was that Manet?

TIDBIT | Hippocrates prescribed vinegar for many ailments, from skin rashes to ear infections to "bad humors."

TIDBIT | Typically, red wine vinegars are slightly more acidic than white wine vinegars

// SOFTWARE ///

2	cups	H$_2$O	
1	cup	cider vinegar	
1	cup	red wine vinegar	
1	medium	onion	chopped
1	large	carrot	chopped
1	tablespoon plus 1 teaspoon	kosher salt	plus additional for seasoning the meat
½	teaspoon	black pepper	freshly ground
2		bay leaves	
6		whole cloves	
12		juniper berries	
1	teaspoon	mustard seeds	
1	3½- to 4-pound	bottom round	
1	tablespoon	vegetable oil	
⅓	cup	sugar	
5	ounces	dark old-fashioned gingersnaps	crushed
½	cup	raisins	(optional)

(1) Combine the water, vinegars, onion, carrot, salt, pepper, bay leaves, cloves, juniper berries, and mustard seeds in a **large saucepan** over high heat. Cover and bring to a boil, then lower the heat and simmer for 10 minutes. Set aside to cool.

(2) Pat the bottom round dry, then rub it with oil and salt on all sides. Heat a **large sauté pan** over high heat; add the meat and brown on all sides, 2 to 3 minutes per side.

(3) When the marinade is cool to the touch, place the meat in a **nonreactive vessel** (a 4-quart stainless-steel pan with a lid is ideal) and pour the marinade over it. Refrigerate for 3 days. If the meat is not completely submerged in the liquid, turn it over once a day.

(4) Heat the oven to 325°F. Add the sugar to the meat and marinade, cover, and cook on the middle rack of the oven until tender, about 4 hours.

(5) Remove the meat from the vessel and keep warm. **Strain** the liquid to remove the solids. Return the liquid to the pan and place over medium-high heat. **Whisk** in the gingersnaps and cook until the sauce has thickened, stirring occasionally. Strain the sauce to remove any lumps. Add the raisins, if desired. Slice the meat and serve with the sauce.

STICKING A FORK IN HOT MEAT...

...IS A BAD THING!

USEFUL STUFF INDEED

▶ Adding a tablespoon of vinegar to poaching water will help eggs to set.

▶ When steaming broccoli, try adding a couple of tablespoons of vinegar to the water, as the evaporating acetic acid will help to set the color.

▶ If you're stuck with some wilted salad greens, just add a bit of white vinegar to the soaking water, and in no time they will be revived.

▶ Equal parts vinegar and water make a righteous glass cleaner. Just wipe dry with crumpled newspaper and your glass will be streak-free.

▶ Copper cookware is nice to use but difficult to clean. No problem. Just dissolve a teaspoon of salt in a cup of white vinegar and stir in enough all-purpose flour to create a thick paste. Rub this on the bottom of the vessel, wait fifteen minutes, rinse, and dry. Behold: new-pot luster!

▶ Since acetic acid is pretty gosh-darn good at killing bacteria, molds, and viruses, white vinegar is great for cleaning cutting boards.

▶ A teaspoon of vinegar can radically improve a chocolate cake batter.

▶ Malt vinegar on fries . . . that's all I'm sayin'.

GRIDDLED ROMAINE SALAD

4 SERVINGS

Acetic acid is highly volatile, molecularly speaking, and has no trouble making the jump from liquid to gas phase, a fact that has forced away many a diner who just can't take the fumes. This application gets around the problem by locking said acid in a (temporarily) solid phase.

// SOFTWARE ///

½	cup	red wine vinegar	
2	hearts	romaine lettuce	
1	tablespoon	olive oil	
	to taste	black pepper	freshly ground
1	cup	Parmesan cheese	finely grated

// PROCEDURE ///

1. Pour the vinegar into a **shallow pan** and freeze it solid. Scrape the frozen vinegar with a fork to create a shaved ice texture, then return it to the freezer until ready to use.

2. Cut each heart of romaine in half lengthwise so that the root keeps each piece together. Lightly **brush** the cut side of the romaine pieces with the oil. Season with the pepper. Place the cheese in a **shallow dish** large enough to lay the romaine in and press the cheese firmly onto the cut side of the romaine so it adheres.

3. Spray a **nonstick griddle** or sauté pan with **nonstick spray** and heat over medium-high heat. Place the romaine in the pan and cook until the cheese turns golden, 1 to 2 minutes. Place the romaine, cheese side up, onto **plates** and sprinkle with the vinegar ice. Serve immediately.

   NOTE: Since I want to keep the uncooked side of the romaine as cool as possible, as it comes off the heat I place it on a reusable chill mat.

THE WAFFLE TRUTH

Few "griddle breads" deliver the goods the way waffles can. Sure, pancakes are fine, crêpes . . . dandy, but for those of us who are golden-brown-and-delicious-obsessed, nothing touches the waffle. And yet, most of us either consume waffles at restaurants (down south we even have a house named after waffles) or turn to insipid factory-made specimens whose quality can merely hint at the promise of the real thing. Some folks have made the argument that my own culinary creed rules out waffle making, as it relies upon the possession of a waffle iron, which they say is undoubtedly a unitasker. True, waffle irons only make waffles, but waffles are in and of themselves so amazingly versatile that the device that makes them cannot be looked upon as a . . . you know. More on that in a moment. Let's get to waffling.

TIDBIT The words *waffle* and *wafer* both derive from the same Old German root word, *Wafel* ("VAY-full"), which is also related to terms meaning "weave" and "honeycomb," both of which nod to the grid pattern found on the modern waffle.

TIDBIT The German *Wafel* became the medieval French *gaufre*, which eventually became *gaufrette*, which is what you shape fresh from the iron into a waffle cone for ice cream.

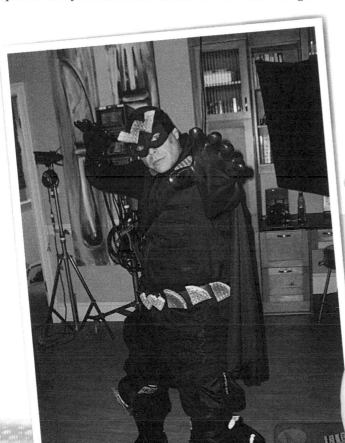

TIDBIT | In 1971 a track coach named Bill Bowerman poured liquid rubber onto his wife's waffle iron, then glued the resulting grid onto a pair of running shoes, thus creating a shoe with low mass but great traction. The resulting footware was named after the Greek goddess of victory, Nike.

OTHER USES FOR WAFFLES:

▶ Use instead of bread to make sandwiches.

▶ Cut into four-grid pieces and toast for croutons.

▶ Leave out to get stale, then tear into chunks for bread pudding.

▶ Make ice cream sandwiches (they freeze well).

NOTE: I have served waffles for every meal of the day, but my favorite application is actually a dinner featuring poultry—fried chicken, to be exact. Simply fry up a batch, toss a couple of pieces in your favorite hot sauce, and serve atop waffles lightly dressed in maple syrup, or if you prefer, cover the whole thing in gravy. Evil, but in a good way.

KNOWLEDGE CONCENTRATE

▷ **A bit of history:** Just in case you doubt that waffles are a gift from God, consider that *wafers* originally meant communion wafers. Back in the gloomy Middle Ages, monastery kitchens were charged with cranking out communion wafers, but since they were one of the few foods that people could actually eat during fasting periods, demand always outstripped supply and eventually secular bakers got into the market and started making them bigger and fancier with elaborate designs and patterns on the top. Such wafers are still associated with certain celebrations in Europe, such as the Twelfth Night feasts in places like Holland, where the original Pilgrims hung out for a decade before coming to the New World and may have picked up a serious waffle habit.

▷ **Two things are needed to produce a waffle:**

1. A waffle iron

2. A batter capable of creating a very crisp and brown exterior while maintaining a light and—dare I say—fluffy interior once placed inside item number 1.

The original waffle irons looked like torture devices composed of two heavy, shaped metal plates and a hinge with a large handle. You heated this device in the coals of a fire, poured in the batter, and closed it up like an iron maiden.

▷ **If there's a big, fat lie in waffledom, it's that good waffles can be made from pancake batter.** Sure, pancakes and waffles both contain eggs, flour, and leavening and they're both served for breakfast. But differences abound. Pancakes may be brown on the outside, but they're floppy, soft, and spongy, with an interior that looks a lot like cake. (I have in fact made some very passable frosted cakes from pancakes.) Waffles, on the other hand, are crisp on the outside and light on the inside, like beignets, funnel cakes, hush puppies, or doughnuts. In short, waffles are fried, only instead of being immersed in hot oil, they are encased in hot-oil-coated metal.

▷ **A few points about waffle batter:**

Waffle batter contains a higher percentage of sugar (for caramelization) than pancake.

Waffle batter includes a bit more fat (for a crisp exterior) than pancake.

Including some whole-wheat flour in the batter increases the roasty-toasty flavor and counteracts some of the sweetness brought on by the extra sugar.

▷ **Concerning assembly:** Thoroughly combining the fat and eggs before introducing the buttermilk will create a smoother batter thanks to the lipoproteins found in eggs yolks, which are powerful emulsifiers and as such will help to bind the fat and water-type liquids together. As is true with all muffin-method mixtures, overmixing is a major cause of waffle malfunction. That's because more mixing produces more gluten, which will toughen waffles and potentially create an inner texture full of long holes, a phenomenon called "tunneling." As with pancake batter, ten to twelve stirs, then just walk away. Yes, there will be lumps.

BASIC WAFFLES

ABOUT 6 (8-INCH ROUND) WAFFLES

// SOFTWARE ///

4¾	ounces	all-purpose flour	
4¾	ounces	whole-wheat flour	
1	teaspoon	baking powder	
½	teaspoon	baking soda	
1	teaspoon	kosher salt	
3	tablespoons	sugar	
3	large	eggs	beaten
4	tablespoons	unsalted butter	melted
2	cups	buttermilk	at room temperature

// PROCEDURE ///

1. Heat a **waffle iron** according to the manufacturer's directions.

2. **Whisk** together the flours, baking powder, baking soda, salt, and sugar in a **medium bowl.**

3. Whisk the eggs and butter together in **another bowl**, and then whisk in the buttermilk.

4. Add the wet ingredients to the dry and whisk to combine.[1] Rest the batter for 5 minutes.[2]

5. Lightly coat the waffle iron with **nonstick spray.**[3] **Ladle** the recommended amount of waffle batter onto the iron according to the manufacturer's recommendations. Close the iron top and cook until the waffle is golden on both sides and is easily removed from the iron. Serve immediately or keep warm in a 200°F oven until ready to serve.[4]

TIP For chocolate waffles, use 7 ounces of all-purpose flour (ditch the whole wheat) and add 1½ ounces Dutch-process cocoa powder to the dry mix Fold in 4 ounces of semisweet chocolate chips to the batter.

[1] Why wet on dry? So that when you beat the mixture, the dry goods won't fly all over the room.

[2] This time will allow the flour granules to hydrate.

[3] There will be smoke. That's okay.

[4] When I'm serving a bunch of folks, I run two matching irons side by side for quicker delivery.

TYPES OF WAFFLES

American waffles are leavened with baking powder and/or soda, are either round or square, and feature small holes or divots.

Most of what are referred to in this country as Belgian waffles are actually Brussels waffles, which are easy to recognize because of their rectangular shape and large divots or pockets. Unlike American specimens, Brussels waffles are light and crisp due to the inclusion of both yeast and whipped egg whites. A second type of Belgian waffle is the Liege waffle, which is rounded, dense, and somewhat chewy. In Belgium, waffles are most often served as a snack or dessert.

Although a pizzelle is cooked from a waffle-style batter in a device much like a waffle iron, this Italian cookie is just that: a big, heavily embossed cookie.

A *stroopwafel* is a delicious Dutch item that features two fine wafflelike cookies sandwiching a layer of syrup, caramel, or honey.

A waffle cone is an ice cream cone made from a cookie (much like a pizzelle) that is cooked in an iron then quickly formed into a cone before it sets into its final crisp configuration.

Regular   Belgian

THE WAFFLE TRUTH

WAFFLING IRONS

When cooktops became the norm in America, ironworkers started cranking out beauties like this, which were a little more convenient to use. You would heat both sides over the cooktop, then you would add the batter on one side, cook it, flip it, cook it, and then take out the finished waffle.

The waffle renaissance in this country had to wait for electricity. You see, after they finished saturating the American market with toasters, appliance manufacturers turned their minds to waffle irons. And by the 1940s, pretty much every household in America had one. Since they got really, really, really hot, these early models weren't very safe, and still aren't. But they are extremely collectable, and models like this with ornate tops are the most desirable. If you are in the market for a new waffle iron, there are a few things to consider.

Today's waffle irons present these basic options:

▶ Square or round

▶ Large grid (Belgian) or small

▶ Plastic or metal chassis

My preferred model is metal and round, which is easier to work with since batter placed in the middle will migrate outward in all directions. (Creating square waffles is tougher, because filling corners requires some finessing. I've also found that round waffle irons typically cook more evenly than square models, probably due to the physical realities of heating coils.) When shopping for a waffle iron, take a close look at the cooking grid. The angles should be sharply indented rather than smooth or rounded. Such an iron will produce crisper edges on its waffles.

I also appreciate the following "bonus" features:

▶ A light that tells you the iron is ready for the batter.

▶ A beeper to tell you when the waffles are done.

▶ A doneness setting to adjust the level of outer browning. In some models this actually changes the heat output of the machine, but in most it simply shortens the time before the beeper beeps.

▶ Someplace to wind the cord.

▶ Upright storage.

NOTE: There is absolutely no doubt that older waffle irons are better than new ones. That's because in the good ole days, waffle iron grids were carbon steel rather than Teflon. Sure, they could stick, but just as a cast-iron skillet puts the best crust on a cornbread, so a steel waffle grid creates the finer crust on a waffle. If you can find a steel model from the 1950s or '60s at a yard sale, you might want to give it a try, but make sure the outlet you plug it into is a GFCI or "ground fault interrupt" outlet (which you should have in your kitchen anyway). Oh, and keep in mind that the exteriors of older irons can get very hot. The need to use caution, however, is a small price to pay for perfection.

GREAT BALLS OF MEAT

EPISODE 139 | SEASON 9 | GOOD EATS

Meatballs are the ultimate multitaskers for carnivores.

Meatballs can be small or big. They can be based on beef, pork, chicken, or any combination thereof, even fish. They can be roasted, simmered, braised, fried, or grilled. They can be lavishly seasoned or left alone in their simplicity. But no matter which way you lead them, a good meatball lies somewhere between sausage and meatloaf and therefore offers a careful balance of flavor and texture. Get it right and you've got good eats.

TRIVIA | The meatball "enorme" that ran over the poor young man at the opening of the show was not meat but rather polystyrene, a.k.a. Styrofoam. We made it look like the guy had been flattened by building a fake floor a few inches above the real one so that only his face and hands stuck out. We're clever that way.

Swedish meatballs always remind me of the parties my parents threw in the '60s.

A FEW FOREIGN MEATBALLS I'VE TRIED AND LIKED OVER THE YEARS:

▶ In Austria they serve fried meatballs called *Fleischlaibchen*.

▶ Chinese meatballs are typically pork and are steamed. Big ones are called "lion's heads."

▶ Greece has the best meatballs, or *keftedes*, which are typically flavored with mint and stewed with onion.

▶ Iran has more meatballs than they know what to do with; it's a Persian thing. They usually go by the name *kufteh*, which means "minced."

▶ In Italy, of course, meatballs are called *polpette*. Pork, beef, garlic, Romano cheese . . . you know the drill. Tiny ones are called *polpettine*.

▶ If you've never had Philippine meatballs served with squash and fried pork cracklin's, you need to fix that.

▶ Down in Latin America meatballs are called *albondigas* and are usually served in a soup.

[1] For most of my daughter's first decade, meatballs were the principal way we snuck spinach into her diet.

Good meatballs require a careful balance of components: meat, binder, filler, seasonings, and the cooking medium (wet or dry—the eternal debate).

THE MEAT: I typically use three meats: pork for texture and fat, beef round or sirloin for flavor, and lamb for what I call "commentary." It's not the primary flavor by any means, but it adds considerable interest. Any of these meats alone results in lackluster meatballs. I should note that my wife often replaces the pork with ground turkey, for health's sake, and I assure you they do taste healthy . . . if you get my meaning. Although I prefer to grind my own pork shoulder, lamb shoulder (or leg), and beef round two times through a medium die, the standard megamart grind will do just fine.

THE BINDER: The binder can be thought of as a kind of glue that holds the entire meatball together into a cohesive whole. What we need for the job is liquid protein glue. Translation: egg. One has more than enough molecular power for one batch of meatballs.

THE FILLER: Originally fillers such as oatmeal, breadcrumbs, cooked rice, farina, and so on were added to meatball and meatloaf recipes as a simple way of bulking up the meal and making up for the fact that the cook either didn't have enough meat or was stingy with it. However, a binder is really necessary for two reasons:

1. A binder captures moisture that might otherwise be squeezed out of the meat by the pressure of heat.

2. Thus moistened, the filler turns into a kind of gel, which smooths out the texture and provides some additional binding power.

Fillers can be vegetal in origin, such as the aforementioned rice, farina, or oats, but a binder can also be something leafy and fibrous like my favorite, cooked spinach.[1] Since I typically have plenty of stale bread around the kitchen, I often go with breadcrumbs, which can be produced simply by taking hunks of stale bread for a spin in the blender.

Another one of my most favorite fillers is chopped dried mushrooms. Since they can take a while to hydrate, I tend to add these only if I have time to let the meat mixture refrigerate for a while before forming.

THE SEASONINGS: This may include any herb, spice, vegetable, cheese, or liquid enhancement (Worcestershire sauce, fish sauce, sriracha, and so on) that you may care to add. Always remember that the name of the dish is *meat*balls, so be careful that enhancement doesn't become concealment.

THE COOKING MEDIUM: There are three choices: wet, dry, and a hybrid of the two. Although I certainly respect the millennia of tradition that go into every single pot of Italian meatballs simmered long and low in a deep pool of tomato sauce on the back burner, I just can't do without the meaty sear that comes as a result of dry cooking. Although this may certainly come courtesy of an oil fry followed by sauce, I find that oven roasting (or in this case baking) does the trick more efficiently and easily.

AB'S BAKED MEATBALLS

4 TO 5 SERVINGS; 20 MEATBALLS

My favorite way to enjoy meatballs is to simply park them atop a nice little bed of pasta tossed with a little olive oil, maybe some grated Parmesan cheese, and freshly cracked black pepper. That said, I've been known to toss them in salads, float them in soup, and of course pile them into meatball sandwiches.

// SOFTWARE //

8	ounces	ground pork	
8	ounces	ground lamb	
8	ounces	ground round	
5	ounces	frozen spinach	thawed and drained
½	cup	Parmesan cheese	finely grated
1	large	egg	
1½	teaspoons	dried basil	
1½	teaspoons	dried parsley	
1	teaspoon	garlic powder	
1	teaspoon	kosher salt	
½	teaspoon	red pepper flakes	
½	cup	breadcrumbs	

// PROCEDURE //

1. Heat the oven to 400°F.

2. Combine the pork, lamb, beef, spinach, cheese, egg, basil, parsley, garlic powder, salt, red pepper flakes, and ¼ cup of the breadcrumbs in a **large mixing bowl**. Using your hands, mix until all ingredients are well incorporated. Use immediately or put in the refrigerator for up to 24 hours.

3. Put the remaining ¼ cup breadcrumbs in a **small bowl**. Cover a **scale** with **plastic wrap**. Weigh meatballs into 1½-ounce portions and place on a **half sheet pan**. Using clean hands, shape the meatballs into rounds, roll in the breadcrumbs, and place the meatballs in **miniature muffin tin cups**. Bake for 20 minutes, or until golden and cooked through.

   N O T E : We often make up big batches of these guys, bake 'em, then cool and freeze 'em in heavy-duty zip-top bags. They'll keep for up to 6 months and can be revived simply by dropping them into a pot of sauce or soup and allowing them to simmer for a few minutes.

TIDBIT The miniature muffin tin helps the meatballs hold their shape while ensuring even cooking.

CLARIFIED BUTTER

Melt a pound of butter in a heavy saucepan over low heat and slowly cook until the bubbling ceases and the liquid turns clear, 30 to 40 minutes. Strain and cool, being sure to leave any solids in the bottom of the pan. Or, once the butter is clear, remove the pan from the heat and quickly add two inches of hot tap water. Since it is less dense than water, the now clarified butter will float to the top. And after a few hours in the refrigerator it will solidify into a big yellow Frisbee that you can lift out and use. Use the clarified butter immediately, wrap it in waxed paper and refrigerate, or add foil and freeze it for up to 2 months.

I've questioned some Swedes quite pointedly about the origins of their delicious meatballs, or *kottbullar* (do not ask me to pronounce this, for not even my Swedish acquaintances can pull it off without producing a great deal of airborne spittle), which have apparently been part of the standard smorgasbord for at least a couple hundred years and are traditionally served in a cream gravy with lingonberries. They were adopted by modern housewives here in the 1950s and '60s because they allowed the use of two beloved attributes of the age: chafing dishes and frilly toothpicks.

// SOFTWARE //

2	slices	fresh white bread	
¼	cup	milk	
3	tablespoons	clarified butter	(left)
½	cup	onion	finely chopped
1	teaspoon plus a pinch	kosher salt	
12	ounces	ground chuck	
12	ounces	ground pork	
2	large	egg yolks	
½	teaspoon	black pepper	freshly ground
¼	teaspoon	ground allspice	
¼	teaspoon	nutmeg	freshly grated[2]
¼	cup	all-purpose flour	
3	cups	beef broth	
¼	cup	heavy cream	

1. Crank your oven to 200°F. Tear the bread into pieces and put it in a **small mixing bowl** along with the milk. Set aside.

2. Heat 1 tablespoon of the butter in a **12-inch straight-sided sauté pan** over medium heat. Add the onion and a pinch of salt and sweat until the onion is soft. Remove from the heat and set aside.

3. Combine the bread and milk mixture, beef, pork, egg yolks, 1 teaspoon kosher salt, the pepper, allspice, nutmeg, and onion in the bowl of a **stand mixer**. Beat on medium speed for 1 to 2 minutes.

4. Cover a **scale** with **plastic wrap**. Weigh meatballs into 1-ounce portions and place on a **half sheet pan**. Using clean hands, shape the meatballs into rounds.

5. Heat the remaining butter in the sauté pan over medium-low heat, or in an **electric skillet** set to 250°F. Add the meatballs and sauté until golden brown on all sides, 7 to 10 minutes. Remove the meatballs to an **ovenproof dish** using a **slotted spoon** and place in the warmed oven.

6. Once all the meatballs are cooked, decrease the heat to low and add the flour to the pan or skillet. **Whisk** until lightly browned, 1 to 2 minutes. Gradually add the broth and whisk until the sauce begins to thicken. Add the cream and continue to cook until the gravy reaches the desired consistency. Remove the meatballs from the oven, cover with the gravy, and serve.

[2] I'm not kidding about this. Real, freshly grated nutmeg is required. If you make the meatballs without it, I'll know, and I won't be happy.

MEATBALL CHAUFFEUR

Believe it or not, *chafing dish* and *chauffeur* have the same root. In old-time France, the chauffeur was the guy who shoveled coal into a steam engine. The original root word is *chaufen*, meaning "to heat" or "to enflame."

Don't own a chafing dish? No problem. Just get yourself some kind of padding material, like some shelf liner, make a little triangle, put some bricks on top of that—just standard household bricks—drop your fuel can in the middle, and then make another triangle of bricks going the other way on top. Fire up your fuel using a long lighter or match, place a cake pan on top of that, and then put water inside that. The water will do the heating. The dish with your meatballs goes on top of that.

A few words to the wise about alcohol gel fuel. When this stuff burns, the flame is very, very tough to see, especially in brightly lit rooms. So always assume that if it is open, it is hot. When it comes time to extinguish it, always smother the flame, either with the lid or, even better, a large metal item with a handle, like a measuring cup. Don't try to blow it out.

Avocados are and always have been my favorite fruit. When I was a kid growing up in California, I often lunched on sliced avocado drizzled with bottled French dressing. As I got a little older I discovered the world of guacamoles. Then avocado-and-Spam sandwiches on rye, then . . . well, let's just say I ate a lot of avocado.

With all that luscious green in my veins, avocado was a no-brain shoo-in for a *Good Eats* episode. Problem is, every time I started writing the show I never could get past guacamole. Who, after all, actually cooks avocado? And so I shelved it. Several times, in fact. But I couldn't admit that avocado had beaten me, and so I decided to break it down into its parts. That's when it hit me: Avocado is mostly fat . . . fabulous, flavorful fat. Why can't it do the things other fats can do?

We began experimenting, and this show came out of those experiments. But first, some interesting facts to know and tell.

KNOWLEDGE CONCENTRATE

▷ **Although dozens of different avocado varieties may, at various times of year, adorn your megamart shelf, they all derive from one of three basic types:**

— Guatemalan

— Mexican

— West Indian

The avocados commercially grown in the western United States are hybrids of Mexican and Guatemalan types, while Florida's crop descends from the West Indian type. Although the West Indian models are lower in calories than those of Central American derivation, they also deliver far less flavor and I personally just won't eat the darned things.

Western-grown avocados include Hass, Fuerte, Reed, and Pinkerton.

▷ **If you've ever wondered why good avocados are on the pricey side, consider that it takes thirteen months for them to mature. Notice I did not use the word *ripen*. That's because avocados never, ever ripen on the tree. They have to be picked before that can happen. This is actually a good thing for growers, because it means they can literally store fruit on the trees for up to seven months. And that is why avocados are available year round.[1]**

Avocados should be heavy for their size, and relatively blemish-free. The level of maturity you seek depends on when you plan to consume them. If you need to keep them for two to three days, buy them as firm as you can. I prefer this scenario because hard fruits are less likely to have suffered bruising. Such specimens will mature to perfection in your kitchen, as long as you do not put them in plastic bags or in the refrigerator, either of which will shut down the metabolism of the fruit, thus halting nature's march to goodness. If you want to purchase the most ready-to-eat specimens possible, try this tiny tip. Just flick off the little stumpy piece of the stem and closely examine the tiny crater it reveals. If you spy green right down in the very bottom, odds are good you have a mature avocado. Of course, you can also give it a gentle squeeze. If it yields like, say, a racquetball and bounces back, you're good to go. But do be gentle.

If your avocados have a couple of days to go to ripen, leave them out at room temperature, but don't pile them up on each other in a bowl or they'll bruise. Recyclable paper beverage holders are the perfect places to stash ripening fruit. If the avocados are already ripe, the refrigerator is a fine idea, because although the cold will prevent unripe avocados from reaching their peak condition, it will also slow the spoiling process in fruits that are already good to go.

Although we have dealt with disassembling avocados before, if my friends who work in emergency rooms are right, it is a lesson worth repeating. Here's how it goes:

Lay the avocado down and take a nice big knife and literally roll the knife across the longitude. Don't do this in your hand; do it down on the board. If the avocado is ripe, you should be able to easily twist it apart. Put the side not containing the pit face down—more on why later. And now, removing the pit is easy: Just pop it with the heel of your blade—

Wait. What's wrong with this picture? Sharp, terrible knife. Soft, pink fingers. Always protect your hand with a mitt or a towel. There. Now we can proceed:

Just take the knife, twist to dislodge the pit, and it will pop right out. Pinch the blade between your thumb and forefinger, and the pit will drop off.

Now, the best way to get the meat out of there is to use a soup spoon. Simply dig your way gently around the outside, turning the avocado and the spoon. The meat will pop right out, leaving you a lovely cup that you can use as a . . . well, nothing, really.

Once you cut into an avocado, an enzyme called phenoloxidase hastens the oxidation of various phenols, which results in rapid browning. If you want to stop the browning, you have two choices. If you have a digitally controlled immersion circulator, you could poach your avocados for a couple of hours at 104°F. That much heat wouldn't damage the texture or flavor, but it would shut down the enzymes that cause browning. Or you could use citric acid, like that found in lemons and limes, which can snap the crankshaft on the enzymatic engine, thus stopping browning in its tracks. Use about half a teaspoon of juice for every avocado's worth of flesh. Keeping O_2 at bay will also help, so wrap or cover with plastic wrap if possible.

NOTE: Okay, avocados do contain a fair amount of fat (about 35g per 7 ounces), which is why they perform the way they do in the following applications. But, as many a dietician has pointed out, a huge majority of this is in the form of monounsaturated fats such as oleic acid, which may be a powerful weapon against high cholesterol. Avodacos also include vitamins K, B_6, and C, folate, potassium, and a bunch of other good stuff that you're not likely to find in butter, lard, or shortening, no matter how hard you look.

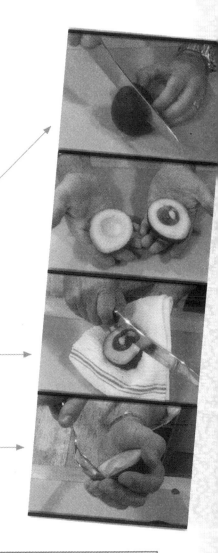

[1] It should be noted that various hybrids have been developed that mature best during different seasons.

AVOCADO COMPOUND BUTTER

ABOUT 8 OUNCES

Compound butter makes a fabulous finish for grilled meats and fish. Why not up the flavor and nutrition ante by subbing out some of that cow stuff with avocado?

// SOFTWARE

6	ounces	ripe avocado meat	about 2 small specimens
1	tablespoon	lemon juice	freshly squeezed
4	tablespoons	unsalted butter	at room temperature
1	clove	garlic	minced
1	tablespoon	fresh cilantro	chopped
2	teaspoons	cumin	freshly toasted and ground
	to taste	kosher salt	
	to taste	black pepper	freshly ground

// PROCEDURE

1. Peel and pit the avocados. Situate all ingredients in the bowl of a **food processor** and process until well combined. **Spoon** the mixture onto a sheet of **parchment paper** and shape into a log.

2. Refrigerate for 3 to 4 hours. Slice and serve with grilled fish or chicken. Store for up to three days in the refrigerator or a week in the freezer.

HASS

Every single Hass tree—and there are millions of them—share a single mother, a very famous tree that recently died. It was planted as a sapling in the backyard of a Whittier, California, postman named Rudolph Hass in 1926. As this tree matured, it produced prodigious amounts of a rich, flavorful fruit. It was so much better than all the other avocados in the area that Hass finally got wise and in 1935 patented the variety. (The patent expired in 1952, the same year of Hass's death.) Now, how do you produce zillions and zillions and zillions of plants from one tree without the fruit changing at all? Well, let's put it this way: Those bumpy green guys have a lot in common with another bumpy green guy, Frankenstein's monster.

TIDBIT | The Aztecs used avocado to add fat to their lean meat selection of turkey, rabbit, dog, and slugs.

TIDBIT In some parts of the world avocados are enjoyed for dessert. In Brazil, they're chilled and then mashed up with sugar and milk, and in Indonesia they're mashed up with coffee.

The way I see it, the linchpin ingredient in great ice cream is the egg. Protein, emulsifiers, fat—it's got everything you need for creating a creamy, rich texture. But check this out: 3.5 ounces of the green stuff gives us a little over 2 grams of protein, 16 grams of fat, and still contains 6.3 grams of carbs for flavor and sweetness. So the trick to using avocados for ice cream is to think of them as eggs. They're even shaped the same. Coincidence? I think not.

// SOFTWARE ///

12	ounces	avocado meat	about 3 medium specimens
1	tablespoon	lemon juice	freshly squeezed
1½	cups	whole milk	
½	cup	sugar	
1	cup	heavy cream	

// PROCEDURE //

1. Peel and pit the avocados. Put the avocado meat, lemon juice, milk, and sugar in a **blender** and puree. Transfer the mixture to a **medium mixing bowl**, add the cream, and **whisk** to combine. Chill the mixture until it reaches 40°F or below, 4 to 6 hours.

2. Process the mixture in an **ice cream maker** according to the manufacturer's directions. This mixture sets up very fast, so count on it taking only 5 to 10 minutes to process. For soft ice cream, serve immediately. Freeze for 3 to 4 hours for a firmer texture.

WHAT'S IN A NAME?

The avocado, like sassafras and bay, is a member of the laurel family, and it is a New World plant that has many, many names. The Incas called it *palta*. The Maya and Guatemalans referred to it simply as *oh*. And Brazilian tribes called it *omichon*. Today, the French call this little guy *l'avocat*, which I'm pretty sure means "lawyer." They do this because the Spanish call it by their word for lawyer, or *abogado*. When Cortez and his crew crashed Montezuma II's party back around 1519, they couldn't say the Aztec word for "avocado," which is *ahuacatl*—which I can barely say. So they used the word that sounded the closest to them. But here's the lovely irony: In Aztec, *ahuacatl* doesn't mean "lawyer," it means "testicle." I just love that.

TIDBIT There is but one fruit that contains more oil than avocados: olives. Avocado oil is one of the best oils for your heart on the face of the earth. And it also has a very high smoke point, over 500°F, so it's perfect for stir-fries and sauteing.

A PIE IN EVERY POCKET

EPISODE 141 | SEASON 9 | GOOD EATS

Hand pies, pocket pies, and turnovers of various shapes and sizes hail from all over the globe. If you've ever had a pierogi in Cleveland, you can thank the Poles who settled there. Empanadas in Texas? Say thanks to Spain, specifically the region of Galicia. Although Louisiana's "hot meat pies" also reflect some Spanish influence, if you look further back you'll see Arab intervention in the form of the triangular *sambusak* pastry. If you've ever traveled the Aegean, you've probably munched on Greece's *kolokotes*. Of course, there's the calzone, which means "pants leg" in Italian . . . not sure about that one.

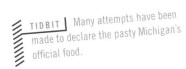

> **TIDBIT** | Many attempts have been made to declare the pasty Michigan's official food.

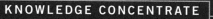

KNOWLEDGE CONCENTRATE

The pocket-pie concept reached its true zenith in the able hands of Cornish housewives, who used to bake up small meat-and-vegetable pies for their coal miner husbands. They'd wrap them, still warm, in a napkin or an old newspaper and stash them in lunchboxes or even right in the jacket pockets of their hubbies.

When lunchtime came, the miner would simply unwrap his parcel. And if his wife used enough newspaper, the pie would probably still be warm. If it wasn't quite warm enough, he would simply place it on the blade of his shovel and warm it over his wee little lantern. If the miner was really lucky, his wife would use two different fillings. She'd put a savory filing in one end of the pie and a sweet filling in the other.

So prevalent was the "pasty" in Cornish cuisine that it is said that the devil himself would not go to Cornwall for fear of being cooked into one of these pies.

A proper pocket-pie crust is characterized by two seemingly contradictory traits, namely flexibility and strength. The flexibility comes from the fact that the crust is actually a foam formed, as all foams are, by tiny bubbles. The strength, as is always the case in baked goods, comes from protein, specifically gluten, which is formed when flour and water are worked together.

How do we get rigidity and flexibility into one dough? By assembling via the biscuit method. Let's review:

1. Combine flour, chemical leaveners, and salt.

2. Rub/cut solid fat (in this case, shortening) into flour.

3. Add liquid to form dough.

4. Knead to smoothness.

5. Cut, roll, form.

It's just that simple.[1]

A few pocket-pie tips:

Fight the urge to overfill. Remember, most fillings are full of water, and water expands when it gets hot—a lot. More than a wee spoonful of filling will essentially blow your pie to smithereens.

Go easy on the egg wash. It's really just protein glue, and you remember the golden glue rule from kindergarten: a little holds better than a lot. Lightly apply with a finger. No need for a brush.

Seal carefully. There's an art to crimping. You want to lay the bowl of the fork down on the counter, and just roll the tines on, until they make that impression.

Always vent. When baking or pan-frying pies I like to cut steam vents with the very tips of my shears, as I believe that does less damage than slashing with a knife. Pies destined for the fryer should be "docked" with a fork: Simply make several shallow pokes across the surface of the pie with just the tips of the tines.[2]

When it comes to immersing the pies in oil, don't just plop them in or you'll be reaching for the burn ointment. Pretend you're releasing a little fish and ease it in. Your hand will come closer to the oil, but there will be less pain in the end because there won't be any flying droplets of doom. Oh, and don't try to fry more than about three at a time.

As is true of most baked goods, cooling is a critical step. It allows the newly gelatinized starches and coagulated proteins to set. Cooling also keeps you from roasting the roof of your mouth off. Believe me, impatience will be punished.

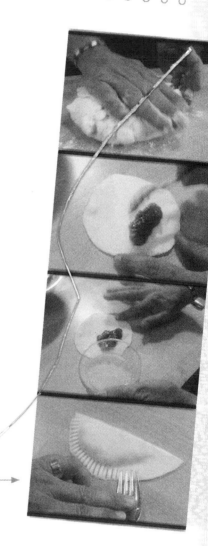

[1] Of course, if it were really that simple, why did it take me the better part of a decade to master my grandmother's biscuits?

[2] The term *dock* comes from the Middle Dutch word *dok*, meaning "to drill."

POP PASTRIES

On September 14, 1964, the hand-pie world changed forever, for it was upon that fateful day that Pop-Tarts were unleashed upon the planet. Like the hand pies of old, this new pastry was meant to be consumed on the go without the aid of utensils. It would fit in a glove compartment, a briefcase, or a purse, and it was perfectly sized to slide right into the most American of all culinary inventions: the toaster. By the time *Sergeant Pepper* hit the airwaves, Pop-Tarts were the most popular manufactured breakfast food in America.

// SOFTWARE

9½	ounces	all-purpose flour	
2	teaspoons	baking powder	
¾	teaspoon	kosher salt	
6	tablespoons	shortening	
¾	cup	milk	
1	large	egg	beaten with 1 teaspoon H_2O
		vegetable or canola oil, or unsalted butter	(optional; for frying)

// PROCEDURE

1. Combine the flour, baking powder, and salt in the bowl of a **food processor**. Pulse for a few seconds, then pour into a **large mixing bowl**.

2. Add the shortening and knead it into the flour with your hands until it is crumbly. Add the milk all at once and mix with a **spatula** until the dough begins to come together. Lightly flour your hands and the countertop and turn the dough out onto the countertop. Knead the dough ball, folding it over 10 to 20 times.

3. If making toaster pastries, skip to that section (right). Otherwise, **roll** the dough to ⅓ to ½ inch thick, and cut into rounds using a **2½-inch ring**. Roll each round as thin as possible, to 5 to 6 inches in diameter. **Spoon** 1 to 2 tablespoons of filling onto the dough, **brush** the edges of one half of the dough lightly with the egg wash, and fold over and seal the edges together with the tines of a **fork**, dipping it into flour as needed. Gently press down to flatten and evenly distribute the filling and **snip** or **cut** 3 slits in the top of the pie. For pies that are going to be deep-fried, dock with a fork instead of snipping or cutting slits.

TO PAN-FRY:

(4) Place a **medium sauté pan** over medium-low heat and add 1 to 2 tablespoons oil or butter. Once heated, place 2 or 3 pies at a time in the pan and sauté until golden on both sides, 3 to 4 minutes per side. Cool the pies for 5 minutes before serving.

TO DEEP-FRY:

(4) Heat vegetable oil in a **deep-fryer or a large heavy pot** to 375°F. Once hot, add 1 or 2 pies at a time and fry until golden brown, 3 to 4 minutes.

TO BAKE:

(4) Crank your hot box to 350°F. Place the pies on a **half sheet pan** and bake for 25 to 30 minutes, until golden brown.

TO MAKE TOASTER PASTRIES:

(4) Heat the oven to 350°F. Divide the dough in half and **roll** out to less than ⅛ inch thick. **Cut** into 4-by-5-inch rectangles. Place 1 to 2 tablespoons of filling in the center of one piece of dough. Lightly coat the edges with egg wash and top with a second piece of dough. Seal the edges by pressing them together with the tines of a **fork**. Gently press down to flatten and evenly distribute the filling and dock the top of the pie. Put the pies on a **half sheet pan**.

(5) Bake for 20 minutes. Remove from the oven, cool completely, and store in **zip-top bags** until ready to toast. The pies will not brown until toasted.

TIP | Got beef or vegetable stew? Then you've got a savory pocket pie waiting to happen. Just fill it up as you would with any other filling for a nice Cornish pastry. Or perhaps you're in the mood for pizza. No problem. Just spoon a little sauce on the pastry rounds and kind of smear it out—not getting too close to the edge—and add your favorite toppings (go light) and a little bit of grated cheese. I like some green onions, but that's just me. Pepperoni's fine, because it's nice and flexible. A few red pepper flakes—again, just don't overstuff, or you'll be sorry later.

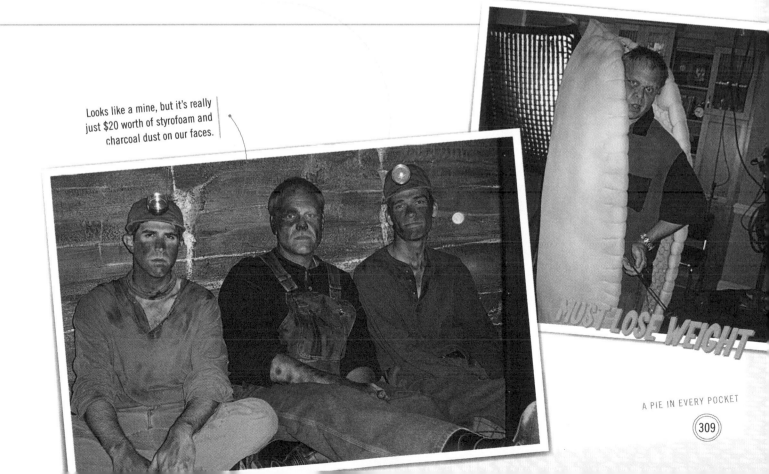

Looks like a mine, but it's really just $20 worth of styrofoam and charcoal dust on our faces.

MUST LOSE WEIGHT

A PIE IN EVERY POCKET

APPLICATION · CHOCOLATE FILLING

ENOUGH FOR 10 TO 15 PIES

I tend to think that a well-designed recipe should be like a good airplane: It should be able to fly itself as long as nobody goes out of their way to crash it. Well, several viewers let us know that this one went down even when they were wide awake at the controls. So we've redesigned it to be more user friendly, adding an egg for binding.

TIDBIT | In France a pocket pie filled with apples is a *chausson aux pommes,* or "apple sock."

// SOFTWARE

1	pound	sugar	
2	ounces	cocoa powder	
	pinch	kosher salt	
1¼	cups	unsalted butter	at room temperature
1	large	egg	lightly beaten

// PROCEDURE

Put the sugar, cocoa powder, and salt in a **large zip-top bag** and shake vigorously to combine. Add the butter and egg and squish until well combined. Cut a hole in one corner of the bag and use it to fill the pastries.

APPLICATION · CURRIED MANGO FILLING

ENOUGH FOR 10 TO 15 PIES

// SOFTWARE

4		mangoes	peeled, pitted, and diced
½	cup	light brown sugar	
½	cup	cider vinegar	
2	teaspoons	curry powder	
¼	cup	lime juice	freshly squeezed

// PROCEDURE

Combine the ingredients in a **small saucepan** over high heat and bring to a boil. Reduce the heat to low, cover, and simmer for 30 minutes, stirring occasionally. Transfer to a **bowl** and place in the refrigerator to cool completely before using as filling.

This was our first alcoholic
beverage episode and featured
the debut of our Good Drinks Bar set.
The way I figure it, beverages go hand in
hand with food, and alcohol goes hand
in hand with beverages . . . at least the
really good ones. Although we knew we'd take on a general cocktail show at some point,
I wanted our first stab at a quaffable to feature some real cooking—and bourbon, and
eggs. And so we come to: Bourbon + Eggs + Cooking = Eggnog.

TIDBIT In 1964 Congress granted bourbon the honor of being the official alcoholic beverage of the United States.

BOURBON

According to the Federal Standards of Identity for Distilled Spirits (C.F.R. 5.22), "bourbon" whisky:

▶ Must be fermented from a grain mixture (mash) containing at least 51 percent corn.

▶ Must be distilled to no more than 80 percent ABV (that's alcohol by volume—multiply by 2 to get the proof).

▶ Must be aged in new, charred oak barrels.

▶ May not be barreled at more than 62.5 percent ABV.

▶ May not be bottled at less than 40 percent ABV.

The steps to making bourbon are deceptively simple:

1. Grind grain (corn and typically wheat).

2. Add water and yeast and ferment in large tanks (open-air tanks render a superior mash).

3. Pump the resulting mash into a still (typically a column rather than pot style) to distill out the alcohol, leaving the solids and chemical impurities behind.

4. Distill the distillate yet again so that the resulting liquid is perfectly clear (this raw liquor is called "white dog" and I happen to like it).

5. Mature said liquid in new, charred oak barrels for several years so that it

can mix and mingle with the wood, thus extracting many of the compounds therein.

World-class bourbons contain complex flavors, thanks in part to natural impurities called congeners. This collection of esters, acids, aldehydes, and higher alcohols is created by the fermentation process, and can also create in overimbibers a seedy set of symptoms known as a hangover. Clear spirits, like vodka and gin, don't contain nearly as many congeners, so they don't typically generate such miserable mornings after. A cure? Well, since eggs contain cysteine, the substance that offsets the toxic acetaldehydes in question, it could be that a glass of eggnog, sans booze, might just help.

TIDBIT The word *nog* was an Old English term for ale, and a *noggin* was the cup from whence it was drunk.

TIDBIT Captain John Smith reported that eggnog was enjoyed in Jamestown in 1607.

▷ **Although most Americans think of eggnog as something they get out of a milk carton during the two-week period leading up to Christmas, eggnog descends from *sack posset*, a strong, thick English beverage built upon eggs, milk, and either a fortified wine (like Madeira) or ale. It was a highly alcoholic beverage, often served so thick it could be scooped. It was also very much an upper-class tipple, as rich folks were usually the only ones who could procure the proper ingredients.**

▷ **Although it is a beverage, eggnog is in fact a stirred custard, very much like an ice cream mix. And as with all custards, the key to success in making eggnog is patience.**

The yolks must be beaten until they lighten and thicken before any sugar is added. This step essentially creates a stable emulsion into which the eggs can be dissolved. But that sugar must be added very slowly. If you rush, you'll end up with nasty little knots of egg protein and sugar (gritty and gross) instead of reaching the ribbon stage (smooth and thick). Once the sugar and eggs have reached the ribbon stage, slowly add the other liquids. Take your time. I believe that working with room-temperature ingredients helps, as they tend to bind more easily than cold ones.

The whites must be free of yolks. Why? Because we wish to beat them into a foam, and a foam is really just a big old pile of bubbles. If you look closely at a bubble you'll see that it's really just a protein matrix trapping little droplets of water. If you could look closely enough at any one of these bubbles, it would look kind of like a window, with the muntins and mullions (or whatever you call those wooden things) serving as protein and the glass acting as the water. The proteins are held together via hydrogen bonds, and that's kind of like, well . . . holding hands. When you beat egg whites, you are essentially unraveling protein strands and stretching them until they can literally reach out and hook up with other protein strands. This creates a stable superstructure for the bubble. If, however, egg yolks or some other fat source crash the party, the bonds become insecure and fall apart, if they form at all.

Although colonial Americans used rum in their nogs, and the English before them brandy or sherry, no self-respecting Southerner would reach for anything but good Kentucky bourbon whisky.[1]

[1] Although many American distillers use the old (and Irish) spelling *whiskey*, the official U.S. spelling is actually *whisky*.

Trying to whip egg whites with yolks in them is like trying to hold hands with greasy gloves. Only frustration can ensue.

The structure of a bubble is a lot like a window.

Protein

H_2O (technically sugar syrup)

Protein

H_2O (technically sugar syrup)

APPLICATION — EGGNOG

6 TO 7 CUPS

// **SOFTWARE** ///

4	large	eggs[2]	separated
⅓	cup plus 1 tablespoon	sugar	
2	cups	whole milk	
1	cup	heavy cream	not half-and-half, not "light" or "coffee" cream; go hard-core here or forget the whole darn thing
1	teaspoon	nutmeg	freshly grated
3	ounces	bourbon	

// **PROCEDURE** ///

1. Beat the egg yolks in a **medium mixing bowl** until they lighten in color. Gradually add the ⅓ cup sugar and continue to beat until it is completely dissolved. Add the milk, cream, bourbon, and nutmeg and stir to combine.

2. Put the egg whites in the bowl of a **stand mixer** fitted with the **whisk attachment** and beat to soft peaks. With the mixer still running, gradually add the 1 tablespoon sugar and beat until stiff peaks form.

3. **Whisk** the egg whites into the yolk mixture. Chill and enjoy.

[2] If you're at all concerned about the possibility of encountering salmonella, by all means purchase pasteurized shell eggs, now available at most megamarts.

FOOD POLICE: (Speaking through megaphone from helicopter above house) Alton Brown, this is the Food Police.

AB: Great Scott!

FP: Come out with your beverages up!

AB: Why don't you guys go pick on somebody else?

FP: We know you've been using raw eggs in there. We don't like it one bit.

AB: I used pasteurized shell eggs. They're perfectly safe.

FP: Yeah, whatever. Put the eggnog in the bucket. (A bucket descends from an unseen chopper)

AB: Okay, okay! (Pours a little bit of eggnog into the bucket) There. Get out of here!

FP: All of it, Brown!

AB: Oh, bother. (Pours in the rest) There. Stinkers! You stinky stinkers!!

FP: Name caller!

AB: Fine. Government says that eggs aren't safe unless they're heated to 160? Fine, we'll do just that.

SCHOOL OF HARD NOGS

6 TO 7 CUPS

// **SOFTWARE** //

4	large	eggs	separated
⅓	cup plus 1 tablespoon	sugar	
2	cups	whole milk	
1	cup	heavy cream	not half-and-half, not "light" or "coffee" cream; go hard-core here or forget the whole darn thing
1	teaspoon	nutmeg	freshly grated
3	ounces	bourbon	

// **PROCEDURE** //

1. **Whisk** the egg yolks and the ⅓ cup sugar together in a **large mixing bowl** until the yolks lighten in color and the sugar is completely dissolved.

2. Combine the milk, cream, and nutmeg in a **medium saucepan** over high heat and bring just to a boil, stirring occasionally. Remove from the heat and gradually stir the hot mixture into the egg yolk and sugar mixture. Return everything to the pan and cook until the mixture reaches 160°F. Remove from the heat, stir in the bourbon, pour back into the mixing bowl, and refrigerate.

3. Beat the egg whites to soft peaks in a **stand mixer** fitted with the **whisk attachment**. With the mixer running, gradually add the 1 tablespoon sugar and beat until stiff peaks form. Whisk the egg whites into the chilled yolk mixture.

N O T E : The cooked version is, of course, a little thicker because of the coagulated proteins. It is a cooked custard. Some folks really dig that shakelike viscosity, but I still prefer the more refreshing texture of the original version. But that's just me.

TIP | A large slotted spoon, perched over a bowl or beaker, makes a fantastic egg separator.

THE ART OF SEPARATING EGGS

If it is a young, fresh egg you're separating, it's very likely that the membrane of the white will want to hang onto the yolk. So, wiggle it back and forth and eventually that membrane will let go.

The yolk goes into bowl number one, the white into bowl number two, and then we inspect the white. If there is no fleck of yolk, it goes into bowl number three. And we repeat with the remainder of the eggs.

EGGNOG ICE CREAM

1 QUART

The holidays are a treacherous time, my friends. People are always just showing up, unexpected and uninvited, wanting to be fed or watered. How can you possibly be prepared for this onslaught? More eggnog, of course. For instance, if you are like me, and you keep around plenty of the cooked custard base without the egg white foam worked into it, well, then you could surprise your various guests with delicious eggnog ice cream. That's right, it's a drink, it's an ice cream base—it's both!

// **SOFTWARE** ///

4	large	egg yolks	
⅓	cup	sugar	
2	cups	whole milk	
1	cup	heavy cream	
1	teaspoon	nutmeg	freshly grated
3	ounces	bourbon	

I always have a nutmeg in my pocket. Really.

// **PROCEDURE** ///

1. **Whisk** the egg yolks and sugar together in a **large mixing bowl** until the yolks lighten in color and the sugar is completely dissolved. Set aside.

2. Combine the milk, cream, and nutmeg in a **medium saucepan** over high heat and bring just to a boil, stirring occasionally. Remove from the heat and gradually stir the hot mixture into the egg yolk and sugar mixture. Return everything to the pan and cook until the mixture reaches 160°F.

3. Remove from the heat, stir in the bourbon, pour into a **medium mixing bowl**, and refrigerate. Chill the mixture until it reaches a temperature of 40°F, 4 to 6 hours.

4. Once it's chilled, process the mixture in an **ice cream maker** according to the manufacturer's instructions. Serve as is for soft-serve or freeze in an **airtight container** for 2 to 4 hours for traditional ice cream.

"SNOW BALL" ISN'T A BRAND. I JUST LIKE NAMING MY APPLIANCES.

This episode marked the return of Sid, the super(?)-agent who represents food items. I'd worked out his sweet potato problem a few episodes earlier and now he was back with an even bigger challenge: Make vanilla glamorous. This would seem a near-impossible task, until you take a closer look. Turns out the poster flavor for bland is as exotic as it comes.

SID: I've got my sights set on a brighter star, a megastar, the biggest flavor on the block! His recognition factor is off the charts! And he's playing every pantry in the country as we speak.

AB: But?

SID: But he has an image problem.

AB: Oh. Bad boy, huh?

SID: I wish. I wish. This guy's image is squeaky clean. Even his biggest fans think he's straightforward, solid, dependable, bland, plain, boring...

AB: Vanilla?

SID: Oh, you know his work. Of course you do. You're the man. See, we both know my client is one fat pod daddy. But he needs a makeover, a new direction, a comeback trail. And I think—oh, nay, nay, I know— you're the man to blaze it.

AB: But vanilla doesn't need me. It's one of the most exotic, spectacular, singular flavors on the planet.

SID: Oh, AB, baby, you're preaching to the choir. But you know what it's like when the congregation loses interest.

AB: No. No, I don't.

SID: I hope you never do. But when you're on that long, lonely slide down, vanilla is the kind of solid culinary player you can count on to be there to soften the blow.

AB: Well...

SID: Fantastic! I'll have a contract over in an hour! Let's make magic! Ciao, baby! (hangs up)

NOT ACTUAL POD SIZE

Of the twenty thousand or so orchid varieties that are living their curious little lives tangled up out there in the tropics, only one produces food for us, the vanilla orchid. It's not unusual for the vines to climb a hundred feet up in the treetops just so the flowers can see the sun. But in order to put on fruit, that blossom must be pollinated. This is a tricky prospect, because it's only available for reproduction one day out of the year and there are only two known natural pollinators: a very small, stingless bee called mellipona, and a rare variety of Central American hummingbird. If neither is available, the job must be done by hand, and it is a tedious task indeed. If the miracle of pollination does occur, pods, or what we call beans, will grow on the vine to full size in about six weeks. Maturation, however, takes up to nine months. And even then, they're still culinarily useless.

That's because, like chocolate, coffee, and tea, vanilla beans have to be cured before they are of any culinary use whatsoever. It's like a long spa treatment:

1. The pods take a nice hot bath in water.

2. They're spread out on a blanket in the midday sun, and left all day long.

3. When night comes, they're rolled up in blankets and left to sweat through the night.

4. The process is repeated every single day for three to four months, or until thoroughly cured.

Although vanilla is commercially grown all over the tropics and in subtropics from Hawaii all the way to New Guinea, there are three classic growing zones:

1. Tahiti: This very, very small, very isolated island actually has its own unique variety. It's called *Vanilla tahitiensis*, and the beans are kind of delicate-looking and extremely fragrant. That's why a lot of folks think they are the cream of the crop worldwide. I happen to think that their flavor is a little bit vanilla, though, and I don't mean in a good way.

2. Mexico: I love Mexican beans. They're the common *Vanilla plantifolia* variety, but look at them. I mean they're fat and they're oily. These things remind me of Cuban cigars. They are right-down funky. The problem with Mexican beans, though, is getting a good-quality supply. They are very erratic. And you never, ever want to use vanilla extracts from Mexico, because they are often processed with parts of the tonka bean, a filler that tastes like vanilla but actually contains some rather dangerous carcinogens.

3. Seventy percent of the vanilla sold here in America comes from Madagascar. These are technically the same beans as in Central America—they were transplanted here in 1840. Oddly enough, these beans are often referred to as "bourbon" vanilla beans: Madagascar used to be called the Isle of Bourbon, because it was discovered during the time of the House of Bourbon, which ruled France off and on until 1848.

No matter where your beans come from, quality is going to be an issue, and it's your responsibility. One thing you can do is always buy them from reliable vendors. I usually buy mine from the Internet. I don't buy them from the megamart because you just don't know how long they've been sitting around on their shelves.

TIDBIT | The vanillin in a bottle of imitation vanilla extract may have come from wood pulp, or may even be a by-product of the coal-mining industry.

TIP | I always store vanilla beans inside plastic bags, and then I keep the bags sealed inside an airtight container, and I keep that in a cool, dark place. Do that, and your beans will stay, well, golden brown and delicious for up to a year.

POD SPOTTING

1. Beware brittleness. Quality beans are always pliant.

2. Quality beans sparkle. You may have to use a magnifying glass, but prime beans are covered with crystallized vanillin, which sparkles under hard light.

3. Quality beans will (when gathered) be uniform in shape, size, and condition.

TIDBIT | Vanilla orchids grow wild in the swamps of south Florida.

FRUIT SALAD WITH VANILLA DRESSING

4 TO 6 SERVINGS

// SOFTWARE

½	cup	plain yogurt	
¼	cup	mayonnaise	
1	teaspoon	lemon juice	freshly squeezed
1	teaspoon	honey	
1	teaspoon	vanilla extract	
¼	teaspoon	kosher salt	
	to taste	black pepper	freshly ground
1		Granny Smith apple	cored and diced
1		pear	peeled, cored, and diced
1		mango	peeled and diced
1		banana	diced
1	cup	seedless grapes	halved
10 to 12	medium	strawberries	halved
⅓	cup	walnuts	chopped and toasted

CONCERNING EXTRACTS

Although pure vanilla extract can, by law, contain things like corn sweeteners and caramel colorings, the best ones contain nothing but alcohol, water, and beans. Pure, single-strength vanilla extract contains a minimum of 35 percent alcohol and 13.35 ounces of bean per gallon. "Natural vanilla flavoring," on the other hand, contains real vanilla beans but no actual alcohol. It is therefore not as potent and cannot be used as a 1:1 replacement in applications.

// PROCEDURE

1. **Whisk** together the yogurt, mayonnaise, lemon juice, honey, vanilla, and salt in a **small mixing bowl**. Season with pepper to taste. Set aside.

2. Put all of the fruit and the nuts in a **large mixing bowl** and toss to combine. Add the dressing, toss, and serve.

VANILLA POACHED PEARS

4 SERVINGS

// SOFTWARE ///

1	750 ml bottle	white wine	Riesling or Viognier
1	cup	H$_2$O	
¾	cup	Vanilla Sugar	(right)
1		vanilla bean	split and scraped
4		firm Anjou, Bartlett, or Bosc pears	peeled, leaving stem intact

// PROCEDURE //

1. Put the wine, water, vanilla sugar, and vanilla bean and its pulp in a **4-quart saucepan** over medium-high heat and bring to a boil.

2. Core the pears from the bottom using a **melon baller**. Decrease the heat to medium-low and put the pears in the liquid, cover, and cook at a gentle simmer for 30 minutes, or until the pears are tender but not falling apart. Remove the pears to a **serving dish**, standing them upright, and refrigerate.

3. Remove the vanilla bean from the saucepan, increase the heat to high, and cook until the syrup is reduced to about 1 cup, 20 to 25 minutes. Do not brown the syrup. Pour the syrup into a **heatproof container** and place in the refrigerator until cool, about 1 hour.

4. Remove the pears from the refrigerator, **spoon** the syrup over the pears, and serve.

VANILLA SUGAR

Split and scrape 1 vanilla bean. Add the seeds and the empty pod to 1 pound of sugar in an airtight container. Leave for at least 1 week, then use as you would plain granulated sugar.

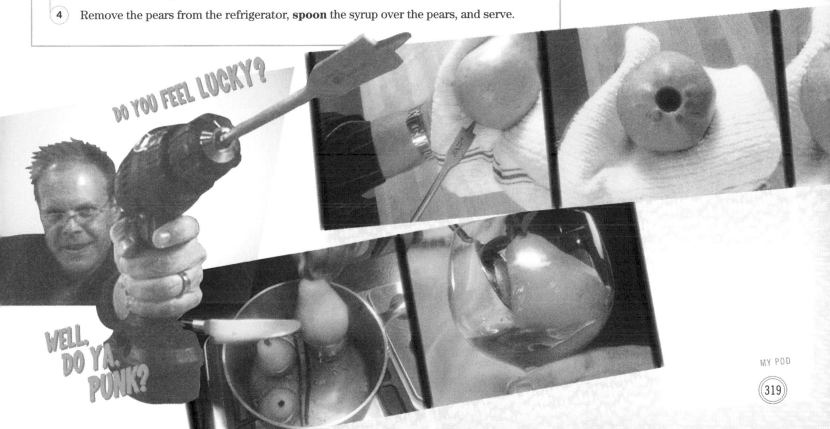

DO YOU FEEL LUCKY?

WELL, DO YA, PUNK?

CRÈME BRÛLÉE

6 SERVINGS

Being a male, I love crème brûlée because I get to burn up something with a torch. When the brûlée rage hit back in the '90s the market was flooded with Lilliputian "brûlée torches," which are nothing more than glorified butane lighters that are hard to fill and grotesquely underpowered, not to mention grotesquely overpriced. Go down to your local hardware store and get yourself an honest-to-goodness propane torch like this:

Oh, and pick up an extra fire extinguisher while you're at it.

NOW THAT'S A TORCH!

// SOFTWARE //

1	quart	heavy cream	
1		vanilla bean	split and scraped
1	cup	Vanilla Sugar	divided, see page 319
6	large	egg yolks	

// PROCEDURE ///

1. Heat the oven to 325°F.

2. Combine the cream and vanilla bean and its pulp in a **medium saucepan** over medium-high heat and bring to a boil. Remove from the heat, cover, and steep for 15 minutes. Remove the vanilla bean (save it for making Vanilla Sugar).

3. **Whisk** together ½ cup of the vanilla sugar and the egg yolks in a medium bowl until they are well blended and the yolks just start to lighten in color. Add the cream a little at a time, stirring continually.

4. Pour the liquid into **6 (7- to 8-ounce) ramekins**. Place the ramekins in a **large cake pan or roasting pan**. Pour enough hot water into the pan to come halfway up the sides of the ramekins. Bake just until the crème brûlée is set, but still trembling in the center, 40 to 45 minutes. Remove the ramekins from the roasting pan and refrigerate for at least 2 hours and up to 3 days.

5. Remove the ramekins from the refrigerator at least 30 minutes prior to serving. Divide the remaining ½ cup vanilla sugar equally among the 6 dishes and spread it evenly on top. Using a **torch**, melt the sugar and form a crisp top. Let the browned sugar set for 5 minutes before serving.

"Luxury: anything which
pleases the senses, is
not necessary for life,
and is also costly or
difficult to obtain, an
expensive rarity."
/////////////////////////////////////
WEBSTER'S, 1913 EDITION

When it comes to food, everyone has a different definition of luxury.

For some, it may be Beluga caviar, or Belgian truffles, or luscious lobster dripping with drawn butter. For me, it's a particular muscle found deep within the back of *Bos taurus*. It's called the tenderloin, and every gram is a feast for the senses. Anyone who's enjoyed filet mignon, chateaubriand, or steak Diane in a top-notch steakhouse will no doubt tell you that, ounce for ounce, beef tenderloin is about as good as good eats get. Beef tenderloin is a luxury for four reasons: It's tender, it's tasty, there isn't much of it, and it's highly desired. But if you know how to shop, cut, and cook, tenderloin can be that rarest of all luxuries: affordable.

TRIVIA No, the plane at the opening of the show isn't mine, but the pilot who busts me is the guy who taught me to fly. His name's Joe, and before he met me he had a lot of hair.

TRIVIA My props guys found the life-size plastic cow at a place that warehoused large outdoor signs. It was hollow, so they had to build the meat and ribs out of felt and Velcro. It's the best meat model I've ever seen. A couple years later we would dress up the cow in fake fleece and pretend it was a sheep.

CROSS-CUT AND ASSEMBLY FOR PORTERHOUSE STEAK

Chine bone

Short loin

Tenderloin

TIDBIT Tenderloin once referred to urban areas where cops on the take could afford tenderloin instead of chuck.

TIDBIT On average, Americans consume 235 pounds of meat per person each year.

TIDBIT Beef Wellington is named for Arthur Wellesley, Duke Wellington, who defeated Napoleon at Waterloo.

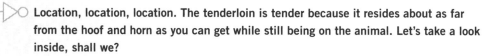

KNOWLEDGE CONCENTRATE

▷○ **Location, location, location.** The tenderloin is tender because it resides about as far from the hoof and horn as you can get while still being on the animal. Let's take a look inside, shall we?

▷○ Between the sirloin primal and the rib primal lies the Fort Knox of beefery, the short loin primal. Here you see the thirteenth rib, and above that the two large loin muscles, which can be treated either as roasts or cut into New York strip steaks. Look beneath these and you'll see these two meaty baseball bats. Those are the tenderloins. They don't really do much of anything, just kind of hang around waiting to be eaten.

▷○ When I purchase tenderloin I buy it in the most economical form: whole in the cryobag, just as it left the packer who processed it. Such a vacuum-packed tenderloin is known in the trade as a PISMO, which stands for "peeled" (of extra fat) and "side meat on" (more on the side meat a little later). Restaurants typically buy PISMOs because they are the best bargain, and if the cryobag remains sealed they can keep in the refrigerator for a month or two.[1]

▷○ If you're only looking to fire up a couple of steaks on a Saturday night, you probably shouldn't look to land a whole PISMO, but if you're willing to perform a little butchery and carefully freeze any leftovers, it's a bargain.

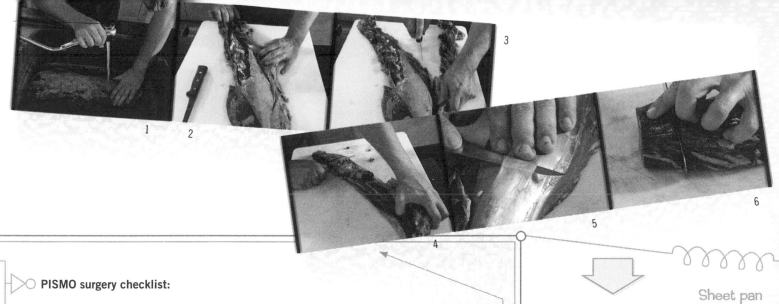

PISMO surgery checklist:

Boning knife for removing side muscle and silverskin.

Big cutting board, the biggest you've got—and make sure it's secure.

Long carving knife for portioning into steaks. My favorite has a 12-inch blade, a rounded tip, and scalloped sides.[2]

Cutting up the PISMO at home:

1. Open the wide end of the bag and dump the meat into your sink to drain. Don't freak out: The liquid is not blood. It's just protein-saturated water that has oozed out of the meat during its time in the bag, but it is a little bit slippery. So spray the meat down with cold water and let it drain while preparing the operating theater.

2. Use your fingers to pull off outside fat and any loose tissue.

3. Use a boning knife to trim off the side meat or "chain" in one piece.[3]

4. Trim away the oval-shaped "head" muscle from the large end of the tenderloin. Set aside.

5. Remove the tough silverskin, the nondissolvable connective tissue that sheaths the main muscle: Line up the tip of your boning knife so that it is perpendicular to the grain of the silverskin and then just kind of wiggle yourself in underneath. Work your finger into the gap, pull taut, angle the knife just ever-so-slightly upward, and then slide. There. Now when it pops out the other end, reach over, pull it taut, and slide the other way. Repeat until as much of it is gone as possible. With practice you'll be able to remove the silverskin without removing much of the good stuff at all.

6. Portioning requires a good, long slicer: You don't want to saw the meat, you want to cut it through in one clean pulling motion.

Even thickness will lead to even cooking, so before I start cutting steaks I break out my big stainless-steel ruler and actually measure out my cuts. Typically I aim for 1½- to 2-inch-thick steaks. What I'm not going to cook, I wrap and freeze sandwiched between two half sheet pans, which help to conduct heat out of the meat.

Now that you're trimmed and portioned, the culinary possibilities are endless (hence part II on page 330).

Sheet pan

Steaks

Sheet pan

To freeze tenderloin steaks, wrap them individually in plastic wrap, sandwiched between two sheet pans, and set them in the freezer. The pans will act as a heat sink, removing heat from the steaks. When they're frozen, place the wrapped steaks in a zip-top freezer bag. Place a small card with the date inside too.

Today

[1] Storing PISMOs in their bags is often referred to as "wet aging," because over time naturally occurring enzymes will tenderize the meat. Unlike dry aging, however, no evaporation takes place and so there is no concentration of meat flavor.

[2] The scalloped indentations on the side of the blade reduce friction, allowing the knife to slide gracefully through the meat with a minimum of pulling or tearing. This type of blade is referred to as a Granton blade, after the Granton Ragg company, which invented it back in the 1920s.

[3] If you know what's good for you, you'll cut this into pieces, pound flat, and use in Philly cheesesteaks.

┌─────────────┐   ┌──────────────────────┐
│ APPLICATION │─┐   ┌──│   STEAK AU POIVRE   │
└─────────────┘ └───┘ └──────────────────────┘

┌──────────────┐
│ 4 SERVINGS │
└──────────────┘

In my opinion nothing rivals the sauté dish known far and wide as steak au poivre. Not only does it taste great, it's also a fine example of two basic skills: sautéing meat and assembling a pan sauce. I also like the dish personally because it features plenty of pepper.

TIP Cognac is a blended brandy. It comes in grades, from VS, or "Very Special," to VSOP, or "Very Superior Old Pale," to the rare and expensive "Napoleon," which we wouldn't waste here. Regular VS performs admirably in pan sauces.

// SOFTWARE

4	6- to 8-ounce	tenderloin steaks	1½ inches thick
	to taste	kosher salt	
2	tablespoons	black peppercorns	
1	tablespoon	unsalted butter	
1	teaspoon	olive oil	
⅓	cup plus 1 teaspoon	Cognac	
1	cup	heavy cream	

// PROCEDURE

1. Remove the steaks from the refrigerator at least 30 minutes and up to 1 hour prior to cooking. Season all sides with salt.

2. Coarsely crush the peppercorns using a **mortar and pestle**, the bottom of a cast-iron skillet, or a mallet and pie pan. Spread the peppercorns evenly on a **plate**. Press the steaks, on both sides, into the pepper until it coats the surface. Set aside.

3. Heat the butter and oil in a **medium skillet** over medium heat. As soon as the butter and oil begin to turn golden and smoke, gently place the steaks in the pan. For medium-rare, cook for 4 minutes on each side. Once done, remove the steaks to a **plate**, tent with **aluminum foil**, and set aside. Pour off the excess fat but do not wipe or scrape the pan clean.

4. Off of the heat, add the ⅓ cup Cognac to the pan and carefully ignite the alcohol with a **long match or firestick**. Gently shake the pan until the flames die. Return the pan to medium heat and add the cream. Bring the mixture to a boil and whisk until the sauce coats the back of a spoon, 5 to 6 minutes. Add the teaspoon of Cognac and season to taste with salt. Return the steaks to the pan, spoon the sauce over, and serve.

REGARDING STAINLESS-STEEL PANS

The types and amounts of ingredients used in the steel—iron, carbon, molybdenum, chromium, manganese, and so on—greatly determine the type of steel you end up with. Culinary stainless is usually rated as 18/8 or 18/10 stainless. The first number refers to the amount of chromium in the recipe, and the second number is the nickel. Nickel provides shine and hardness, while chromium provides corrosion resistance. It does this by mixing with oxygen in the air and creating a very thin, invisible layer of oxide right on the surface. This barely molecule-thick envelope of gas protects the pan from rusting, and some folks, myself included, believe that this layer of oxide may actually assist browning, as do the microfissures present on the surface of the seal itself.

When I was a kid, my dad always

walked through the door at precisely 6 o'clock. He'd make a beeline for the bar and mix up a pitcher of cocktails. The sound of the ice in the pitcher was like this civilized signal announcing to the world, "The workday is over." The problem these days, of course, is that the workday is never really over. Ever. But that doesn't mean that I'm going to allow the art of the homemade cocktail to slide into obscurity. "Too late!" you say? Rubbish! If you're willing to master just three simple drinks, you will then be in possession of, oh, I don't know, 80 percent of all the mixology you will ever need. So belly up to the bar, because although they may not be food, cocktails are most definitely good eats.

TRIVIA | Our production designer Todd played my dad, and Carmi from culinary played my mom. I don't remember my parents doing this, but I did have an early bedtime.

ICE

In Cocktail Town you can never have too much ice. That's because it functions not only as software but as hardware. Sure, it makes things cold. But it also provides very good agitation when set in motion. Kind of like the little steel ball bearing inside the can of spray paint. Of course, when alcohol hits it, it starts to melt, and the little bit of water that melts off of it helps the other ingredients to meld. Since flavor is a pretty big deal when it comes to ice, I usually like to freeze bottled water or filtered water in ice cube trays and then move the cubes to zip-top bags and keep them in my freezer so they won't get funky-tasting. When I'm going to have a really big party, I'll either pick up a few bags of ice at the local grocery store or I'll go old school and chip away at a thirty-pound block.

KNOWLEDGE CONCENTRATE

An Incredibly Brief History of the Cocktail:

1764: England's King George seeks to make some extra cash by passing the Revenue Act, which places heavy taxes on Madeira, America's favorite alcoholic beverage. Crafty colonists fight back by convening in taverns to create a new country as well as mixed-up concoctions called cocktails after the French word *coquetel*, which means "mixed-up concoction." Within a century, American barmen create hundreds of juleps, toddies, fizzes, sours, and slings, including the Daiquiri in Cuba, the Mint Julep in Kentucky (or maybe Maryland), and the Martini in either California or New York, depending on who you ask.

1920: The Volstead Act and Prohibition. Alcohol becomes illegal, and drinking becomes more popular than ever. Only now, instead of drinking in bars most Americans drink their cocktails, especially those based on bathtub gin, at home. After a couple of world wars, vodka invades the party, making many high-octane, low-character drinks available to all.

1977: The nadir of the cocktail, as dazed disco dancers quench their polyester-clad infernos with sickly sweet umbrella drinks. Thankfully, retro-hipsters of the '90s rediscovered Sinatra and Martinis, thus spawning a cocktail renaissance.

When mixologists concoct a new cocktail, they often think in terms of a base, modifiers, and accents, the goal being to create a harmonious chord.

The first note, the root of the chord, is provided by the BASE, which is usually a spirit—bourbon, tequila, vodka, gin, what have you—or sometimes even a wine.

The MODIFIERS have to harmonize with the base. A lot of things can fit the modifier role, from fortified wines like vermouth, to juices, flavored syrups, colas, sodas, you name it. Many classic drinks stop right here (Gin and Tonic, Scotch and Soda). If this is the case, then what you have is referred to in the trade as a "highball."

ACCENTS are where a bartender can really strut his or her stuff. These are generally subtle amounts of powerful ingredients. Citrus would certainly be a good example, as would aromatic bitters and complex flavored liqueurs, all of which provide the defining characteristic of a drink. Sometimes there are three-note chords, sometimes the chord has just two notes, sometimes five or more.

FOUR SCORE AND SEVEN DRINKS AGO...

BASIC BAR HARDWARE

1. A set of OLD-FASHIONED GLASSES.

2. A set of HIGHBALL (or COLLINS) GLASSES.

3. COCKTAIL GLASSES: These last two are stemmed vessels, and what goes in them traditionally does so sans ice. The stem provides a handle, thus keeping hot hands from warming the beverage. Although many sizes are available, anything over 6 ounces is just plain gauche.

4. CHAMPAGNE FLUTES (unless you never plan on serving anything containing bubbles).

5. A JIGGER/PONY COMBO: This holds an ounce and a half on one side and an ounce on the other.

6. A SHAKER: You'll be tempted to buy something that looks like this: Don't. They leak, the lids jam, and the little built-in strainers are rarely the right size. It's a flat-out bad design, plain and simple. If you want proof, go to your neighborhood bar or tavern and watch professionals mix. They never use these things. What they do use is this:

7. These two metal cups, one 28 ounces and the other 16, unite to form what's called a BOSTON SHAKER. You pour everything into the large cup, including the ice, then clamp the smaller one down onto it. The air inside the enclosure quickly chills and contracts, forming a very efficient vacuum. You hold the large cup in one hand with a couple of fingers extending across the bottom of the smaller cup and shake. Then just tap the side against the lip of the bar to break the seal. To strain into a glass, hold it like this:

8. A STRAINER (optional): Some folks prefer to strain through a Hawthorne strainer. That's the thing that looks like a space-age bolo paddle. Although I had one on the show, I'd never own one for real, because it's a unitasker.

9. For muddled drinks that contain much smaller bits and pieces, you may want to consider a julep strainer. You can also use this to strain sauces or smallish portions of pasta.

10. A MUDDLER: It looks like a little baseball bat, and it's used to crush or "muddle" herbs and/or spices and sugar and the like in the bottom of an Old-Fashioned or highball glass. It's a must-have if mojitos or juleps are on your mind.

⊐⊐⊐⊐ **AB'S MARTINI**

1 DRINK

Frederick Henry, Hemingway's hero in *A Farewell to Arms*, says of a Martini, "I had never tasted anything so cool and clean. They made me feel civilized." I like that.

// SOFTWARE //

1	cup	crushed ice	plus extra for the glass
½	ounce	dry vermouth	
2½	ounces	gin	
1		olive	

// PROCEDURE //

1. Put some crushed ice into a **Martini glass** and set aside.

2. Put the 1 cup crushed ice in a **cocktail shaker**. Pour in the vermouth and swirl it around, making as much contact as possible with the ice. Strain the vermouth out. Add the gin to the ice and stir well to combine.

3. Remove the ice from the serving glass and put the olive in the glass. Strain the gin into the serving glass.

TIP Substitute a black olive for the green olive and you've got a Buckeye. Use a cocktail onion and you have a Gibson. Add a shot of scotch and you have a Smoky Martini, and a few drops of the brine from the olive jar would give you a Dirty Martini. I occasionally like to sneak in a few flakes of smoked sea salt for a kind of Dirty Smoky Martini.

APPLICATION ⊐⊐⊐⊐ **DAIQUIRI**

1 COCKTAIL

// SOFTWARE //

2	cups	crushed ice	plus extra for the glass
2	ounces	light rum	
1	ounce	lime juice	freshly squeezed and strained
½	ounce	simple syrup[1]	

// PROCEDURE //

1. Put some crushed ice into a **Martini glass** and set aside.

2. Put the 2 cups crushed ice in a **cocktail shaker**. Pour the rum, lime juice, and simple syrup over the ice, cover, and shake well. Remove the ice from the serving glass and strain the drink into it. Serve immediately.

[1] For simple syrup, simply combine 2 cups sugar with 1 cup water in a saucepan and bring to a boil over high heat, stirring often. When it reaches a boil, turn down the heat to a simmer and let it cook for 3 to 5 minutes. This process will literally break apart some of the sucrose molecules into their components, fructose and glucose. This is called an invert sugar. It will resist crystallization and is actually sweeter than the original sugar.

MINT JULEP

Some of the oldest cocktails were born at the hands of apothecaries, who would grind up herbs and spices and roots and whatnot as medicine. They'd add a little bit of sweet liquor to, you know, make the medicine go down a little more easily. Well, I don't know if the Mint Julep was born that way, but I do know it's good for what ails you, if what ails you happens to be the hot old sun and a three-piece suit in the middle of summer.

// **SOFTWARE** ///

10	leaves	fresh mint	plus 1 sprig for garnish
1½	teaspoons	superfine sugar[2]	
		seltzer water	
		crushed ice	
2½	ounces	Kentucky bourbon whisky	Must be from Kentucky . . . absolutely

// **PROCEDURE** //

Put the mint leaves in the bottom of an **Old-Fashioned glass** and top with the superfine sugar. **Muddle** these together until the leaves begin to break down. Add a splash of seltzer water, fill the glass three quarters full with crushed ice, and add the bourbon. Top with another splash of seltzer, stir, and garnish with a sprig of mint. Serve immediately.

[2] You can make this by simply taking some sugar for a spin in a small food processor.

Beef tenderloin is so gosh-darned versatile that we had to give it a second show. Although we did recap some of the basic info for folks who missed the first episode, most of what you have here is straightforward cooking. These applications are all fan favorites.

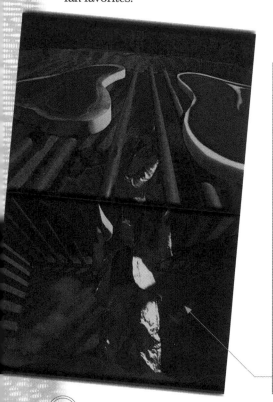

KNOWLEDGE CONCENTRATE

▷○ **Following the Steak au Poivre experiment (delicious, wasn't it?) from episode 144, we had plenty of tenderloin remaining, including:**

— A small roast cut from the head of the main muscle;

— The side or chain meat; and

— About 24 ounces of the main muscle, enough to cut into a chateaubriand, that being a famous small roast, supposedly invented by a French chef named Montmireil and named for his boss, the Vicomte de Chateaubriand.

▷○ **Due to its unique composition, beef tenderloin responds well to high doses of dry heat. The challenge (whether broiling, sautéing, frying, smoking, roasting, or grilling) is temperature control. You see, once the internal temperature of the tenderloin moves into the 140°F range, the going gets risky. That's because the meat can go from juicy and delicious to mealy and desert-dry in no time flat. I get around this by using a dual-temperature method. With larger roasts I start low and finish high, but for tenderloin I start high and finish low.**

HEAT CONTROL

Drop a big juicy steak onto a grill and it will immediately go to sizzling and hissing. And that is because three different types of heat have gone to work, the most dramatic of which is conduction. You see, if you've properly preheated your grill, those metal grates will be very, very, very hot, and through direct contact that heat will move into the meat, which is how you get those nice handsome grill marks; very effective, conduction. But there is a lot more going on here. For instance, there is radiant energy, heat waves moving straight off the burning charcoal or the gas flames, emanating upward. They are what heated the grates to begin with, and now they are going to work on the exposed parts of the meat. And of course there's convection. You see, there's a lot of air down here, and as it gets hot from being near the coals or flames, it gets energized and moves upward, and that also creates a nice, dry heat on the exposed surfaces of the meat. And of course the spaces between the grates are important, because they allow moisture to leave the meat and fat to drip down onto the coals or flames. That creates a flavorful smoke that drifts upward almost like an airborne marinade. The grill is a very complicated and unique environment that cannot be imitated in its entirety. You can, however, mimic certain portions of it.

Take a look at those raised ridges. They will do some mighty fine searing, much like grill grates. The metal in the cut-out trench areas will give out a good bit of radiant energy, and of course those are also nice places for juices from the meat to gather. And when they gather down there, they'll get hot enough to actually partially pyrolysize—that is, burn and turn into smoke. And that smoke will go up and further flavor the meat.

When shopping for a grill pan, the following are some attributes that I recommend you keep your eyes peeled for:

- Cast iron. I don't think that there's any metal on earth that can suck up heat and dose it out the way cast iron does.

- Very delineated grill ridges, for sharp hatch marks.

- Low sides. The way I see it, high sides would only get in the way of tongs or spatulas. It's not like we're going to be deep-frying in this thing.

- Square shape. For reasons that will soon reveal themselves.

- And I personally really dig a handle that snaps on and off.

CENTER-CUT TENDERLOIN ROAST

2 OR 3 SERVINGS

This is a very straightforward but elegant preparation perfect for small dinner parties. The cumin adds funk but doesn't try to sing lead. The goal of cooking it twice is to create a solid sear while maintaining an even doneness within.

// SOFTWARE //

1½	teaspoons	kosher salt	
1½	teaspoons	black pepper	freshly ground
1	teaspoon	cumin seeds	freshly toasted and ground
1	1- to 1¼-pound	beef tenderloin	cut from the center of the whole tenderloin
1	teaspoon	vegetable oil	

// PROCEDURE //

1. Heat the oven to 250°F.

2. Combine the salt, pepper, and cumin in a **shallow dish**. Roll the roast in the seasonings, coating well. Leave the roast at room temperature for 30 minutes.

3. Heat a **cast-iron grill pan** over high heat. When the pan is good and hot, **brush** the roast with the oil and sear it in the pan on all sides for 8 to 10 minutes total. Remove the roast to a **platter** and cover with **aluminum foil** to rest for 10 to 15 minutes.

4. Return the roast to the grill pan, put it in the oven, and cook until it reaches an internal temperature of 135°F, about 20 minutes. Remove from the oven, wrap in foil, and let it rest for 30 minutes before slicing and serving.

MONTMIREIL

The roast that Montmireil made famous was meant to be sliced thick and served, with béarnaise sauce, to two people in love. (Which is kind of odd when you consider the fact that *mignon* means "little" or "delicate" in French. *C'est la boeuf.*) Back then searing was out of fashion, so Montmireil wrapped the roast in thin cuts of lesser-quality beef. He roasted the whole thing and then threw the outer steaks to the dogs. Eventually, the steaks were replaced with slices of bacon. Now we Americans have shrunk the chateaubriand and turned it into a roast for one, which we call the filet mignon.

STUFFED TENDERLOIN

4 SERVINGS

Although any blue cheese will do here, these days I'm leaning toward Roquefort. Oh, and by the way, this may be my favorite tenderloin application of all time.

// **SOFTWARE** //

1	1- to 1½-pound	head roast of beef tenderloin	
	to taste	kosher salt	
	to taste	black pepper	freshly ground
		olive oil	
3	ounces	veined cheese	such as blue or Roquefort, crumbled

// **PROCEDURE** ///

1. Heat the oven to 450°F.

2. Slice the roast open lengthwise to create a pocket in the middle, being careful not to slice all the way through. Season the meat on all sides with salt and pepper.

3. Heat a **cast-iron grill pan** over high heat. When the pan is good and hot, **brush** the roast with the oil and sear it in the pan on all sides for 8 to 10 minutes total. Remove the roast to a **platter** and cover with **aluminum foil** to rest for 10 to 15 minutes.

4. After the meat has rested, stuff the pocket with the cheese. Tie the whole thing closed with **kitchen twine**. Return the tied meat to the grill pan, place in the oven, and cook until it reaches an internal temperature of 125°F, 20 to 25 minutes. Remove from the oven, wrap in foil, and let it rest for 15 minutes before slicing and serving.

APPLICATION	BEEF CARPACCIO

4 SERVINGS

Once upon a time there was an Italian renaissance painter named Vittore Carpaccio, and he was famous for the brilliant use of red in his compositions. An exhibit of his work during the 1950s inspired the owner of Harry's Bar in Venice, Giuseppe Cipriani, to invent a dish that would capture just that hue. He named it, aptly enough, "carpaccio," and it was built on a bed of raw beef.

// SOFTWARE

8 to 10	ounces	beef tenderloin	from the tip end of the roast
4	handfuls	arugula	or other mixed greens
		vinaigrette	such as the one on page 419 (for the Lentil Salad)
	to taste	kosher salt	
	to taste	black pepper	freshly ground
		Parmesan cheese	shaved

// PROCEDURE

1. Wrap the tenderloin in **plastic wrap** and freeze for 2 hours.

2. Unwrap the tenderloin and slice the beef into ⅛- to ¼-inch pieces. Lay out sheets of plastic wrap and place each slice on a sheet of plastic. Top with another piece of plastic and gently pound the meat with a **meat mallet** until paper thin. Repeat until all of the meat is sliced and pounded. Divide the meat evenly among **4 chilled plates**. Serve with the arugula, vinaigrette, salt, pepper, and Parmesan cheese.

   NOTE: Since the arrival of mad cow disease on the scene, the popularity of carpaccio has slackened off not one bit, as near as I can tell. Still, my attorneys Itchy and Twitchy insist that I reiterate the possible dangers of consuming raw meat. So there. I've never heard tell of anyone, ever, in the annals of recorded culinary history catching a disease (much less a deadly one) from carpaccio, but you know how lawyers are.

TRIVIA | I've had my share of bumps, scrapes, sprains, and gashes requiring stitches while working on *Good Eats*, but this tackle by my attorneys broke my butt . . . plain and simple.

Not really blood.

WHEN LAWYERS ATTACK!!!

CHAIN OF BULL CHEESESTEAKS

2 SANDWICHES

I learned to appreciate the "chain" while cooking in restaurants where PISMO tenderloins are the norm. The ragged but delicious piece is always trimmed from the main muscle before cutting steaks, so it ends up in the family meal—that is, it feeds the staff. Unless you buy PISMOs you'll never know the pleasure of this cut . . . and that would be a shame.

// SOFTWARE ///

1	6- to 8-ounce	chain section from a beef tenderloin	trimmed, plus any other meaty scraps from trimming the tenderloin
2	teaspoons	olive oil	
	to taste	kosher salt	
	to taste	black pepper	freshly ground
1	medium	onion	julienned
2	ounces	Mimolette cheese	
2		hoagie rolls	

// PROCEDURE ///

1. Remove the beef from the refrigerator 1 hour before cooking.

2. Heat a **cast-iron grill pan** over high heat.

3. Lightly pound the chain with a smooth **meat mallet** until it is an even thickness throughout. Toss the meat with 1 teaspoon of the oil and season with salt and pepper. When the pan is hot, put the chain in the pan and cook on both sides until cooked through, 3 to 4 minutes per side. (If necessary, cut the chain in half or thirds to fit in the pan.) Remove the chain from the pan, wrap in **aluminum foil**, and rest the meat.

4. Add the remaining teaspoon of oil to the pan, along with the onions. Sauté until they are tender and beginning to brown, 7 to 10 minutes.

5. Slice the beef into small strips and divide it evenly among the hoagie rolls. Pour any accumulated juice from the meat onto the hoagie as well. Top the meat with the cheese, followed by the onions. Wrap the sandwiches in foil for 10 minutes, then serve.

PHILLY

Once upon another time, I think it may have been 1930, in southern Philadelphia, a guy named Olivieri had a little sandwich shop. And one day he got hungry; he wanted to make some lunch. But he didn't want to cook up any of the stuff that he could sell to customers. So he looked around and noticed a few scraps of steak that he had been kind of hoarding over a few days. He chopped them up and threw them onto this little griddle that he cooked on there by the street. A couple minutes later, a cabbie stopped by, smelled it, and said, "Wow. I want some of that." So Olivieri said, "Okay." He got a hoagie roll and put some of the meat on there, and he gave it to him. And the cabbie said, "Hey, you know, Olivieri, your hot dogs aren't too good, but this stuff is great!" And off he went. So this is why we, today, have the Philly steak sandwich. In 1948, Olivieri added cheese to the equation, giving us the Philly cheesesteak.

From time to time on this program we journey onto another plane; a plane that happens to be rather lacking in one dimension. I speak, of course, of the unique realm of flat food. Here we find the pizza, the flank steak, the pancake. Yet rarely do we see an entire creature.

That is because, with the possible exception of those of us who live on television, most animals are three-dimensional . . . except, of course, the flatfish. Have a look at our live specimen, won't you?

See him? Of course not. Lurking just beneath the sea floor, the flatfish not only finds protection from passing predators, he gets the jump on any dinner that might come drifting by. Since most of his swimming is done in short, sudden bursts, flatfish musculature is mostly of the fast-twitch variety—like chicken breast—and is therefore finely textured, flaky, and mild in flavor when cooked. This is especially true of the flounder, whose body is relatively easy to dismantle and offers a large, bone-free canvas on which an even modestly skilled cook can create a myriad of culinary designs.

TIDBIT | Flatfish by any other name: brill, dab, plaice, fluke, hogchoker.

KNOWLEDGE CONCENTRATE

There are over five hundred species of flatfish, all belonging to the order *Pleuronectiformes*, which is Latin for "side swimmer." Flatfish begin their lives the way roundfish do, swimming upright. But early on in their development, one eye starts to migrate over by the other, the mouth gets longer, and the body starts listing to one side, until eventually they're swimming 100 percent horizontal. If that weren't strange enough, some species can even alter their pigmentation to mimic the color of their surroundings like freaky ninja bathmats—and in the case of Pacific halibut very large bathmats indeed. Come to think of it, halibut deserve their own episode. So we'll concentrate on smaller fish here, ones that are reasonably purchased whole.

A good fishmonger will generally offer a wide variety of flatfish options, including but not limited to black back flounder, petrale sole, Dover sole, turbot, yellowtail flounder, lemon sole, grey sole, halibut, and dab. Or at least that's what the signs will say. Truth is, most of the fish that are sold as sole, including grey sole, lemon sole, and petrale sole, are basically flounders. And by the way, if your fishmonger tells you he has "American" Dover sole: run. Dover sole only lives in certain European waters and what does make it to American markets hails from England or Holland.

If you're going to buy whole, I'd go with the grey-sole size of flounder, which is about a pound and a quarter and large enough to hang off the sides of a large dinner plate, which means it can easily feed a couple of people.

If you prefer not to deal with whole flatfish, you'll typically have two different fillet options: half of a fish, where you get a top and a bottom of one side, or the smaller quarter sides.

Most Americans live long, happy lives without ever cutting up a fish. But what if one day your fishmonger was home sick? Or what if you were walking down the street and someone said, "Here, have a flounder"? You would want to be able to break it down, wouldn't you? Well, of course you would. And it's as easy as fish cutting gets. Let's observe my cutting station, shall we?

When it comes to cutting up critters, be they aquatic or terrestrial in origin, you'll need a good BONING KNIFE in hand. Boning knives are distinguished by the curved tip, which allows for a better working angle and helps prevent point gouging. They come in various lengths and can be stiff or flexible. Flexible blades are good for maneuvering around bones, but they're a lot trickier to control. So until you get the hang of fish cutting I suggest a six-inch, stiff or semi-rigid boning knife, which you can augment with a thin, flexible blade later on. Although forged knives are the standard for chef's knives, I tend toward cheaper "stamped" blades when it comes to boning blades because a heavy spine and bolster would just get in the way. Stamped blades also tend to carry ergonomic, no-slip handles, which is good when handling potentially slimy customers. •

I have a large, restaurant-grade CUTTING BOARD right next to the sink. (It's very helpful to cut next to running water because it's just about the only substance on earth that can herd fish scales.) •

I have a TRASH RECEPTACLE in one side of the sink. •

I've got a LANDING SPOT for my fillets.

I've got my HONING STEEL in case my edge gives out.

I've got a small HAND TOWEL.

And I like to work with GLOVES. These are oyster gloves. I think they give me a little more traction. •

HOW TO NOT FLOUNDER IN FLOUNDER DISSECTION

The subject is a two-pound female flounder, probably Floridian in origin. Let's cut, shall we?

1. I am right-handed so I begin with the fish facing to the right, belly facing the top of the board.

2. I begin with a cut from the belly to the shoulder. You'll notice this is a diagonal cut, which allows me to miss the very small bunch of guts that this fish happens to have.

3. Next I kind of unzip the skin, moving across the back toward the tail and then sliding the knife off the tail there.

4. Then I basically let the knife just float right on top of the ribs, and peel off the top part of the fillet.

5. When I get to the spine, I flip the knife over and use just the tip to get down on the other side of it.

6. And then I continue just wiping that knife right over the top of the ribs. Remember to lift the meat away as it is freed. In no time you'll have yourself a big, luscious fillet.

7. To remove the skin, make a small cut right at the tail, then get a grip on the skin. Hold your knife in one place, pointing down, and just jiggle and pull the skin. I don't push the knife at all, but rather pull the skin against the knife with a bit of a jiggling motion. With practice, you'll get it to come away in one piece.

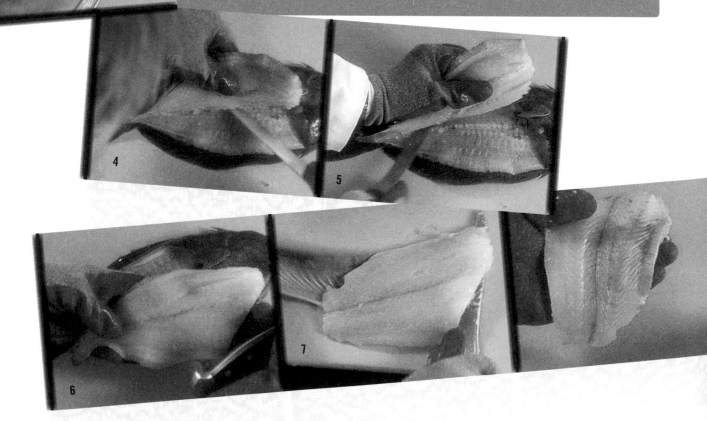

BAKED STUFFED FLOUNDER

4 TO 6 SERVINGS

When it comes to cooking flatfish—and on cooking shows it usually does—there are myriad opportunities. But, you know, I really prefer to stick with methods that take particular advantage of this *poisson*'s peculiar physiology. For instance, he's very *flat*, he's very *thin*, and his flesh is therefore very *flexible*. This means he can be wrapped around things . . . such as a filling.

// SOFTWARE //

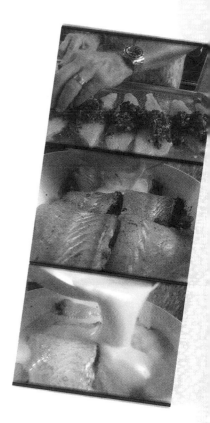

2	tablespoons	unsalted butter	
1	medium	onion	chopped
½	teaspoon	kosher salt	plus extra for seasoning
1	clove	garlic	minced
1	10-ounce package	frozen spinach	thawed and squeezed
1		lemon	zested
¼	teaspoon	black pepper	freshly ground
2	tablespoons	fresh parsley	chopped
1	cup	heavy cream	
¼	cup	white wine	
10	ounces	cheddar cheese	grated
2	cups	cooked rice	leftovers are great
1½ to 2	pounds	flounder fillets	

// PROCEDURE //

1. Heat the oven to 350°F.

2. Melt the butter in a **medium sauté pan** over low heat, add the onion and a pinch of salt, and sweat until translucent. Add the garlic and continue to cook for another minute. Add the spinach and lemon zest and cook until just heated through. Season with the ½ teaspoon salt and the pepper, add the parsley, and stir to combine. Remove from the heat and keep warm.

3. Put the cream and wine in a **medium saucepan** over medium heat. Once the mixture begins to simmer, gradually add the cheese and stir until melted. Set aside and keep warm.

4. Cut any large fillets in half. Season each piece on both sides with salt and pepper. Divide the spinach mixture evenly among the fillets and roll the fish around the mixture. Spread the rice evenly in a **2½-quart casserole dish**. Place each roll on top of the rice, seam side down. Pour the cheese sauce over the rolls and bake for 25 minutes. Cool for 5 minutes before serving.

OIL-POACHED FLOUNDER

4 TO 6 SERVINGS

Flatfish, such as flounder, are extremely lean, a condition that poses a challenge for cooks: without fat to enhance texture, dryness sets in quickly. A lot of cooks try to get around this via poaching. Problem is, 180°F water or wine can overcook a fish just as fast as 500°F air or 350°F oil. This isn't to say that I don't believe in either oil or poaching. I like them a lot. But in this case I suggest poaching in oil, a method that the French refer to as *confit*. Why? Three reasons:

1. Oil hates water. The fish is full of water, and if we cook it completely submerged in oil, well, the oil is a lot less likely to coax water out of the fish, right?

2. Oil "feels" moist in the mouth. So even if the fish were to overcook a tad, as long as it takes a little bit of oil along the way, it'll feel moist to the mouth.

3. Oil carries flavors. Oh, yes, it does, children.

// SOFTWARE ///

3	cups	olive oil	not extra virgin
1½ to 2	pounds	flounder fillets	
	to taste	kosher salt	
	to taste	black pepper	freshly ground
2		lemons	thinly sliced
1	small bunch	fresh parsley	rinsed and thoroughly dried[1]

// PROCEDURE //

1. Heat the oven to 350°F. Heat the oil to 300 to 310°F in a **medium saucepan** over low heat.

2. While the oil is heating, season the flounder fillets on all sides with salt and pepper. Lay half of the lemons and half of the parsley in the bottom of a **cast-iron skillet** large enough to hold the fillets in a single layer without overlapping. Lay the fillets on top of the lemons. Top with the remaining lemons and parsley. Once the oil has reached temperature, gently pour it over the fillets, then put the skillet in the oven and poach for 10 minutes. Cool the fish in the oil for 5 minutes before serving. The oil can be strained and saved for other fishy applications.

NOTE: Once chilled, these leftovers make a nice lunch served over greens with a simple vinaigrette.

[1] Hot oil is going to be poured on this, and any water can cause popping, which can cause . . . discomfort.

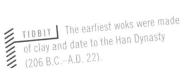

YOUR PAD THAI OR MINE

EPISODE 148 | SEASON 9 | GOOD EATS

For me, certain meals are almost like travel in that they can convey me directly into the heart of another culture—only without leaving my kitchen. This is certainly true of the Thai dish known far and wide as pad thai. Besides the fact that it's delicious, pad thai is interesting because it's a nationalistic dish that was endorsed and promoted by Prime Minister Luang Phibunsongkhram in the 1930s and '40s as a way to curb rice consumption during shortages and to strengthen his country in turn. What makes pad thai *Good Eats* worthy (other than the aforementioned deliciousness) is that it handily sums up the Thai pantry and cooking methodology.

TIDBIT The earliest woks were made of clay and date to the Han Dynasty (206 B.C.–A.D. 22).

TIDBIT In Thailand, new woks are traditionally seasoned with pork fat.

WOK THIS WAY

Authentic ingredients are all fine and good, but they'll come to naught without a heapin' big helping of heat delivered all fast and furious like. And nothing doles out said helpin' better than a wok.

The wok shape is perfect for stir-fry, as the heat can be tightly focused right at the bottom. Due to the lens-like shape, the heat then rapidly dissipates as it conducts up and out toward the rim. A skilled wok-meister uses this to his or her advantage by pushing cooked ingredients up the sides, where they'll stay warm without overcooking.

Although the Internet has become the premiere place to land a wok,

a little research may reveal a brick-and-mortar restaurant supply store that specializes in Asian hardware where instant gratification will only be complicated by an overwhelming range of choices and unbelievably cheap prices.

Top-quality woks are easy to spot. They are deep and well rounded. They are sturdy in construction. They're composed of high-carbon steel, and the handles are attached via large rivets or welds. Some surfaces even show marks where a hand-wielded hammer was used for final shaping. For everyday stir-frying at home, a 14-inch wok will probably do you fine. But if you're going

to be doing any kind of entertaining, I think a 16-inch is a far better thing. As for handles, the double-looped style is very popular in restaurants because they stay out of the way, making the wok less likely to get accidentally knocked over. But to tell the truth, for the average home kitchen or backyard scenario I think the single hollow metal handle is better for pan handling. As for surfaces, remember: No real wok will have a nonstick surface . . . ever. Nor will it feature any stainless steel, which is, relatively speaking, a crappy conductor of heat.

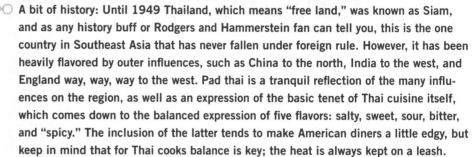

▷○ **A bit of history: Until 1949 Thailand, which means "free land," was known as Siam, and as any history buff or Rodgers and Hammerstein fan can tell you, this is the one country in Southeast Asia that has never fallen under foreign rule. However, it has been heavily flavored by outer influences, such as China to the north, India to the west, and England way, way, way to the west. Pad thai is a tranquil reflection of the many influences on the region, as well as an expression of the basic tenet of Thai cuisine itself, which comes down to the balanced expression of five flavors: salty, sweet, sour, bitter, and "spicy." The inclusion of the latter tends to make American diners a little edgy, but keep in mind that for Thai cooks balance is key; the heat is always kept on a leash.**

▷○ **When dealing with exotic dishes I tend to break the parts list into three categories: "familiar," "somewhat familiar," and "what the . . . ?"**

In this case the list looks like this:

FAMILIAR:	SOMEWHAT FAMILIAR:	WHAT THE . . . ?:
peanuts	mung bean sprouts	fish sauce (*nam pla*)
garlic	tofu (bean curd)	dried shrimp (*goong haeng*)
dried chiles	rice noodles	tamarind paste (*ma kahm*)
eggs		palm sugar
scallions		salted cabbage (*tung chai*)
rice vinegar		
peanut oil		
limes		

Everything in the first list is easy, and most major megamarts will offer everything on the second. Some might even offer up the "what the . . . ?" parts as well, though I wouldn't count on it.[1] Since they're all long-keeping pantry items you can buy them off the Internet as I have done from multiple purveyors without mishap. But what fun is that? Click, click, password, click, credit card number, click. The second option is much more fun: Get thee to an Asian market. Yes, it will seem odd (unless you're Asian, of course), but look at it this way: Shopping there is like travel, only you don't need a passport. Either way, here are a few notes on the list.

If you can't find small (but fiery) THAI CHILES, go with the smallest specimens you can find.

You can tell MUNG BEAN SPROUTS from alfalfa sprouts because the sprout part is much thicker. Mung beans are packed with nutrition and are ridiculously easy to grow at home. But we're going to save that for our "Survival Eats" show.

Pad Thai is technically a stir-fry, and when it comes to TOFU for stir-fries you should always go with extra-firm tofu over the custardy silken tofu served as dessert in Japan. So I'd avoid the stuff in the aseptic carton and go with the block floating in liquid in the see-through box.

Dried RICE NOODLES are usually called "rice sticks," and they come in a lot of different sizes and shapes. What you want is the narrow version, which looks almost like angel hair pasta in the bag.

NAM PLA is Thai for "fish sauce," or, to be more precise, "fish water." This stuff is as crucial to the cuisines of Southeast Asia as soy sauce is to those of China or Japan. To make it, you basically take a bunch of little fish, usually anchovies, and you layer them in a big box with salt, and you let it just sit there and ferment for up to a year. You then squeeze out the liquid, strain it, and bottle it. If you're thinking that this might have a pungent aroma, by golly, you'd be right. Luckily, the fragrance mellows when cooked.[2] Quality fish sauce is always reddish brown and clear, never murky.

Tam kho thuong hang, a.k.a. DRIED SHRIMP, is as common in Thai cuisine as black pepper in ours. They're nothing more than tiny, sun-dried shrimp, yet the flavor is very concentrated, very briny.

The crazy-looking TAMARIND pod houses both seeds and a sweet-sour paste that I can only describe as raisins soaked in lime juice. Since all we really need is to produce the flavorful liquid from this, we might as well forgo the hard labor of harvesting and just buy tamarind in paste form. Simply soak in boiling water, force through a sieve, and you're good to go.

PALM SUGAR is made from sap that drips from the buds of the sugar palm. After collection, the sap is boiled down until all that remains is a sticky sugar, kind of like maple sugar. To use, just break off a hunk and use it as you would any other sugar.

PRESERVED OR SALTED CABBAGE can be called either *tung chai* or *tianjin* (after the city that is apparently famous for producing this dish). It's little more than cabbage and salt, but it lends an amazing flavor and, of course, texture to stir-fries, soups, and whatnot.

Even if my cooktop could properly accommodate a wok, which it can't, I wouldn't stir-fry in the house, unless it was in the dead of winter and the furnace wasn't working.

I usually use an outdoor gas burner to heat my wok, and that's still my very favorite way of stir-frying. But if you have a wok ring, which looks like this:

. . . you can also do the job atop charcoal. Whatever method you use it's hard to overemphasize the need for high heat and very speedy cooking.

Of course, my legal team has asked me to remind you that, like swimming, playing golf, or sitting still on your sofa, grilling can be a hazardous pastime, so make sure you comply with all local, state, and federal guidelines for this kind of activity, and at all times obey the manufacturer's instruction booklet. I'd like to add that I never grill without a multi-purpose fire extinguisher within easy reach.

TIDBIT The Thai food philosophy can be summed up in two words: *arroy*, meaning "delicious," and *sanuk*, meaning "fun."

WOK

[1] I'd really love to see a grocery store with a "what the . . . ?" aisle.

[2] This style of fish sauce is reminiscent of garum, the ketchup of ancient Rome and precursor of Worcestershire sauce.

2 SERVINGS

// SOFTWARE ///

1	ounce	tamarind paste	
¾	cup	boiling H_2O	
2	tablespoons	fish sauce	
2	tablespoons	palm sugar	
1	tablespoon	rice vinegar	
4	ounces	rice stick noodles	
6	ounces	Marinated Tofu	(right)
1 to 2	tablespoons	peanut oil	
1	cup	scallions	chopped
2	teaspoons	garlic	minced
2	large	eggs	beaten
2	teaspoons	salted cabbage	
1	tablespoon	dried shrimp	
3	ounces	mung bean sprouts	divided
½	cup	peanuts	roasted and salted, chopped
		dried red chiles	freshly ground
1		lime	cut into wedges

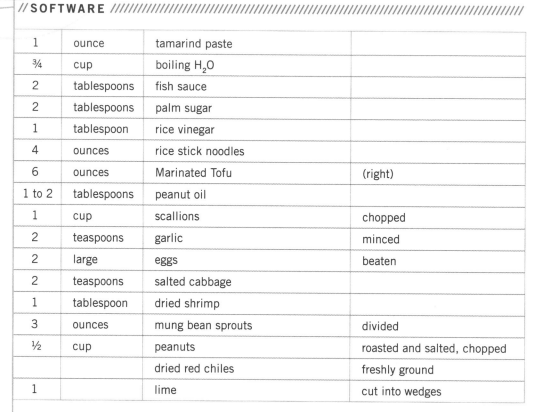

// PROCEDURE ///

1. Put the tamarind paste in the boiling water and set aside.

2. Combine the fish sauce, palm sugar, and vinegar in a **small bowl** and set aside.

3. Put the noodles in a **mixing bowl** and cover with **hot water**. Set aside while you prepare the remaining ingredients. When the other ingredients are measured out into **separate bowls**, drain the water from the noodles and set them aside. Cut the tofu into ½-inch-wide strips, about the size of French fries.

4. Press the tamarind paste through a **fine-mesh strainer** and add it to the fish sauce mixture. Stir to combine.

TIP | Pad thai is a stir-fry, and stir-fry happens fast. Once you start, there's no getting off the ride, so proper preparation is key. And if I've said it once, I've said it, I don't know, seven times: "Organization will set you free."

5. Heat a **wok** over high heat. Once hot, add 1 tablespoon of the oil. Heat until it shimmers, then add the tofu. Cook the tofu until golden brown, moving it constantly, for no longer than 1 minute. Remove the tofu to a **small bowl** and set aside.

6. If necessary, add some more oil to the pan and heat until shimmering. Add two thirds of the scallions and then the garlic; cook for 10 to 15 seconds. Add the eggs. Once the eggs begin to set up, in 15 to 20 seconds, stir to scramble them. Add the remaining ingredients in the following order and toss after each addition: noodles, sauce mixture, cabbage, shrimp, and two thirds of the bean sprouts and peanuts. Toss everything until heated through, but no longer than 2 minutes total. Transfer to a **serving dish**. Garnish with the remaining scallions, bean sprouts, and peanuts. Serve immediately with the ground chiles and lime wedges.

TIDBIT They say that in Thailand there is a different pad thai recipe for every cook.

SUB-APPLICATION	⎍	MARINATED TOFU
		6 OUNCES

// SOFTWARE ///

6	ounces	extra-firm tofu	not silken
1½	cups	soy sauce	
1	teaspoon	Chinese five spice	

// PROCEDURE ///

1. Wrap the tofu tightly in a **tea towel**. Put the wrapped tofu in an **8-inch cake pan**. Top with **another cake pan** and weigh down with a **5-pound weight**. (Bags of dried beans or grains work well.) Refrigerate for 12 to 15 hours, or overnight.

2. Put the pressed tofu in a **2-cup container**. Combine the soy sauce and five spice and pour the mixture over the tofu. Cover and refrigerate for 30 minutes, turning once. Remove the tofu from the marinade and use immediately or store in the refrigerator for up to 3 days.

YOUR PAD THAI OR MINE

345

Scallops are hands down my favorite seafood. The fact that God put this perfect buttery yoyo-shaped muscle right inside this pretty shell is proof he loves us. But, as with all simple things, the devil lurks in the details. You must shop carefully and cook carefully, or all that goodness will rise up and bite you.

TRIVIA From an entertainment standpoint, this is my favorite episode of *Good Eats*, for no other reason than it goofs, rips, samples, and swipes at every turn from *Jaws*, which is my favorite guy movie of all time. Those of you who are fans of the show will no doubt notice that the gentleman playing Captain Squint is Daniel Petrow, who has played my neighbor Chuck and Rusty the flamboyant cowboy.

SCALLOP PARTS

Spooky eyes

Gills

Small, "smooth" muscle (usually removed)

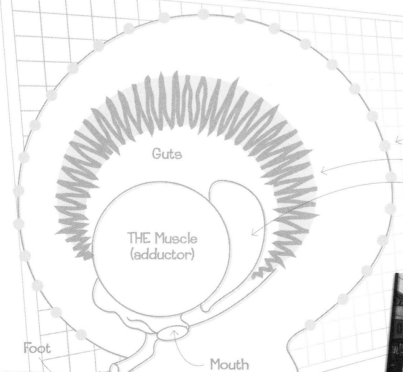

Guts

THE Muscle (adductor)

Foot

Mouth

346

Unlike mussels, oysters, or clams, scallops can move—*really* move—by rapidly flapping their symmetrical, fan-shaped shells open and closed like seagoing castanets. This is made possible by a hinge at the base of the shell assembly and a large muscle called an "adductor," which provides the power for propulsion. It is this muscle we culinarians seek. It is in fact the only part of the scallop we consume, and we generally do so in a cooked state, though scallops are often served as sushi and sashimi.

In most major markets, you'll find two types of scallops:

SEA SCALLOPS (*Plactopecten magellanicus*) run from marshmallow size to doorknob girth, which means there can be anywhere from 10 to 40 in a pound. Sea scallops have various aliases, including king scallops, great scallops, and jumbo scallops.

BAY SCALLOPS (*Argopecten irradians*) are much smaller than sea scallops, running anywhere from 70 to 100 per pound. Although they're fine for salads and mousses, they're tough to sear because they tend to overcook so quickly. They also go by the occasional alias, including cape scallops, queen scallops, and Nantucket scallops (which has a particularly nice ring to it).

Since they are highly perishable, the method by which scallops are captured greatly affects their freshness. Ships that dredge the open ocean floor for scallops don't just mangle the sea bed; they also have to stay out for quite a while in order to make the trip worth their time. So they either shuck and freeze their catch or they treat it with chemicals. Either way, the quality is compromised. Boats that go out in the morning and return to dock in the evening deliver far fresher scallops, referred to as "day boat" scallops. As for "diver" scallops, see the sidebar.

When it comes to shopping for fresh scallops, especially sea scallops, one must exercise caution. Specifically, you must develop the ability to spot the difference between dry and wet scallops. Dry scallops are usually ivory, or slightly pink, or even orange in color. They are never white. And, of course, they don't actually look dry. The term refers to the fact that these lovely lozenges have not been soaked in chemicals such as sodium tripolyphosphate, which is applied to help scallops retain moisture when frozen. Now, there's nothing wrong with that per se, unless the scallop in question is not going to actually be frozen. You see, treating fresh scallops with STP causes them to gain moisture, making them heavier, which could be a good thing for a retailer but is seldom any good for a cook: Once this stuff is inside the scallop, it becomes very difficult to cook that scallop properly, and impossible to sear it.

Although bay scallops are being raised in aquicultural environments in China and Japan, some 95 percent of the scallops consumed in the United States are harvested wild from American and Canadian waters.

Keep fresh scallops in an airtight container, devoid of excess moisture, and preferably surrounded by ice that can freely drain as it melts. Scallops should be cooked and consumed within a day or two of purchase. Frozen scallops can be kept two to three months in the deep freeze. Overnight thawing in the refrigerator is highly recommended.

In cooking, "scallop" doesn't always mean a scallop. The French word *escalope* (which has almost the same pronunciation) means a thin piece of meat that's been pounded even flatter with the side of a knife or a mallet. For a look at this kind of scallop, check out episode 146, "Flat Is Beautiful III." To further complicate matters, there's scalloped potatoes, which are potatoes cut into thin "scallops" (as in *escalope*), stacked, and baked with cheese and breadcrumbs in a casserole. There are no scallops in scalloped potatoes, or in veal scaloppini for that matter. Aren't cooking words fun?

Although waiters tend to throw the term around as though it were an actual variety or statement of size, "diver" scallops are simply scallops that have been harvested by scuba divers by hand. Since this kind of harvesting is an editorial process, "divers" tend to be the cream of the crop in both size and quality. And since the sea bottom isn't raped and pillaged in the process, diver scallops are a good ecological choice. The downside? You pay through the nose . . . although true scallop lovers don't mind. I only have them a couple times a year, but when I do I sear them in a hot, black steel pan with butter and eat them with some coarse sea salt. That's it.

APPLICATION   ⌐_⊓_⊓_⌐   **SEARED SCALLOPS**

4 SERVINGS

The secret to cooking scallops, besides finding the right ones, is simple: Sear them. This little guy is all muscle, like a tiny tenderloin. It's packed with amino acids and a substance called glycogen, which is a chemical combo that muscles use to store glucose. This substance browns up beautifully as long as it gets a high dose of heat from the right kind of surface.

// SOFTWARE //

1 to 1¼	pounds	dry sea scallops	about 16
2	teaspoons	unsalted butter	
2	teaspoons	olive oil	
	to taste	kosher salt	
	to taste	black pepper	freshly ground

TIP If you're searing scallops in two batches, clean the pan in between and start with fresh fat.

// PROCEDURE ///

1. Remove the small side muscle from each scallop, rinse with cold water, and thoroughly pat dry.

2. Put the butter and oil in a **12- to 14-inch sauté pan** over high heat. Salt and pepper the scallops. When the fat begins to smoke, gently add the scallops, making sure they are not touching each other. Sear the scallops for 1½ minutes on each side. The scallops should have a ¼-inch golden crust on each side while still being translucent in the center. Serve immediately.

SHELL GAME IV

348

SCALLOPS ON THE HALF SHELL

4 SERVINGS

Fresh bay scallops are even sweeter than sea scallops and can stand up to considerable herbal accompaniment.

// SOFTWARE ///

8	ounces	bay scallops	
2	tablespoons	unsalted butter	
1	tablespoon	garlic	minced
¼	teaspoon	kosher salt	plus extra for seasoning
1	cup	fresh breadcrumbs	or crushed crackers
2	medium	tomatoes	very ripe, finely chopped
¼	cup	fresh parsley	chopped

// PROCEDURE ///

1. Heat the oven to 450°F.

2. Remove the side muscle from each scallop, rinse with cold water, and thoroughly pat dry.

3. Melt the butter in a **medium sauté pan** over medium heat. When the butter is melted, add the garlic and a pinch of salt and cook for 30 seconds. Remove the pan from the heat and toss in the breadcrumbs until well combined. Set aside.

4. Toss together the tomato, parsley, and ¼ teaspoon salt in a **small bowl**. Evenly divide the tomato mixture among **4 ovenproof ramekins or scallop shells**. Set the scallops over the tomato mixture and top with the breadcrumb mixture. Bake for 8 to 10 minutes, or until golden brown on top. Serve immediately.

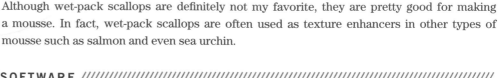

| APPLICATION | | SCALLOP MOUSSE |
| 35 TO 40 HORS D'OEUVRES |

Although wet-pack scallops are definitely not my favorite, they are pretty good for making a mousse. In fact, wet-pack scallops are often used as texture enhancers in other types of mousse such as salmon and even sea urchin.

// SOFTWARE //

1	pound	wet sea scallops	muscle removed, rinsed and patted dry
2	large	egg whites	
1	teaspoon	kosher salt	
¼	teaspoon	white pepper	
¼	teaspoon	nutmeg	freshly grated
½	teaspoon	lemon zest	
½	teaspoon	fresh parsley	chopped
¼	cup	heavy cream	very cold
35 to 40		mini phyllo shells	

// PROCEDURE //

1. Heat the oven to 350°F.

2. Put the scallops in the bowl of a **food processor** and pulse 4 or 5 times. Add the egg whites and pulse until combined. Scrape down the sides of the bowl and add the salt, white pepper, nutmeg, lemon zest, and parsley. Pulse to incorporate.

3. While the machine is running, slowly add the cream. Scrape down the sides of the bowl one last time, put the lid back on, and run for 5 more seconds.

4. Arrange the mini phyllo shells on a **half sheet pan**. Put the mousse in a **pastry bag or a zip-top bag** with the tip snipped off and pipe into the phyllo shells. Bake for 10 minutes. Cool the mousse cups for 2 to 3 minutes before serving.

   N O T E : Try to keep the mousse as cold as possible while working with it. I keep a bag of ice nearby and park the bag in it every few minutes.

 In the painting *The Birth of Venus*, the goddess of love is seen rising from the ocean in a giant scallop shell.

 According to French mythology, Saint James rescued a knight who fell into the ocean and emerged covered with scallops, which is why the French call that bivalve *coquille Saint-Jacques* to this day.

 According to FDA regulations, any scallop with a water content of 82 percent or higher must be labeled as "water-added product." And those scallops with a water content above 86 percent cannot be marketed at all.

OLIVE ME

The ubiquitous olive is the fruit (a drupe, to be exact) of a small tree in the Oleaceae family, which includes ashes, lilacs, forsythia, and jasmine. Although there are only six subspecies worldwide, there are thousands of cultivars. Some experts believe that Italy alone is home to three hundred different types.

The olive is perhaps the most historically significant fruit in history, and if you don't believe me you haven't spent much time reading the works of the likes of Homer and Horace, or Apicius, and you definitely haven't spent much time with the Quran or the Bible, which are jam-packed with olive references.

TIDBIT | The idea of stuffing the hole left by pitting goes back to the eighteenth century.

CONCERNING THE PITTING OF OLIVES

▶ **DIFFICULT:** Green Cerignola, black Cerignola, Thasos, cracked green, Picholine

▶ **MODERATE:** Sun-dried black, Mt. Pelion

▶ **EFFORTLESS:** Kalamata, Alfonso, Manzanilla

To pit olives, place a bench scraper on top and pop with your fist.

First thing to know is that this episode is only concerned with eating olives. Olive oil will have to wait in line for its own show. Okay, now some facts:

The only difference between a green olive and a black olive is time. A black olive is the fully ripe fruit, whereas green olives are harvested when they are full size but still immature.

Black olives are graded by size: medium, large, extra large, jumbo, colossal, and (believe it or not) SUPERCOLOSSAL, which I suppose is really big, at least for an olive.

All green olives must be treated with a lye solution in order to eliminate a very bitter substance called oleuropein, a glucoside that's just about the gnarliest thing you can put in your mouth. Black, ripe olives can skip the lye and be cured by one of the following processes:

WATER CURING: Olives are soaked, rinsed, soaked, rinsed, over and over for so long that the method is no longer widely used.

BRINE CURING: Soaked for 2 to 6 months in a salt solution (like a turkey, only a lot longer). Brine-cured olives are usually shiny, plump, and, more often than not, purple or black.

DRY CURING: Packed in a mixture of dry salt and herbs for several months, most often resulting in a wrinkled rather than smooth fruit.

OIL CURING: Soaked in some type of oil for several months, also wrinkled.

Once upon a time, average Americans had access to two types of olives: green ones in jars with red things stuck in them and black ones in cans. Typically the green, a.k.a. Spanish, olives are Manzanilla olives that have been soaked in lye then bottled with lactic acid and brine, which grants them their particular flavor and crispness. As for those flavorless black olives, a.k.a. "California," "imperial," or "ripe" olives, they're preserved by the cooking that comes with the canning process. That shiny black finish comes courtesy of oxidation and a dip in a ferrous gluconate solution. Yum.

Luckily, things have changed. Here are a few types to keep an eye out for:

MANZANILLA: Yes, although they're the ones most often in the jar, these brine-cured Spanish olives have a caperlike sharpness that plays well in many cooked dishes.

LIGURIA: Italian, jet black, brine cured, strong.

NICOISE: French, small, black, often packed with herbs. Good meat-to-pit ratio, brined.

GAETA: Italian, black, dry cured then rubbed with oil, wrinkled, mild flavor, often packed in herbs. Also available brine cured and smooth.

KALAMATA: Greek, large, purple or black, typically split and cured in red wine vinegar brine. Flavor ranges from soft to sharp with considerable smokiness.

PICHOLINE: French, green, brine cured, mild.

CERIGNOLA: Italian, green, huge, brine cured, size makes them good for stuffing.

MOROCCAN: North African, black, can be salt or oil cured, deeply wrinkled, salty, bitter.

TAPENADE

1 TO 1½ CUPS

No dish delivers olivey goodness quite like the olive paste of Provence: tapenade. Now I realize that innumerable permutations of this dish exist. I think the real secret is in creating not only a contrast of flavors, but a contrast of textures. I do this by using a combination of soft-flesh, easy-to-pit olives and firm-flesh, not-so-easy-to-pit olives. Super-soft olives, like, say, kalamatas, can often be pitted simply by rolling them around in a tea towel while exuding a bit of downward pressure. Tougher olives may just require a thwack from one of my favorite multitaskers: the bench scraper.

Traditionally, tapenade is made via mortar and pestle. But if you look to your food processor for labor relief, I, for one, won't tell.

// SOFTWARE ///

8	ounces	mixed olives	pitted
2		anchovy fillets	rinsed
1	small clove	garlic	minced
2	tablespoons	capers	
2 or 3	leaves	fresh basil	
1	tablespoon	lemon juice	freshly squeezed
2	tablespoons	extra virgin olive oil	

// PROCEDURE ///

Thoroughly rinse the olives in cool water. Combine all of the ingredients in the bowl of a **food processor**. Process to combine, stopping to scrape down the sides of the bowl, until the mixture becomes a coarse paste, 1 to 2 minutes total. Transfer to a bowl and serve with chips or on a steak, or shaken with oil and vinegar for a dressing, or smeared on toast, or shaken into a Martini. It's a floor wax, it's a dessert topping—no, it's both.

THE LEGACY OF THE LADY OF THE REFRIGERATOR

Portrayed by dietician Carolyn O'Neil, she's strictly here to explain nutritional elements. Although the character is conceptually sampled from the Lady of the Lake (you know . . . King Arthur), I have absolutely no memory of why I thought to stick the poor lady back there in that gown with all that chilly dry ice fog.

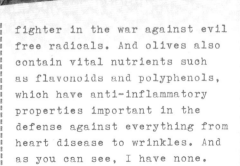

LADY OF THE REFRIGERATOR: Hello, Alton.

AB: It is the Lady of the Refrigerator. And I thought she only existed in legend, myth, story, and song.

LR: That's true, I do. But olives are also mentioned many times in myths, legends, fables, stories, and song. Not to mention the Bible.

AB: How many times?

LR: A lot. And listen, riddle me this: If, as you say, olives are so bad for you, why have they been so important to mankind, and why are doctors so crazy about olive oil, hmm?

AB: I don't know.

LR: Let me tell you a few things about olives and nutrition. Olives are a fine source of gloriously good monounsaturated fats and vitamin E, which is a mighty fighter in the war against evil free radicals. And olives also contain vital nutrients such as flavonoids and polyphenols, which have anti-inflammatory properties important in the defense against everything from heart disease to wrinkles. And as you can see, I have none.

AB: (blushing) No. You're beautiful.

OLIVE ME

// SOFTWARE

17	ounces	all-purpose flour	
3	teaspoons	baking powder	
12	ounces	mixed olives	pitted and roughly chopped
⅓	cup	Tapenade	see page 353
2	large	eggs	beaten
½	cup	olive oil	
1	cup	whole milk	
1	tablespoon	honey	
1¼	teaspoons	kosher salt	

TIDBIT | In ancient Greece, cutting down an olive-tree was punishable by death.

TIDBIT | In 1774 Thomas Jefferson planted olives at Monticello. They died.

// PROCEDURE

1. Heat the oven to 375°F. Spray a **9¼-by-5¼-inch nonstick loaf pan** with **nonstick spray**, line with **parchment paper**, and set aside.

2. Put the flour and baking powder in the bowl of a **food processor** and pulse for 5 seconds. Pour the dry ingredients into a **large mixing bowl**. Stir in the olives and tapenade.

3. **Whisk** together the eggs, oil, milk, honey, and salt in a **medium bowl**. Add to the dry ingredients and stir just to combine; do not mix until smooth. Pour the mixture into the prepared loaf pan and bake for 75 to 80 minutes, until the internal temperature is 210°F or a **toothpick** inserted in the center comes out clean.

4. Remove the loaf from the pan and cool completely on a **cooling rack**.

I'm betting there's a Mexican restaurant

just down the street from your house. You know the one—
in the strip mall, sombreros on the wall over the cash register,
soccer on the TV over the bar. There's a cactus on the outside
of the menu and a bunch of numbers on the inside. And here's a
shocker, America, delicious though that number 16 combo may be, it's about as authenti-
cally Mexican as the Frito Bandito. There is, however, one solid piece of Meso-Americana
here, the tortilla.

Indeed, it could be argued that, besides being a staple food for half the planet, this
humble flatbread is one of the edible linchpins of human history. Delectable though they
are, the average gringo would no more attempt to make tortillas at home than to take
up flamenco guitar. And that's a shame, because the tortilla is truly a-maize-ing, and way
more American than apple pie. Healthful, easy to concoct, versatile as vise grips, and
eminently qualified to be good eats.

My assistant |

Assistant to the
assistant manager |

Assistant editor |

OLÉ!

KNOWLEDGE CONCENTRATE

Want fresh tortillas? You have three options:

1. Buy them from the factory: Just about every city and large town in the United States with a Latin American community has a tortilla factory. Besides offering truly great tortillas—which, I might add, freeze fabulously if left in the bag and then double-wrapped in aluminum foil—most factories are more than happy to sell you all the maize, cal, nixtamal, or masa dough you need to make your own tortillas at home. In this case, you'll still need a griddle and a tortilla press. (See page 359.)

2. Make quasi-homemade tortillas: Purchase instant masa mix at your local market. There's no shame in this, as you'll still have to press and griddle tortillas. There will, however, be a serious downgrade in flavor . . . but then, you knew that.

3. Make them from scratch:

Step 1: Land a pound (about 2 cups) of dried field or flint corn, which can be found at health food stores, co-ops, and, of course, on that new-fangled World Wide Web thing.

Step 2: Rinse the corn and move it to a stainless-steel pot large enough to hold the corn plus 6 cups water and ½ ounce (2 tablespoons) calcium hydroxide. Canners call this pickling lime; builders call it slaked lime; Mexican cooks call it cal, which I think is a far, far nicer name. (Both the corn and cal are easily obtained at a Latin market or a megamart with a well-stocked international aisle.)

Step 3: Bring this slowly to a boil. You want it to take about 30 to 40 minutes. And make sure you use a stainless-steel vessel and a stainless-steel spoon, because the cal can discolor metals and bleach wood. When your corn hits a boil, cover the pot, kill the heat, and stash the pot someplace out of the way overnight. Do not refrigerate.

Step 4: Pop the top the next day and you'll immediately see that your lime solution has loosened up the hulls on your maize. Rub the kernels under lukewarm running water for 5 to 6 minutes to remove the hulls, then soak in clean water for 2 minutes. Change the water, and soak it for another 2 minutes.

Now you've got nixtamal and can continue with the application for corn tortillas.

TIDBIT | *Tortilla* literally means "little tart."

TIDBIT | Southern grits are ground from hominy, a white corn version of nixtamal.

TIDBIT | Things the Aztecs put in tortillas: water bugs, frogs, salamanders, algae, and tiny lake worms.

One of my favorite models—nixtamalization!

CORN TORTILLAS

14 TO 16 TORTILLAS

Sure, you can buy masa dough mix at the megamart, but hey, what fun is that?

// SOFTWARE ///

1½ to 2	pounds	nixtamal
4 to 5	tablespoons	lukewarm H_2O
1	teaspoon	kosher salt

// PROCEDURE //

1. Put the nixtamal in the bowl of a **food processor** and pulse 10 to 15 times. Add 2 tablespoons of the water and pulse 8 to 10 times, stopping to scrape down the sides of the bowl once or twice. Add 2 more tablespoons water along with the salt and pulse until a dough begins to form. If the dough is still dry and somewhat crumbly, add the remaining tablespoon of water and pulse several times. Turn the dough out onto the counter and shape into a ball. Wrap the ball of dough in **plastic wrap** and let rest for 30 minutes.

2. Heat a **cast-iron griddle** over medium-high heat until it reaches 400°F.

3. Divide the dough into 1½-ounce portions, shape into balls, and keep covered with a **damp tea towel**.

4. Cut a **1-gallon zip-top bag** in half and line the base of a **tortilla press** with one of the plastic bag halves. Place one ball at a time on the press and top with the other half of the plastic. Close the press and push down firmly several times until the tortilla is flattened. Remove the plastic from the tortilla and put the tortilla on the cast-iron skillet; cook for 1 minute on each side. Remove the tortilla to a **plate lined with a tea towel**. Cover the tortilla with a **second towel** to keep it warm. Repeat with all of the dough. Use immediately or store in a zip-top bag in the refrigerator for up to 1 week.

> **TIDBIT** Traditionally in Mexico, the tortillas are cooked on a special griddle made of either earthenware or thin cast iron and called a *comall* ("COMB-all") or *comal* ("co-MALL"), depending on where you are.

> **TIDBIT** In Spain *tortilla* often refers to an open-face omelet.

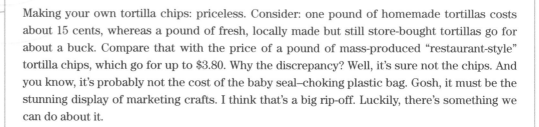

APPLICATION — LIME TORTILLA CHIPS

40 CHIPS

Making your own tortilla chips: priceless. Consider: one pound of homemade tortillas costs about 15 cents, whereas a pound of fresh, locally made but still store-bought tortillas go for about a buck. Compare that with the price of a pound of mass-produced "restaurant-style" tortilla chips, which go for up to $3.80. Why the discrepancy? Well, it's sure not the chips. And you know, it's probably not the cost of the baby seal–choking plastic bag. Gosh, it must be the stunning display of marketing crafts. I think that's a big rip-off. Luckily, there's something we can do about it.

// SOFTWARE

¼	cup	lime juice	freshly squeezed
2	teaspoons	kosher salt	
10		fresh corn tortillas	cut into quarters
2	quarts	peanut oil	

// PROCEDURE

1. Combine the lime juice and salt in a **small mixing bowl**. One at a time, dip the tortilla quarters into the mixture and lay on a **cooling rack** set inside a **half sheet pan**. Dry the tortillas for 1 hour, or until there are no visible signs of moisture on them.

2. Heat the oil in a **5-quart pot or Dutch oven** to 365° to 375°F. Gently lower the chips, 5 or 6 at a time, into the oil and fry for 20 to 30 seconds (or 1 to 1½ minutes if using tortillas made from the previous application). Using a **slotted spoon or spider**, remove the chips to a **newspaper-lined half sheet pan**. Cool the chips for 3 to 4 minutes before serving with queso, salsa, whatever.

MONTEZUMA'S LAST LAUGH

In 1519, Hernando Cortez landed in what is today Veracruz, Mexico. He had a serious jones for some shiny, which he soon found in the Aztec city-state of Tenochtitlán, which was, at the time, probably the most splendid city on earth. Aided by cannons, horses, smallpox, and a legend that made him out to be a returning god, Cortez captured the city's ruler, Montezuma, and decimated his civilization. Had Cortez stopped for a moment to consider how it was that such heathen savages were able to erect such a bling-encrusted metropolis, he might have discovered that the answer was a different type of gold: maize.

The Aztecs lived on a starchy version of maize that came with a rock-hard outer hull, or pericarp. These early Americans learned that if they soaked and cooked the maize in water with wood ashes in it, the hulls would just slip right off due to the high alkalinity of the ash.

Unbeknownst to the cooks of the time, the alkaline essentially unlocked a huge portion of the grain's nutrition, making it available for whatever human might consume it. Suddenly the Indian diet was packed with amino acids such as lysine and tryptophan and vitamin B₃, better known as niacin. When you consider how much corn was in their diet it's clear that without this process, dubbed nixtamalization, the Aztecs wouldn't have had the energy to build that magnificent empire of theirs.

When the Old World got its mitts on maize, it skipped nixtamalization altogether. Those who made maize their main grain eventually suffered from pellagra, which causes the three dreaded Ds: diarrhea, dementia, and death.

I HEADED DOWN TO THE DUNGEON TO SEE IF MY DUNGEON MASTER HAD ANY HARDWARE DEVICES...

DM: Greetings, Master. How might I serve your impudence?

AB: I need a tortilla press.

DM: Ah, want to put a little squeeze on something, eh?

AB: Tortillas.

DM: Right, tortillas. Say no more, Master.

AB: Look, if this is going to be some big hassle, I'll just go to a kitchen store.

DM: Ha, ha, ha, ha. That's rich. Would Master wish to mashy-mashy something up a little old school? Here we have a traditional wooden press. The victim...whatever...goes in here. Then this slab comes down and the handle applies the pressure.

AB: What else is it good for?

DM: Other than eliciting confessions, it's just good clean fun.

AB: Got anything a little more twentieth century?

DM: Oh, yes. Here we have an electric model. This one presses and cooks at the same time. The only thing this baby's missing is spikes. Here we have a couple of metal presses. One in aluminum, the other in iron. The aluminum one is nice and light, but not heavy enough to inflict serious damage. Not like our iron friend here. I might also point out, this one comes in a bigger model in case Master would wish to mashy something a bit larger.

AB: Like, maybe, a flour tortilla?

DM: Or a Madagascar cockroach. Slam! Dah! Heh heh heh.

AB: (takes the larger iron tortilla press)

I gotta go.

DM: Oh, very well. Thanks for coming down. Drop in anytime.

You know, before wheat, rye, buckwheat, millet, or, some even say, rice, barley was cultivated and gathered on almost every continent on this planet. It was roasted, boiled, toasted, ground, simmered, and, of course, malted, that is, sprouted and then roasted. Sound yummy? Well, kind of depends on the delivery system. Although the average American consumes plenty of barley in liquid form (read: beer), few folks take advantage of its qualities as a full-blown culinary multitasker. But that, my food friends, is all about to change.

TIDBIT Noise level in decibels: normal breathing = 10, rainfall = 50, average grain mill = 80, air raid siren = 130.

TIDBIT Hull-less barley contains two to three times the protein of an equal portion of rice.

MY BROTHER, B.A.

HULL =

PROTECTIVE COATING

America, meet *Hordeum vulgare*: barley. Consumed in many forms throughout the ages from Egypt to Greece, Japan to Britain, India to Italy, where barley was fed to gladiators to keep them strong, hence their nickname, *barbarian hordearii* ("barley eater").

Barley facts to know and tell:

Barley isn't very picky about where it grows. As a result, it is grown commercially in twenty-seven states.

Barley is the fourth-largest grain crop in the world, after wheat, rice, and corn.

Fifty-one percent of the U.S. barley crop is used as animal fodder; 44 percent is malted (sprouted and roasted) for yummy beverages like beer. Mmmmm, beer.

Some historians have argued that the presence of wild barley in prehistoric Eurasia may have given the peoples of those regions a nutritional and therefore a political and economic jump on the rest of the human race.

Barley varieties:

COVERED barley is barley with the inedible outer hull still intact. Not much use to you and me in the kitchen.

HULLED barley has been abrasively treated just to remove the outer coat. Most of the bran (where a majority of the nutrition resides) and germ (which contains most of the grain's fat content) remain, as well as the starchy endosperm. Depending on where you shop, you should be able to find hulled barley in multiple forms, including:

berries (kernels)   grits (also marketed as "bits")

flakes (rolled like oats)   flour or meal

If you really want to take full culinary advantage of barley, you will want to use coarse cracked kernels—or barley grits—and barley flour. Various hand-powered grain mills are capable of grinding these, but if you're going to get more whole grains into your diet (and you know you should), you'll want to spring for an electric grain mill. That said, many megamarts and most health food stores these days have freestanding mills that you can just walk up to and grind away on.

HULL-LESS barleys don't cling to their outer hulls, which fall off during harvesting. This means they can be prepared with almost all of the bran intact. Hull-less varieties are therefore more nutritious because less of the good stuff has been processed away. Hull-less barley is typically available in the same forms as hulled.

PEARLED OR SCOTCH barley is hulled barley that has been abrasively polished down to the starchy endosperm. Although this is the most popular and quickest cooking of the kernels due to the absence of the bran, it's also the least nutritious form. That said, unlike wheat or spelt or most other grains whose fiber content rests in the outer layers, barley's fiber runs all the way through the grain.

TIDBIT Barley kernels, or "barley-corns," were used as units of measurement as early as the sixth century.

Protective crust

Inner shield (bran)

Fuel packets (endosperm)

Capsule (germ)

Hordeum Vulgare

BAKED BARLEY

4 TO 6 SERVINGS (ABOUT 4 CUPS)

If you're interested in giving hulled barley a try, this is about the easiest try you'll ever find.

// SOFTWARE ///

1	cup	hulled barley	
1	tablespoon	unsalted butter	
1	teaspoon	kosher salt	
2	cups	boiling H₂O	

// PROCEDURE ///

1. Heat the oven to 375°F.

2. Put the barley in a **1½-quart ceramic or glass baking dish** and add the butter, salt, and boiling water. Stir to combine. Cover the dish tightly with **aluminum foil** and put the lid on top of the foil. Bake on the middle rack of the oven for 1 hour.

3. After 1 hour, remove the cover, fluff with a fork, and serve immediately.

   NOTE: Proper fluffing is crucial, because when it first comes out of the oven the starch on the surface of each kernel hasn't set yet and is very vulnerable. Work it hard and you'll make a brick. Always fluff with a large fork or even chopsticks to minimize mashing.

// SOFTWARE //

3	tablespoons	orange juice	freshly squeezed
	to taste	kosher salt	
2	tablespoons	extra virgin olive oil	
3½ to 4	cups	barley	cooked and cooled
1	small head	fennel	julienned
¼	cup	pine nuts	toasted
½	cup	Parmesan cheese	grated
4	slices	bacon	cooked and crumbled
2	tablespoons	fresh parsley	chopped
	to taste	black pepper	freshly ground

// PROCEDURE //

1. **Whisk** together the orange juice and a pinch of salt in a **small bowl**. Add the oil and whisk to combine. Set the dressing aside.

2. Combine the barley, fennel, pine nuts, cheese, bacon, and parsley in a **large mixing bowl**. Add the dressing and stir to combine. Season to taste with salt and pepper. Devour immediately or refrigerate for up to 1 hour.

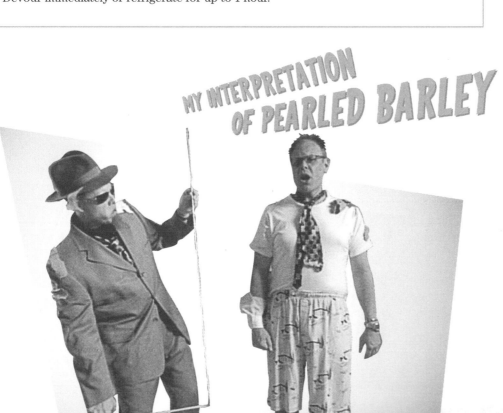

MY INTERPRETATION OF PEARLED BARLEY

BARLEY AND LAMB STEW

4 TO 6 SERVINGS

// SOFTWARE ///

2	pounds	boneless lamb shoulder	trimmed of fat and cut into bite-size pieces
¼	teaspoon	kosher salt	
1	teaspoon	black pepper	freshly ground
1	teaspoon	all-purpose flour	
1	tablespoon	olive oil	divided
3	medium	carrots	cut into ¼-inch rounds
1	cup	barley grits	
4	cups	chicken broth	
2	teaspoons	fresh oregano	chopped

// PROCEDURE ///

1. Toss the lamb in the salt, pepper, and flour in a **medium mixing bowl**.

2. Heat half of the oil in a **4- to 5-quart Dutch oven** set over medium-high heat until it shimmers. Add half of the lamb and brown it on all sides, 7 to 8 minutes total.

3. Remove the lamb to a **clean bowl** and repeat with the remaining oil and lamb. Remove the second batch of lamb to the bowl and add the carrots to the pot. Sauté the carrots for 3 to 4 minutes, stirring occasionally. Return all of the lamb to the pot, along with the barley grits, and stir to combine. Add the broth and bring to a boil. Decrease the heat to low, cover, and simmer for 30 to 45 minutes, until the liquid is absorbed and the lamb and grits are tender.

4. Five minutes before the stew is finished, add the oregano. Taste for seasoning and add salt and pepper as desired. Serve in bowls.

APPLICATION — BARLEY BREAD

8 TO 10 SLICES

// SOFTWARE

10	ounces	barley flour	
1	teaspoon	kosher salt	
1	ounce	baking powder	(about 2½ tablespoons)
2	tablespoons	honey	
¼	cup	canola oil	plus extra for the pan
2	large	eggs	
1	cup	whole milk	

// PROCEDURE

1. Heat a **gas grill** on low heat for at least 10 minutes.

2. Lightly rub the sides and bottom of a **4- to 5-quart Dutch oven** with oil and set aside.

3. **Whisk** together the flour, salt, and baking powder in a **medium mixing bowl**. Whisk together the honey, oil, eggs, and milk in a **small mixing bowl**. Add the wet ingredients to the dry ingredients and stir until combined.

4. Pour the batter into the prepared Dutch oven but do not cover with the lid. Put the Dutch oven on the grill and close the lid of the grill. Cook with the grill lid shut for 35 to 40 minutes, until the internal temperature of the bread reaches 190°F. Cool the bread in the Dutch oven for at least 5 minutes before turning out onto a **cooling rack**.

   N O T E : If you're using a traditional oven, bake at 350°F for 25 to 30 minutes, until the bread reaches an internal temperature of 190°F.

Dry Team   Wet Team

Cinnamon buns. I don't really see why we need say more. I could prevaricate, insisting that it's all in the name of science, that we must examine how yeasts react to high levels of sugar and concentrations of coumarin, which alters the little beasties' respiration. But that would all be a shammy charade avoiding the simple truth that . . . Cinnamon buns. I don't really see why we need say more.

TIDBIT February 21 is National Sticky Bun Day.

TIDBIT In the United States and Canada, cassia may be legally marketed and sold as "cinnamon." In most of Europe. it cannot.

CINNAMON
Feathery, thin, subtle

CASSIA
Hard, thick, sharp

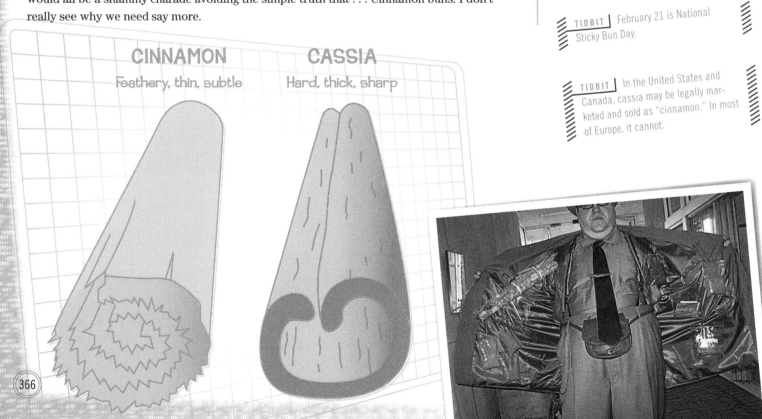

Cinnamon buns are born of yeast dough just like baguettes or pizza dough. The CO_2 produced by the yeast provides lift, enhances texture, and brings a twangy sourness to the flavor that helps to balance the sugar and spice. What's different about rich, sweet dough is the effect that fat and sugar have on traditional yeasty doughs. The fat tenderizes the dough by preventing gluten bonds from forming.

Sugar also tenderizes, by locking on to water and preventing it from evaporating. That's why sweet dough products don't get stale as quickly as savory baked goods. The sugar (almost 10 percent of the weight of the flour in this application) poses a challenge to the yeast. Sure, yeast gets charged up by small amounts of sweetness—after all, it eats the stuff. But the hygroscopic nature of the sugar can prevent the yeast from getting the water it needs to do its business. As a result, sweet doughs require longer to rise. But that's okay, because I always give them overnight in the fridge.

Here in the United States, the term *cinnamon* can be legally applied to the rolled or ground inner bark of two members of the laurel family:

Cinnamomum zeylanicum, a.k.a. "true" or "Ceylon" cinnamon, has rolled bark or "quills" that are light tan, long, and almost feathery at the ends. The flavor and aroma are sweet and subtle. It's easily ground to powder via a coffee mill. Most Americans will live out their lives never having tried this kind of cinnamon. Although I appreciate this spice in beverages and certain cookies, in strongly flavored applications I prefer cinnamon's coarser cousin, cassia.

Cinnamomum aromaticum, called "Chinese" cinnamon or simply "cassia," is what most of us know as cinnamon. Those hard orange sticks we grate or put in hot drinks? Cassia. The reddish brown powder we buy at the megamart? Cassia. I prefer its sharper, more in-your-face flavor in baked goods, but I'm really picky about the quality. I don't try grinding those hard quills except (occasionally) for coffee, because the good stuff comes in pieces far too big for me to grind. And since the essential oils (specifically cinnamic aldehyde) that give cassia and cinnamon their distinct flavors are highly volatile, I won't buy the ground stuff at the megamart, where I can ascertain neither the age nor the quality of the product. I purchase small portions, ground to order, from Internet-based spice merchants who deal in specific types of cassia.

VIETNAMESE SAIGON (my personal favorite) contains the highest percentage of volatile oils. It is therefore the most expensive. It's complex and sweet stuff, and I use it in cakes and cookies.

INDONESIAN KORINTJE is grown on the island of Sumatra and is available in grades A, B, and C. It is the mildest of the cassias and makes the nicest quills of the bunch. I keep Korintje A quills around for making mulled wine.

CHINESE TUNG HING is the most potent of the bunch and it's my choice for cinnamon buns; it can stand up to the intense sweetness and the flavors produced by the yeast.

ORIGINS: NOT

Once upon a time spice merchants made up rather fanciful mythologies regarding the origins of cinnamon in order to scare away anyone who might get the wise idea of going out and finding it themselves. Here are a couple of dandies.

Cinnamon grows only in valleys infested with venomous serpents and can be harvested only by those with stout hearts and sturdy souls. After each harvest the foragers must build a cinnamon altar for the sun, who then consumes the costly pile in a single fiery gulp.

Ancient Arabian raptors used cinnamon to build their clifftop nests. To get at them, spice men would tempt the ravenous ravens with big hunks of meat. The greedy birds took these back to their nests, which shattered under the weight. The traders had only to pick up their prize and flee before they were ripped asunder.

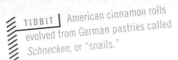

TIDBIT | American cinnamon rolls evolved from German pastries called *Schnecken*, or "snails."

// SOFTWARE

FOR THE DOUGH

4	large	egg yolks	at room temperature
1	large	egg	at room temperature
2	ounces	sugar	
6	tablespoons	unsalted butter	melted
¾	cup	buttermilk	at room temperature
20	ounces	all-purpose flour	plus additional for dusting
1	envelope	instant dry yeast	(that's ¼ ounce, people)
1¼	teaspoons	kosher salt	

FOR THE FILLING

8	ounces	light brown sugar	
1	tablespoon	cinnamon	ground
	pinch	kosher salt	
1½	tablespoons	unsalted butter	melted

FOR THE ICING

2½	ounces	cream cheese	
3	tablespoons	milk	
5½	ounces	confectioners' sugar	

// PROCEDURE

1. Make the dough: Combine the egg yolks, whole egg, sugar, butter, and buttermilk in the bowl of a **stand mixer fitted with the whisk attachment** on medium speed. Add about half, or 10 ounces, of the flour, along with the yeast and salt; whisk until moistened and combined.

2. Remove the whisk attachment and replace it with a **dough hook**. Add all but 4 ounces of the remaining flour and knead on low speed for 5 minutes. Check the consistency of the dough, and add more flour if necessary; the dough should feel soft and moist but not sticky. Knead on low speed for 5 minutes more, or until the dough clears the sides of the bowl. Turn the dough out onto a lightly floured work surface; knead by hand for about 30 seconds. Lightly oil a **large bowl**. Transfer the dough to the bowl, lightly oil the top of the dough, cover, and let rise until doubled in volume, 2 to 2½ hours.

3. Make the filling: Combine the brown sugar, cinnamon, and salt in a **medium bowl**. Mix until well incorporated. Set the sugar mixture and the butter aside until the dough is fully risen.

4. Butter a **9-by-13-inch glass baking dish**. Turn the dough out onto a lightly floured work surface. Gently shape the dough into a rectangle with the long side nearest you. Roll into an 18-by-12-inch rectangle. **Brush** the dough with the butter, leaving a ½-inch border along the top edge. Sprinkle the brown sugar mixture over the dough, leaving a ¾-inch border along the top edge; gently press the filling into the dough. Beginning with the long edge nearest you, roll the dough into a tight cylinder. Firmly pinch the seam to seal and roll the cylinder seam side down. Very gently squeeze the cylinder to create an even thickness. Using a **serrated knife**, slice the cylinder into 12 (1½-inch) rolls. Arrange the rolls cut side down in the baking dish; cover tightly with plastic wrap and store in the refrigerator overnight, or up to 16 hours.

5. Remove the rolls from the refrigerator and put them in a turned-off oven. Fill a **shallow pan two thirds full of boiling water** and set it on the rack below the rolls. Close the oven door and let the rolls rise until they look slightly puffy, about 30 minutes. Remove the rolls and the pan of water from the oven.

6. Heat the oven to 350°F. Bake the rolls on the middle rack of the oven until they are golden brown and the internal temperature reaches 190°F, about 30 minutes. Let cool while you make the icing.

7. Make the icing: Whisk the cream cheese in the bowl of a stand mixer until creamy. Add the milk and whisk until combined. Sift in the sugar and whisk until smooth. Spread over the rolls and serve immediately.

A NOSE FOR FOOD

Ever try a cinnamon bun when you have a cold? It tastes like a chewy mouthful of . . . nothing. That's because the human tongue can only detect salty, sweet, sour, and bitter (and maybe umami, depending on whom you ask). Most of the magic of spices like cinnamon doesn't register on the tongue but upstairs in your nose. The human schnozz can detect some ten thousand different types of aromas. How does it work?

Let's say for a moment that this is a cinnamon molecule: airborne, of course. And you breathe in, and it's drawn in until it reaches something called the olfactory epithelium, a big bundle of nerves that is unique because it's the only part of the brain that is actually exposed to the air. When the little cinnamon guy hooks up with one of these little nerve endings, it creates an electrical charge that your brain interprets as an aroma. Now, what's

important—to an eater, at least—is that this is not the only way these guys can get in. They can come up, huge blocks of them, from the back of the throat when you chew. When they meet up with these nerves, the brain marries that information to the information from your tongue and bingo, you've got what we call flavor. And that explains why it's hard to taste your food when you have a stuffed-up nose.

Monkey bread, a.k.a. bubble bread, became all the rage during the 1950s but was probably born during America's western expansion, when, I imagine, the stacking of small yeast dough balls in a Dutch oven was just a smart use of time, space, heat, and materials. Although some historians like to attach deeper meaning to the moniker, I think that some observant home baker thought her kids pulled at it like monkeys at the zoo pulled on . . . well, something. Whatever the origins, this is one baked good that fosters a primal response—at least in me. This application, by the way, has been voted by my crew the best *Good Eats* baked good of all time. And we know from baked goods.

// SOFTWARE ///

FOR THE DOUGH

4	large	egg yolks	at room temperature
1	large	egg	at room temperature
2	ounces	sugar	
6	tablespoons	unsalted butter	melted
¾	cup	buttermilk	at room temperature
20	ounces	all-purpose flour	plus additional for dusting
1	envelope	instant dry yeast	
1¼	teaspoons	kosher salt	

FOR THE TOPPING

1	cup	unsalted butter	
8	ounces	light brown sugar	
½	teaspoon	ground dried rosemary[1]	
3	ounces	golden raisins	

FOR THE COATING

5	tablespoons	unsalted butter	melted
1	teaspoon	ground dried rosemary	

// PROCEDURE ///

1. Make the dough: Combine the egg yolks, whole egg, sugar, butter, and buttermilk in a **stand mixer fitted with the whisk attachment** on medium speed. Add about half, or 10 ounces, of the flour, along with the yeast and salt; whisk until moistened and combined.

2. Remove the whisk attachment and replace it with a **dough hook**. Add all but 4 ounces of the remaining flour and knead on low speed for 5 minutes. Check the consistency of the dough, and add more flour if necessary; the dough should feel soft and moist but not sticky. Knead on low speed for 5 minutes more, until the dough clears the sides of the bowl. Turn the dough out onto a lightly floured work surface; knead by hand for about 30 seconds. Lightly oil a **large bowl**. Transfer the dough to the bowl, lightly oil the top of the dough, **cover**, and let rise until doubled in volume, 2 to 2½ hours.

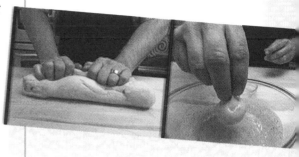

3. Make the topping: Combine the butter, brown sugar, rosemary, and raisins in a **small saucepan** over medium heat. Cook, stirring occasionally, until the butter is melted and the sugar is dissolved. Pour half of the topping into the bottoms of **2 bundt pans** and set aside. Cover and store the other half of the topping in the refrigerator until the next morning.

4. Make the coating: Combine the butter and rosemary in a **medium shallow bowl**. Once the dough has risen, turn it out onto a lightly floured surface. Portion the dough into 1-ounce pieces; roll each piece into a ball. (You should have about 36 balls.) Roll the balls in the melted butter and rosemary.

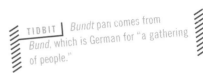

TIDBIT | *Bundt* pan comes from *Bund*, which is German for "a gathering of people."

5. Divide the balls evenly between the bundt pans. Cover with **plastic wrap** and place in the refrigerator overnight, or up to 16 hours.

6. Remove the bread from the refrigerator and place in a turned-off oven. Fill a **shallow pan two thirds full of boiling water** and set it on the rack below the bread. Close the oven and let the bread rise until slightly puffy looking, 20 to 30 minutes. Once the bread has risen, remove it and the pan of water from the oven.

7. Heat the oven to 350°F. Bake the bread on the middle rack of the oven until it is slightly golden on top and the internal temperature reaches 190°F, 25 to 30 minutes. Meanwhile, reheat the remaining topping in a **small saucepan** over medium heat until the mixture is pourable, about 5 minutes. Fifteen minutes into baking, pour the topping over the bread, and finish cooking. Let cool on a cooling rack for 5 minutes, then invert onto a platter or cutting board. Serve immediately.

[1] This stunning innovation came from Carmi Adams, one of my culinary team, whose baked goods are so otherworldly that a few hundred years ago she would have been burned as a witch. Before this I'd never thought of seasoning a sweet application with rosemary. Now I eat it on Cap'n Crunch.

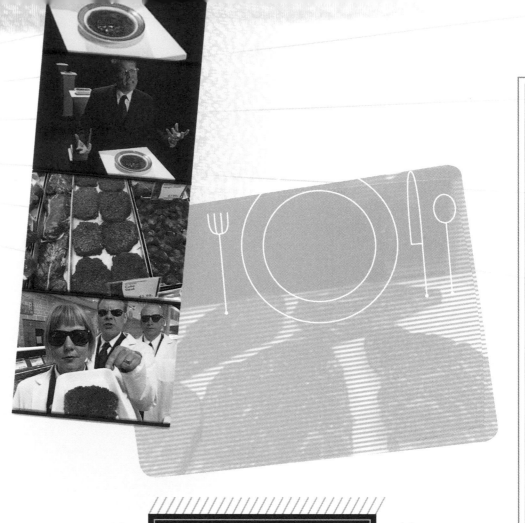

Welcome once again to the Food Gallery.

Tonight, let us stroll through the Hall of Home-Cooked Horrors. Liver and onions are on permanent display here, along with other suppertime nightmares of our youth—like beets. And who could forget Mom's "Don't ask, don't tell" casserole? These, of course, pale in comparison to the horrors of cube steak. In any sane universe, this prodigiously perforated montage of mismatched meat would be used to patch tires rather than fill stomachs. Most moms make matters worse by encasing each slab in a thick morass of flavorless, fried flour, which they then top with "gravy." But like many a monster from childhood mythology, the only thing cube steak needs is a little love, a little consideration, a little homespun knowhow. Because when it's treated right, even the cheapest cutlet in town can cast a tall culinary shadow. Whether it's slow-cooked or chicken-fried, cube steak can and will be good eats.

KNOWLEDGE CONCENTRATE

▷○ **Cube steak:** It's a bit of a misnomer, if you ask me, seeing as how there isn't really anything cubist about it. But I guess it sounds better than "perforated meat," which is what cube steak actually is. Why would you perforate a perfectly good piece of meat? To convert a flavorful but tough hunk of meat into something that is flavorful and potentially tender, or at least tenderer. Now where might you find such a bit of goodness? Of all the primal cuts, I would say that the round is the best candidate. Round is divided into the top round, the bottom round, and the knuckle, and of these the bottom round is best suited to the mission. It's lean and, since it does a fair amount of work, full of flavor. Best of all, it can be had at a reasonable price.

▷○ **When shopping for a cube steak, you're probably going to run across two different types: cube steak and special cube steak. What's the difference?**

According to the North American Meat Processors Association, item #1100, a.k.a "cube steak," can be prepared from any portion of the carcass excluding the shank and heel meat. However, item #1101, a.k.a. "beef cube steak, special," is to be prepared exclusively from the round, loin, rib, or chuck sections. Additionally, the knitting together of two or more pieces of meat, or the folding of the meat during the cubing process, is permissible only in the cut sold as "cube steak," not "cube steak, special."

That's right, "knitting." In this case, we're not talking about making a sweater but rather the process whereby the processor physically melds multiple pieces of meat into one single Frankensteak. Folding is more about making one, skimpy long piece, which may be riddled with holes, into something that looks like you might want to cook it. I avoid "cube steak" at all costs. I will purchase "cube steak, special" if it's on sale or if I'm in a hurry, but I'd just as soon buy a two-pound bottom roast and do the perforating myself. Once you've chosen a roast, go ahead and ask your butcher to cut it into half-inch slices . . . unless you want to do that part, too.

If you're going to do your own cubing, you will need a device, a device of lethal cunning capable of going medieval on a piece of meat. As is true of most culinary endeavors, there are many choices. Odds are good that somewhere in your kitchen, in the back of a drawer, is something that looks like this:

The toothed side is called a "tenderizer," but it ought to be called a "musher" or "mangler," because that's what it does. Promise me you will never use it on a piece of meat. Promise! Thank you.

On the other end of the spectrum we have the professional countertop "needler," which can be found in small butcher shops. It's armed with nearly a thousand cutting edges and can tenderize, needle, and knit just about anything you run into it. including your hand if you're not careful. It goes for $1,500. Overkill? Perhaps.

Hunters are fond of running bits and pieces of deer, elk, and the like through crank "cubers," but since the blades actually rotate in and out of the meat they do more damage than I'd like.

Here's what I use, and I like to think of it as my own little personal secret. It's a manual needler and it uses forty-eight sharp metal spikes to break up fibers and connective tissue, thus tenderizing the meat. It only cost about twenty bucks and is easily found via the Internet.

Now, if you want to research cube steak, then you really ought to get yourself down to your local roadside diner, because all the great cube steak applications were either born or perfected there. Of course, you would no doubt also find that cube steak–related nomenclature changes radically with the topography. For instance, in North Carolina ordering country-fried steak will get you a cube steak that has been dredged in flour, seared, and then braised in a brown sauce. A little farther north, in Maryland, this might be served to you as Salisbury steak, which is odd because I'm pretty sure that Dr. Salisbury himself designed his dish around ground meat. Up in Minnesota the same dish might be served to you as Swiss steak, even though it doesn't have any onions or tomatoes on it the way it does out west. And in the great state of Texas, ordering a chicken-fried steak will get you a battered cube steak, pan-fried and served with a pepper cream gravy. In other words, no matter where you roam, cube steak confusion is sure to follow. And so in the name of culinary clarity, I'm going to stick out my neck and declare that a cube steak, lightly dredged in flour, pan-fried, and then braised in a brown sauce, is country-style steak. It's a beautiful tune and here's how it goes.

Medieval-brand meat tenderizer

If found please contact THOR

If you took everything useful out of your kitchen tool drawer, this culinary cruel cudgel would remain.

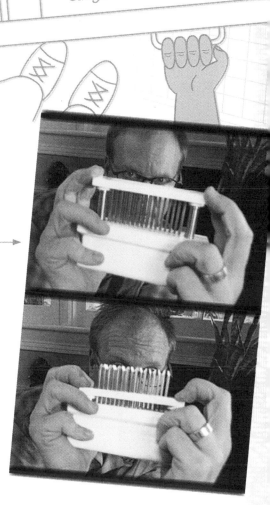

COUNTRY-STYLE STEAK

4 TO 6 SERVINGS

// SOFTWARE

2	pounds	beef bottom round	trimmed of excess fat
2	teaspoons	kosher salt	
1	teaspoon	black pepper	freshly ground
¾	cup	all-purpose flour	
¼	cup	vegetable oil	or bacon drippings
2	cups	chicken broth	
1	teaspoon	dried thyme	

// PROCEDURE

1. Heat the oven to 300°F.

2. Cut the meat with the grain into ½-inch-thick slices and season on both sides with salt and pepper. Put the flour in a **pie pan**. Dredge the pieces of meat on both sides in the flour. Tenderize the meat, using a **needling device**, until each slice is ¼ inch thick. Dredge in the flour again and set aside.

3. Add enough of the oil to just cover the bottom of a **4- to 5-quart Dutch oven** set over medium-high heat. When the oil begins to shimmer, add the steaks to the pan, being careful not to overcrowd. Cook until golden brown on both sides, about 2 minutes per side. Remove the steaks to a **plate** and repeat until all of the steaks have been browned.

4. Add the broth and thyme to the pot, and **whisk** until the liquid just comes to a boil. Return the steaks to the pot and make sure they are all submerged in the liquid. Cover the pot and bake on the middle rack of the oven for 1½ to 2 hours, until the meat is tender and falling apart.

STARCH THICKENING EXPLAINED

Starch granules

When starch granules "pop"

CHICKEN-FRIED STEAK

4 TO 6 SERVINGS

CFS, or chicken-fried steak, is the unofficial state dish of Texas, and it's based on Wiener schnitzel. How did a nice little German cutlet become the cornerstone of Lone Star cuisine? Cultural adaptation. During the nineteenth century, thousands of Germans emigrated into the Hill Country of central Texas, and when they got there they found there was lots of beef but very little veal. So they just adapted their Wiener schnitzel recipe by tenderizing tougher cuts of meat. Even the light gravy they put on their CFS has roots in German cuisine, in the form of ramen schnitzel, a fried cutlet with cream sauce. Over time, chuck wagon cooks started making it, and that resulted in the myriad varieties we have today.

TIDBIT According to the Texas Restaurant Association, some 800,000 orders of chicken-fried steak are served daily.

// SOFTWARE ///

2	pounds	beef top round	trimmed of excess fat
2	teaspoons	kosher salt	
1	teaspoon	black pepper	freshly ground
1	cup	all-purpose flour	
3	large	eggs	beaten
¼	cup	vegetable oil	
2	cups	chicken broth	
½	cup	whole milk	
½	teaspoon	fresh thyme	

// PROCEDURE ///

1) Heat the oven to 250°F.

2) Cut the meat with the grain into ½-inch-thick slices. Season each piece on both sides with the salt and pepper. Put the flour in a **pie pan**. Put the eggs in a **separate pie pan**. Dredge the meat on both sides in the flour. Tenderize the meat, using a **needling device**, until each slice is ¼ inch thick. Dredge the meat again in the flour, followed by the egg, and finally in the flour again. Repeat with all the pieces of meat. Place the meat on a **plate** and allow it to sit for 10 to 15 minutes before cooking.

3) Cover the bottom of a **12-inch slope-sided skillet** with the oil and set over medium-high heat. When the oil begins to shimmer, add the meat in batches, being careful not to overcrowd the pan. Cook each piece on both sides until golden brown, about 4 minutes per side. Remove the steaks to a **cooling rack set in a half sheet pan** and place in the oven. Repeat until all of the meat is browned.

4) Add the remaining oil, or at least 1 tablespoon, to the pan. **Whisk** in 3 tablespoons of the flour left over from dredging. Add the broth and deglaze the pan. Whisk until the gravy comes to a boil and begins to thicken. Add the milk and thyme and whisk until the gravy coats the back of a **spoon**, 5 to 10 minutes. Season to taste. Serve the gravy over the steaks.

*Or, The Stuff You Really Might Want to Know about Water Despite the Fact That You're Pretty Sure You Know Enough Already

This program has long made a mission of exploring

the plain, ordinary ingredients of everyday life: dried pasta, steak, potatoes, salt, biscuits, peas . . . that sort of thing. And yet up to this point we'd never taken more than a sideways glance at the most basic and universal ingredient of them all, an ingredient that plays a role in every edible on earth. I speak, of course, of dihydrogen monoxide, H_2O, the simple yet unfathomably significant lopsided arrangement of one oxygen and two hydrogens that we call "water."

TIDBIT | Although America makes up just 5 percent of the world's population, we consume 15 percent of the world's fresh water. To put that into context, the average you or me goes through 105 gallons of water a day. The average African, 15.

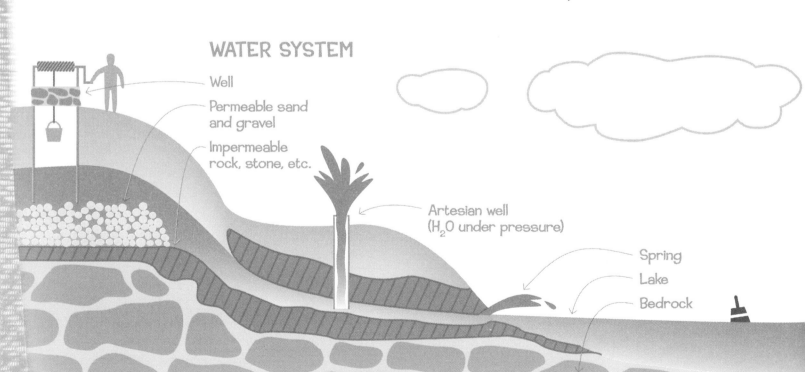

WATER SYSTEM

Well

Permeable sand and gravel

Impermeable rock, stone, etc.

Artesian well (H_2O under pressure)

Spring

Lake

Bedrock

The most significant number in all of human existence may be 104.45, the angle at which one oxygen atom bonds with two hydrogen atoms to form the compound water. This arrangement is "polar" in nature, meaning it has a negative charge on one end and a positive charge on the other. This makes water something of a molecular magnet. Just as an actual magnet can pick up ferrous compounds, water can pick up calcium, magnesium, radium, lead, and hundreds of other polar compounds. Water is a powerful if not universal solvent, which makes it useful for washing your hair, making coffee, and a lot of other things in between.

Water exists in four places: inside living things (you, me, kittens, geckos, small shrubs), in the atmosphere (that big puffy thing slowly crossing the sky), on the surface of the earth (rivers, ponds, streams, lakes, seas, oceans), and in the ground (aquifers, as in permeable sand, gravel, and anything else down there that water can move through).

The last two sources are of interest because that's where the stuff comes from when you open the faucet (an amazingly convenient thing, when you think about it).

SURFACE WATER: Decades of beer advertising have conditioned us to believe that when it comes to purity, you just can't beat a cold, fast-moving mountain stream. But the truth is, they're chock-full of every kind of microbial life there is: protozoa, parasites, viruses, bacteria. How do they get there? Animals (including man) come to drink, and sometimes when they make withdrawals, they make deposits. And, of course, since most surface water moves, it's a handy place to throw things you don't want—like industrial waste. Although large-scale dumping is pretty much a thing of the past, at least in the United States, surface waters are still vulnerable, especially to runoff from things like insecticides, fertilizers, and various nastiness from boats, tankers, and so on.

GROUNDWATER: Anyone who has ever pulled a bucket of water out of a well has tapped into groundwater contained in a geological formation called an aquifer. The U.S. mainland sits over eleven aquifers, which contain a staggering 1 quintillion gallons of H_2O. That's "1" followed by eighteen zeroes: 1,000,000,000,000,000,000.

Rainwater and runoff from mountains seep down into underground sand and gravel, and pool on top of less permeable layers such as clay and shale. The top of this pool is called the water table, and its level changes with the weather, which is why wells that tap into it run the risk of running dry during droughts. However, deep groundwater can flow between the impermeable layers in the even deeper bedrock. These confined aquifers move very slowly, and water drawn from them has often been underground for centuries, or even millennia. If you tap into an aquifer that's under pressure, the water will come to the surface all on its own, sometimes with considerable force. That would be an artesian well. Most groundwater, however, seeps to the surface in the form of springs.

Since they're protected from seepage from above, and filtered by years of moving through sand and rock, waters from confined aquifers are considered to be as clear and clean as water can get in nature, which is not to say that they are safe to drink. In fact, regardless of whether you're talking about surface water or groundwater, safe drinking water is actually pretty hard to come by. Why? Well, it all comes back to 104.45 degrees.

LIFE WILL FIND A WAY

America enjoys the safest, cheapest, tastiest, and most reliable tap water in the world. And still, as Dr. Malcolm put it in *Jurassic Park*, "life will find a way." Occasionally, even the best system can develop a chink in its armor. For instance, in 1999, a relatively new bug, called *Cryptosporidium*, crept through a water treatment plant in Milwaukee, Wisconsin, leaving fifty people dead. Which may explain, at least in part, why millions are willing to spend billions on alternative sources of drinking water.

TIDBIT | Bad, bad water bugs: *Escherichia coli, Cryptosporidium, Giardia lamblia*.

TIDBIT | Water makes up about 85 percent of your brain, 80 percent of your blood, and 70 percent of your muscle.

THE PROBLEM WITH WATER

Because it's a highly potent solvent, water can dissolve and hold on to a great many substances. This can be a good thing in the case of calcium, iron, potassium, and manganese, but not so good in regards to the likes of lead, arsenic, mercury, or radium. It's also not a good thing when manmade stuff—industrial waste, pesticides, fertilizer, petroleum—dissolves in the water. And of course bacteria, viruses, and all manner of other microscopic nasties find water ever so pleasant and refreshing. In fact many of the world's great historic plagues have been waterborne, including cholera, which has wiped out more human life than all the world's wars put together. Luckily we have ways of dealing with them.

Although there are plenty of mechanical and physical processes that can kill viruses, bacteria, and whatnot, good old chlorine is still the best and cheapest way for big systems to produce safe water. Chlorine is a powerful oxidant that can break down cell walls of microbial troublemakers like siege guns pounding castle walls. And best of all, chlorine has what's called "residual effectiveness," meaning that, if the dose is right, it can continue killing nasties right up to the moment your water comes out of the tap.

WATER FILTRATION AND YOU

If you live in the continental United States and receive your water from a municipal source (as opposed to a well), odds are amazingly good that your supply is safe. However, that doesn't mean it tastes good, or that it's capable of functioning to its full potential as a solvent. Your water may require filtration or some type of chemical alteration, such as the process known as "softening."

When it comes to filtration, we home consumers generally have three options: pitcher filters, under-sink installed systems, or whole-house systems. Each of these usually employs multiple systems or "stages" to make your water better.

Fine-mesh filters remove suspended particles that make water murky. These are essentially fine strainers that capture very tiny bits and pieces.

Activated charcoal or "active charcoal" is a special form of carbon that is so riddled with little cracks, nooks, and crannies that a mere gram of it possesses the surface area of not one but two tennis courts. Activated charcoal can catch and hold on to organic compounds, pesticides, benzene, certain metals, radon, and chlorine gas through a process called adsorption (basically, they stick to it). This is a very effective detoxifying medium and is often used in respirators and old-fashioned gas masks. Activated charcoal alone can make your water taste much better.

Inorganic compounds such as arsenic, cadmium, chromium, and radium don't adsorb to carbon. For that we need ion exchange beads. Think of these tiny beads as little suitcases full of ions, charged particles that can pull (not all, but most) inorganic compounds right off and exchange them for good ions. It's like a weapons-exchange program where hand grenades are exchanged for . . . um . . . baby bunny rabbits.

But what about spores? Spores and their close cousins, cysts, are hard, tiny capsules inside of which certain bacteria stash their nasty little offspring (if you could even consider them offspring, which you can't). At 1 to 2 microns in diameter, they're too small to filter out with typical filtration screens designed to remove particulate matter in the 4- to 5-micron range. Spores are also inconveniently resistant to chlorine, so they occasionally sneak their way into municipal water-treatment facilities. Typically this is not a big deal, because the kinds of critters we're talking about, such as *Cryptosporidium* and *Giardia*, have to attack in large numbers in order to make you sick. But if you have small children in your household, or seniors, or folks with immune-system issues, or if you're just plain paranoid, you might want to install a spore-filtration system. If that's the case, you'll want to look for these phrases on the box: "absolute" pore size of 1 micron, or NSF (National Sanitation Foundation) standard 53 (or 58) for cyst removal.

The new high-tech option is something called reverse osmosis, or RO, which uses semipermeable membranes to filter out just about everything, including the minerals that actually make water taste good. Water bottlers often use RO systems in conjunction with ultraviolet (UV) light to make their products as spiffy-clean as possible.

From the beginning of recorded time, waters issuing from deep within the earth have been credited with possessing medicinal—if not magical—properties. Pliny the Elder, for instance, wrote of springs that supposedly could make women conceive, could change your voice, or could convert black sheep into white sheep (which, I suppose, could be useful).

Throughout the eighteenth and nineteenth centuries—actually, right up into the twentieth century—it was not unusual for respected physicians to ship their patients off to various spas and springs to take the waters as treatment for many a malaise, some real, some utterly imagined.

The groovy thing is that these cures sometimes actually worked. As it turns out, water containing high levels of iron is very good for treating what the doctors used to call "female troubles." Sulfur waters can, under the right conditions, quell skin disease. Carbonated or "carbonic" waters can settle a wide range of tummy troubles. And certain alkaline mineral waters are good for gout.

Even if the substances dissolved in the water didn't cure the particular ailment for which it had been prescribed, odds were the health of the patient would improve, if only because the water at the springs was so much cleaner than that available in the cities. You have to remember, the concept of sanitation didn't really exist before the twentieth century, and in cities like Paris it wasn't unusual for wells to be dug right next to open cesspools.

Although the rich could afford to come hang out at springs and spas for weeks, it didn't take long for the owners to spread their net ever wider by bottling their wares for distribution to those who couldn't. By the 1880s, you could walk into a quality grocer or general store in just about any city in the world and buy waters from New York, France, or Italy. The burgeoning middle class, who couldn't afford to take off time for travel, was nonetheless willing to shell out for these waters—which were not cheap—because of their potential health virtues. Water thus became status, and here we are today . . . bottles in hand, just to cross the room.

Before purchasing a bottle of water, please keep in mind that tap water is regulated by the Environmental Protection Agency, while bottled agua is part of the Food and Drug Administration's extremely mind-bogglingly long list of products. There is absolutely no reason to think that bottled water is safer than tap, and when you consider how many thousands of times more expensive the bottled stuff is . . . well, you've just got to wonder.

About 30 percent of the bottled water on store shelves, including many national brands, is harvested from municipal sources. In short, it's tap water. In most cases it's been distilled to remove any and all mineral content before a special recipe of "branded" minerals is added back. So at best it's great-tasting designer tap water. And you're shelling out billions of dollars a year for it.

And then there's all that plastic. Most of those bottles we seem hell-bent on carrying everywhere we go are composed of polyethylene terephthalate, or PET, which was developed by a couple of British chemists back in the 1940s. PET is strong, PET is light, PET is stable, chemically speaking, and above all PET is clear. It's also completely recyclable. But, my fellow Americans, there's a catch: PET bottles are utterly incapable of rolling themselves to the recycling center. Just thought you should know.

BOTTLED WATER LABELS

▶ **SPRING WATER** must be taken from an underground aquifer, from which water naturally flows to the surface at a specific location.

▶ **WELL WATER** means that the water has been pumped out of a hole in the ground, drilled by man. If the water issues forth from the manmade hole via natural pressure, the resulting water may be labeled "artesian" or "artesianal water."

▶ **NATURALLY SPARKLING WATER** contains enough dissolved CO_2 in it to come to the surface in a naturally effervescent state. No carbonation may be added.

▶ **MINERAL WATER** contains in excess of 250 parts per million of total dissolved solids—that is, minerals. Most of the expensive European imports are mineral waters, and they have very distinct flavors.

WATER WORKS — HARD WATER

In some parts of the country, groundwater passes through limestone, chalk, dolomite, or marble, picking up considerable amounts of calcium and magnesium along the way. These can react with stearates in soap, creating a kind of insoluble scum in tubs, sinks, and your hair and making it really, really hard to froth up any suds, which is why they call it "hard" water. And it gets worse. The calcium can precipitate out of the water, creating hard, white scales on things like the insides of electric kettles, water heaters, and the spray arms inside your washing machine. One time, in Utah, I saw a shower head that looked like it had stalactites hanging off it.

Water-softening systems coax the hard water to trade in these excess minerals for microscopic amounts of salt. For those concerned about their salt intake, potassium-based softening systems are also available, though the water they produce tastes a bit off to me.

WATER WORKS — WATER AND HEAT, PART I

Ever wonder why it takes so gosh-darned long for a pot of water to come to a boil? Because water has a very high specific heat. That means it can absorb a vast amount of energy without actually undergoing a change in temperature. What's going on? Under normal circumstances, the average water molecule makes and breaks a few dozen hydrogen bonds per second (with other water molecules and whatever else happens to be around). Pour on more energy, and this number goes up considerably, yet the temperature goes up very slowly. This is good news because it means that once a cooking solution reaches a desired temperature, it's a lot easier to maintain that temperature than it would be in, say, oil. This is why we bake delicate custards in a hot water bath. The water absorbs heat from the oven without delivering it all to the cups. Once water reaches 212°F (100°C)—at sea level, of course—the temperature stops climbing and the water begins to boil. That is, the hydrogen bonds are building and breaking so quickly that the water molecules break out into a vapor state.

WATER WORKS — WATER AND HEAT, PART II

Everybody knows that most everything contracts, becoming dense, when it's cold, right? Well, water is no exception. As the energy drops, the molecules get closer and closer and closer and closer together, until they drop below 39°F (4°C). Then they do something really strange. Like a marching band at dress right, they line up and spread out in a uniform pattern. Eventually, all movement ceases, and the solid called ice is formed. What's interesting is that this crystalline form is actually less dense than the liquid, which is why ice floats.

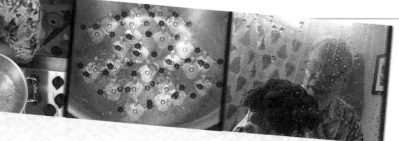

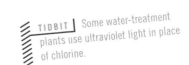

TIDBIT | There are more than 55,000 community water systems in the United States.

TIDBIT | Some water-treatment plants use ultraviolet light in place of chlorine.

LOCATION
LOCATION
LOCATION

What can I say about this episode? No food stuff here, really, no applications or useful techniques. Just a lot of meta stuff, almost all of which was completely made up. Fabricated, faked.

But I promised my publisher that there would be a chapter here for each show, and I'm not about to let that poor woman down. So, sit back and enjoy a mini-gallery of never-before-published, behind-the-scenes images, including a snazzy 360-degree panorama of the set, all smartly annotated, of course.

The set from outside the porch area.

Outside the "house." See the trees "shower curtain"?

The porch. We made the wooden fish for the tuna episode.

OPEN THE POD BAY DOOR, HAL!

The first oven-cam shot required a freestanding oven.

Inserting the host into a cabinet for the "swingdown" sequence of "Raising the Steaks."

Because we can't show any real packaging or product logos, we make up our own. This baking powder is named for our soundman's daughter.

STAY-FRESH CONTAINER
New!!
DEVIN'S
BAKING POWDER
Double Acting
Aluminum Free!
NET WT. 12 OZ (340 GRAMS)

Here is a 360-degree view of the set, which is a 90 percent replica of the real kitchen where we used to shoot. Most of the cabinets don't open—drawers either, now that I think about it.

Cabinet cam— my view.

People always ask about the chicken. She came from a store in Chapel Hill, North Carolina. She's papier-mâché, has a P.M. parachute connected to her back, and is getting pretty beat up.

The bar is backless. Beyond it you can see a prep fridge with a drawing of our culinary lead's dog. The T. rex skeleton (with custom breastbone) is from season one.

What I see.

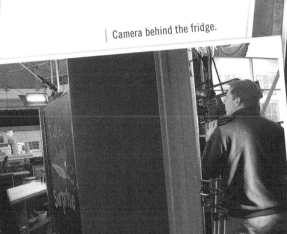

Camera behind the fridge.

Paul draws all the fridge art.

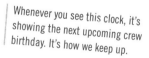

Whenever you see this clock, it's showing the next upcoming crew birthday. It's how we keep up.

Ah, the bongos. Most tool holders flare out at the top, which lets things flop and fall. This is way better.

The "grid" above the set holds the lights and allows us to "fly" stuff and people into the set.

Peaches have always been one of my favorite fruits. When I was a kid, I used to dream about being James in *James and the Giant Peach*, only in my version of the story, inside the peach pit we had a complete galley at our disposal.

KNOWLEDGE CONCENTRATE

▷ **Despite the fact that peaches didn't really take root in the United States until the abolition of slavery made growing cotton a bit of a difficult proposition, now the United States grows a quarter of the world's peach crop, some 3 billion pounds a year. Not bad, when you consider that they're not even from this side of the planet. Peaches are in fact native to China, where they've been cultivated since at least 2000 B.C. Those early peaches were small, hard, and very pitty, but that didn't stop the Chinese from treasuring them, not only as cuisine but as Taoist symbols of longevity.**

From China the peach migrated west to Persia, which is probably why the peach's scientific name is *Persicum mala*, "Persian apple." From there it was just a quick hop to Greece, and then Rome, where the peach was considered a high delicacy, often going for four or even five bucks a pop (that's in today's dollars). Like a great flock of birds, the Romans scattered their pits across Europe, so that by the sixteenth century English, French, and Spanish explorers could sail the peach westward, toward the dark, rich, fertile earth of the American South. By the time the Civil War broke out, states such as Georgia and South Carolina were well-established peach growers. (Several peach orchards served as backdrops for some very bloody battles, including Shiloh and Gettysburg.)

TIDBIT | California, South Carolina, and Georgia are the three largest peach-producing states.

TIDBIT | Production of peaches is second only to apples in the United States.

It's hard to classify a fruit that's as genetically diverse as peaches, but essentially they all fall into two basic categories.

The flesh of CLINGSTONE peaches clings to the pit, or stone, like bad hair on Donald Trump. Tasty though they are, most clingstones end up being frozen, canned, pureed, or otherwise mangled for commercial uses, which is okay come winter, when I reach for bagged frozen peaches for fruit smoothies.

FREESTONE peaches gladly relinquish their stones and so are considered the best out-of-hand peaches, despite the fact that they're often on the dry side and rather lacking in flavor (James certainly did not ride on a freestone).

Peaches can also be classified by color. For instance, Muir, Lovell, and the original Georgia peach, Elberta, all have yellow flesh, a trait developed in the United States in the nineteenth century. The color comes from an abundance of carotenoid pigments, including beta-carotene, which we all like.

White peaches have a lower acid content, which may make them taste a little less peachy but also renders them insanely sweet. Some common white varieties include Mountain Rose, Alexander, Old Mixon, and Summer Snow.

Most peaches are at their peak between June and September, but once they are plucked the sugar content locks and the clock begins to tick. Even with modern shipping techniques, ripe peaches will not last more than ten days to two weeks post-harvest, which explains why it's best to pick your peaches as close to the tree as possible.

Take a look at a truly ripe peach.

Notice that the shoulders are round and full, evidence of sufficient time on the tree. The background color is yellow-orange, no green. This specimen displays considerable blush, which has nothing to do with ripeness. It's just proof that the fruit has spent a good bit of time in direct sunlight, except, of course, here at the top, where it was shaded by the stem. The suture is pronounced, and the cheeks are plump and barely yielding. Why, it's almost too much for a good Southern boy to bear.

Less-than-ripe specimens can be stashed in a paper bag at room temperature for a few days to soften. Notice I did not say "ripen." That is because "ripen" suggests an increase in sugar development, and that is impossible once fruit departs tree. Time, however, can concentrate flavor components and allow the flesh to soften, becoming more juicy.

Aside from the usual fiber and vitamins and whatnot, peaches (nectarines) contain phenols, powerful antioxidants that help to block a most unpleasant process called photoaging, wherein the sun's rays mobilize free radicals, thus aging your skin well before its time.

TIDBIT | Dried peaches have up to three times as much vitamin A as fresh peaches.

PUTTING THE FREEZE ON PEACHES

When the days grow short and cold, home-preserved peaches sure can crack old Jack Frost's steely grasp. The problem is, the cooking required for the process saps peaches of their fresh flavor and ruins their meaty texture. But this summer goodness can easily be preserved by proper freezing. If you toss your chunks in sugar, which likes to hug water on a molecular level, moisture will be pulled out to form a syrup. When the syrup freezes, the sucrose will hold on to some of the water, preventing the ice crystals from getting so big that they trash all the cells. I'd say ¾ cup sugar would be perfect for 1½ pounds peaches.

Neither sucrose nor freezing will prevent your peaches from browning, which can only be counteracted by an antioxidant such as vitamin C. Crush a 500-milligram tablet, dissolve in 3 tablespoons water, and mix into the peaches before adding the sugar. Rest at room temp for 15 minutes, so that a thick syrup forms. Transfer to zip-top freezer bags and freeze for up to 6 months. If you bake with them, hold back about a quarter of the total sugar in whatever application you're using.

I have always felt the combining of cake and fruit to be powerful magic, especially when the elements in question are kept subtly segregated. A good example of this approach is the single-serving peach upside-down cake, which just might be my favorite breakfast food of all time.

// **SOFTWARE** ///

3	tablespoons	unsalted butter	
¼	cup	light brown sugar	
2	medium	peaches	peeled
1	ounce	crystallized ginger	chopped
2½	ounces	all-purpose flour	
1	teaspoon	baking powder	
⅛	teaspoon	baking soda	
⅛	teaspoon	kosher salt	
⅓	cup	sugar	
½	cup	buttermilk	at room temperature
½	teaspoon	vanilla extract	
		whipped cream or vanilla ice cream	optional

// **PROCEDURE** ///

1. Heat the oven to 350°F.

2. Divide 2 tablespoons of the butter among **4 (6-ounce) ramekins**. Melt the remaining 1 tablespoon butter and set aside. Evenly divide the brown sugar among the ramekins, sprinkling it into the bottoms of the dishes. Cut each peach into 12 to 14 pieces. Lay the peaches on top of the sugar, evenly dividing them among the dishes, and sprinkle with the ginger. Set aside.

3. **Whisk** together the flour, baking powder, baking soda, and salt in a **medium bowl**. In a **separate bowl**, whisk together the sugar, buttermilk, vanilla, and melted butter. Add the wet mixture to the dry mixture and stir until just combined. Pour the batter over the peaches, dividing the mixture evenly among the dishes. Bake on the middle rack of the oven for 20 to 25 minutes, until the cake reaches an internal temperature of 190°F.

4. Remove from the oven to a **cooling rack** and let cool for 5 minutes. Run a knife around the edge of each dish and turn it upside down onto a **serving plate**. Serve immediately with whipped cream or ice cream, if desired.

At the turn of the last century, Dame Nellie Melba was the most famous opera soprano in the world—and back then, opera famous was seriously famous. Nellie was known for three things: her angelic voice, her attention-grabbing persona, and her obsessive adoration of peaches. To honor Nellie's 1893 performances in Paris, chef Georges-Auguste Escoffier, of the Savoy Hotel, no less, designed a dessert that combined ice cream, raspberry sauce, and poached peaches that would eventually become known as Peach Melba. We change things up a bit by taking the cooking al fresco.

// SOFTWARE ///

¾	cup plus 1 tablespoon	sugar	
¾	cup	H_2O	
2	tablespoons	lemon juice	freshly squeezed
1		vanilla bean	split and scraped
4	medium	peaches	peeled, pitted, and halved
8	ounces	frozen raspberries	thawed
4	scoops	vanilla ice cream	

// PROCEDURE ///

1. Heat a **grill** to medium-high heat.

2. Place the ¾ cup sugar, the water, 1 tablespoon of the lemon juice, and the seeds from the vanilla bean in a **small saucepan** and set over high heat. Bring the mixture to a boil and boil for 1 to 2 minutes. Remove from the heat. Add the peaches, spooning the sauce over them. Set aside.

3. Combine the raspberries, the remaining 1 tablespoon lemon juice, and the tablespoon of sugar in a **food processor** and puree. Pass the mixture through a **fine-mesh strainer** into a **small bowl**. Cover and refrigerate.

4. When the grill is hot, place the peaches over direct heat and grill on each side for 3 to 4 minutes, until tender. Return the peaches to the pan with the syrup and cover with **aluminum foil** for 5 minutes.

5. To serve, put the ice cream in **4 serving bowls** and top each bowl with 2 peach halves. Drizzle each bowl with the raspberry sauce and serve immediately.

At the top of the show, AB is considering taking on one of Sid the food agent's new clients.

> AB: You know, Sid, I'm impressed that you would even take on a client like okra. It's an art-house choice. He's the Steve Buscemi of the vegetable world.
>
> SM: Are you kidding? He's my most important client.
>
> AB: Yeah, I'll bet he's also your only client.
>
> SM: Yes, but we have a bit of an image problem. It's the, er...
>
> AB: Slime.
>
> SM: Exactamundo! I begged him to get some rehab.
>
> AB: Are you kidding? It's not his fault. It's bad cooking.

Okra, the seed pod of *Abelmoschus esculentus*, is a member of the Malvaceae family, which includes the marsh mallow, whose gooey interior was once the basis for the eponymous treat, the marshmallow. When the weather turns hot in the summer, okra plants grow very quickly indeed, moving from flower to full-grown pod in only about a week. Since mature pods are tough and fibrous, the best specimens are harvested at between two and three inches in length. When buying okra, look for bright, firm pods with uniform color. Green is certainly the norm, but red, white, and purple varieties are also available. But don't be spooked: They all taste the same.

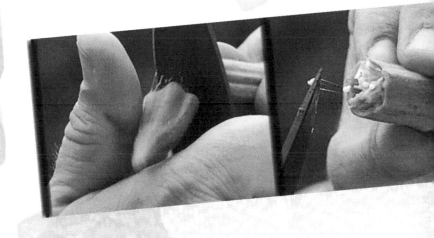

Inside the okra pod is a substance called mucilage, an apt word for a rather gooey material composed of carbohydrate molecules tangled up with proteins. The mucilage's job is to help retain water and store energy. It's the same stuff that makes cacti such successful desert dwellers. Culinarily speaking, it's interesting stuff, because when it comes into contact with hot liquid the starch granules absorb water, swell, and ultimately burst, releasing amylose and amylopectin, starches that grab the surrounding water and thicken it. And so okra can serve as both a vegetable and an effective thickening agent, which is why gumbo just wouldn't be gumbo without okra.[1]

TIDBIT | Each September, Checotah, Oklahoma, hosts Okrafest, a celebration of all things . . . you know.

To store okra, keep it cool and keep it as dry as possible, because surface moisture greatly hastens decomposition, and avoid plastic bags whenever possible. Regardless of the care you take, okra goes south quickly, so use it within a couple days of purchase.

[1] Unless, of course, the cook chose to use powdered sassafras leaf, or "gumbo file," as the thickener, which would never be used in conjunction with okra—not around here, anyway.

As if being delicious wasn't enough, okra is a mighty fine source of dietary fiber, and it packs a significant hit of vitamin A and vitamin C, as well as folate, which is especially important in the development of the fetus during pregnancy.

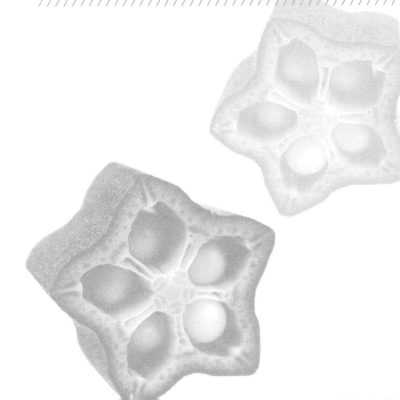

OKRAPHOBIA

PICKLED OKRA

4 PINTS

Due to its firmness and high fiber content, okra takes especially well to pickling.

// SOFTWARE //

2	pounds	young, small okra	
4	small	dried chiles	split in half
2	teaspoons	mustard seeds	
12	sprigs	fresh dill	
4	cloves	garlic	
1	teaspoon	black peppercorns	
¼	cup	kosher salt	
2	cups	rice vinegar	
2	cups	filtered H$_2$O	

// PROCEDURE //

1. Thoroughly wash **4 pint-size canning jars**, **rings**, **lids**, **tongs**, **ladle**, and **funnel** with hot, soapy water. Rinse.

2. Pile everything except the lids in a **large pot**. Cover with hot water by at least 1 inch and bring to a boil. Maintain a boil for 10 full minutes to sterilize. Kill the heat, wait 5 minutes, then add the lids. Leave everything in place until you're ready to can.

3. Wash the okra and trim the stem to ½ inch. Place one chile, ½ teaspoon mustard seeds, 3 sprigs of dill, 1 clove garlic, and ¼ teaspoon peppercorns in the bottom of each jar. Divide the okra evenly among the 4 jars, standing them up vertically, alternating stems up and down.

4. Bring the salt, vinegar, and water to a boil in a **medium saucepan** over medium heat. Pour the boiling mixture over the okra in the jars, leaving space between the top of the liquid and the lid. Seal the lids. Set in a cool, dry place for 2 weeks.

```
SM: (tastes a pickled okra)
Umm. Fresh, crisp, just a
little spicy. A little naughty,
a little nice. And no slime!

AB: No slime.

SM: Ohh, we're going to hit the
'cukes on the condiment aisle.
Think of the picnic possibili-
ties. Ohhh, and the fast food!
Got to get on the horn!
```

```
AB: (to the okra) You know,
if Sid has his way, you're
never going to be able to
just, you know, be yourself.
You're never going to be able
to show what's inside. I tell
you what, don't worry. I'm
going to make sure that people
know the real you, okay?

(Okra gives AB a hug)
```

WET FRIED OKRA

4 SIDE SERVINGS

What okraphobes may not know is that the pods' inner gooiness can be put to excellent use.

// **SOFTWARE** //

1	pound	okra	stems removed
½	cup	cornmeal	
		vegetable oil	for frying
	to taste	kosher salt	

// **PROCEDURE** //

1. Cut the okra into ¼-inch pieces and put them in a **colander**. Rinse under cold water and drain only slightly.

2. Put the cornmeal in a **1-gallon zip-top bag**. Add the okra and shake to coat thoroughly.

3. Add enough oil to a **cast-iron or stainless-steel skillet** to completely cover the bottom of the pan. Place over medium heat and heat until the oil reaches 370°F. Add the okra all at once and fry, without disturbing, until golden brown on one side, 6 to 7 minutes. Turn the okra with a **spatula** and do not disturb until the majority of the other side is golden brown as well, 3 to 4 minutes. Stir occasionally until all of the okra is golden on all sides, another 3 to 4 minutes. Remove the okra from the pan with a **slotted spoon or spatula** to a **cooling rack** set over a **half sheet pan** lined with **newspaper**. Cool for 1 to 2 minutes, season with salt, and serve.

SM: Ewww, that still looks slimy to me. You said no slime!

AB: No, I said that we would make the...

SM: ...slime...

AB: ...work for us.

SM: Uh huh.

AB: Alright, for the okraphobes out there, I can make a couple of small changes that will produce a...well...we'll say "fried okra light" that'll still taste great.

DRY FRIED OKRA

4 SIDE SERVINGS

A small variation in technique from the previous page results in a whole new dish.

// **SOFTWARE** //

1	pound	okra	stems removed
½	cup	cornmeal	
		vegetable oil	for frying
	to taste	kosher salt	

// **PROCEDURE** //

1. Rinse the whole okra pods under cold water, drain, pat dry, trim, and cut into ¼-inch pieces. Set aside.

2. Put the cornmeal in a **1-gallon zip-top bag**. Add the okra and shake to coat thoroughly. Return the okra to a **dry colander** and shake off excess cornmeal.

3. Add enough oil to a **12-inch stainless-steel sauté pan** to completely cover the bottom of the pan. Place over medium-high heat and bring the oil to 370°F. Add the okra and fry until golden brown on one side, 5 to 6 minutes. Stirring occasionally, continue cooking until the okra is golden brown on all sides, 5 to 6 minutes longer. Remove the okra from the pan with a **slotted spoon or spatula** to a **cooling rack** set over a **half sheet pan** lined with **newspaper**. Cool for 2 minutes, season to taste with salt, and serve.

OKRA AND TOMATOES

4 TO 6 SERVINGS

Most culinary historians believe that okra's birthplace was at the Abyssinian center, a region that includes parts of Ethiopia, Eritrea, and the Sudan. From there, it migrated westward across Africa and then, finally, and against its will, across the Atlantic to the American South. With this in mind, I offer a very African application.

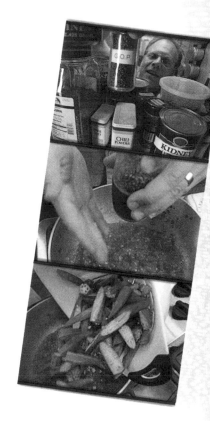

// SOFTWARE //

1	pound	okra	rinsed and trimmed
3	tablespoons	olive oil	
1½	cups	red onion	finely chopped
1½	teaspoons	kosher salt	
1	tablespoon	garlic	minced
2	cups	tomatoes	peeled and chopped
1	tablespoon	fresh ginger	minced
1	teaspoon	grains of paradise[2] or black pepper	freshly ground
½	teaspoon	cardamom	freshly ground

// PROCEDURE //

1. Cut each okra pod in half lengthwise and set aside. If there are any pods longer than 4 inches, cut them in half crosswise and then lengthwise.

2. Heat the oil in a **4-quart saucepan** over medium heat until shimmering. Add the onions along with the salt and cook until they begin to turn golden, about 4 minutes. Add the garlic and cook for 1 minute longer. Add the tomatoes and bring the mixture to a boil. Decrease the heat to low and add the ginger, pepper, cardamom, and okra. Stir to combine. Cook, uncovered, for 20 minutes. Remove from the heat, taste, and adjust the seasoning as desired. Serve immediately.

[2] For more on grains of paradise, a.k.a. *Aframomum melegueta* or Guinea peppers, see the sidebar on page 417.

SM: (tasting the okra) Mmmm. Slimy, oh, but good. So, okra is a foreign food.

AB: That's right, Sid. In fact, the word *okra* comes from ancient Ghana.

SM: Eh?

AB: In Africa.

SM: Oh, ohhh. Fantastic. My boy is multicultural.

AB: Yep.

SM: He is international.

AB: International.

SM: We can sell that. Too bad about the slime, though.

AB: Oh, bother.

SQUID PRO QUO II

Squid have always been

favorites in the international market, but until recently I would bet that most Americans would side with the captain in this episode. Luckily, back in the 1990s calamari crashed our shores, converting many a squid-phobe into a fan.

Open to the deck of a ship. A low boat horn sounds.

AB: Thanks for having me aboard, Captain.

BOAT CAPTAIN: Whatever. Your check cleared. That's all that matters.

AB: Ahh, good, good, good. So, this is a real, live squid ship.

BC: Aye, but this ain't no pleasure cruise, Mr. Brown. Why are you so eager to ship out on a hard-working research vessel?

AB: Well, Captain, the truth is I feel like I owe a debt to squid. See, I work on this cooking show, and a long, long time ago, we did an episode about squid.

BC: Where I'm from, they call that "bait."

AB: Well, everything's bait to something. Anyway, I got so caught up in doing these cutesy little skits, I hardly did any cooking. I didn't even make the world's most popular restaurant appetizer.

BC: Ahhh, spicy wings. I love 'em!

AB: Actually I was thinking calamari.

BC: Isn't that a Hindu god?

AB: No, I don't—actually, now that you mention it...Look, what's important is that squid is probably the most culinarily versatile critter on the entire planet, and I mean to do it justice.

BC: Whatever. Be dark soon. Best get to your quarters, Mr. Brown, and start cooking up some...

 TIDBIT The word *calamari* comes from the Latin word *calamus*, or "reed pen."

TIDBIT Some squid can swim at over 23 miles per hour.

Let's meet some squid.

Behold, *Loligo opalescens*, a.k.a. Pacific market squid. This is the squid you will most often find in western states.

The common eastern varieties, the Atlantic long-finned and short-finned, which pretty much taste exactly the same (although I have been told that the short-finned are considered by some to be a little more on the chewy side).

Regardless of variety, I like to buy my squid whole, but only if I know that I'm going to cook them within hours. Even on ice or in a cold refrigerator, high-protein squid decompose with amazing speed and dexterity. When choosing from fresh or thawed product, use your nose. If they smell stinky, pass. The skin should be slightly slimy, not dry, and the color ought to be dark and mottled, never pink. Cleaned, cut frozen squid are the standard of the restaurant industry in the United States, and that's okay by me, because squid freezes fabulously. With squid in the freezer, calamari is never more than a few minutes away.

A quick lesson in anatomy

Let us examine today's dinner. Here we have the tube, the fins, and the head in the middle. Kind of odd, but that's how it is. There are the two eyes, and then, of course, the tentacles. Our first cut is going to be to separate the tentacles from the head. So just kind of feel around. There will be a little lump where the beak is; cut there. If you just squeeze the tentacles, the beak will pop out. Believe it or not, this is the only part of the squid that is not digestible. (The first evidence that scientists had of giant squids were the beaks the size of human heads found inside the stomachs of sperm whales.)

Next, move your fingers up into the tube, get hold of the head, and gently pull straight out. There's one more part to remove from inside: Feel around for something kind of plastic-y. Pull it out. That's the quill, the closest thing a squid has to a bone. To remove the skin, I get a little incision going and then just pull it off. And there you have it. (Some people like to pull off the fins; I usually leave them on.) To prep for frying, simply cut the tube into narrow rings with a sharp knife.

Tentacle

Fin

Tube
(posterior
surface)

Collar

Funnel

Eye

Head

Arm

WET FRIED CALAMARI

4 APPETIZER SERVINGS

Calamari is the plural of *calamaro*, which is Italian for "squid." Some folks argue that calamari are actually a specific type of squid, but around most of the Mediterranean for centuries and America for a few decades, *calamari* has come to mean a specific preparation of squid in which small pieces (tentacles and rings) are quickly fried and served with dipping sauce.[1] Calamari-acs generally recognize two specific styles of the dish, wet and dry. I happen to like them both.

// SOFTWARE ///

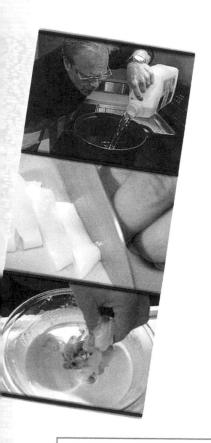

2	quarts	peanut oil	
1	pound	squid	tubes and tentacles
1	large	egg	
1	cup	ice H_2O	
1	cup	all-purpose flour	
	to taste	kosher salt	
	to taste	black pepper	freshly ground

// PROCEDURE //

1. Heat the oil in a **4- to 5-quart Dutch oven** over medium-high heat until it reaches 375°F.

2. Rinse the squid thoroughly and pat dry. Cut the tentacles in half lengthwise and the tubes into ½-inch rings. Set aside.

3. Put the egg, water, and flour in a **bowl** and **whisk** thoroughly to combine. In small handfuls, dip the squid in the batter and shake off the excess. Gently lower the squid into the hot oil. Cook for 1 minute. The squid will not be browned, but lightly golden in color. Remove the squid and transfer to a **cooling rack** turned upside down and set over a **half sheet pan** lined with **newspaper**. Season with salt and pepper as desired. Repeat until all of the squid is cooked. Make sure to check the temperature of the oil before each batch to ensure it is 375°F. Serve immediately.

[1] Technically speaking, the dish is "fried calamari," not just "calamari," but I think we all know what we're talking about here.

DRY FRIED CALAMARI

For the squid purists out there, a dredge-only version with a cornmeal crunch.

// SOFTWARE ///

2	quarts	peanut oil	
1	pound	squid	tubes and tentacles
½	cup	all-purpose flour	
½	cup	cornmeal	
	to taste	kosher salt	
	to taste	black pepper	freshly ground

// PROCEDURE ///

1. Heat the oil in a **4- to 5-quart Dutch oven** over medium-high heat until it reaches 375°F.

2. Rinse the squid thoroughly and pat dry. Cut the tentacles in half lengthwise and the tubes into ½-inch rings. Set aside.

3. Combine the flour and the cornmeal in a **medium bowl**. In small handfuls, dredge the squid in the flour and cornmeal mixture and shake off the excess. Gently lower the squid into the hot oil. Cook for 1 minute. The squid will not be browned, but lightly golden in color. Remove the squid and transfer to a **cooling rack** turned upside down and set over a **half sheet pan** lined with **newspaper**. Season with salt and pepper as desired. Repeat until all of the squid is cooked. Make sure to check the temperature of the oil before each batch to ensure it is 375 °F. Serve immediately.

TRIVIA Like the scallop show before it, this episode took place almost completely below decks on a boat. But unlike the scallop show, which was filmed completely on location, we decided to build this boat from scratch on a gimble, a big seesaw, so that it could rock back and forth, especially during the giant squid attack. Fans will no doubt note that this is the second time I've been accosted by a cephalopodic leviathan. What can I say . . . I really liked *20,000 Leagues Under the Sea*.

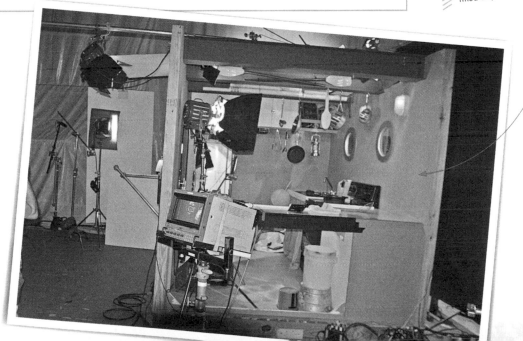

SQUID-STUFFED SQUID

4 SERVINGS

My dislike, disregard, and disgruntlement regarding the stuffing of poultry is well documented. I feel that in 99 percent of all poultry cases the stuffed are made to suffer to the betterment of the stuffing. This, however, is not the case with squid, which are perfect for stuffing because the meat is thin and elastic and, well, something needs to go in there. The way I see it, it might as well be more squid.

// SOFTWARE ///

1	tablespoon	olive oil	
¼	cup	onion	finely chopped
½	teaspoon	kosher salt	
1	clove	garlic	minced
8 to 10		whole squid	
2	ounces	raw shrimp	
¼	cup	breadcrumbs	
14	ounces	tomato sauce	
2	teaspoons	lemon zest	grated
2	teaspoons	fresh ginger	grated
¼	teaspoon	black pepper	freshly ground

PROCEDURE ///

1. Heat the oven to 375°F.

2. Heat the oil in a **medium sauté pan** over medium heat until shimmering. Add the onion and salt and sweat until the onion is translucent, 1 to 2 minutes; do not brown. Add the garlic and continue to cook for 1 minute. Transfer the mixture to a **medium bowl** and set aside to cool.

3. Rinse the squid thoroughly. Remove and discard the heads. Turn the tubes inside out (since the outside skin tends to curl outward, it'll hold the stuffing better inside out), put in a **bowl**, and set in the refrigerator until ready to use.

4. Put the tentacles and shrimp in a **food processor** and pulse 6 to 8 times, until there are no large pieces visible; do not process until smooth. Transfer to the bowl with the onion and garlic. Add the breadcrumbs, two tablespoons of the tomato sauce, the lemon zest, ginger, and pepper. Stir to combine well.

5. Spoon the mixture into a **1-gallon zip-top bag** and snip off one corner. Pipe the stuffing into the tubes, dividing the mixture evenly among them; do not overstuff.

6. Place the stuffed tubes in an **8-by-11-inch glass baking dish** and cover with the remaining tomato sauce. Cover tightly with **aluminum foil** and bake for 30 minutes. Serve immediately.

SEASIDE SQUID SALAD

4 SERVINGS

Despite my deep abiding love of fried calamari, this steamed application is actually my favorite squid dish because it's unexpected, fast, and easy. I've served it as a salad course, a light dinner, and lunch. Once cooked, mixed, and cooled, it will keep for several days in the refrigerator.

// SOFTWARE ///

1½	pounds	squid	tubes and tentacles
2	tablespoons	lemon juice	freshly squeezed
2	tablespoons	extra virgin olive oil	
¾	teaspoon	kosher salt	
¼	teaspoon	black pepper	freshly ground
¼	teaspoon	ground cumin	
⅛	teaspoon	ground cayenne	
¾	cup	tomato	seeded and finely chopped
¼	cup	red onion	finely chopped
2	tablespoons	capers	drained
¼	cup	fresh cilantro	chopped

// PROCEDURE ///

1. Thoroughly rinse the squid under cold water and pat dry. Cut the tentacles in half lengthwise. Cut the bodies in half lengthwise and then into ½-inch-thick pieces. Set aside.

2. Bring ½ inch of **water** to a boil in a **6-quart saucepan** over high heat. Decrease the heat in order to maintain a simmer. Put the squid in a **steamer basket** and gently set it over the simmering water. Cover and steam for 2 to 4 minutes. Remove the steamer basket from the pot and plunge the squid into **ice water** to stop the cooking. Remove from the water and drain thoroughly. Set aside.

3. **Whisk** together the lemon juice, oil, salt, black pepper, cumin, and cayenne in a **large bowl**. Add the squid, tomato, onion, capers, and cilantro and toss until combined. Cover and refrigerate for 1 hour before serving.

POP ART

EPISODE 161 | SEASON 10 | GOOD EATS

John Wayne ate popcorn. In fact, if there's a snack food any more American, I can't think of it. After all, corn, or maize, as the rest of the world calls it, is the most important New World food of all time, and popcorn is certainly the most American form of the grain. It tastes great, it's good for you, and it goes off like fireworks when you cook it. But like so many crucial elements of Americana, we've allowed popcorn to fall from grace. Today's poppers are grown for yield rather than flavor, so we make up for it by dumping on noxious flavorants and enough salt to make a mini Lot's wife. Heck, we don't even pop it ourselves anymore unless it's to toss an envelope with a picture of a shriveled old man in a bow tie on it in the nuker. Well, I say it's time for popcorn lovers to take back the snack and return it to its rightful place.

TRIVIA | I worked through a couple years of college as a professional popcorn popper. I produced it by the bushel and used so much noxious flavoring that my fingernails were stained yellow for months afterward. I was fired from the job for writing morbid little poems on the sides of the bags. Strange days.

POPCORN AND MOVIES

In the old days, theater owners used to rent space outside their places to local popcorn vendors, who would move their carts around the city. It wasn't until the Depression, when a five-cent bag of popcorn seemed like an affordable luxury, that movie theater owners got wise and started popping their own. Today, a vast majority of a theater's profits comes from popcorn.

TIDBIT | At movie theaters in South America, people eat roasted ants instead of popcorn.

(400)

The next time you set out to purchase popcorn, consider the criteria of the big popcorn growers. Yield per acre, size of popped kernel, and number of unpopped kernels in a batch. What about flavor and texture? Well, believe it or not, they don't really enter the equation, which, if you ask me, is a darn good reason to seek out the old varieties, which come in two basic shapes, pearl (smooth and round) and rice (tear-shaped and kind of pointy).

Some of my favorites include Pink Diamond, Purple Amethyst, Baby Black Pearl, Southwest Gold, Baby Blue Sapphire, Baby Pearl, Red Ruby, Baby Yellow Topaz, Blue Sapphire, and Petit Princess Amber, each of which possesses a distinct flavor, texture, and size when popped. But don't be deceived by the color. Except for the white varieties, which will always pop up white, they're all yellow deep down where it counts.

Ever wonder why popcorn explodes? Well, let's ponder some of the parts involved.

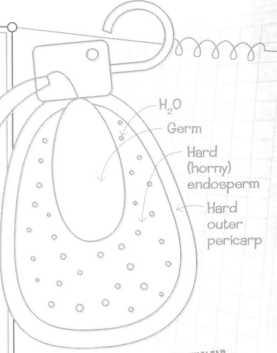

H₂O

Germ

Hard (horny) endosperm

Hard outer pericarp

First, there's the pericarp. All grains have this hard outer shell, but in the case of popcorn it is unusually hard. And it's unique in that it can absorb and radiate high amounts of heat to the interior of the kernel without actually burning.

All grains also have an interior fuel tank, or endosperm, composed of two different types of starch: hard and soft. Popcorn, however, possesses an unusually high percentage of the hard type of starch.

The last ingredient you need is water—say, between 13 and 15 percent—to act as an explosive agent.

When heat is applied, the water inside turns into steam, which in turn creates a tremendous amount of pressure inside the kernel. Eventually, the steam combines with the starch to create something akin to lava. When the pressure finally reaches a critical point . . . KABLAM!

The pericarp ruptures, spewing hot liquid starch in every direction. As the pressure is released, the corn-lava cools and sets into these curious shapes, no two of which are alike (take that, snowflakes!).

LIKE ANY EXPLOSIVE (EXCEPT FOR NUCLEAR WEAPONS, OF COURSE), POPCORN IS ALL ABOUT THE PRESSURE OF RAPIDLY EXPANDING GASSES RUPTURING A RIGID, FRAGMENTING ENCLOSURE.

PRIMITIVE POP

The caverns of Bat Cave, in Catron County, New Mexico, once housed an ancient agrarian society that was heavily dependent upon maize for nutrition. Because of the cool, dry microclimate inside the caverns, you can still find kernels of ancient popcorn lying around. When soaked for a while in water, they still pop! The residents of Bat Cave as well as other ancient Americans popped popcorn not in hot oil but in hot sand. When the corn popped it rose to the top, where it could be picked out, blown clean, and consumed.

TIDBIT | Popcorn didn't become popular in the eastern United States until nineteenth-century whalers brought it back from Chile.

TIDBIT | Why does popcorn taste so darn good? That would be pyrazines, phenols, pyrroles, carbanols, and furans.

PERT-NEAR PERFECT POPCORN

3½ TO 4 QUARTS

// SOFTWARE //

3	tablespoons	peanut oil	
3	ounces	popcorn kernels	
½	teaspoon	popcorn salt[1]	
3	tablespoons	unsalted butter	

// PROCEDURE ///

1. Put the oil, popcorn, and salt in a **6-quart metal mixing bowl**. Cover with **heavy-duty aluminum foil** and poke 10 slits in the top with a **knife**.

2. Place the bowl over medium heat and shake constantly using **tongs** to hold the bowl. Continue shaking until the popcorn finishes popping, about 3 minutes.

3. Remove the bowl from the heat and carefully remove the foil. Stir in any salt that is on the side of the bowl.

4. Melt the butter in a microwave oven. Slowly drizzle it over the popcorn while spinning the bowl. Serve immediately.

TIP | For the more gourmet-minded of you out there, try stirring in 1 teaspoon each of finely chopped fresh thyme and fresh rosemary to the popcorn before adding the butter. (I've actually served this as an appetizer at a dinner party.)

[1] Popcorn salt is ground very fine so that it will stick handily to the nooks and crannies of the popped kernels. If you buy it you're crazy. One cup of kosher salt goes into a food processor. And I think about 10 three-second pulses should perfectly smash this, or rather pulverize it, to the correct consistency.

A HEALTHIER SNACK

Popcorn is high in fiber, which we all know is a good thing. Dentists dig it because it is a sugarless snack. And although pediatricians warn against serving popcorn to toddlers because of potential choking hazards, they do like home-popped corn for older kids because it doesn't contain additives, dyes, preservatives, or other, you know, *stuff*. Microwaved and butter-flavored movie popcorn could possibly be another story, so pop your own. It's good, it's good for you, and it's more fun than a barrel full of M.D.s.

SLACKER JACKS

4 TO 6 SERVINGS

Due to its size, hand-friendly shape, and multiple crags, popcorn has long been used as a canvas onto which confectioners have applied a wide range of goodness. Kettle corns are probably the best known and are typified by a burnt sugar coating, sometimes with spices, sometimes with nuts. One particular version became immortal when it was mentioned in a song called "Take Me Out to the Ballgame." This one's just as good—but you'll have to supply the prize.

// SOFTWARE //

3	ounces	popped popcorn	(left)
½	cup	unsalted butter	
16	ounces	dark brown sugar	
¼	cup	dark corn syrup	
½	teaspoon	vanilla extract	
1	cup	salted peanuts	

// PROCEDURE //

1. Heat the oven to 250°F.

2. Spray a **half sheet pan** with **nonstick spray** and line it with **parchment paper**. Spray the parchment paper with nonstick spray as well and set aside.

3. Set the popcorn aside in a **large bowl**.

4. Melt the butter in a **medium saucepan** over medium heat. Add the brown sugar, corn syrup, and vanilla and stir to combine. Heat the mixture until it reaches 250°F, about 10 minutes.

5. Quickly add the peanuts to the syrup, pour it over the popcorn, and stir to combine. You will need to work quickly, because the syrup hardens rapidly. Spread the mixture onto the prepared sheet pan and bake for 1 hour. Cool completely.

6. Break into pieces and serve immediately or store in an airtight container for 2 to 3 days.

THE EVOLUTION OF "POPPERS"

Popcorn popping was popularized after the Civil War, when popcorn poppers were developed and marketed. (If that's not American marketing, I don't know what is.) Back then, poppers were hearth-based appliances; that is, they were meant to be used over the fire. Early models were little wire mesh boxes with wooden handles, and they typically burned more corn than they popped. The next development was something I like to call "the Bed-Warmer Popper," which featured a solid bottom that facilitated the addition of cooking fat. Today there are oil poppers, hot-air poppers, and all manner of unitaskers meant to do nothing more than pop corn, and what's ironic is that none of them does as good a job as a metal mixing bowl and some heavy-duty foil.

MAJOR PEPPER

EPISODE 162 | SEASON 10 | GOOD EATS

PEPPER PRIMES AGE OF DISCOVERY

Sick and tired of buying over-priced peppercorns from the Venetian cartel, the Portuguese crown in 1494 sent Vasco da Gama to find a sea route to India. He eventually worked his way around the Cape of Good Hope and into the Indian Ocean, and within a decade the Portuguese were the new kings of spice. Later, the Dutch and the English would overturn that monopoly. By the end of the eighteenth century, most European pepper was run through Salem, Massachusetts, whose speedy clipper ships made thousands of runs to pepper ports along the island of Sumatra, making pepper affordable to all.

Salt and pepper have stood, side by side, on the American table since, well, forever. Like the bride and groom atop a wedding cake, they complete the table's sense of mise en scene. What I want to know is why. How is it the king of spices came to play a pre-ground Tonto to salt's Lone Ranger? I suspect that food processors, during the Industrial Revolution, cashed in on pepper's cache by grinding it up and mixing it up with coal dust and pencil shavings, thus increasing their profits and lowering the flavor expectations of generations of cooks and eaters alike.

Well, I'm here to say, it's got to stop. If you have a pepper shaker on your table, I want you to pick it up. I want you to go over to the window. Open the window and yell, "I'M MAD AS . . . " You know, on second thought, maybe you can make it into a cinnamon shaker for your cappuccino.

True peppercorns are the fruits of a tropical vine, *Piper nigrum*, commonly found climbing up palms, eucalyptus trees, and often even manmade trellises. The fruits themselves are packed into dense little spikes, containing fifty or more berries that start out green before eventually turning yellow, then red as they mature. These berries can render multiple products, depending on how they're processed.

If you pick the pepper prior to maturity, then ferment and dry it, you have the classic BLACK PEPPERCORNS, which are graded geographically. The most famous are Malabar and Tellicherry peppercorns from India.

Harvest the berries when they're completely ripe and remove the skins, and you're left with the lonely heart of the fruit, known as WHITE PEPPERCORNS. Although not as fragrant or as flavorful as their fully dressed cousins, white peppercorns are a color-coordinated complement to light-colored dishes.

GREEN PEPPERCORNS are just like black peppercorns, but they're pickled in a brine before being bottled or dried. The dried versions are nice in and on certain cheeses, but I find that there's nothing the wet ones can do that a caper can't do better.

PINK PEPPERCORNS are not actually peppercorns at all. They're processed from the berries of a South American plant, *Schinus terebinthifolius*. Look pretty, taste mild.

SZECHUAN PEPPERCORNS aren't proper peppers either, but rather the dried berries of the prickly ash, *Zanthoxylum simulans*. They have a peppery citrus aroma, and the taste is rather tangy. But you'll only notice that for a moment, because your mouth will start to tingle and then go kinda numb due to hydroxy-alpha-sanshool, which is an item of considerable interest among anesthesiology researchers.

When the pepper fruit is allowed to ferment and is then dried, the outer skin wrinkles, oxidizes, and turns black. That is a sign that it has captured a wide range of aromatic compounds, called terpines, and they give the spice a kind of a woodsy, citrusy, cologney kind of vibe. If we breach the fruit, by either cracking it or grinding it, we release a volatile oil, called piperine, in the process. The piperine and the various terpines on the surface come together to give pepper its pleasantly pungent flavor.

Piperine is a member of the vanilloid family, but unlike its fiery chile cousin, capsaicin, piperine leaves only a faint aftertaste on the tongue. It does, however, stimulate taste buds, increasing the flow of saliva and gastric juices and thus improving digestion. Fortunately for the cook, the essential oils involved here are not only tasty and aromatic, but soluble in many different substances, which is just another way of saying they're good at flavoring things.

PEPPER VODKA

1 (750 ML) BOTTLE OF VODKA

I think it could be argued that one of the biggest trends in alky-hol in the last few years has been toward flavored spirits, and one of the spirits most often flavored is, of course, vodka (which is really perfect for this kind of treatment, because, let's face it, it doesn't have much flavor of its own). This is a good thing if you like pepper vodka, because black pepper is full of alcohol-soluble flavorants, which means you don't have to go out and buy yourself a bottle of pepper vodka; you can make your own.

// SOFTWARE //

2	tablespoons	whole black peppercorns	slightly cracked
1	750 ml bottle	vodka	

// PROCEDURE //

1. Add the peppercorns to the vodka and set in a cool, dark place for 7 days. Stir or gently shake to combine every few days.

2. Strain through a **fine-mesh strainer** to remove the peppercorns. Place in a **glass container** with a lid and store in a cool dark place. Use for Bloody Marys or for finishing your spaghetti sauce.

ON PEPPER MILLS

Although I suspect that a controlled sonic pulse system is the key to perfect pepper grinding, almost every pepper mill currently on the planet is based upon a design introduced in 1874 by Jean-Pierre and Jean-Fredrique Peugeot, who, at the time, were best known for manufacturing hand saws, of all things. Their design featured a wooden tube that fed the pepper into a rotary mill, composed of a grooved male head and a grooved female ring. Although steel has long been the norm, ceramic mechanisms, which are quieter, and, I think, more precise, are now coming onto the scene. In another new development, some mills are replacing the classic drive shaft with a mill housing that allows the entire container to be turned.

Regardless of the model, there are a few things to keep in mind when mill shopping. One, it has to be easy to load. If the refill slot isn't much bigger than a peppercorn, it's useless. You want a high capacity, because you don't want to be refilling it every week. The grind has to be consistent. If, upon testing, you notice that there are big old chunkies mixed in with, you know, pepper powder, you need to keep looking.

You might also want to look for indexed grind settings for everything from very, very fine to very, very coarse. Oh, and about one-handed electric mills: You know, this is a good concept, but I have never seen it executed properly. Of course, I am working on a little something of my own . . .

BLACK PEPPER MANGO SORBET

1 QUART

A great deal of the pleasure that we extract from pepper is actually sensed by the schnozz. All of that aroma comes from volatile chemicals that are mostly carried by the essential oils of the plant. Now, a great many plants have essential oils, and they can be extracted, either by being distilled or being cold-pressed out of the seed itself. Most of the essential oils out there are used for things like aromatherapy and massage, but a few of them actually do have culinary uses, and black pepper is one of them. The beauty of an essential oil is that you can use it in a dish where you wouldn't really want little bits and pieces of pepper, like, for instance, I don't know, a sorbet.

// SOFTWARE ///

2½ to 3	pounds	ripe mango flesh	about 4 large specimens
¼	cup	lime juice	freshly squeezed
¼	cup	Pepper Vodka	(left)
¼	teaspoon	black pepper essential oil	optional
12	ounces	sugar	

// PROCEDURE ///

1. Process the mango in a **food processor** until smooth. Add the lime juice, vodka, essential oil, and sugar and process for an additional 5 to 10 seconds. Pass the mixture through a **fine-mesh strainer** and place in the refrigerator to chill until the mixture reaches 40°F or below, 2 to 3 hours.

2. Process the sorbet in an **ice cream maker** according to the manufacturer's instructions, 20 to 25 minutes. Place in the freezer for 3 hours, or overnight, before serving.

FOUR-PEPPER DEVILED EGGS

12 DEVILED EGGS

The flavors in pepper come mostly in the form of oils, and oils love getting together with other forms of fat, such as those found in egg yolks. Which, of course, is what you use to make deviled eggs. The term *deviled egg* comes from eighteenth-century England, where the word *deviled* meant anything that was stuffed with a spicy filling.

// SOFTWARE ///

6		hard-cooked eggs	cooled and peeled
1	teaspoon	whole pink peppercorns	divided
½	teaspoon	whole white peppercorns	
½	teaspoon	whole black peppercorns	
½	teaspoon	whole green peppercorns	
½	teaspoon	caper brine	
¼	cup	mayonnaise	
1	teaspoon	Dijon mustard	
½	teaspoon	kosher salt	
	pinch	sugar	

// PROCEDURE //

1. Slice the eggs in half from top to bottom. Scoop the yolks into a **medium bowl** and set the whites aside.

2. Set aside ½ teaspoon of the pink peppercorns and combine all of the remaining peppercorns in a **spice grinder** and process until finely ground. Add the ground peppercorns, caper brine, mayonnaise, mustard, salt, and sugar to the egg yolks and, using a **fork**, stir to thoroughly combine.

3. Put the mixture in a **zip-top bag** and snip off one corner. Pipe the mixture evenly into the egg white halves. Coarsely grind the reserved pink peppercorns and use to garnish the top of each egg. Chill in the refrigerator for at least 1 hour before serving.

FRY TURKEY FRY

There are maybe ten *Good Eats* episodes that I'm actually proud of. This is #1, not because it's a great half hour of entertainment, or even because it produces great food. I'm proud of it because we figured out how to safely fry a turkey. The day that a small group of firemen came up to me and thanked me for making this show was the proudest day of my professional life.

Each year, more and more cooks decide to deep-fry the turkey, and every year, more and more cooks end up in deep, deep trouble. Since hot oil is so efficient at conducting heat, it can produce a tasty bird in a fraction of the time required by any other cooking method, but deep-frying is a potentially dangerous business. Each holiday season, sirens sound and flames, and sometimes poultry, fill the sky. Can we break this cycle of destruction? I think we can. We just have to be willing to get creative with the physical realities of the situation. Sure, it's going to take a little effort, but the results will indeed be good eats.

KNOWLEDGE CONCENTRATE

THE TURKEY DERRICK

▷ Ask any professional firefighter, and he or she will tell you that every Thanksgiving they answer a slew of emergency calls as variations on the scene above play out at hundreds of homes across America.

This happens primarily because:

— Oil pot is too full.

— Oil is too hot.

— Turkey is wet or contains ice.

In the interest of preserving humanity, wooden decks, and Thanksgiving dinner, we offer the Turkey Derrick. ▸

▷ **WARNING: Failure to follow these instructions could result in fire or explosion, which could cause property damage, personal injury, or death—not to mention ruin a perfectly good turkey.**

▶ 1 sturdy, high-quality outdoor propane gas burner unit with accessories: burner base should be stable, four-legged, and welded (not bolted); there should be double rings of gas jets, and an air-flow adjuster

▶ 1 heavy-duty outdoor cooker pot with lifter/spindle insert: 30- to 34-quart capacity, at least 15 inches tall

▶ 1 (8-foot) fiberglass ladder

▶ 15 feet of heavy-duty cotton sash cord (not synthetic rope; it can't take the heat)

▶ 2 (2-inch) pulleys, one with swivel top (I have taken to using heavy-duty screw-closure carabiners, which, while more expensive, are multitaskers)

▶ 1 (3-inch) quick link or carabiner (a real one, not a key chain that looks like one)

▶ 2 (75-pound-test) plastic cable ties (I actually use a 10mm-wide Dynex climbing runner because it's reusable and strong as all get-out)

▶ 1 (6-inch) window shade cleat (or you can use a small boat cleat if you have one lying around)

▶ 2 (1-by-¼-inch) bolts

▶ 2 (¼-inch) nuts

▶ 1 thermometer with clip attachment to measure oil temperature

▶ 1 instant-read meat thermometer

▶ 1 fire extinguisher

▶ 1 tank of propane fuel filled to the shoulder of the tank

▶ 4 feet of fuel line

▶ 1 (3-foot) piece of aluminum foil

▶ 1 heavy wooden coat hanger

▶ Optional but recommended: spinning emergency beacon (D-battery version) for the top of the ladder, to warn of deep-frying in the vicinity.

1. Thoroughly read—and then reread—the instructions that came with your burner unit. Assemble the burner unit as instructed in the manual.

2. Illustration (right), inset D: Bolt the cleat to the right side of the ladder with the 2 bolts and nuts; tighten securely.

3. Inset A: Tie one end of the sash cord to the top rung of the left side of the ladder with a bowline knot (very important knot to know; it cannot come untied).

4. Inset B: Secure a pulley to the top rung of the right side of the ladder with 2 cable ties.

5. Inset C: Thread the sash cord through pulley 1 and then pulley 2; feed out enough cord to allow pulley 1 to center over the middle point beneath the ladder, about 4 feet off the ground; secure the cord to the cleat, wrapping in a figure-8 fashion several times and tying it off so it cannot slip.

6. Inset C: Attach the quick link or carabiner to pulley 1.

7. Wrap the gas supply line with aluminum foil to protect it in case of any overflow.

8. Place the burner unit under pulley 1, centered beneath the ladder, with the propane tank on the ground as far from the burner unit as possible.

Large-vessel frying is serious business. It matters a lot where you stage this operation. Be sure you are at least 10 feet—yes, feet—away from any structure like your house, your garden shed, your wooden fence, your deck, your carport, or your garage.

Also essential is a level surface—but not a wooden deck or a paved or concrete driveway; these will show oil splatters, and kids like to play there. A patch of grass or dirt that is level and free of toys and other obstacles is ideal.

You will also need to keep everyone at a safe distance from your base of operations—10 feet away. This is no place for kids, and no time to start any holiday drinking.

Until your bird is done and delivered to the table, no alcohol allowed. Period.

Your base of operations should include a chair (because you are not going to leave this site until your turkey is done and the fire is out), a table containing your heat-resistant gloves, a timer, a stick-type lighter, a meat thermometer, a beverage (remember, nonalcoholic), and, most important of all, your trusty fire extinguisher.

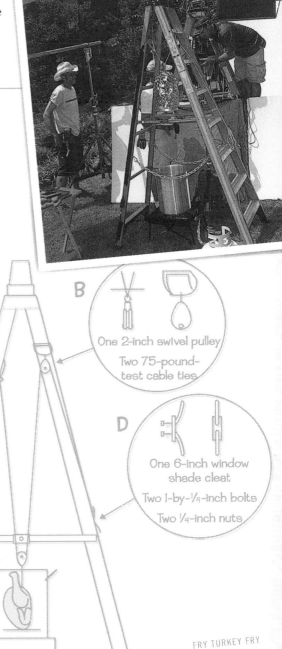

SIDE VIEW

Beacon light

8-foot ladder

Maximum turkey weight: 14 pounds

Propane gas cylinder with control and regulator hose (hose wrapped in aluminum foil)

Fryer

Cooker

SECTION VIEW

A One 15-foot cotton sash cord with a bowline knot

B One 2-inch swivel pulley
Two 75-pound-test cable ties

C One 2-inch pulley
One 3-inch quick link

D One 6-inch window shade cleat
Two 1-by-¼-inch bolts
Two ¼-inch nuts

KNOWLEDGE CONCENTRATE

TURKEY

Here we see an approximation of the space a **COMMERCIAL TURKEY** has to call its own. Now, some folks feel better about buying free-range birds, which they assume live happily in the open, playing poultry games and developing a lot of flavor. But, according to the USDA, "free-range" birds are required only to have access to the outdoors. How much space they have, and how long they spend outside, is up to the grower.

PASTURE-RAISED birds are free to roam around and eat bugs and grass and whatnot, which is closer to what nature intended. The problem is, the word *pasture* is no more regulated than the word *range*, and one man's pasture could be another man's postage stamp.

HERITAGE TURKEYS are descendants of the birds that were strutting around America back when the *Mayflower* landed. Raised on small farms, these rare varieties, like Bourbon Red and American Bronze, look nothing like factory Frankenbirds, nor do they taste like them. Although I love a heritage bird, they're not for everyone, as increased flavor often comes at the price of juicy tenderness—and they're pricey.

If you are a fan of this show, then brining is probably not an alien concept to you. The idea is that by soaking your bird in a salt solution you can actually denature some of the internal proteins, which will ensnare moisture, helping the bird keep moist during the cooking process. Of course, the seasoning doesn't exactly hurt the flavor, either.

APPLICATION — DEEP-FRIED TURKEY

6 TO 8 SERVINGS

// SOFTWARE ///

6	quarts	hot H_2O	
1	pound	kosher salt	
1	pound	dark brown sugar	
5	pounds	ice	
1	13- to 14-pound	turkey	thoroughly thawed, giblets removed
4 to 4¼	gallons	peanut oil	

// PROCEDURE ///

1. Brine the turkey: Put the hot water, salt, and brown sugar in a **5-gallon upright drink cooler** and stir until the salt and sugar dissolve completely. Add the ice and stir until the

FRY TURKEY FRY

mixture is cool. Gently lower the turkey into the container. If necessary, weigh down the bird to ensure that it is fully immersed in the brine. Cover and set in a cool place for 8 to 16 hours.

2. Prepare a **Turkey Derrick** as described on page 410, under "Construction."

3. Fry the turkey: Insert the lifter spindle in the turkey cavity, legs up and wings/breast down. You may need to tie the wings in with cotton butcher's twine to keep them from flopping out and getting caught on the pot edge.

4. In your kitchen sink, lower the turkey and spindle down into the empty pot you'll be frying in and fill it with water, one gallon at a time, until the bird is just covered; remove the spindle and turkey, then mark the water fill level from the top edge of the pot so you know how much oil will be needed. Pour out the water and dry the pot thoroughly.

5. Out at your base of operations, clip the carabiner to the top of the lifter spindle, suspending the turkey about 30 inches above the burner surface.

6. Set the empty pot on the burner unit, attach the thermometer to the side of the pot, and fill with the peanut oil to the measured level; the thermometer tip must be immersed in the oil; do not overfill.

7. Following the instruction manual carefully, light the gas burner and adjust the gas and air flow; do not put a lid on the pot. Have a seat and wait for the oil to reach 250°F.

8. When the oil reaches 250°F, untie the cord from the cleat and slowly lower the turkey into the hot oil; don't hurry this. Quickly dropping the turkey in is dangerous, and it lowers the oil temperature dramatically, which is not good. When the base of the lifter spindle touches the bottom of the pot, raise it 1 inch, and securely tie off the cord on the cleat.

9. Raise the burner heat to bring the oil up to 350°F, then set the timer for 30 minutes—and do not leave the pot.

10. Closely monitor the oil temperature: It will start to climb above 350°F as moisture cooks out of the turkey; reduce the gas flow accordingly to keep at 350°F. This is very important. Allowing the temp to go higher could result in a dangerous inferno.

11. After 30 minutes, untie the cord from the cleat, raise the turkey out of the oil, tie off the cord, and insert an instant-read meat thermometer. The turkey will be ready to remove when the internal temp is 151°F: Take a reading at the breast, thigh, and leg to be sure all parts of the bird have reached 151°F.

12. When the turkey has reached 151°F, raise it well above the pot and securely tie off the cord at the cleat. Turn off the gas supply and put the lid on the pot. Set the timer for 30 minutes and have a seat. Do not leave your base of operations; you want to defend your bird from hungry animals (and neighbors?), and it is still cooking. Carryover heat will raise the temperature to an ideal 161°F—perfect golden doneness. Continue to keep everyone away even though the flames have been extinguished; the oil is still very hot.

13. When the turkey has reached 161°F, lower the turkey to rest upon the pot lid and unclip the carabiner from the spindle; hook a heavy coat hanger through the top of the spindle and lift the turkey away to a kitchen full of awestruck family and friends.

14. When the oil has cooled to below 80°F, remove the lid and filter the oil back into its original containers; it may be used once more. To dispose of the oil, take it to a local collection point for recycling as biodiesel fuel.

PANTRY RAID VI: LENTILS

EPISODE 164 | SEASON 10 | GOOD EATS

Historians and poets through the ages have been rough on the lentil, citing it for being irritating, gassy, and flavorless, for causing poor eyesight and even nightmares. I suspect the real problem is that they've long been associated with poverty and there's never been a lentil PR campaign to repair the image. And that's a shame, because whether you're rich or poor, vegetarian or carnivore, Eastern or Western, lentils are good eats.

TIDBIT | In the sixteenth and seventeenth centuries, the word *lentils* also referred to freckles.

THE ADVENT OF THE AMERICAN LENTIL

Ninety-eight percent of all lentils grown in the United States come from a tiny patch of fertile volcanic soil in the Pacific Northwest, an area called the Palouse. The lentil industry originally grew up there as a means of feeding a local population of mostly vegetarian Seventh-Day Adventists. This makes sense when you consider the nutritional power of lentils. High in fiber, low in fat, a good source of B vitamins, folate, magnesium, and potassium, they're easy to digest, meaning they don't produce as much gassy by-product as other legumes.

Of course, there's also the protein: Of all edible plants, only soybeans contain more. Proteins are like long trains made up of molecules called amino acids. There are twenty amino acids, and what a particular protein does depends on which aminos are in it and in what order they appear along the train. Our bodies require thousands of different proteins to operate, and when we consume protein in food our digestive system breaks down the amino acids and reassembles them into the protein trains that we need. The

body can also synthesize certain amino acids, but there are nine known as the essential amino acids, including lysine, that must come from the outside world—that is, from food. Most animal protein sources, like eggs and meat, are complete, meaning that they contain all those nine essential amino acids. But some legumes, such as soybeans and lentils, come very, very close—and without any of the saturated fat associated with most meats. And of course lentils only cost about a buck eighty-nine a pound.

Behold the lentil, _Lens culinaris._ One might assume that the lenslike shape inspired the name, but in fact it's the other way around: The lentil's Latin moniker actually inspired the name of the device I am looking through. •

Like peas and beans, lentils are legumes, but they've got one really big advantage over the other members of the family, and that is that they cook very quickly due to their unusual shape.

Lentils come in many sizes and colors, simply because they've been around so long. Lentils were one of man's earliest crops and were domesticated in Mesopotamia more than eight thousand years ago. As the plant spread around Europe, Asia, and Africa, farmers selected the colors they liked and cultivated those. So the modern lentil color wheel is a record of cultural preferences.

The cuisines of the Indian subcontinent have embraced the lentil like no other, and dozens of varieties are regularly cooked there. Some of the most famous are _dal_ or _masoor dal_—split red lentils . . . very good at soaking up moisture and therefore very popular in soups. (_Dal_, by the way, is Hindi for "split" lentil, the whole version being "gram.")

SPANISH PARDINAS and ITALIAN USTICAS, which are very small, hold their shape well when cooked; when you eat them they pop kind of like caviar.

BROWN LENTILS are the standard megamart variety. Khaki-colored and large, they tend to turn mushy easily. Although they're okay in salads, let's face it . . . who wants khaki food?

RED LENTILS are small and fast cooking. Although they lose some of their red, turning gold in the pot, they're a great addition to soups and stews.

VERTE DE PUY (green lentils) are a specialty of the Haute-Loire region of France, where volcanic soil and an ideal climate grow ze perfect lenti (or so sayeth the French). Verte de Puy were the first vegetables to be granted _appellation d'origine controlée_ certification, which means that only lentils from Puy get to be called Puy.

Unless you really like your dentist, the first thing you should do when cooking lentils is to check for pebbles, as even the most secure processing facility will occasionally let a little lentil look-alike slip through. You should also give your lentils a rinse—they're very often covered in dust, especially if they are organic.

TIDBIT Americans were asked to substitute lentils for meat during World War I in order to support the war effort.

TIDBIT Hippocrates prescribed a dish of lentils and sliced dog as a treatment for liver ailments.

SAY IT!

BASIC COOKED LENTILS

6 TO 8 SERVINGS; ABOUT 6 CUPS

// SOFTWARE ///

1	pound	brown or green lentils	picked over and rinsed
1	small	onion	halved
1	clove	garlic	halved
1		bay leaf	
1	teaspoon	kosher salt	or to taste
¼	pound	salt pork	optional
¼	teaspoon	black pepper	freshly ground

// PROCEDURE ///

1. Combine the lentils with the onion, garlic, bay leaf, salt, and salt pork, if using, in a **6-quart saucepan** and cover with water by 2 to 3 inches. Set over high heat and bring just to a rolling boil. Reduce the heat to low, cover, and simmer until the lentils are tender, 25 to 30 minutes.

2. Drain off any remaining liquid and discard the onion, garlic, bay leaf, and salt pork. Stir in the pepper and season with more salt if necessary. Serve immediately.

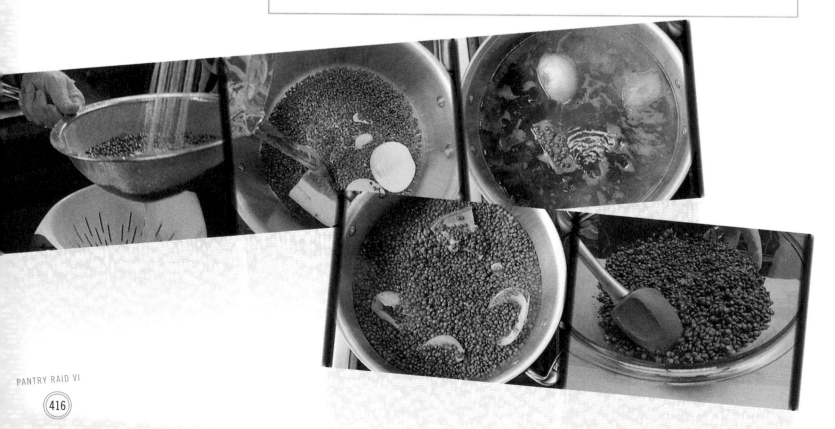

LENTIL SOUP

6 TO 8 SERVINGS

// SOFTWARE ///

2	tablespoons	olive oil	
1	cup	onion	finely chopped
½	cup	carrot	finely chopped
½	cup	celery	finely chopped
2	teaspoons	kosher salt	
1	pound	lentils	picked over and rinsed
1	cup	tomatoes	peeled and chopped
2	quarts	chicken or vegetable broth	
½	teaspoon	coriander	freshly ground
½	teaspoon	cumin	freshly toasted and ground
½	teaspoon	grains of paradise	freshly ground (right)

// PROCEDURE //

1. Heat the oil in a **6-quart Dutch oven** over medium heat. Add the onion, carrot, celery, and salt and sweat until the onion is translucent, 6 to 7 minutes. Add the lentils, tomatoes, broth, coriander, cumin, and grains of paradise and stir to combine. Increase the heat to high and bring just to a boil. Reduce the heat to low, cover, and cook at a low simmer until the lentils are tender, 35 to 40 minutes.

2. Using an **immersion blender**, puree to your preferred consistency. Serve immediately.

GRAINS OF PARADISE

Melegueta pepper, commonly known as grains of paradise, hails from tropical West Africa and is cultivated primarily in Ghana. The small, red-brown seeds, which come from the wrinkled pod of a reedy cousin of ginger, were especially popular as a spice from the time of Elizabeth I to George III. Interestingly enough, the name comes from an old Portuguese word meaning "jellyfish." Ever since discovering several sources on the Internet for grains of paradise, I have found myself grinding it onto and into many dishes instead of black pepper. I even keep a grinder set aside just for it.

Western Africa

• Ghana

> TIDBIT | Royal Egyptian tombs were stocked with lentils so the dead would have something to nosh in the afterlife.

Dehydrating my neighbor Chuck to make a point.

LENTIL COOKIES (YES, REALLY)

4 ½ DOZEN

Lentils are very good at playing, well, not lentils. For instance, they've long been used as meat substitutes. You might even say that they are the penitent man's protein, since anybody who couldn't afford fish used to eat lentils during Lent. And no, the names are not related, but it would really be cool if they were. Anyway, what if I told you that lentils also work and play well in the world of baked goods?

// SOFTWARE //

9½	ounces	whole-wheat pastry flour[1]	
1	teaspoon	baking powder	
1	teaspoon	kosher salt	
1½	teaspoons	cinnamon	ground
½	teaspoon	allspice	ground
8	ounces	sugar	
¾	cup	unsalted butter	at room temperature
1	large	egg	
2	teaspoons	vanilla extract	
1½	cups	Lentil Puree	(right)
3½	ounces	rolled oats	
4	ounces	dried fruit	
2¼	ounces	coconut	unsweetened dried shredded

// PROCEDURE //

1. Heat the oven to 375°F.

2. Combine the flour, baking powder, salt, cinnamon, and allspice in a **medium bowl**.

3. Cream together the sugar and butter on medium speed in the bowl of a **stand mixer**. Add the egg and mix until just incorporated. Add the vanilla and lentil puree and mix until combined. Add the flour mixture and blend on low speed until just combined. Remove the bowl from the mixer and stir in the oats, dried fruit, and coconut.

4. Form the dough into balls about 2 teaspoons in size and place them 1 inch apart on a **half sheet pan** lined with **parchment paper**. Bake for 15 to 17 minutes, until the cookies reach an internal temperature of 195°F. Cool for 10 minutes before devouring. Store in an airtight container for up to 5 days.

[1] If desired, a quarter of the whole-wheat flour can be substituted with lentil flour for a denser, more strongly flavored cookie.

SUB-APPLICATION — LENTIL PUREE

1 ½ CUPS

TIDBIT | The obelisk standing in St. Peter's Square was shipped from Egypt packed in 3 million pounds of lentils.

// **SOFTWARE** //

4	ounces	lentils	picked and rinsed
2	cups	H$_2$O	

// **PROCEDURE** //

Combine the lentils and water in a **small pot** over medium heat. Bring to a simmer, cover, and simmer for 30 to 40 minutes, until the lentils are tender. Remove from the heat and puree. If using immediately, let cool. The puree may be stored in the refrigerator for 3 to 4 days or in the freezer for 2 to 3 months.

APPLICATION — LENTIL SALAD

6 TO 8 SERVINGS

This is my very favoritest of all lentil applications.

// **SOFTWARE** //

½	cup	red wine vinegar	
¼	cup	olive oil	
2	teaspoons	Dijon mustard	
1	teaspoon	kosher salt	
½	teaspoon	black pepper	freshly ground
¼	cup	fresh parsley	finely chopped
1	teaspoon	fresh thyme	finely chopped
1	application	warm Basic Cooked Lentils	see page 416
6 to 8	rashers	thick-sliced bacon	cooked and chopped

// **PROCEDURE** //

Whisk the vinegar, oil, mustard, salt, pepper, parsley, and thyme together in a **large bowl**. Add the lentils and bacon and stir to combine. Serve warm or at room temperature.

FINAL THOUGHTS

... continued from volume 1

1. While there are no people who can't cook, there are plenty of people who won't cook.

2. It's very difficult to taste food through the TV.

3. The most important tool in the kitchen is the table. Without a good kitchen table to feed folks at, it's all just show biz.

4. Favorite spice? Bacon.

5. In cooking, the most misunderstood ingredient is time.

6. I still have trouble making a really great cup of coffee.

7. If you can possibly keep chickens, keep chickens. You haven't had an egg until you've had an egg laid by your own chicken.

8. I think, just maybe . . . we've gone overboard on this whole washing everything thing.

9. No chocolate chip cookie tastes as good as the dough it was made from.

10. When it comes to cooking, the more you know the less you need.

11. An infrared thermometer is a great investment. Not only will it accurately tell you the temperature of any surface, but dogs and cats love to chase that red laser dot.

12. I've always been able to get my daughter to try new foods simply by telling her she can't have any.

13. If you wouldn't seal a food up in a pot of water and cook it for an hour or two, then you probably shouldn't buy it canned either. Think about it: beans . . . asparagus. See?

14. In the end, you cannot teach anyone to cook. You can point them in the right direction, arm them with the proper tools, give them good groceries. But in the end it's like dancing: You either find the groove or you don't.

CONVERSION CHARTS

// WEIGHT EQUIVALENTS //////////////////////////////////

The metric weights given in this chart are not exact equivalents, but have been rounded up or down slightly to make measuring easier.

Avoirdupois	Metric
¼ ounce	7 grams
½ ounce	15 grams
1 ounce	30 grams
2 ounces	60 grams
3 ounces	90 grams
4 ounces	115 grams
5 ounces	150 grams
6 ounces	175 grams
7 ounces	200 grams
8 ounces (½ pound)	225 grams
9 ounces	250 grams
10 ounces	300 grams
11 ounces	325 grams
12 ounces	350 grams
13 ounces	375 grams
14 ounces	400 grams
15 ounces	425 grams
16 ounces (1 pound)	450 grams
1½ pounds	750 grams
2 pounds	900 grams
2¼ pounds	1 kilogram
3 pounds	1.4 kilograms
4 pounds	1.8 kilograms

// VOLUME EQUIVALENTS ///

These are not exact equivalents for American cups and spoons, but have been rounded up or down slightly to make measuring easier.

American	Metric	Imperial
¼ teaspoon	1.2 milliliters	—
½ teaspoon	2.5 milliliters	—
1 teaspoon	5.0 milliliters	—
½ tablespoon (1½ teaspoons)	7.5 milliliters	—
1 tablespoon (3 teaspoons)	15 milliliters	—
¼ cup (4 tablespoons)	60 milliliters	2 fluid ounces
⅓ cup (5 tablespoons)	75 milliliters	2½ fluid ounces
½ cup (8 tablespoons)	125 milliliters	4 fluid ounces
⅔ cup (10 tablespoons)	150 milliliters	5 fluid ounces
¾ cup (12 tablespoons)	175 milliliters	6 fluid ounces
1 cup (16 tablespoons)	250 milliliters	8 fluid ounces
1¼ cups	300 milliliters	10 fluid ounces (½ pint)
1½ cups	350 milliliters	12 fluid ounces
2 cups (1 pint)	500 milliliters	16 fluid ounces
2½ cups	625 milliliters	20 fluid ounces (1 pint)
1 quart	1 liter	32 fluid ounces

// OVEN TEMPERATURE EQUIVALENTS ///

Oven Mark	°F	°C	Gas
very cool	250–275	130–140	½–1
cool	300	150	2
warm	325	170	3
moderate	350	180	4
moderately hot	375–400	190–200	5–6
hot	425–450	220–230	7–8
very hot	475	250	9

INDEX

COPYRIGHT

Published in 2010 by Stewart, Tabori & Chang
An imprint of ABRAMS

Library of Congress Cataloging-in-Publication Data
Brown, Alton, 1962-
  Good eats 2 : the middle years / Alton Brown.
    p. cm.
  title: Good eats two
  Includes index.
  ISBN 978-1-58479-857-6 (alk. paper)
 1. Cookery. 2. Good eats (Television program) I. Good eats (Television
 program) II. Title. III. Title: Good eats two.
TX651.B7272 2010
641.5–dc22

                    2010015852

Editors: Kate Norment and Liana Krissoff
Designers: Galen Smith and Danielle Young
Production Manager: Tina Cameron

The text of this book was composed in ITC Century, Trade Gothic,
Vintage Typewriter, and Typography of Coop.

Printed and bound in the United States
10 9 8 7 6 5 4 3 2

Stewart, Tabori & Chang books are available at special discounts when purchased in quantity for
premiums and promotions as well as fundraising or educational use. Special editions can also be
created to specification. For details, contact specialsales@abramsbooks.com or the address below.

THE ART OF BOOKS SINCE 1949

115 West 18th Street
New York, NY 10011
www.abramsbooks.com